Snow White with the Red Hair

SORATA AKIDUKI

16

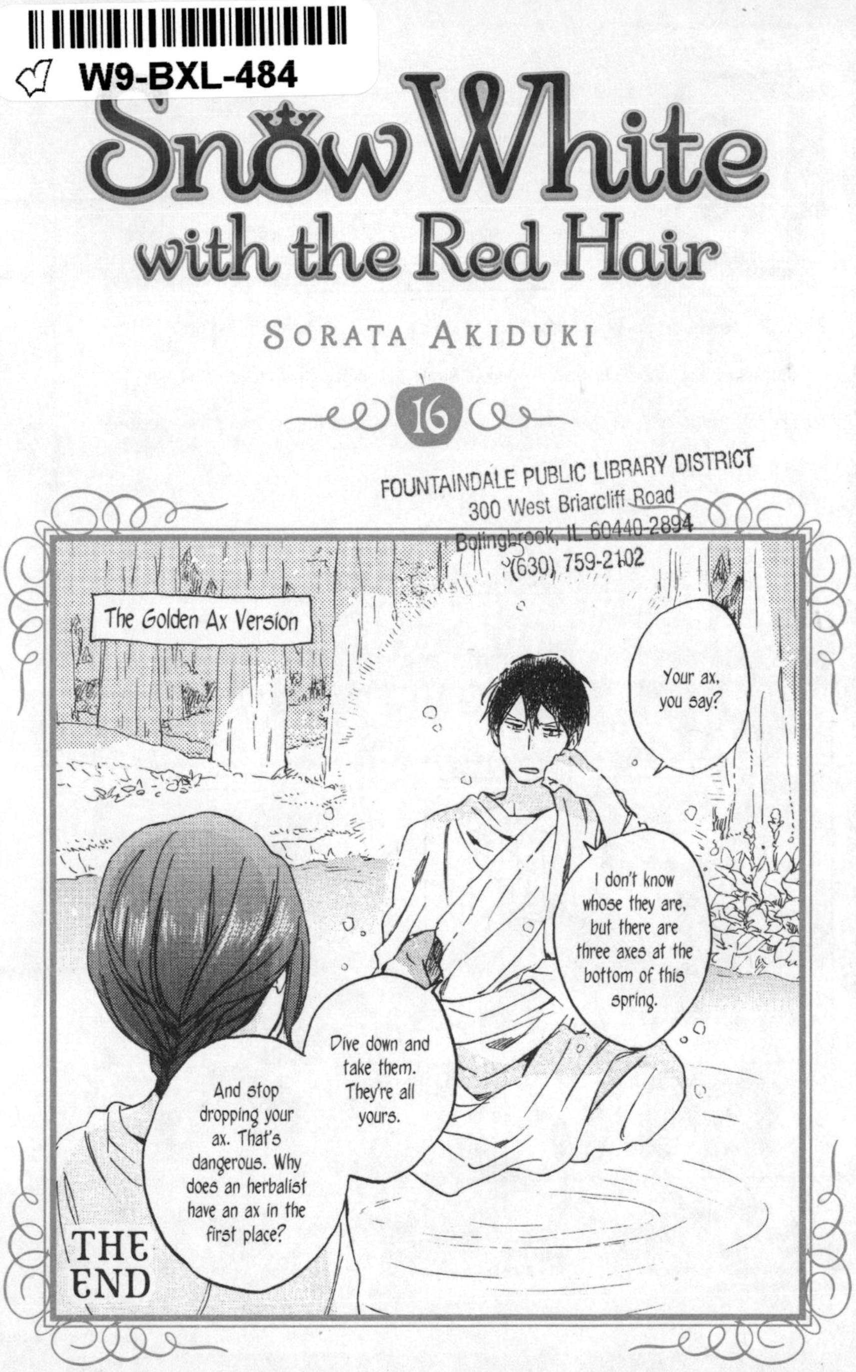
The Golden Ax Version
Your ax, you say?
I don't know whose they are, but there are three axes at the bottom of this spring.
Dive down and take them. They're all yours.
And stop dropping your ax. That's dangerous. Why does an herbalist have an ax in the first place?
THE END

THE STORY

Shirayuki was born with beautiful hair as red as apples, but when her rare hair earns her unwanted attention from the notorious prince Raj, she's forced to flee her home. A young man named Zen helps her in the forest of the neighboring kingdom, Clarines, and it turns out he is that kingdom's second prince! Shirayuki decides to accompany Zen back to Wistal, the capital city of Clarines.

Shirayuki has met all manner of people since becoming a court herbalist, and her relationship with Zen continues to grow, as the two have finally made their feelings known to each other.

"They say that red is the color of destiny."

SHIRAYUKI

Working as a court herbalist. Has feelings for Zen—feelings that he shares.

ZEN WISTERIA

Prince of Clarines and brother to the king.

RYU

Shirayuki's boss. A brainy kid who became a court herbalist at a young age.

MITSUHIDE & KIKI

Zen's aides. They're good friends who share a strong bond.

OBI

Former assassin. Currently, Zen's underling. Served as Shirayuki's bodyguard for part of her stay in Lilias.

VOLUME 16

TABLE *of* CONTENTS

After becoming a full-fledged court herbalist, Shirayuki takes a work trip to the northern city of Lilias with her boss, Ryu. When a mysterious illness starts spreading, they put their skills to use and figure out what's causing it.

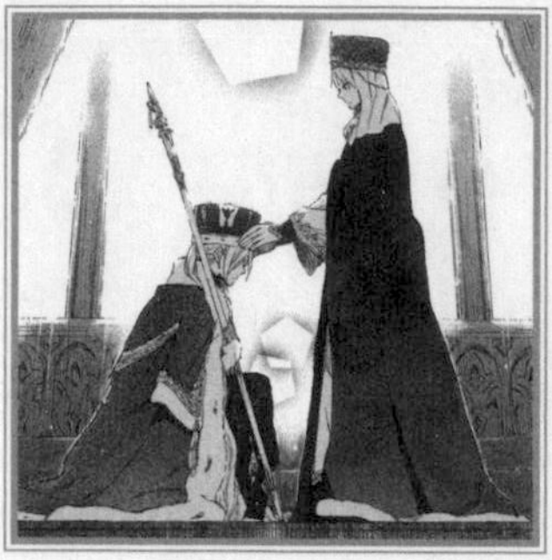

Once back in Wistal, the newly crowned king Izana orders Shirayuki and Ryu to return to Lilias. But this time, it's no mere business trip—it's a personnel transfer for two whole years. Still, Shirayuki finds the resolve to do what she must to advance her career. Zen also dispatches Obi to Lilias, where the capital trio begin their new lives.

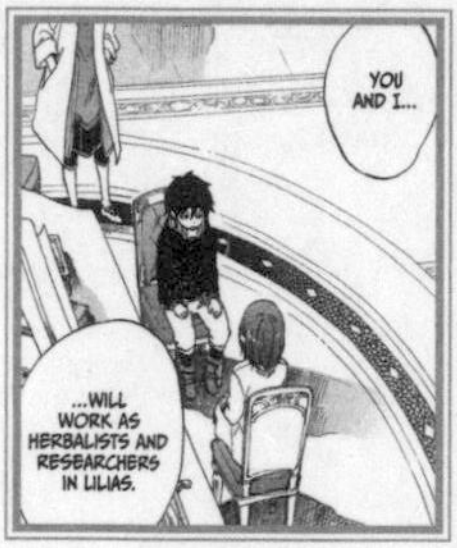
YOU AND I...
...WILL WORK AS HERBALISTS AND RESEARCHERS IN LILIAS.

Shirayuki starts researching how to neutralize the toxin of the glowing orimmallys—the same plant that caused the earlier outbreak—but she and her colleagues can't figure out how to retain the glowing properties of the seeds once the toxin is removed. They decide to search for scholars who deal with light and heat, which leads the group to a noble named Rata Forzeno, who studies wunderocks.

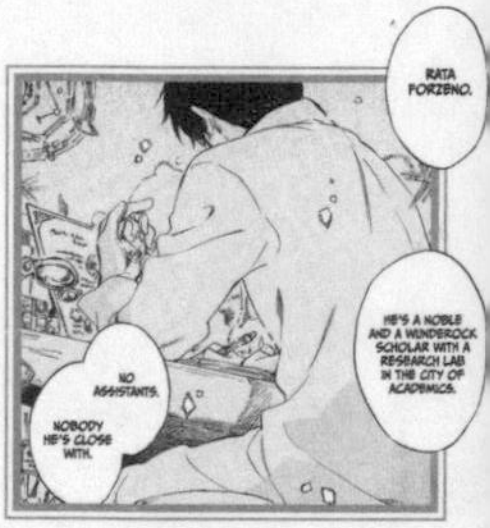
RATA FORZENO.
HE'S A NOBLE AND A WUNDEROCK SCHOLAR WITH A RESEARCH LAB IN THE CITY OF ACADEMICS.
NO ASSISTANTS.
NOBODY HE'S CLOSE WITH.

With Rata's guidance, Shirayuki and friends manage to create wunderocks that apply continuous heat to the seeds. At long last—after seemingly endless experimentation—they achieve a method for breeding seeds with more of the light-producing substance. These new seeds should glow just as brightly as the original orimmallys, but without the toxin.

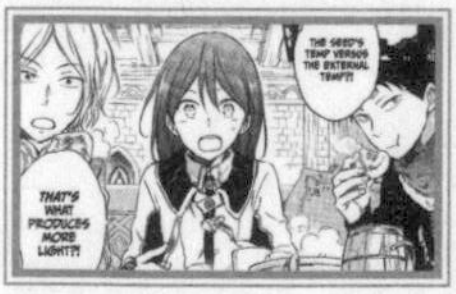
THE SEED'S TEMP VERSUS THE EXTERNAL TEMP?!
THAT'S WHAT PRODUCES MORE LIGHT?!

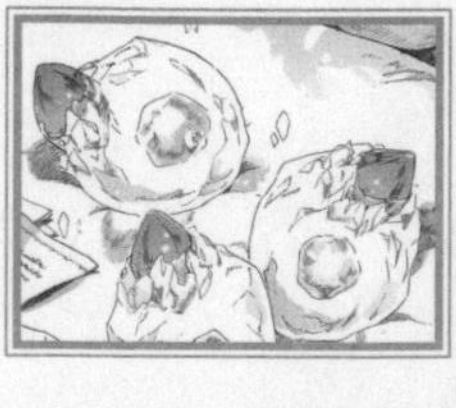

Snow White
with the
Red Hair

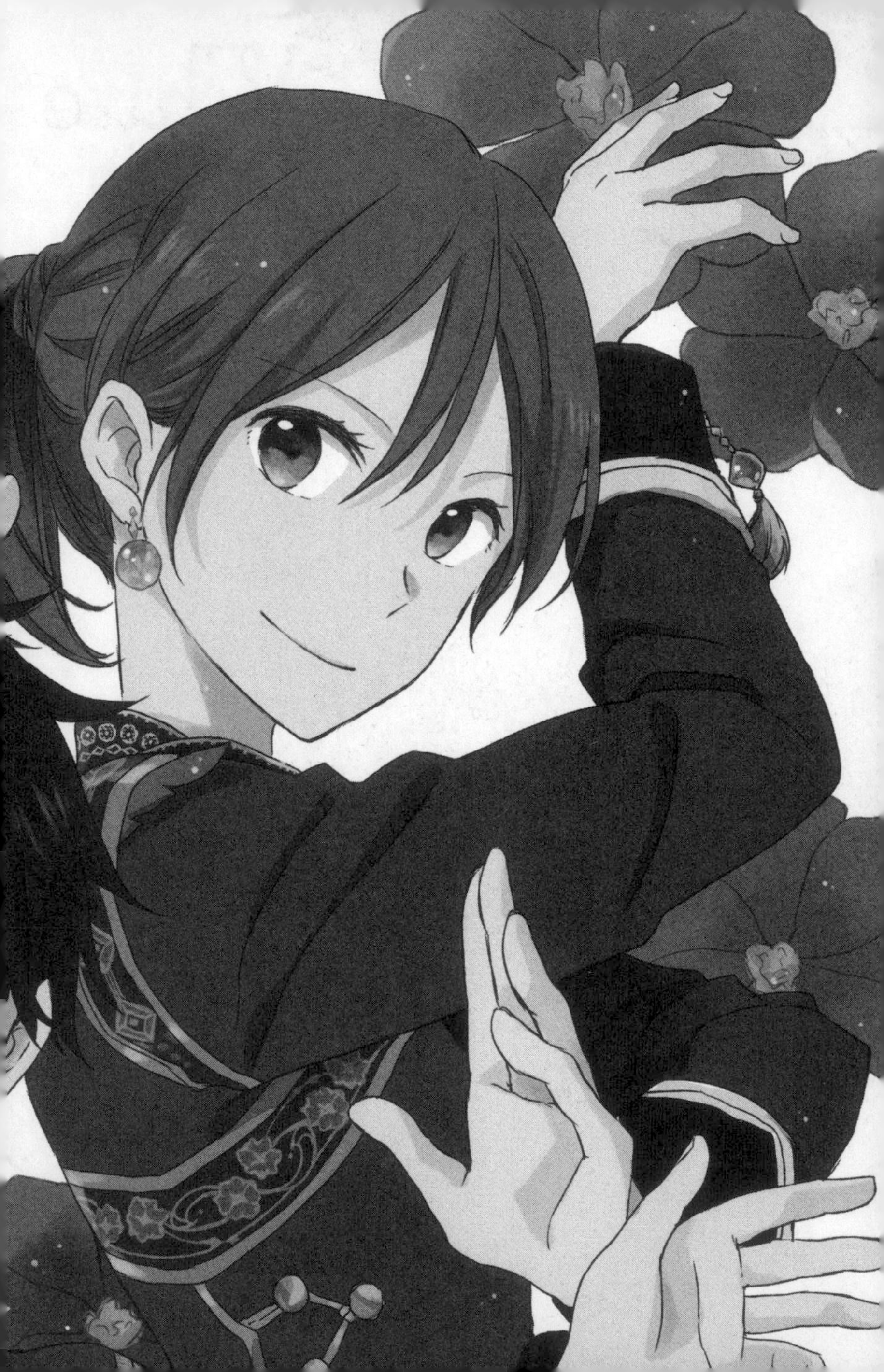

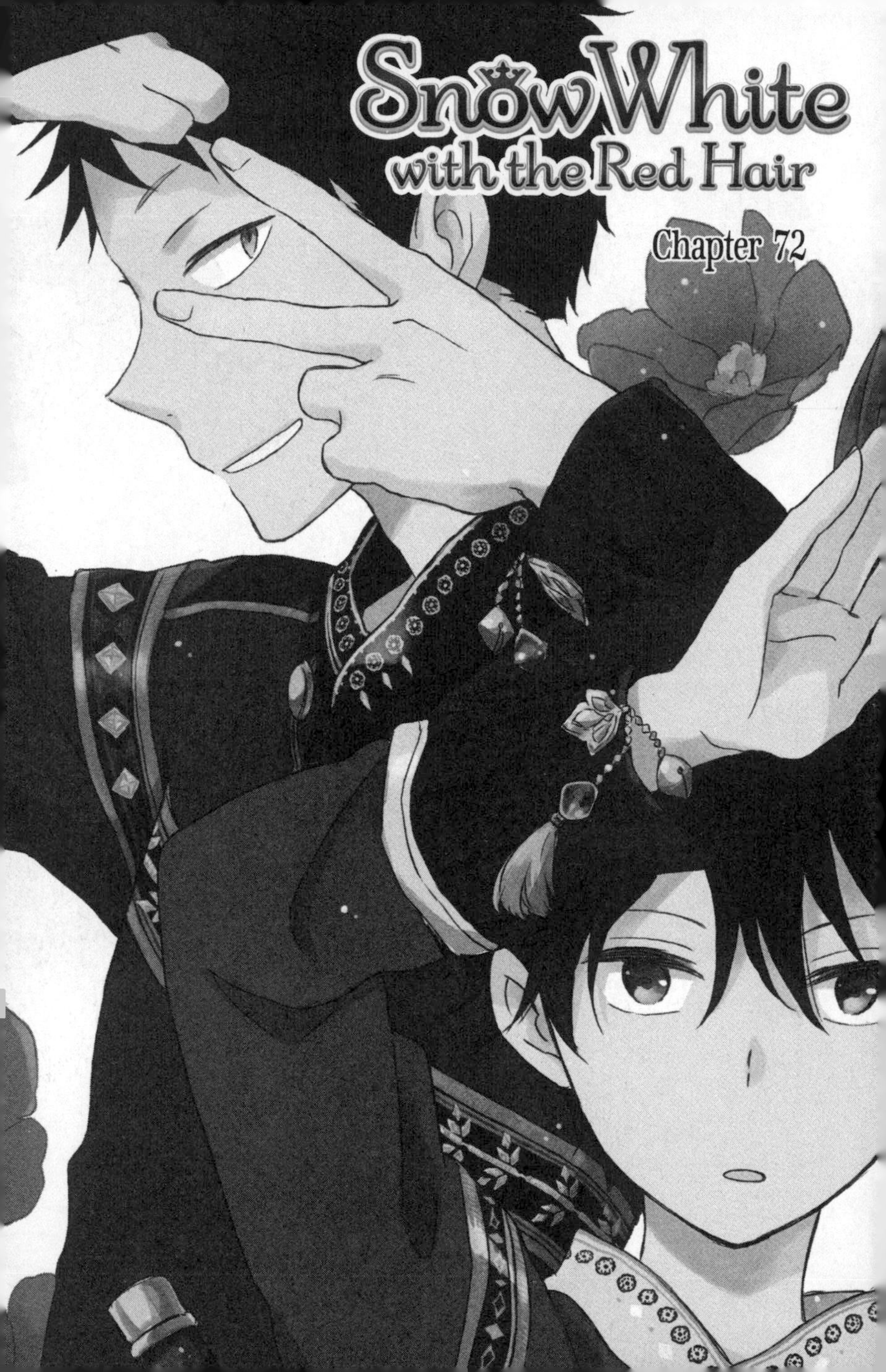
Snow White
with the Red Hair
Chapter 72

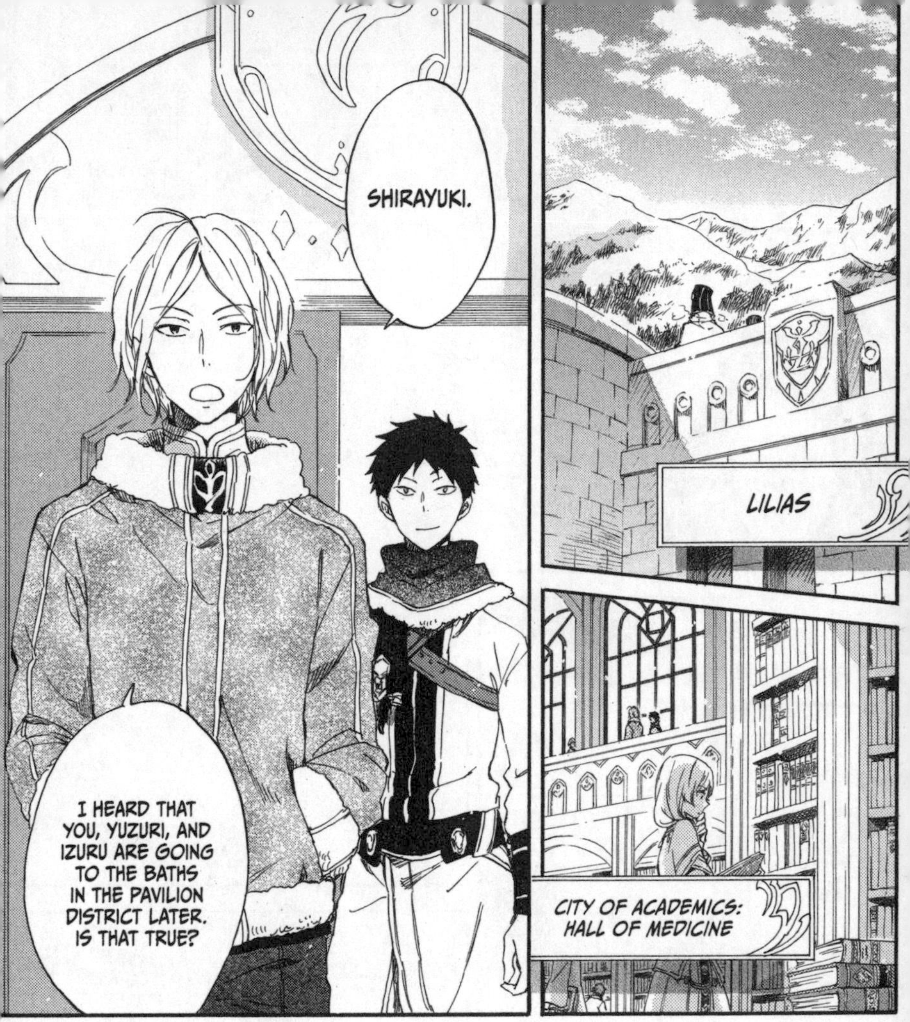
LILIAS
CITY OF ACADEMICS: HALL OF MEDICINE
SHIRAYUKI.
I HEARD THAT YOU, YUZURI, AND IZURU ARE GOING TO THE BATHS IN THE PAVILION DISTRICT LATER. IS THAT TRUE?

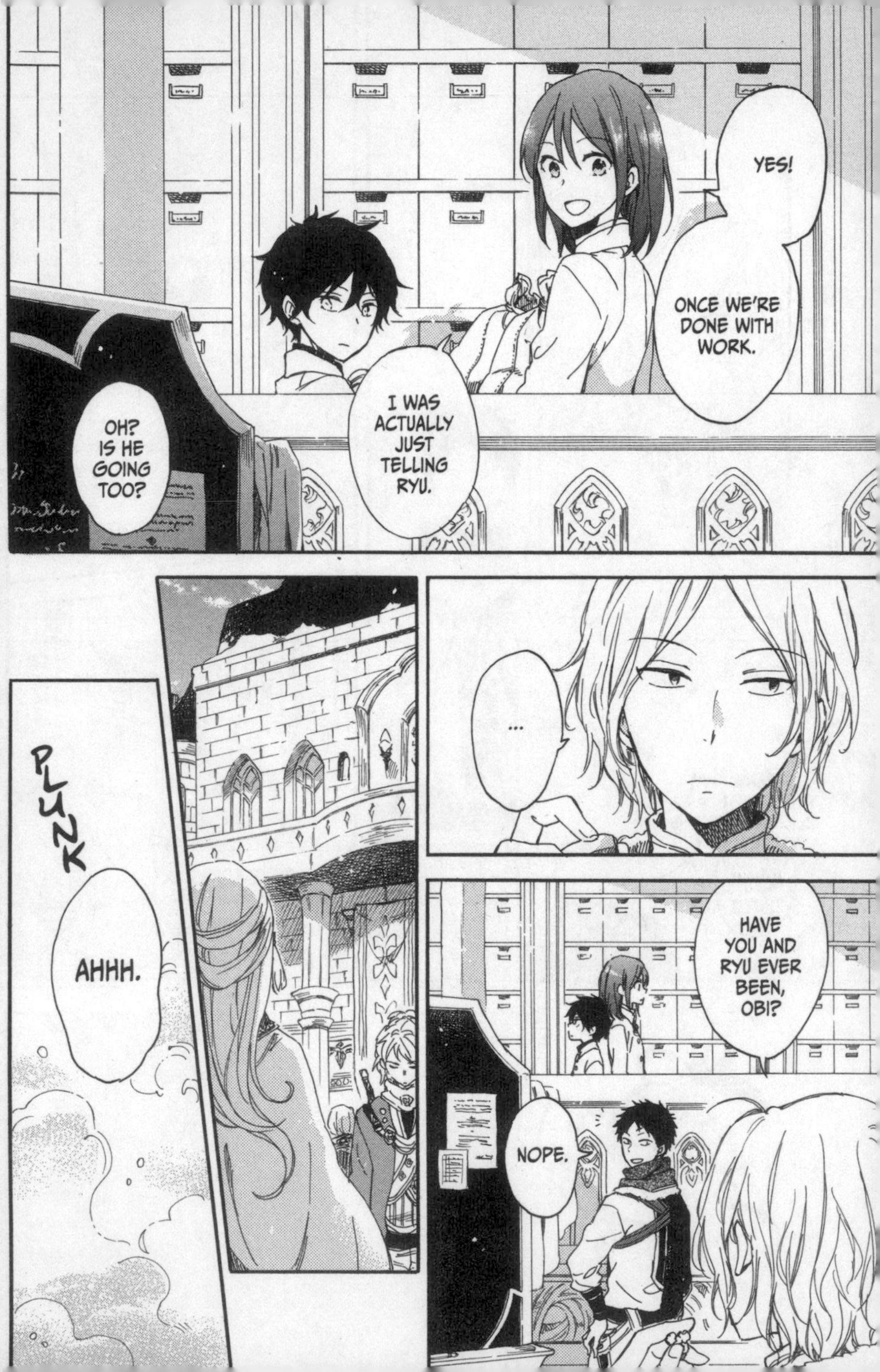
YES!
ONCE WE'RE DONE WITH WORK.
I WAS ACTUALLY JUST TELLING RYU.
OH? IS HE GOING TOO?
...
HAVE YOU AND RYU EVER BEEN, OBI?
NOPE.
PLUNK
AHHH.

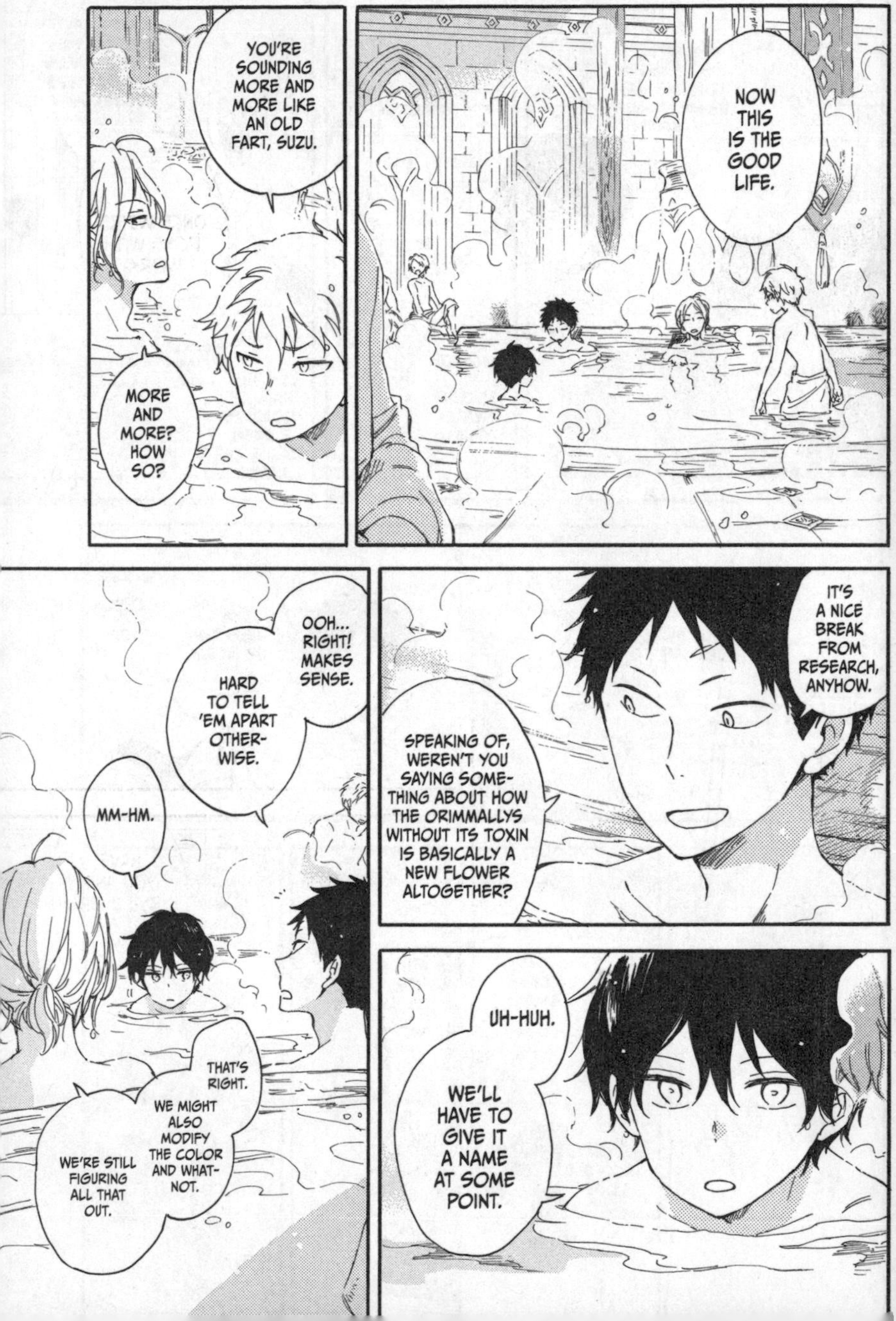
NOW THIS IS THE GOOD LIFE.
YOU'RE SOUNDING MORE AND MORE LIKE AN OLD FART, SUZU.
MORE AND MORE? HOW SO?
IT'S A NICE BREAK FROM RESEARCH, ANYHOW.
SPEAKING OF, WEREN'T YOU SAYING SOME-THING ABOUT HOW THE ORIMMALLYS WITHOUT ITS TOXIN IS BASICALLY A NEW FLOWER ALTOGETHER?
UH-HUH.
WE'LL HAVE TO GIVE IT A NAME AT SOME POINT.
OOH... RIGHT! MAKES SENSE.
HARD TO TELL 'EM APART OTHER-WISE.
MM-HM.
THAT'S RIGHT.
WE MIGHT ALSO MODIFY THE COLOR AND WHAT-NOT.
WE'RE STILL FIGURING ALL THAT OUT.

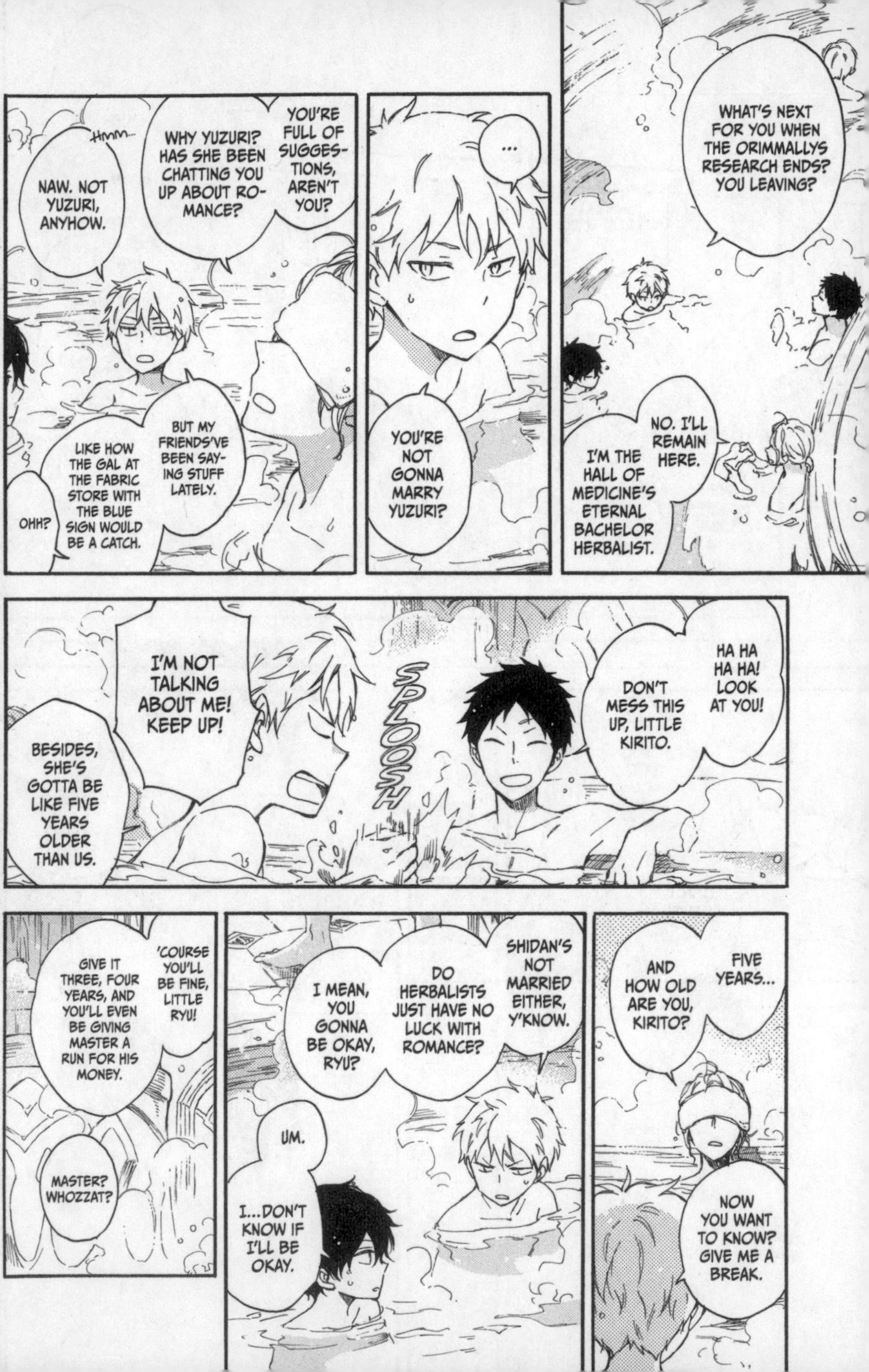
WHAT'S NEXT FOR YOU WHEN THE ORIMMALLYS RESEARCH ENDS? YOU LEAVING?
NO. I'LL REMAIN HERE.
I'M THE HALL OF MEDICINE'S ETERNAL BACHELOR HERBALIST.
...
YOU'RE NOT GONNA MARRY YUZURI?
YOU'RE FULL OF SUGGES-TIONS, AREN'T YOU?
WHY YUZURI? HAS SHE BEEN CHATTING YOU UP ABOUT RO-MANCE?
Hmm...
NAW. NOT YUZURI, ANYHOW.
BUT MY FRIENDS'VE BEEN SAY-ING STUFF LATELY.
LIKE HOW THE GAL AT THE FABRIC STORE WITH THE BLUE SIGN WOULD BE A CATCH.
OHH?
HA HA HA HA! LOOK AT YOU!
DON'T MESS THIS UP, LITTLE KIRITO.
SPLOOSH
I'M NOT TALKING ABOUT ME! KEEP UP!
BESIDES, SHE'S GOTTA BE LIKE FIVE YEARS OLDER THAN US.
FIVE YEARS...
AND HOW OLD ARE YOU, KIRITO?
NOW YOU WANT TO KNOW? GIVE ME A BREAK.
SHIDAN'S NOT MARRIED EITHER, Y'KNOW.
DO HERBALISTS JUST HAVE NO LUCK WITH ROMANCE?
I MEAN, YOU GONNA BE OKAY, RYU?
UM.
I...DON'T KNOW IF I'LL BE OKAY.
'COURSE YOU'LL BE FINE, LITTLE RYU!
GIVE IT THREE, FOUR YEARS, AND YOU'LL EVEN BE GIVING MASTER A RUN FOR HIS MONEY.
MASTER? WHOZZAT?

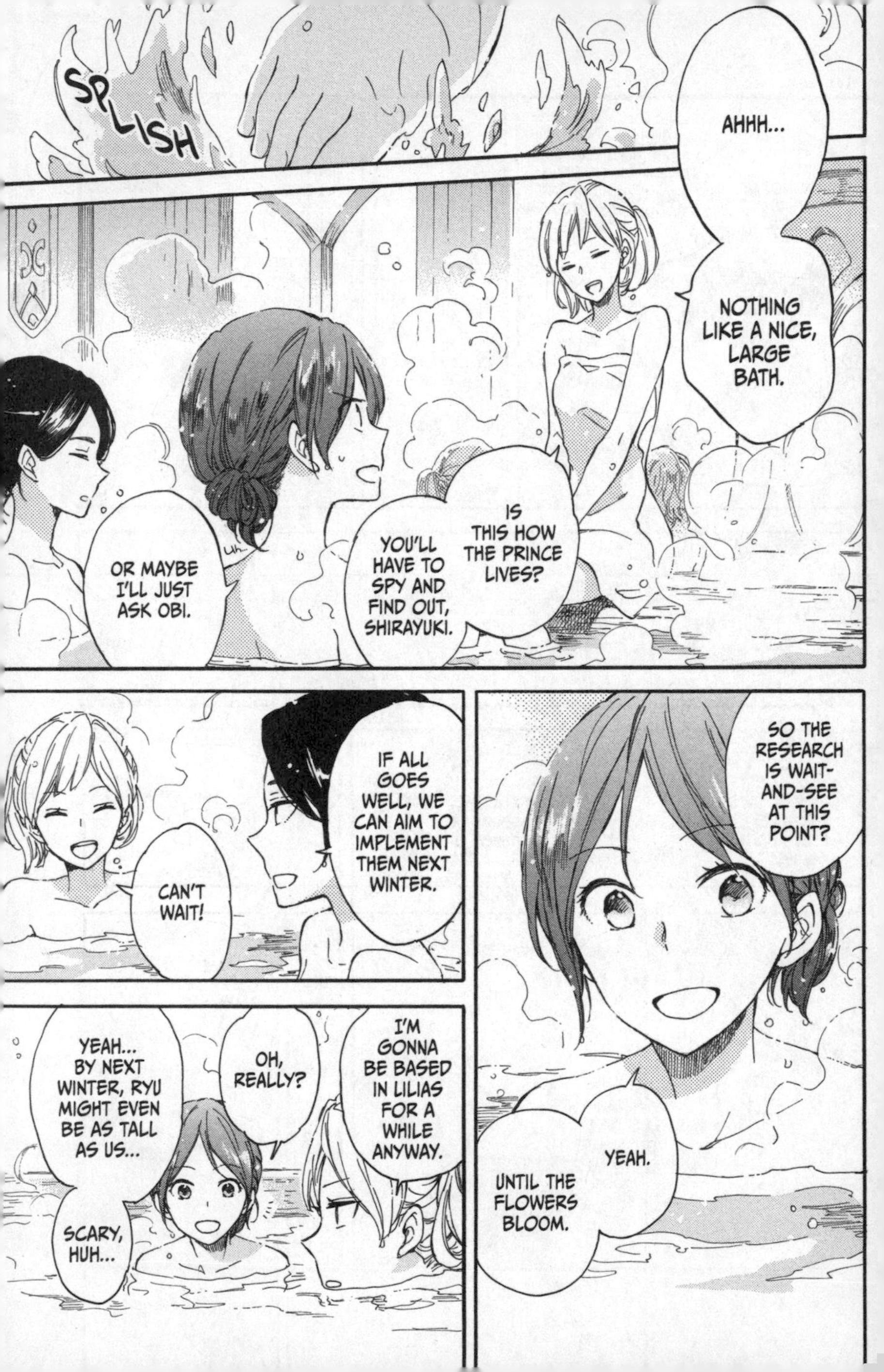
SPLISH
AHHH...
NOTHING LIKE A NICE, LARGE BATH.
IS THIS HOW THE PRINCE LIVES?
YOU'LL HAVE TO SPY AND FIND OUT, SHIRAYUKI.
Uh...
OR MAYBE I'LL JUST ASK OBI.
SO THE RESEARCH IS WAIT-AND-SEE AT THIS POINT?
YEAH.
UNTIL THE FLOWERS BLOOM.
IF ALL GOES WELL, WE CAN AIM TO IMPLEMENT THEM NEXT WINTER.
CAN'T WAIT!
I'M GONNA BE BASED IN LILIAS FOR A WHILE ANYWAY.
OH, REALLY?
YEAH... BY NEXT WINTER, RYU MIGHT EVEN BE AS TALL AS US...
SCARY, HUH...

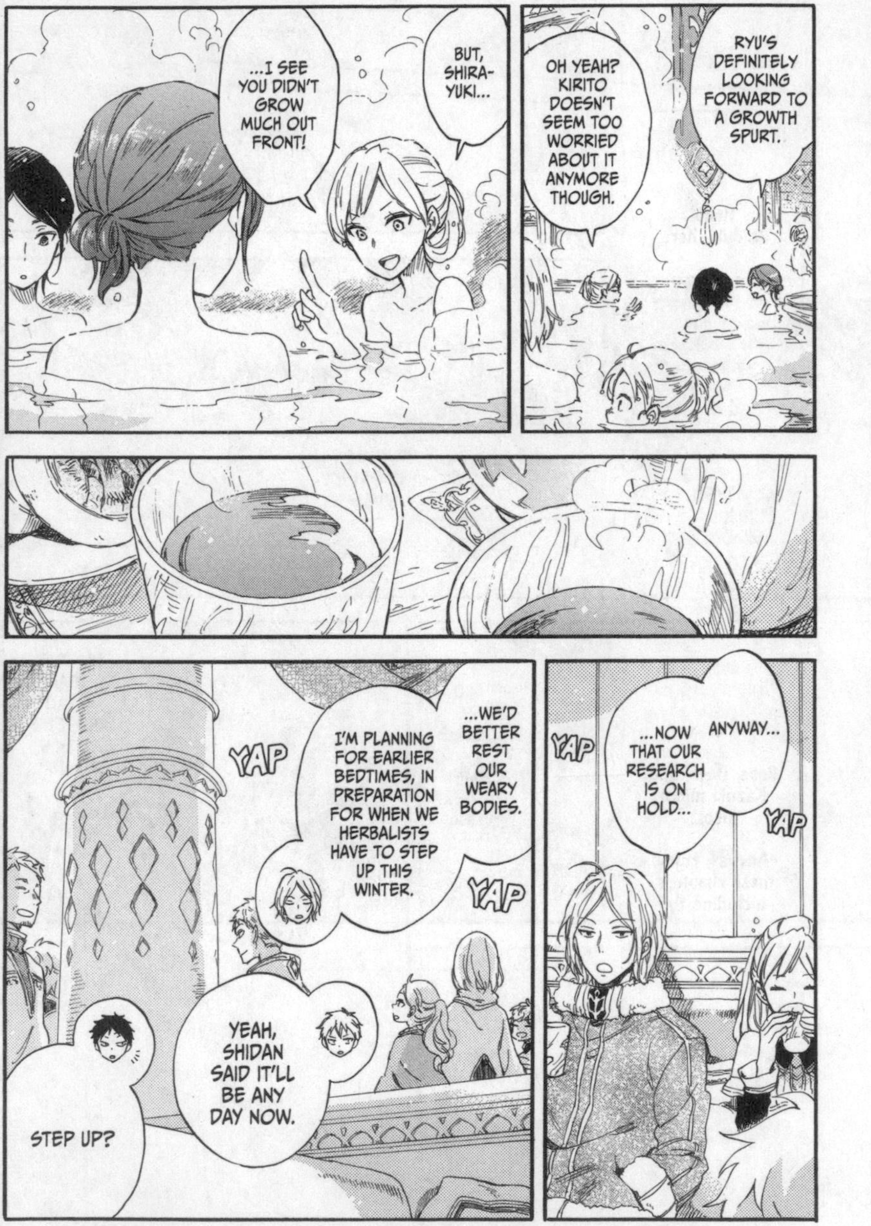

RYU'S DEFINITELY LOOKING FORWARD TO A GROWTH SPURT.
OH YEAH? KIRITO DOESN'T SEEM TOO WORRIED ABOUT IT ANYMORE THOUGH.
BUT, SHIRA-YUKI...
...I SEE YOU DIDN'T GROW MUCH OUT FRONT!
ANYWAY...
...NOW THAT OUR RESEARCH IS ON HOLD...
YAP
YAP
...WE'D BETTER REST OUR WEARY BODIES.
I'M PLANNING FOR EARLIER BEDTIMES, IN PREPARATION FOR WHEN WE HERBALISTS HAVE TO STEP UP THIS WINTER.
YAP
YAP
YEAH, SHIDAN SAID IT'LL BE ANY DAY NOW.
STEP UP?

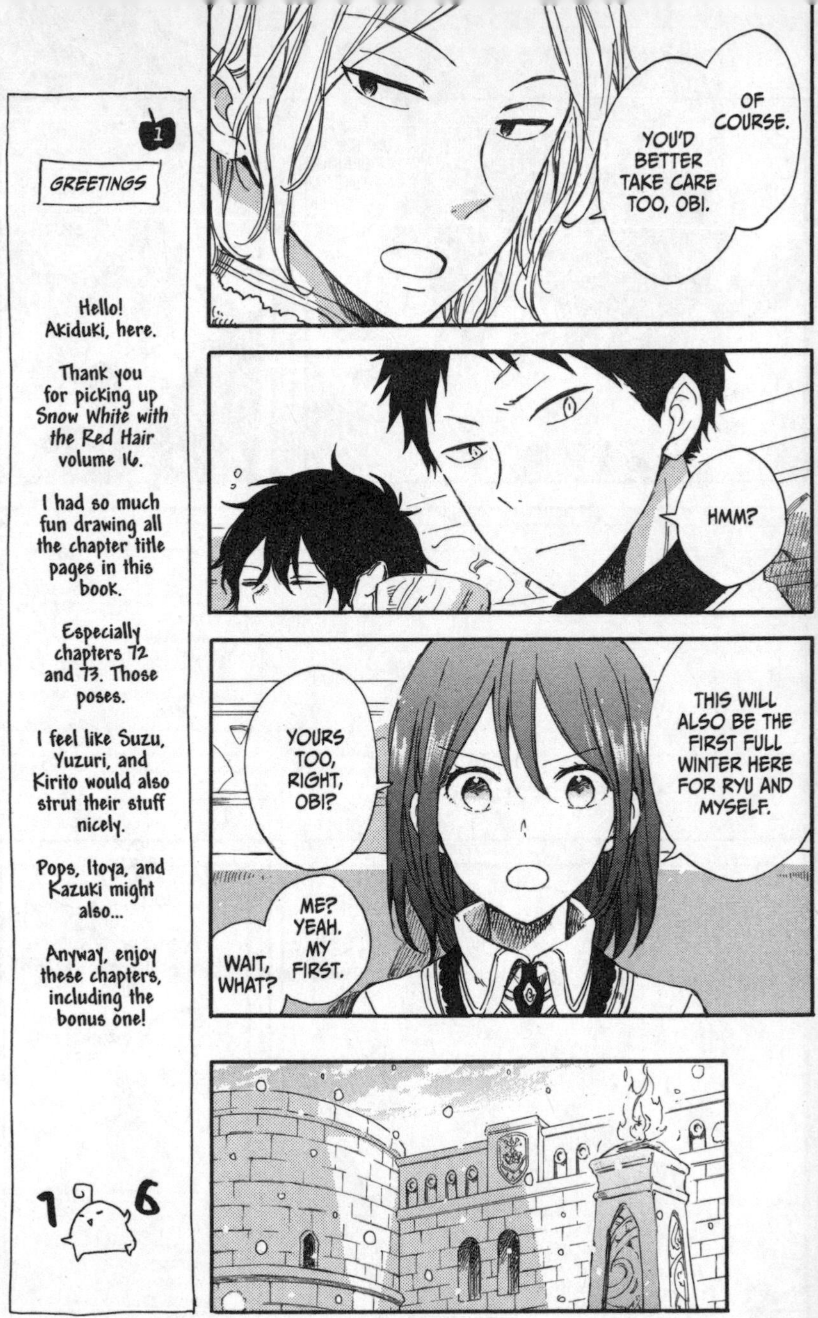
OF COURSE.
YOU'D BETTER TAKE CARE TOO, OBI.
HMM?
THIS WILL ALSO BE THE FIRST FULL WINTER HERE FOR RYU AND MYSELF.
YOURS TOO, RIGHT, OBI?
ME? YEAH. MY FIRST.
WAIT, WHAT?

1

GREETINGS

Hello! Akiduki, here.

Thank you for picking up Snow White with the Red Hair volume 16.

I had so much fun drawing all the chapter title pages in this book.

Especially chapters 72 and 73. Those poses.

I feel like Suzu, Yuzuri, and Kirito would also strut their stuff nicely.

Pops, Itoya, and Kazuki might also...

Anyway, enjoy these chapters, including the bonus one!

16

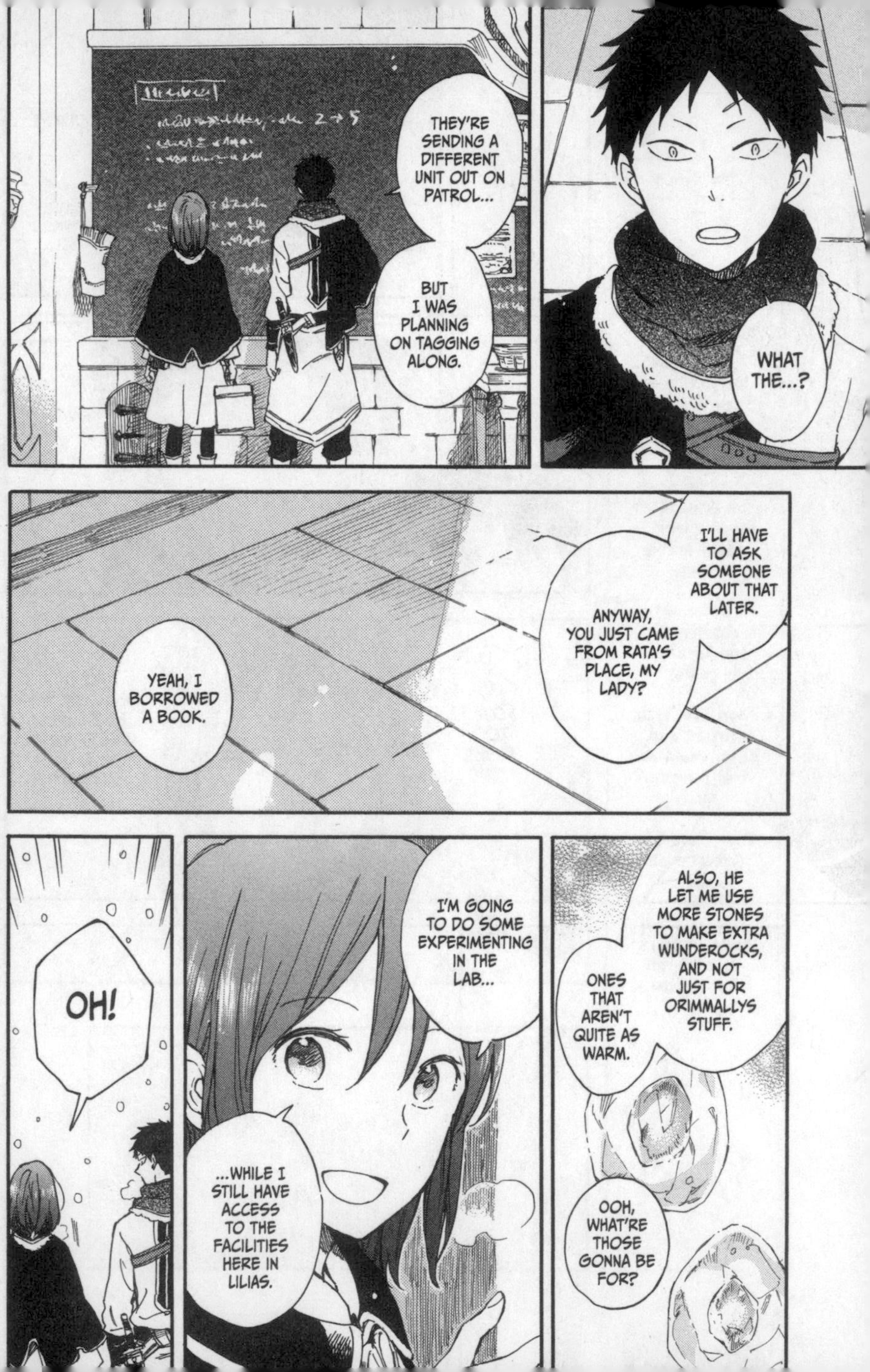
WHAT THE...?
THEY'RE SENDING A DIFFERENT UNIT OUT ON PATROL...
BUT I WAS PLANNING ON TAGGING ALONG.
I'LL HAVE TO ASK SOMEONE ABOUT THAT LATER.
ANYWAY, YOU JUST CAME FROM RATA'S PLACE, MY LADY?
YEAH, I BORROWED A BOOK.
ALSO, HE LET ME USE MORE STONES TO MAKE EXTRA WUNDEROCKS, AND NOT JUST FOR ORIMMALLYS STUFF.
ONES THAT AREN'T QUITE AS WARM.
OOH, WHAT'RE THOSE GONNA BE FOR?
I'M GOING TO DO SOME EXPERIMENTING IN THE LAB...
...WHILE I STILL HAVE ACCESS TO THE FACILITIES HERE IN LILIAS.
OH!

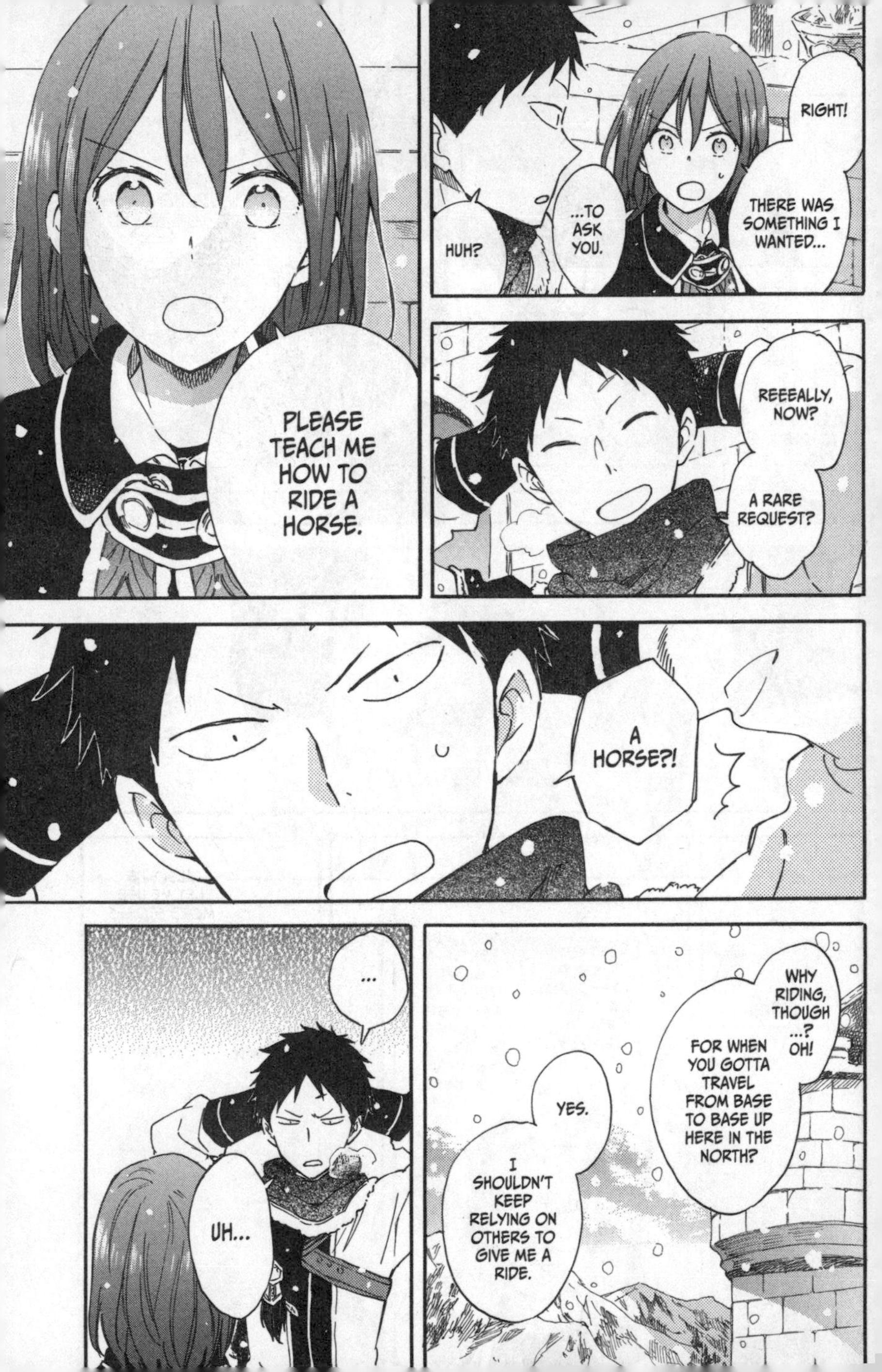
RIGHT!
THERE WAS SOMETHING I WANTED...
...TO ASK YOU.
HUH?
REEEALLY, NOW?
A RARE REQUEST?
PLEASE TEACH ME HOW TO RIDE A HORSE.
A HORSE?!
WHY RIDING, THOUGH ...? OH!
FOR WHEN YOU GOTTA TRAVEL FROM BASE TO BASE UP HERE IN THE NORTH?
YES.
I SHOULDN'T KEEP RELYING ON OTHERS TO GIVE ME A RIDE.
...
UH...

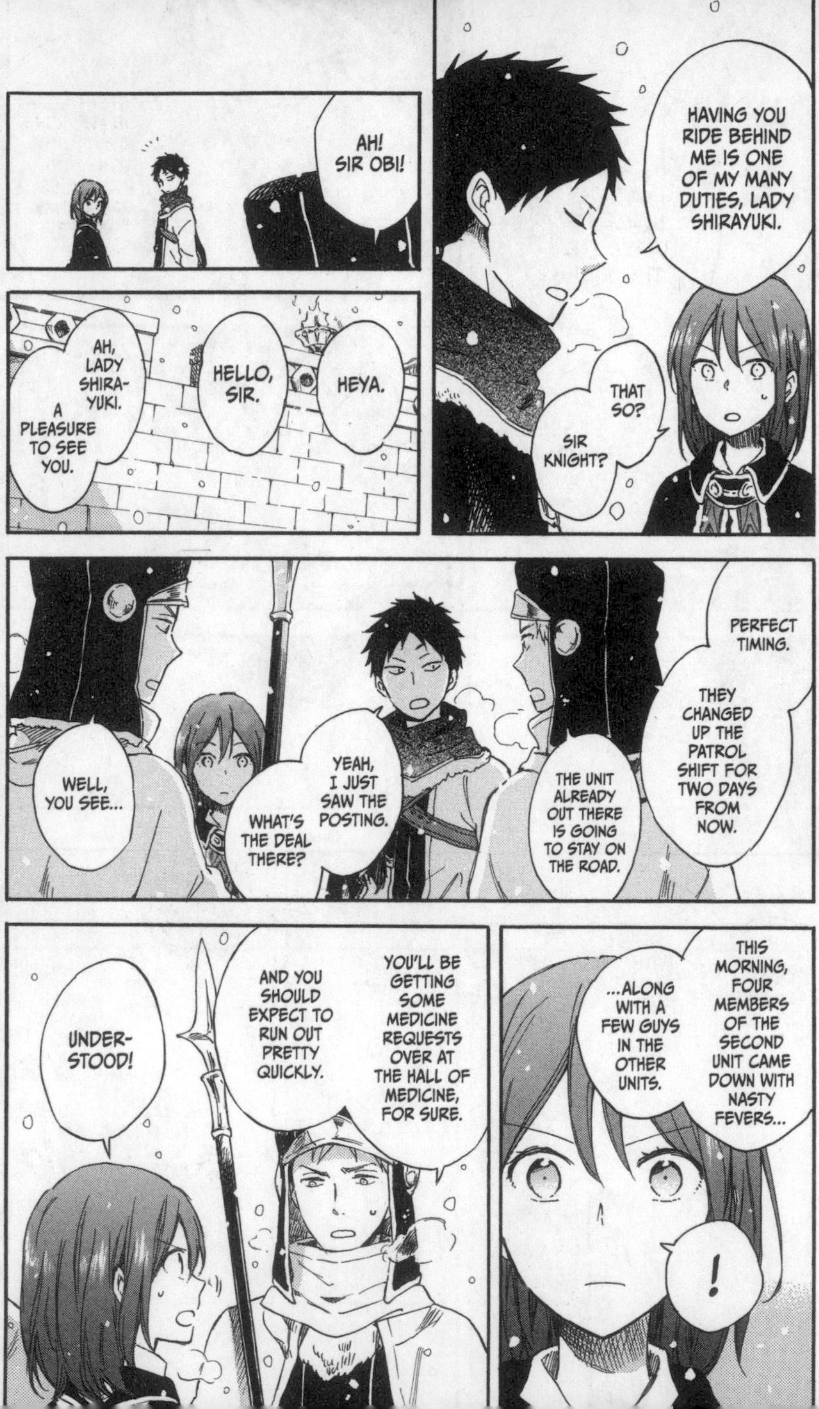
HAVING YOU RIDE BEHIND ME IS ONE OF MY MANY DUTIES, LADY SHIRAYUKI.
THAT SO?
SIR KNIGHT?
AH! SIR OBI!
HEYA.
HELLO, SIR.
AH, LADY SHIRA-YUKI.
A PLEASURE TO SEE YOU.
PERFECT TIMING.
THEY CHANGED UP THE PATROL SHIFT FOR TWO DAYS FROM NOW.
THE UNIT ALREADY OUT THERE IS GOING TO STAY ON THE ROAD.
YEAH, I JUST SAW THE POSTING.
WHAT'S THE DEAL THERE?
WELL, YOU SEE...
THIS MORNING, FOUR MEMBERS OF THE SECOND UNIT CAME DOWN WITH NASTY FEVERS...
...ALONG WITH A FEW GUYS IN THE OTHER UNITS.
!
YOU'LL BE GETTING SOME MEDICINE REQUESTS OVER AT THE HALL OF MEDICINE, FOR SURE.
AND YOU SHOULD EXPECT TO RUN OUT PRETTY QUICKLY.
UNDER-STOOD!

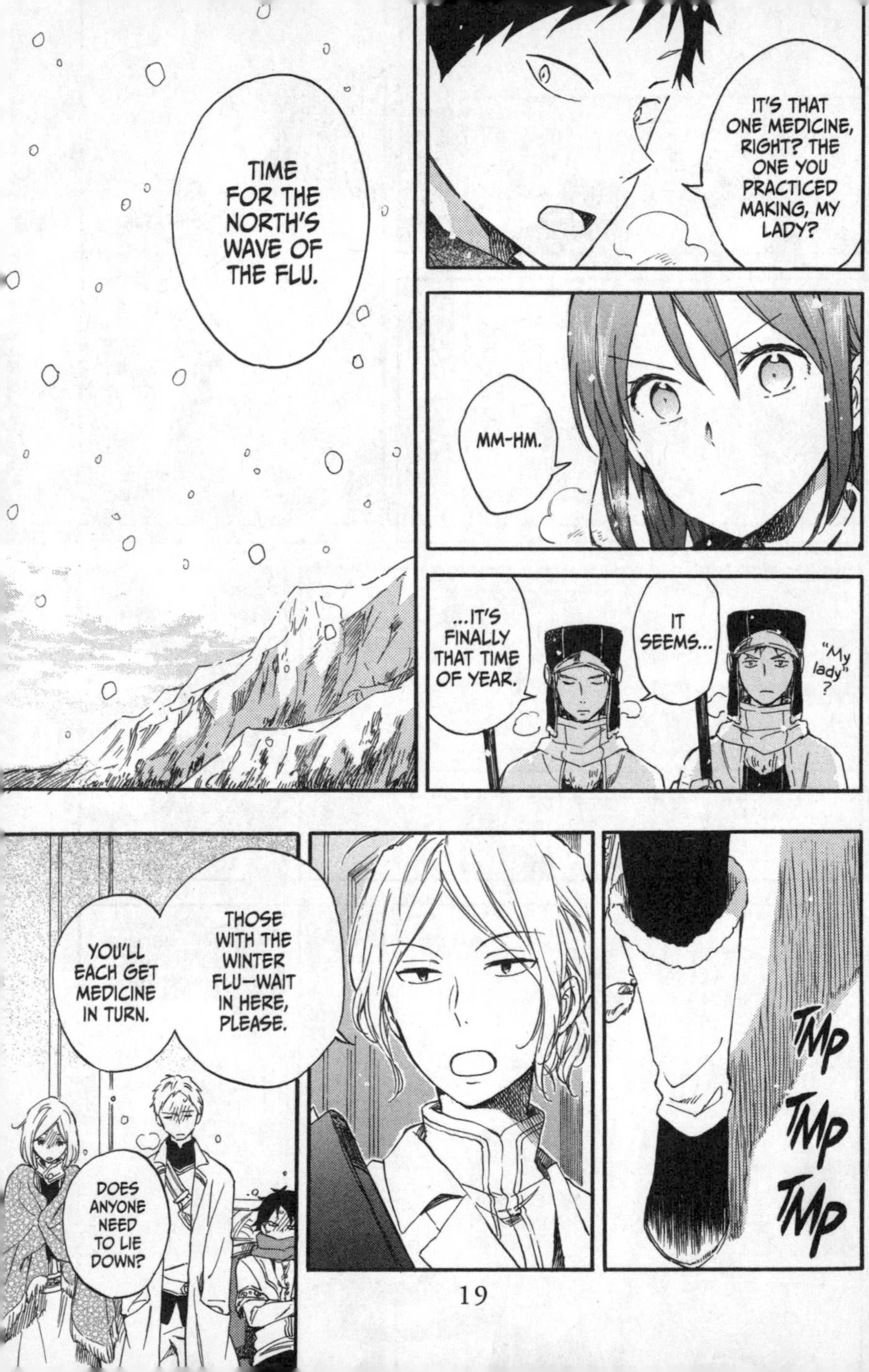
IT'S THAT ONE MEDICINE, RIGHT? THE ONE YOU PRACTICED MAKING, MY LADY?
MM-HM.
"My lady"?
IT SEEMS...
...IT'S FINALLY THAT TIME OF YEAR.
TIME FOR THE NORTH'S WAVE OF THE FLU.
TMP TMP TMP
THOSE WITH THE WINTER FLU—WAIT IN HERE, PLEASE.
YOU'LL EACH GET MEDICINE IN TURN.
DOES ANYONE NEED TO LIE DOWN?

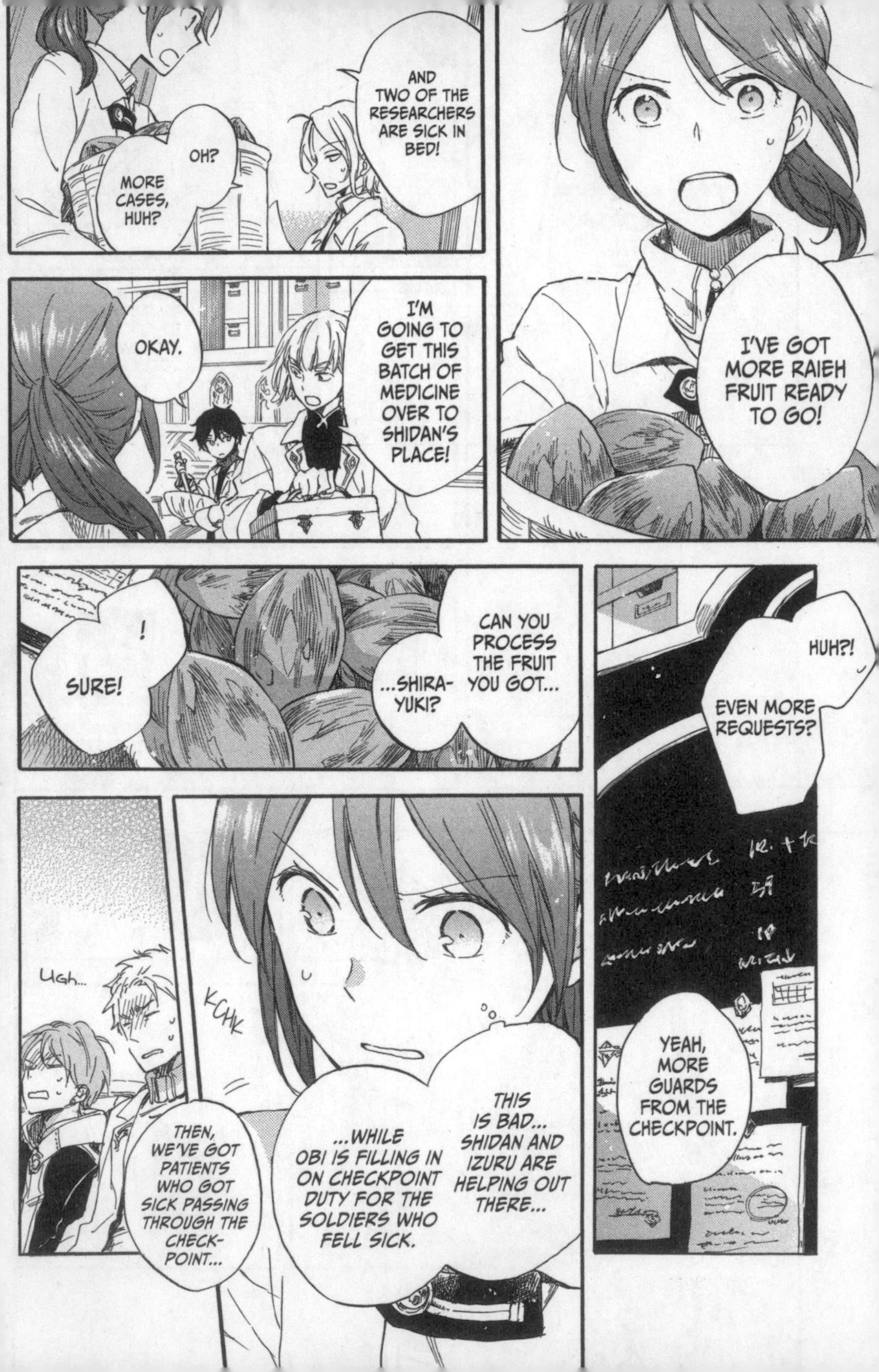
I'VE GOT MORE RAIEH FRUIT READY TO GO!
AND TWO OF THE RESEARCHERS ARE SICK IN BED!
OH?
MORE CASES, HUH?
I'M GOING TO GET THIS BATCH OF MEDICINE OVER TO SHIDAN'S PLACE!
OKAY.
HUH?!
EVEN MORE REQUESTS?
YEAH, MORE GUARDS FROM THE CHECKPOINT.
CAN YOU PROCESS THE FRUIT YOU GOT...
...SHIRA-YUKI?
!
SURE!
THIS IS BAD... SHIDAN AND IZURU ARE HELPING OUT THERE...
...WHILE OBI IS FILLING IN ON CHECKPOINT DUTY FOR THE SOLDIERS WHO FELL SICK.
THEN, WE'VE GOT PATIENTS WHO GOT SICK PASSING THROUGH THE CHECK-POINT...
KCHK
Ugh...

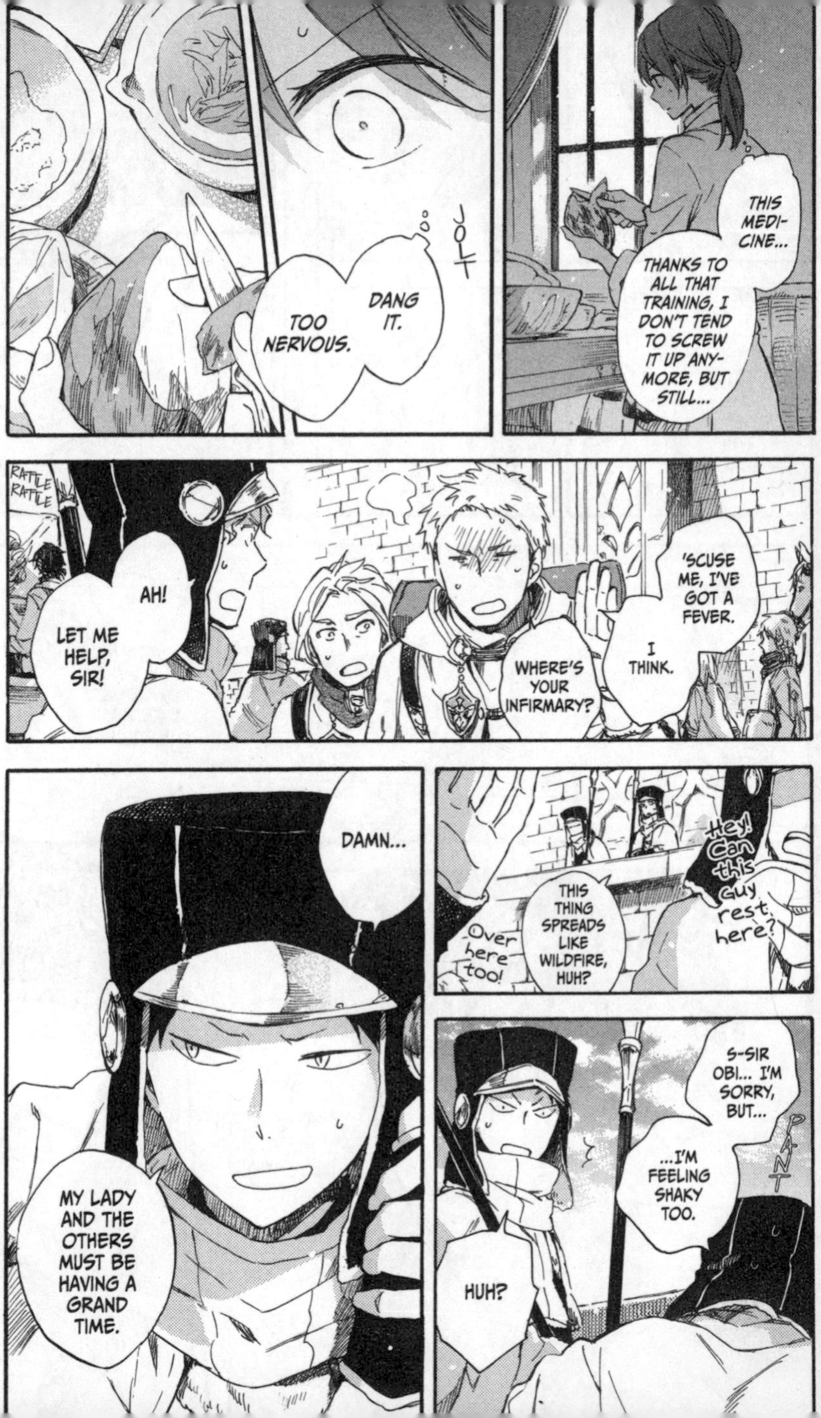
THIS MEDI-CINE...
THANKS TO ALL THAT TRAINING, I DON'T TEND TO SCREW IT UP ANY-MORE, BUT STILL...
JOLT
DANG IT.
TOO NERVOUS.
'SCUSE ME, I'VE GOT A FEVER.
I THINK.
WHERE'S YOUR INFIRMARY?
AH!
LET ME HELP, SIR!
RATTLE RATTLE
Hey! Can this guy rest here?
THIS THING SPREADS LIKE WILDFIRE, HUH?
Over here too!
S-SIR OBI... I'M SORRY, BUT...
...I'M FEELING SHAKY TOO.
PANT
HUH?
DAMN...
MY LADY AND THE OTHERS MUST BE HAVING A GRAND TIME.

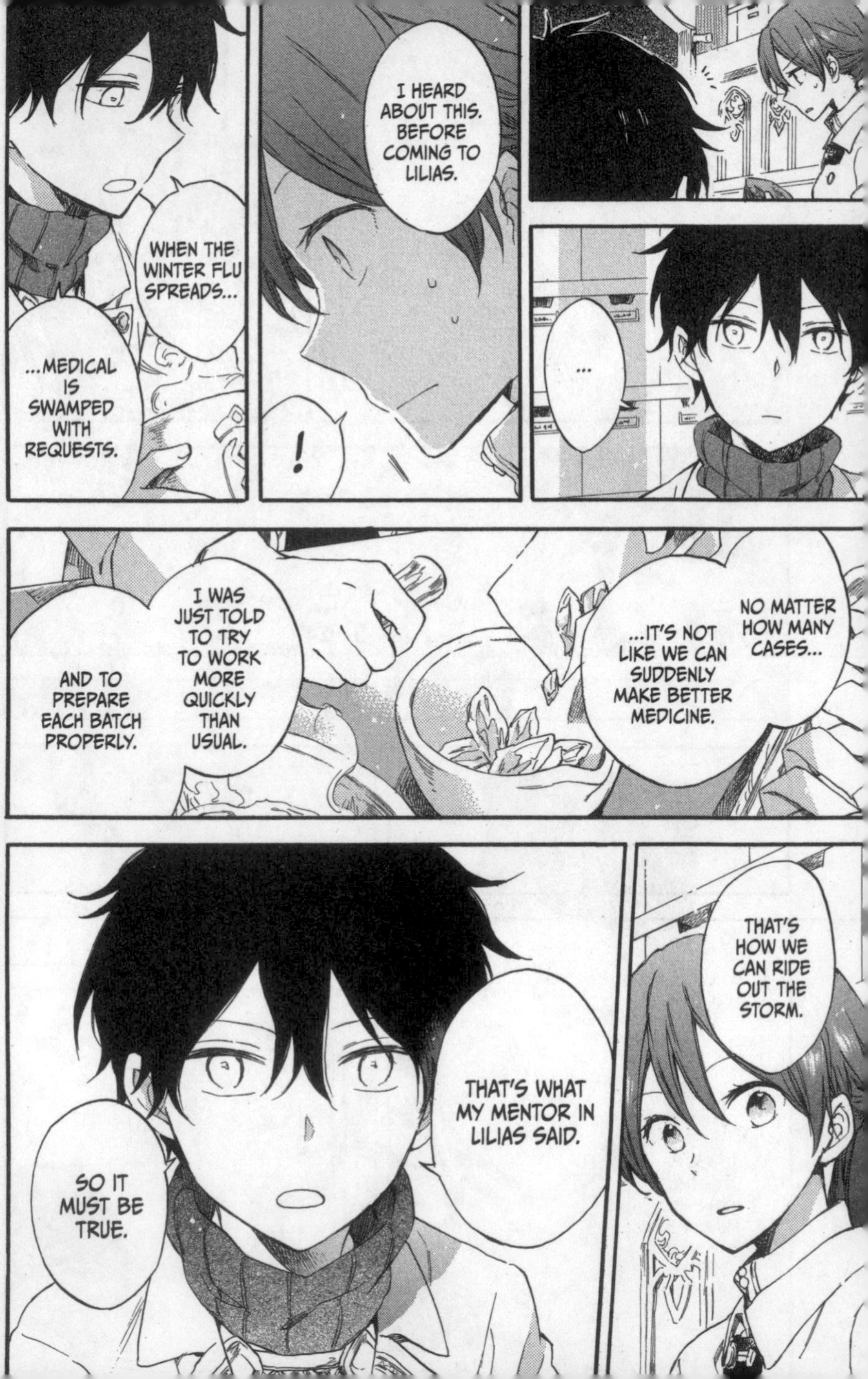
...
I HEARD ABOUT THIS. BEFORE COMING TO LILIAS.
!
WHEN THE WINTER FLU SPREADS...
...MEDICAL IS SWAMPED WITH REQUESTS.
NO MATTER HOW MANY CASES...
...IT'S NOT LIKE WE CAN SUDDENLY MAKE BETTER MEDICINE.
I WAS JUST TOLD TO TRY TO WORK MORE QUICKLY THAN USUAL.
AND TO PREPARE EACH BATCH PROPERLY.
THAT'S HOW WE CAN RIDE OUT THE STORM.
THAT'S WHAT MY MENTOR IN LILIAS SAID.
SO IT MUST BE TRUE.

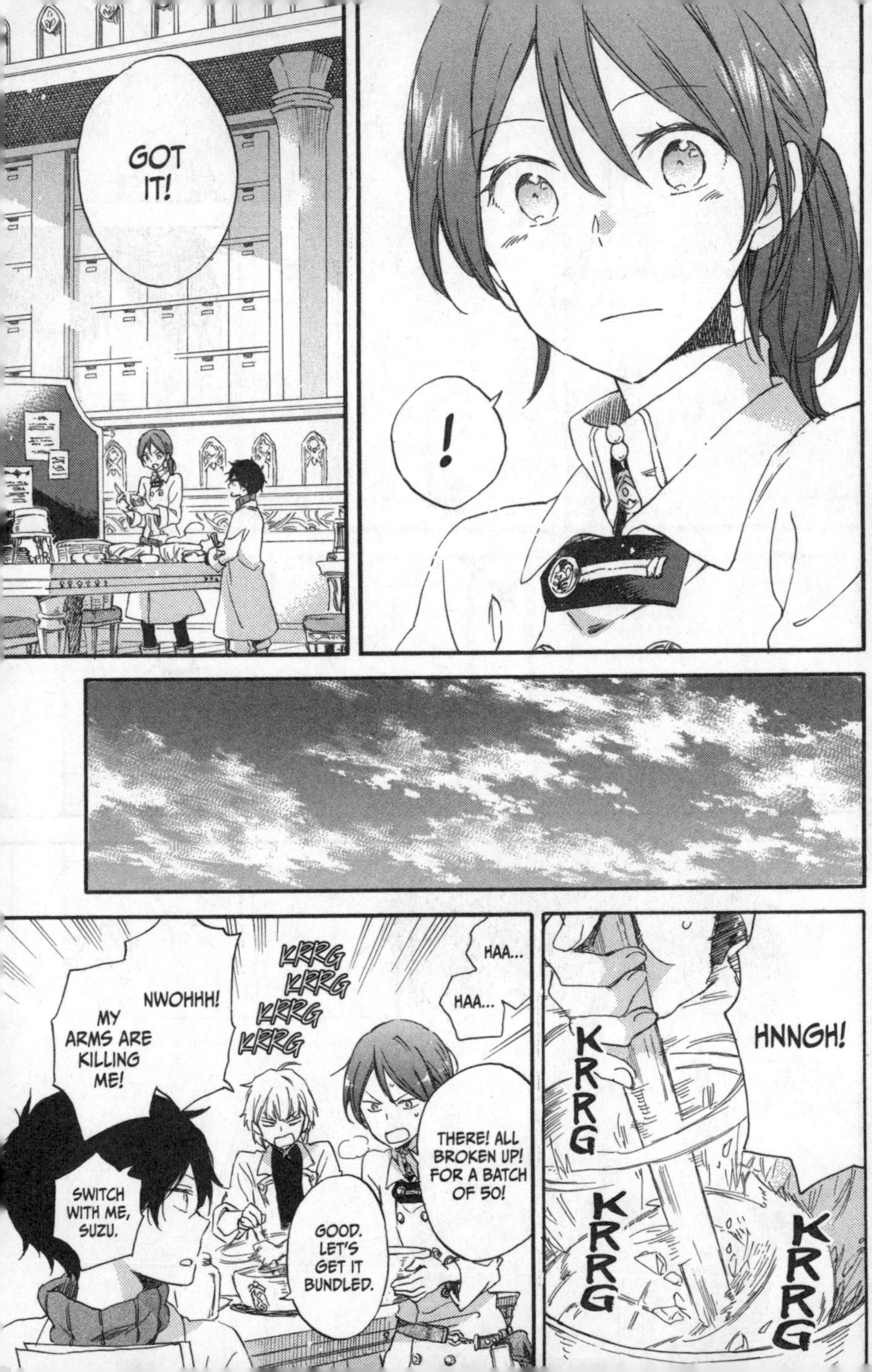
!
GOT IT!
HNNGH!
KRRG
KRRG
KRRG
HAA... HAA...
KRRG KRRG KRRG KRRG
NWOHHH! MY ARMS ARE KILLING ME!
THERE! ALL BROKEN UP! FOR A BATCH OF 50!
GOOD. LET'S GET IT BUNDLED.
SWITCH WITH ME, SUZU.

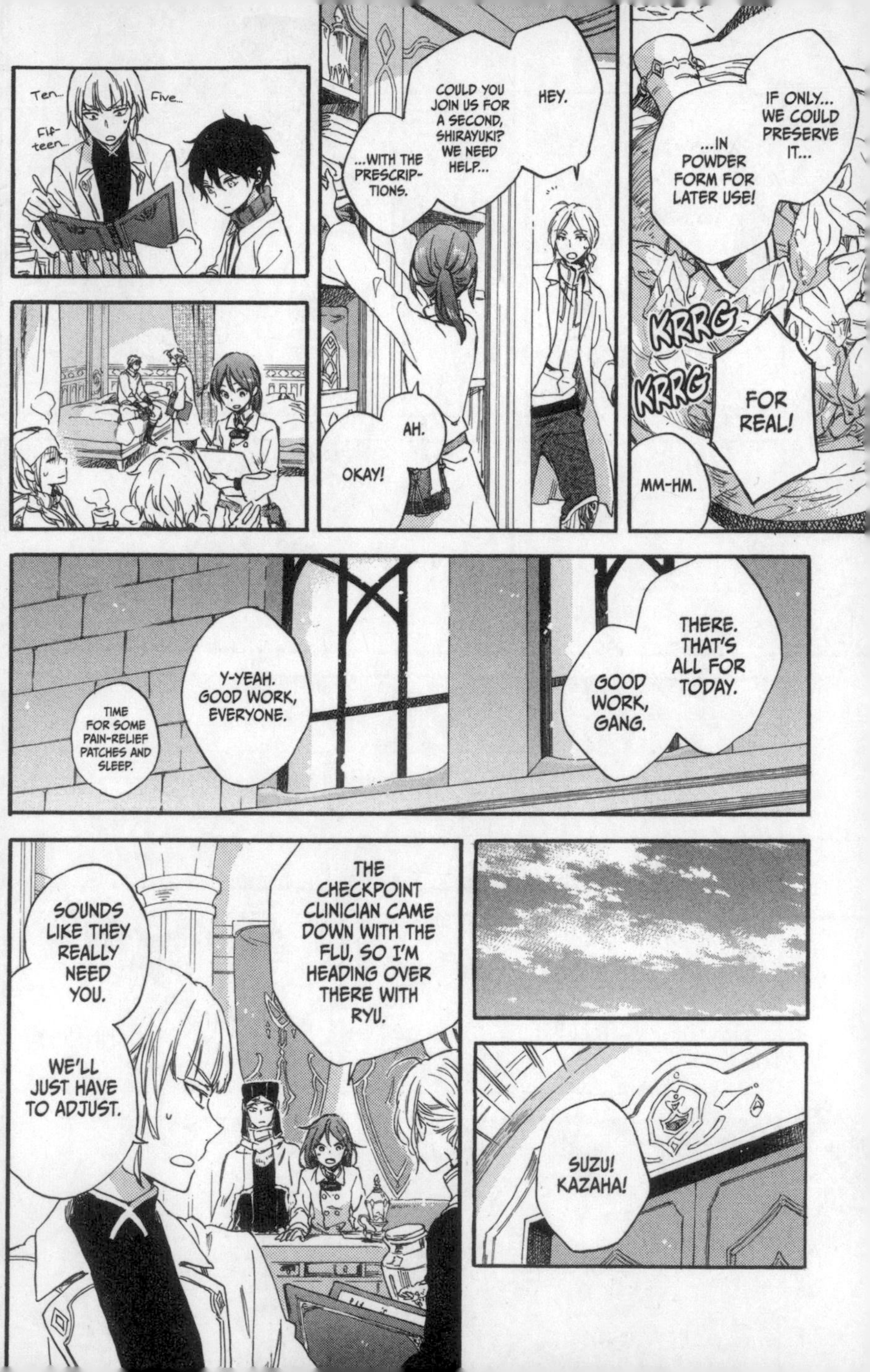
IF ONLY... WE COULD PRESERVE IT...
...IN POWDER FORM FOR LATER USE!
KRRG
KRRG
FOR REAL!
MM-HM.
HEY.
COULD YOU JOIN US FOR A SECOND, SHIRAYUKI? WE NEED HELP...
...WITH THE PRESCRIP-TIONS.
AH.
OKAY!
Five...
Ten...
Fif-teen...
THERE. THAT'S ALL FOR TODAY.
GOOD WORK, GANG.
Y-YEAH. GOOD WORK, EVERYONE.
TIME FOR SOME PAIN-RELIEF PATCHES AND SLEEP.
SUZU! KAZAHA!
THE CHECKPOINT CLINICIAN CAME DOWN WITH THE FLU, SO I'M HEADING OVER THERE WITH RYU.
SOUNDS LIKE THEY REALLY NEED YOU.
WE'LL JUST HAVE TO ADJUST.

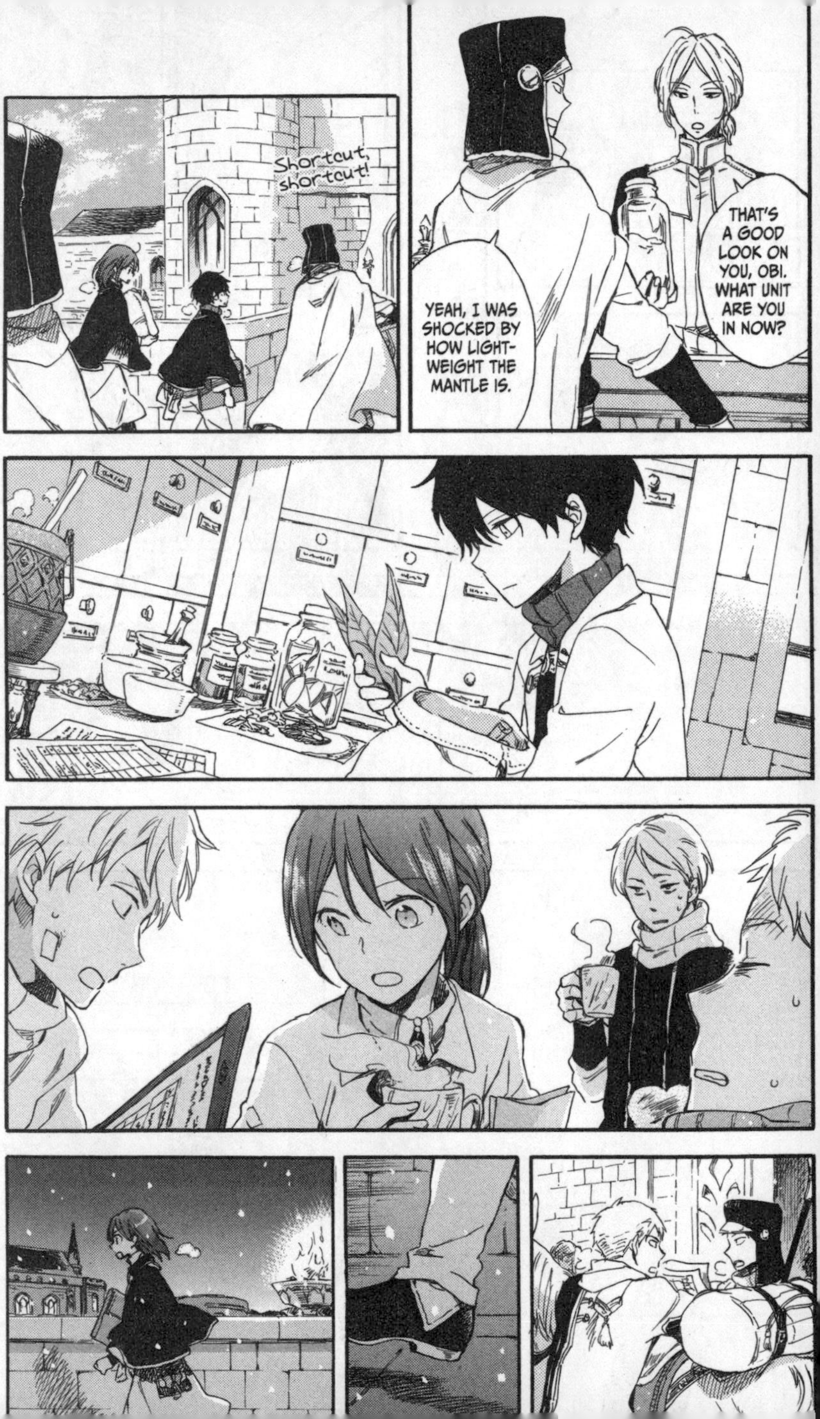
THAT'S A GOOD LOOK ON YOU, OBI. WHAT UNIT ARE YOU IN NOW?
YEAH, I WAS SHOCKED BY HOW LIGHT-WEIGHT THE MANTLE IS.
Shortcut, shortcut!

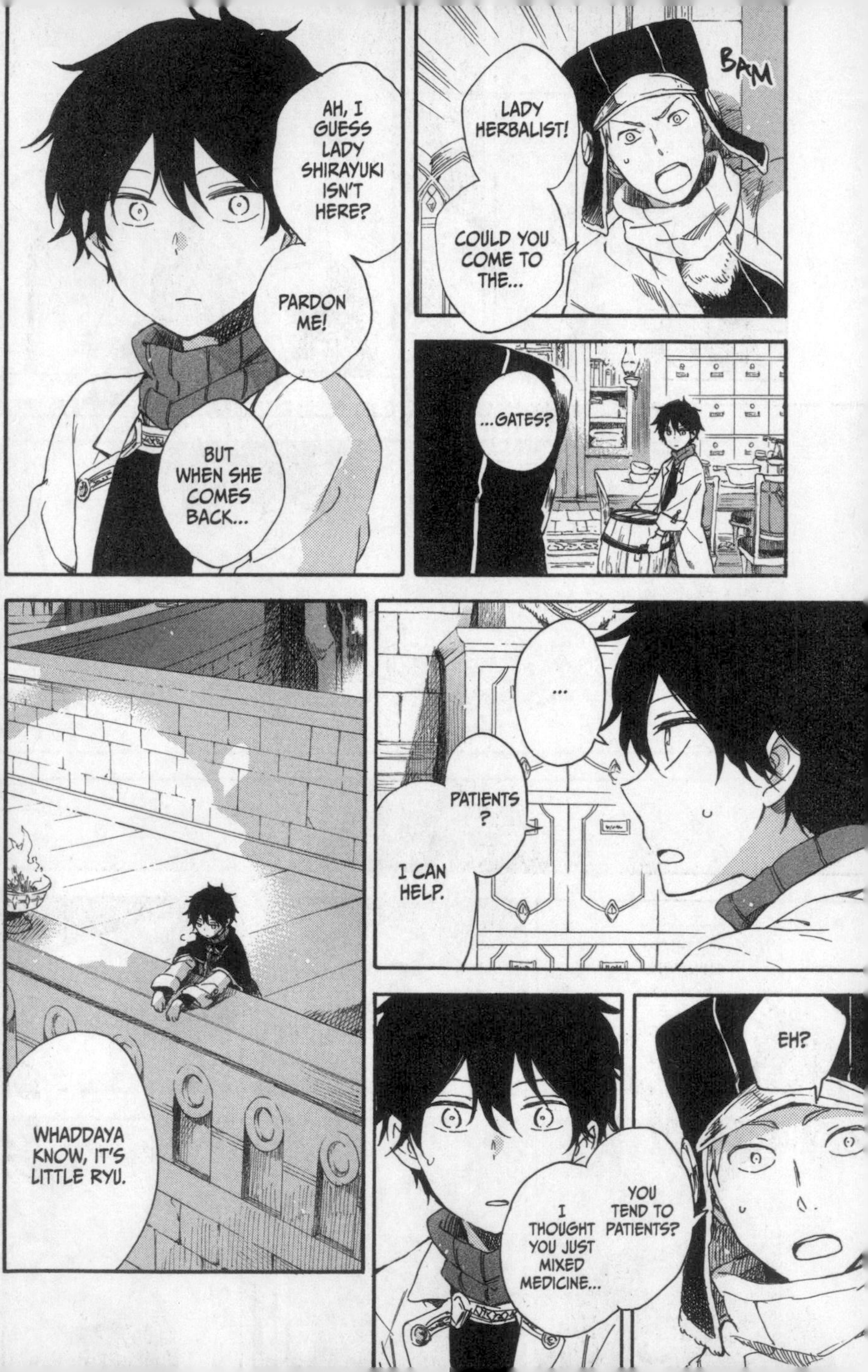
BAM
LADY HERBALIST!
COULD YOU COME TO THE...
...GATES?
AH, I GUESS LADY SHIRAYUKI ISN'T HERE?
PARDON ME!
BUT WHEN SHE COMES BACK...
...
PATIENTS?
I CAN HELP.
EH?
YOU TEND TO PATIENTS?
I THOUGHT YOU JUST MIXED MEDICINE...
WHADDAYA KNOW, IT'S LITTLE RYU.

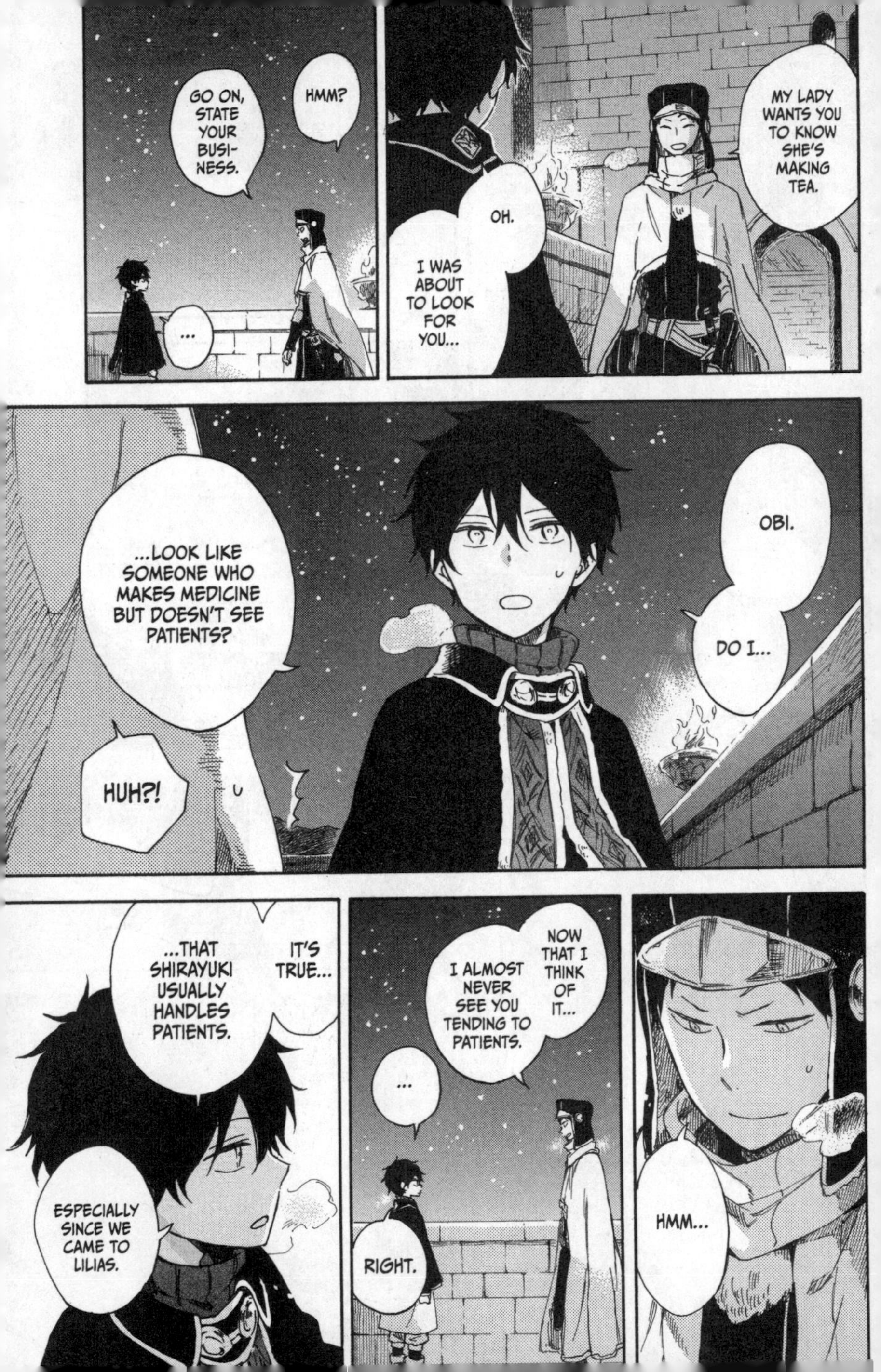
MY LADY WANTS YOU TO KNOW SHE'S MAKING TEA.
OH.
I WAS ABOUT TO LOOK FOR YOU...
HMM?
GO ON, STATE YOUR BUSI- NESS.
...
OBI.
DO I...
...LOOK LIKE SOMEONE WHO MAKES MEDICINE BUT DOESN'T SEE PATIENTS?
HUH?!
HMM...
NOW THAT I THINK OF IT...
I ALMOST NEVER SEE YOU TENDING TO PATIENTS.
...
RIGHT.
IT'S TRUE...
...THAT SHIRAYUKI USUALLY HANDLES PATIENTS.
ESPECIALLY SINCE WE CAME TO LILIAS.

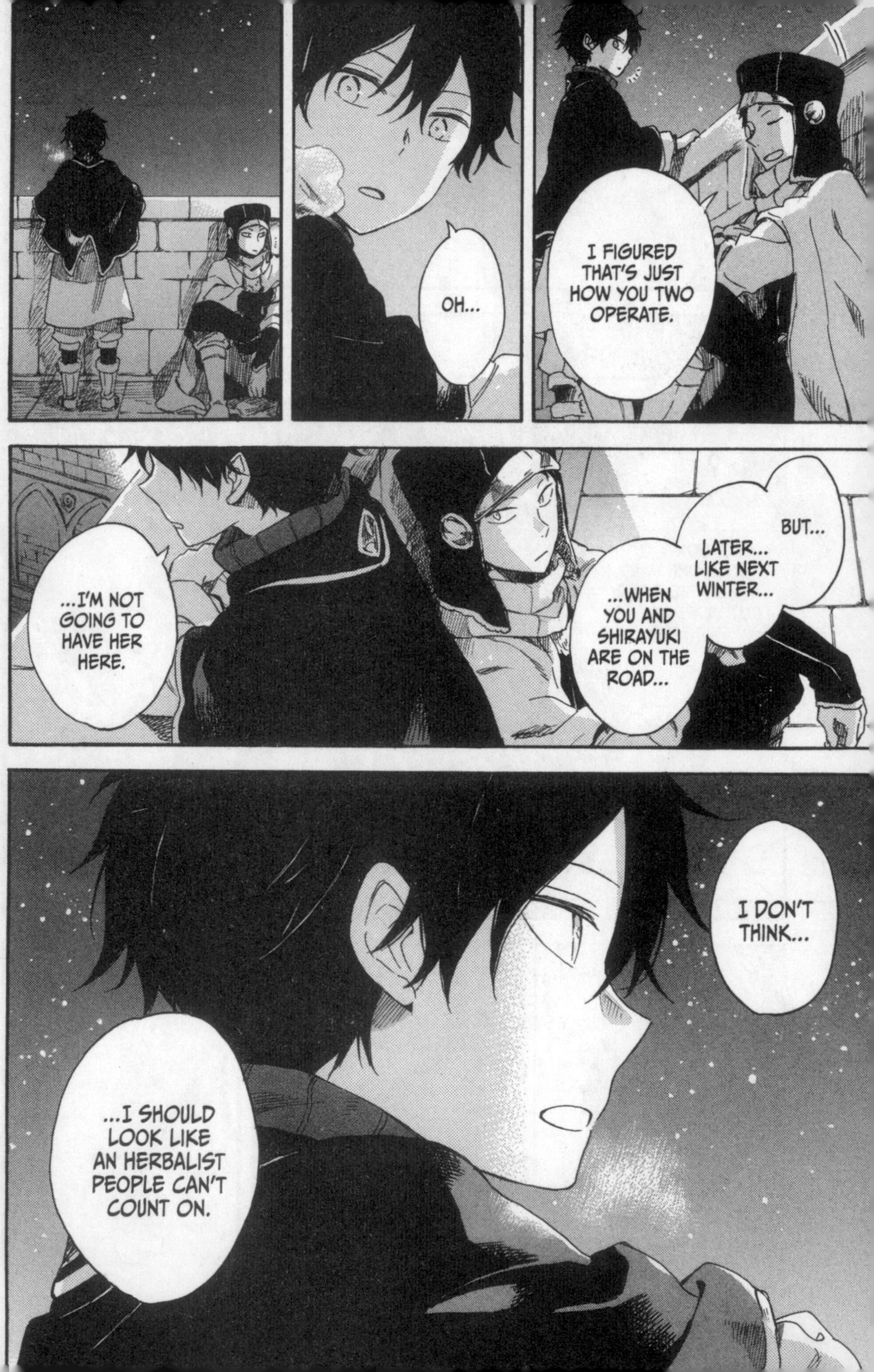
I FIGURED THAT'S JUST HOW YOU TWO OPERATE.
OH...
BUT...
LATER... LIKE NEXT WINTER...
...WHEN YOU AND SHIRAYUKI ARE ON THE ROAD...
...I'M NOT GOING TO HAVE HER HERE.
I DON'T THINK...
...I SHOULD LOOK LIKE AN HERBALIST PEOPLE CAN'T COUNT ON.

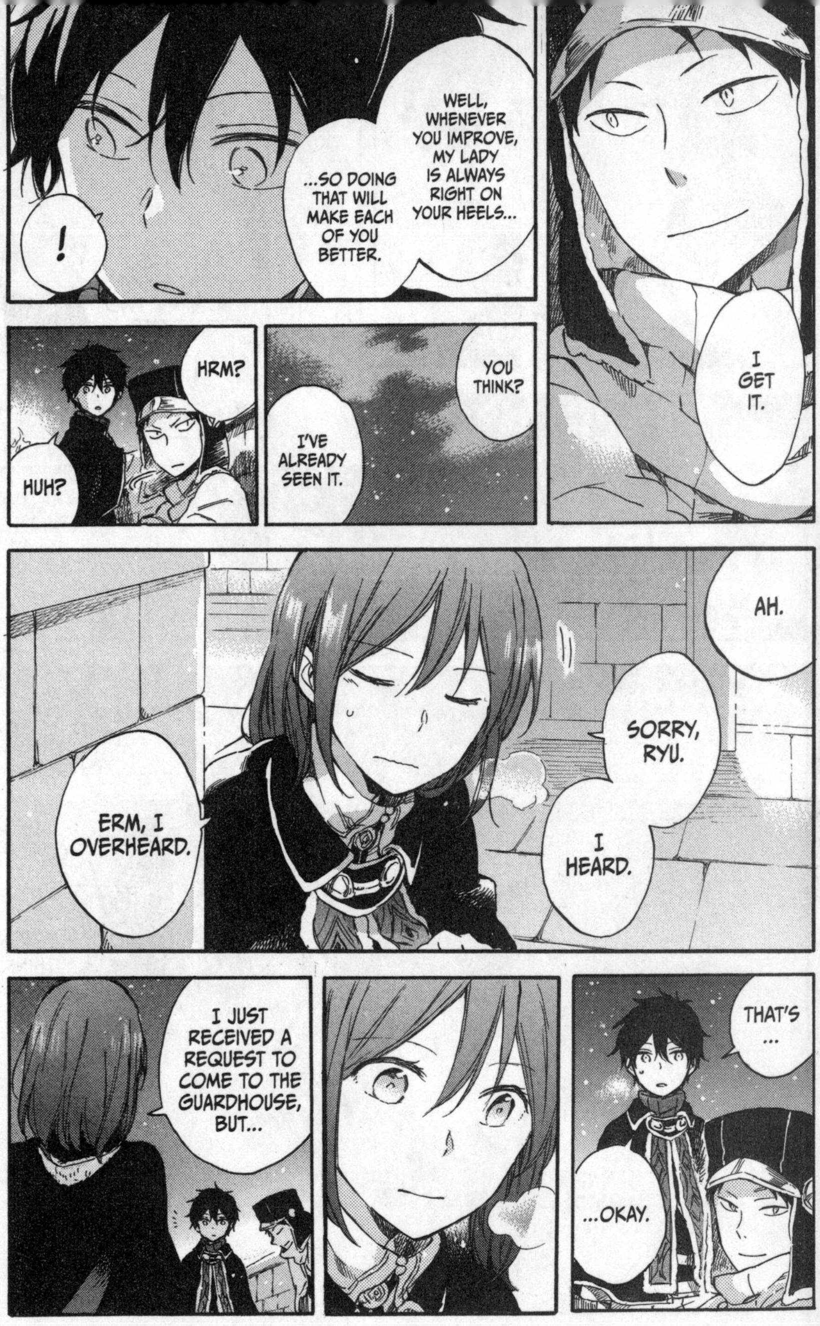
WELL, WHENEVER YOU IMPROVE, MY LADY IS ALWAYS RIGHT ON YOUR HEELS...
...SO DOING THAT WILL MAKE EACH OF YOU BETTER.
!
I GET IT.
YOU THINK?
I'VE ALREADY SEEN IT.
HRM?
HUH?
AH.
SORRY, RYU.
I HEARD.
ERM, I OVERHEARD.
THAT'S ...
...OKAY.
I JUST RECEIVED A REQUEST TO COME TO THE GUARDHOUSE, BUT...

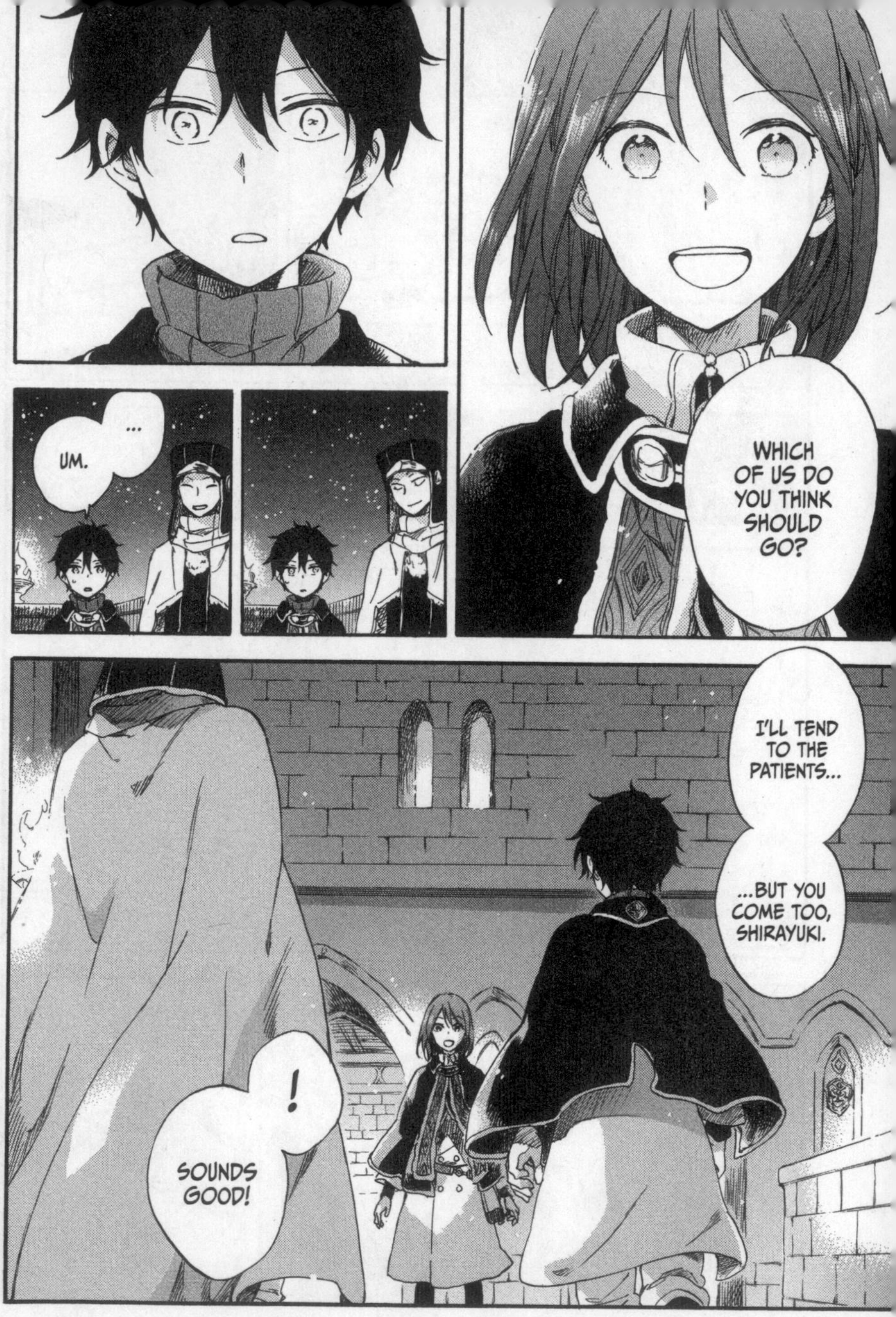

WHICH OF US DO YOU THINK SHOULD GO?
...
UM.
I'LL TEND TO THE PATIENTS...
...BUT YOU COME TOO, SHIRAYUKI.
!
SOUNDS GOOD!

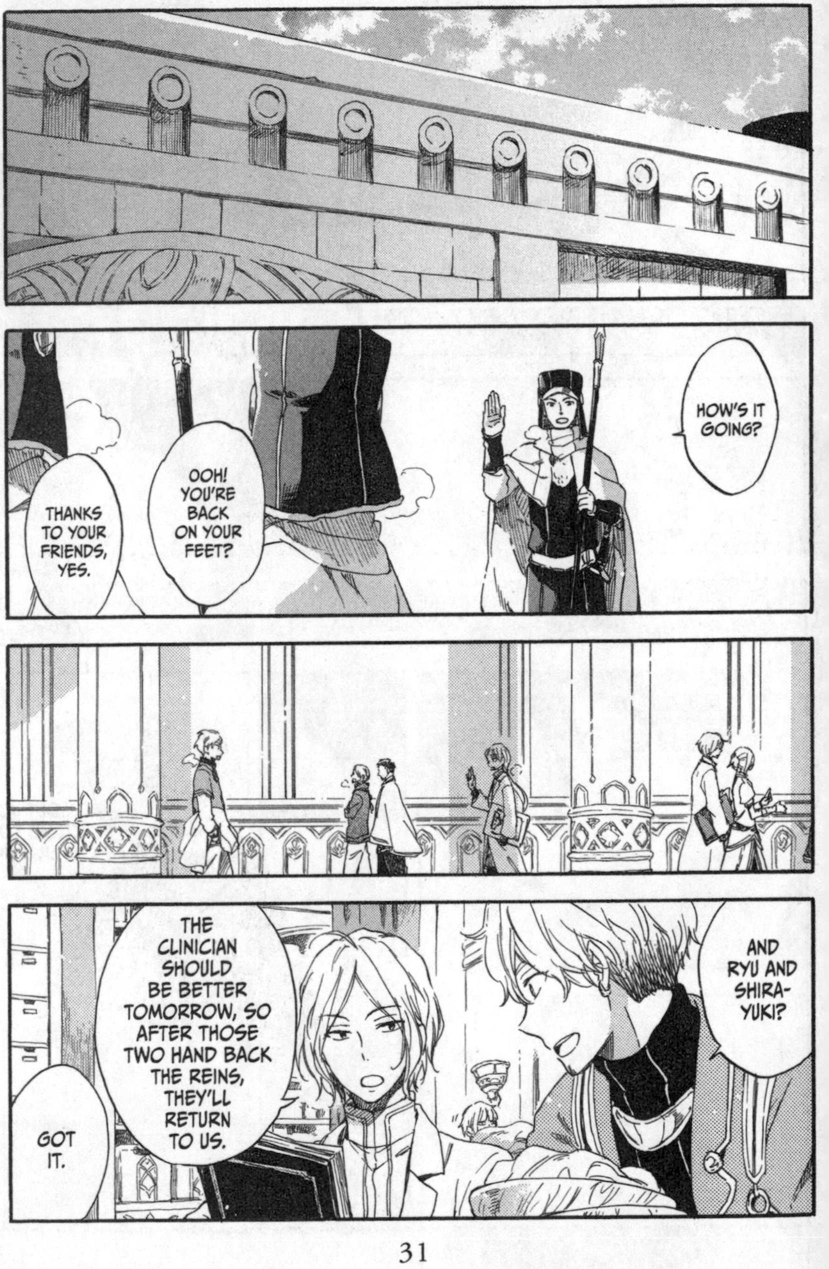
HOW'S IT GOING?
OOH! YOU'RE BACK ON YOUR FEET?
THANKS TO YOUR FRIENDS, YES.
AND RYU AND SHIRA-YUKI?
THE CLINICIAN SHOULD BE BETTER TOMORROW, SO AFTER THOSE TWO HAND BACK THE REINS, THEY'LL RETURN TO US.
GOT IT.

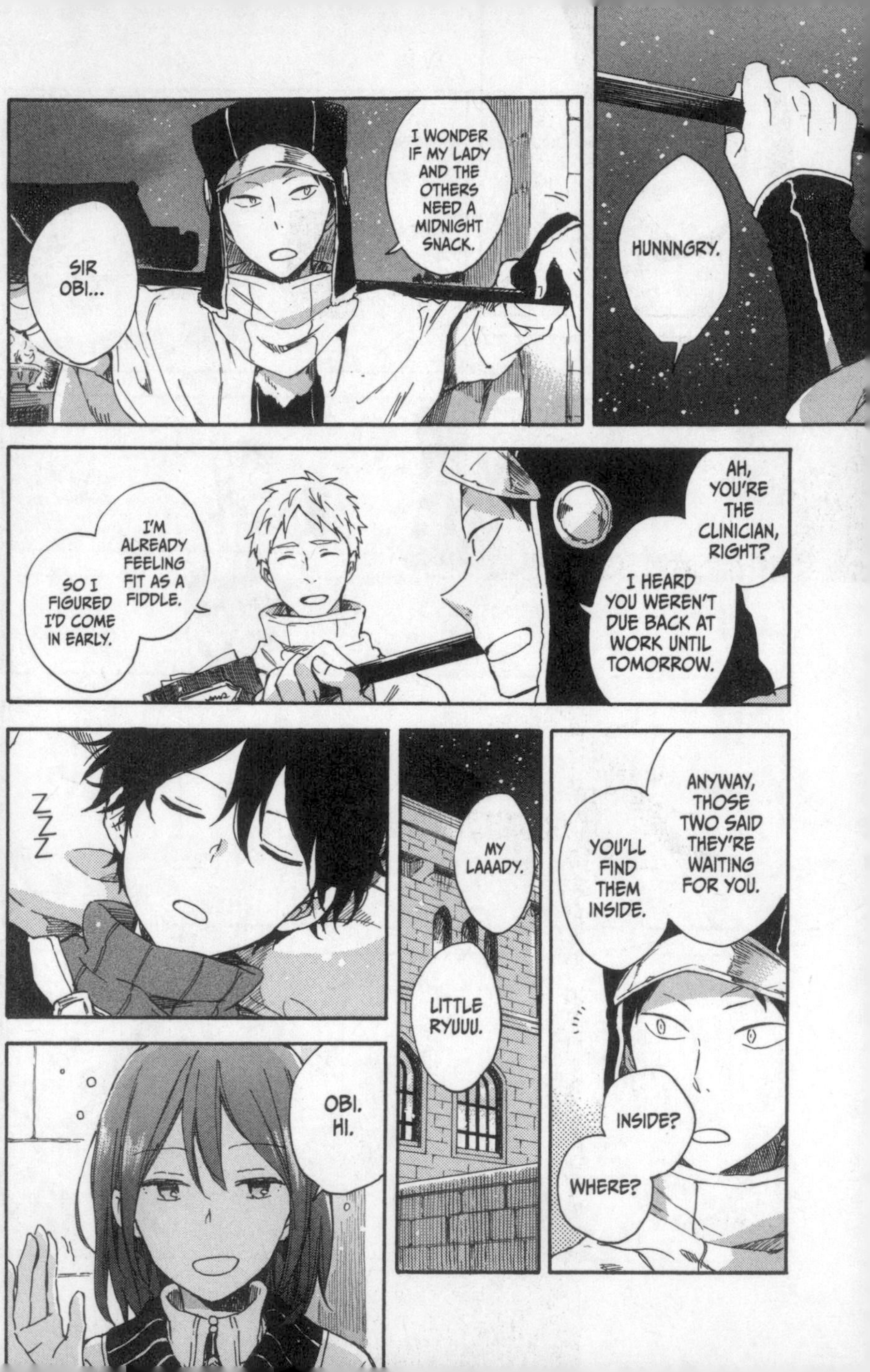
HUNNNGRY.
I WONDER IF MY LADY AND THE OTHERS NEED A MIDNIGHT SNACK.
SIR OBI...
AH, YOU'RE THE CLINICIAN, RIGHT?
I HEARD YOU WEREN'T DUE BACK AT WORK UNTIL TOMORROW.
I'M ALREADY FEELING FIT AS A FIDDLE.
SO I FIGURED I'D COME IN EARLY.
ANYWAY, THOSE TWO SAID THEY'RE WAITING FOR YOU.
YOU'LL FIND THEM INSIDE.
INSIDE?
WHERE?
MY LAAADY.
LITTLE RYUUU.
ZZZ
OBI. HI.

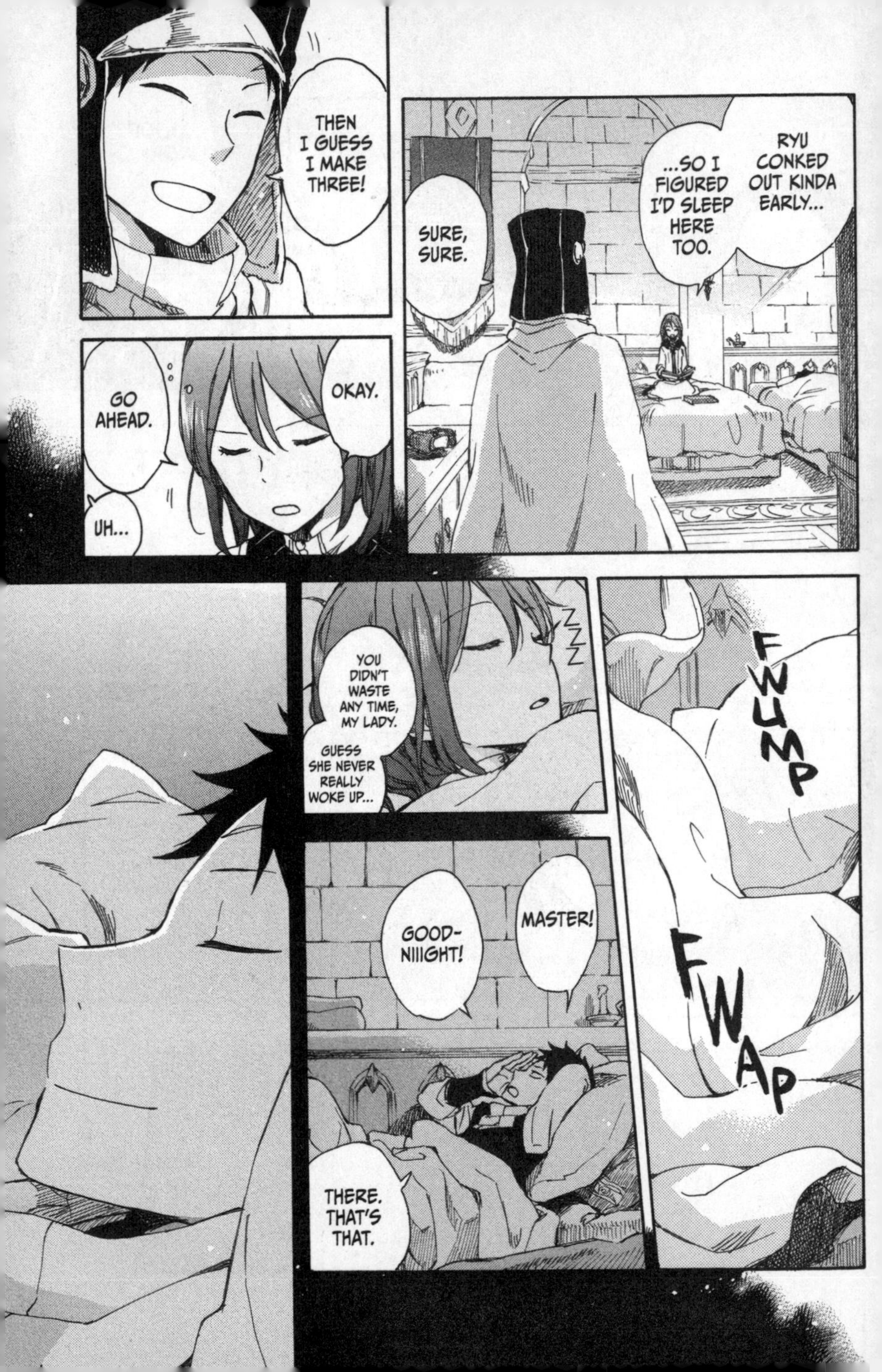
RYU CONKED OUT KINDA EARLY...
...SO I FIGURED I'D SLEEP HERE TOO.
SURE, SURE.
THEN I GUESS I MAKE THREE!
OKAY.
GO AHEAD.
UH...
FWUMP
FWAP
ZZZ
YOU DIDN'T WASTE ANY TIME, MY LADY.
GUESS SHE NEVER REALLY WOKE UP...
MASTER!
GOOD-NIIIGHT!
THERE. THAT'S THAT.

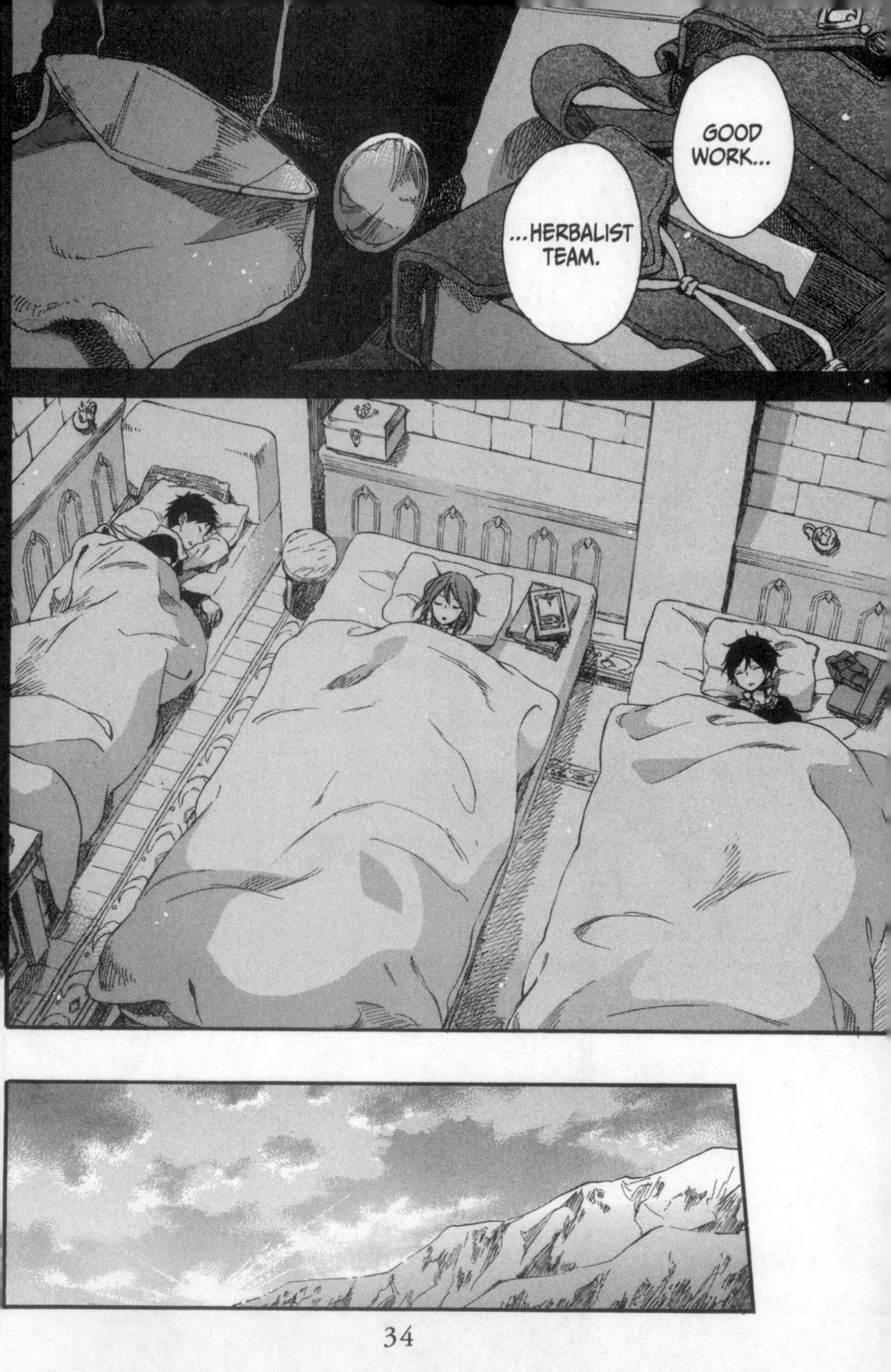
GOOD WORK...
...HERBALIST TEAM.

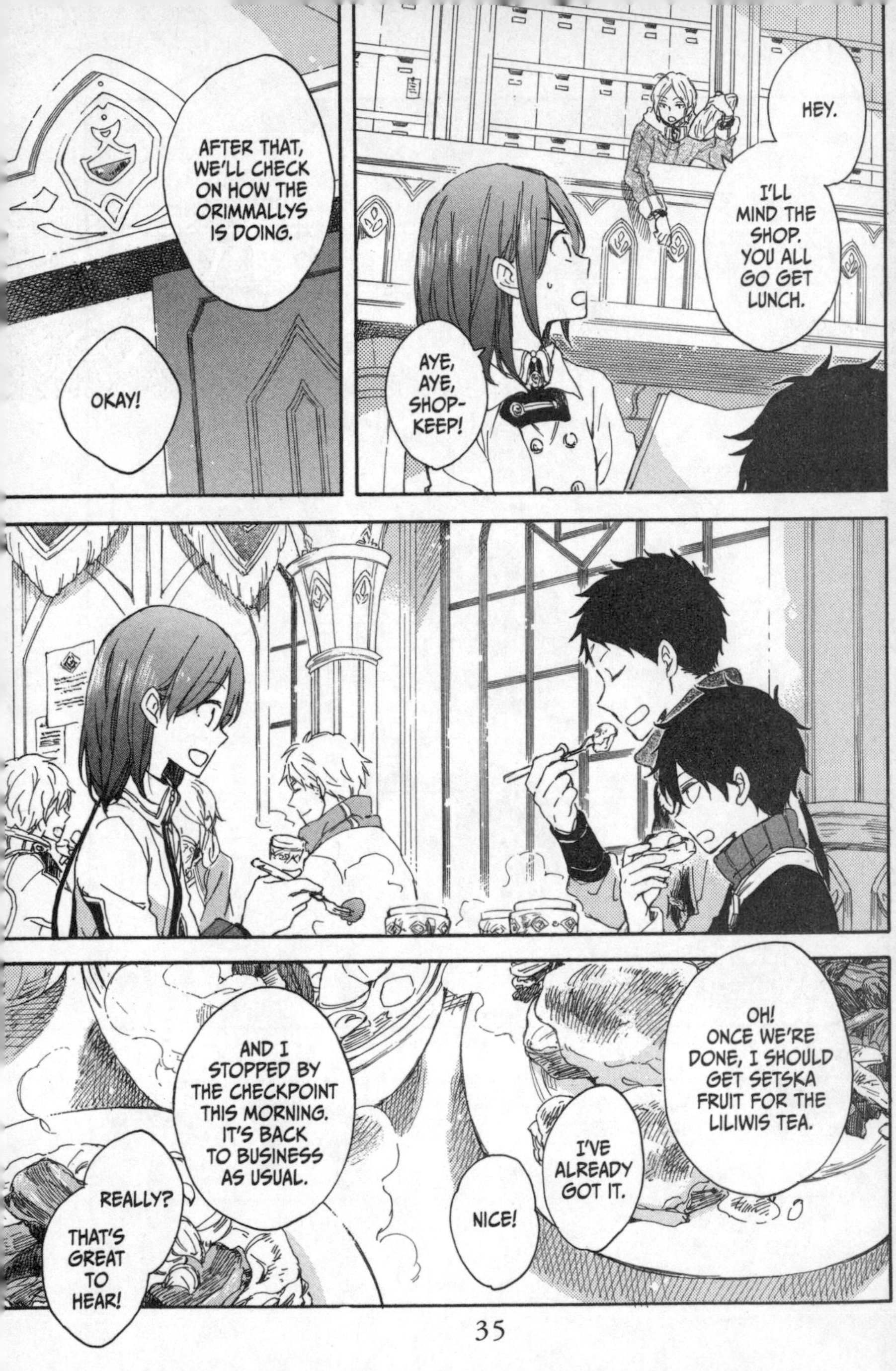
HEY.
I'LL MIND THE SHOP. YOU ALL GO GET LUNCH.
AYE, AYE, SHOP-KEEP!
AFTER THAT, WE'LL CHECK ON HOW THE ORIMMALLYS IS DOING.
OKAY!
OH! ONCE WE'RE DONE, I SHOULD GET SETSKA FRUIT FOR THE LILIWIS TEA.
I'VE ALREADY GOT IT.
NICE!
AND I STOPPED BY THE CHECKPOINT THIS MORNING. IT'S BACK TO BUSINESS AS USUAL.
REALLY?
THAT'S GREAT TO HEAR!

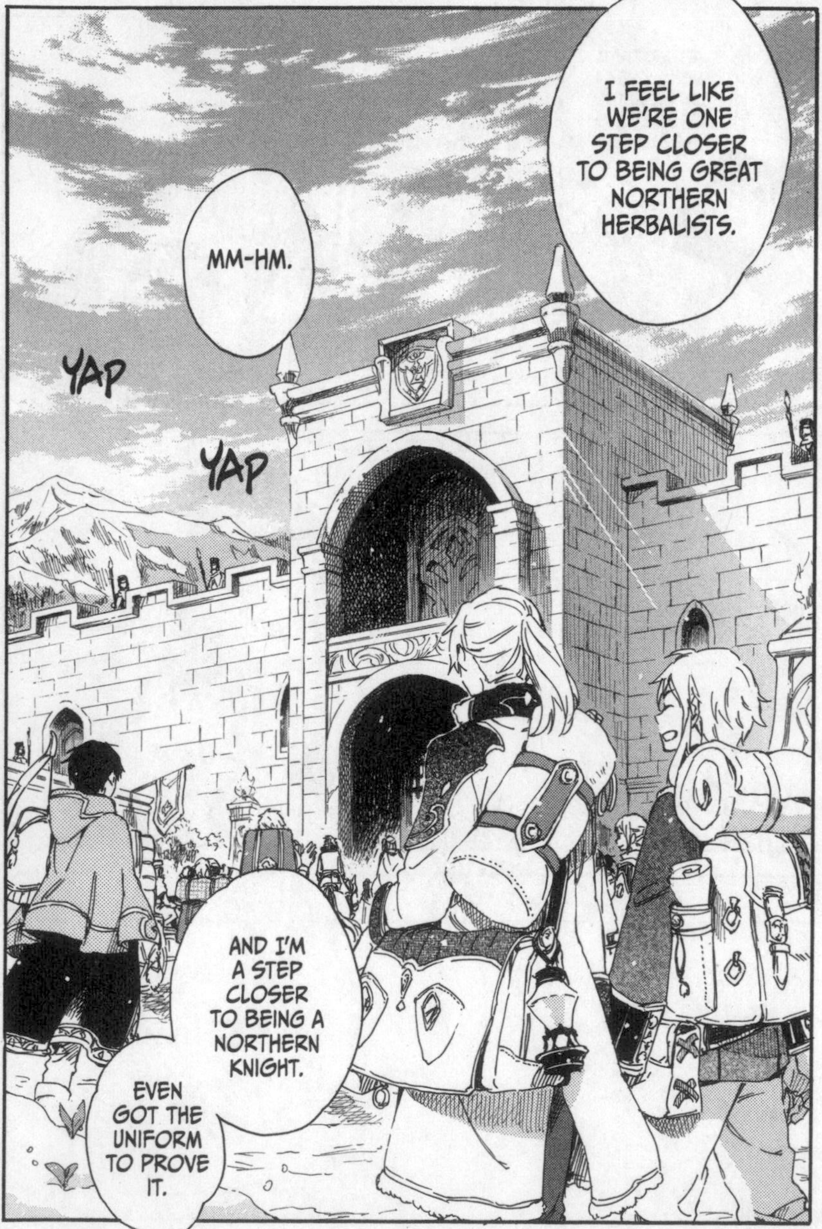
I FEEL LIKE WE'RE ONE STEP CLOSER TO BEING GREAT NORTHERN HERBALISTS.
MM-HM.
YAP
YAP
AND I'M A STEP CLOSER TO BEING A NORTHERN KNIGHT.
EVEN GOT THE UNIFORM TO PROVE IT.

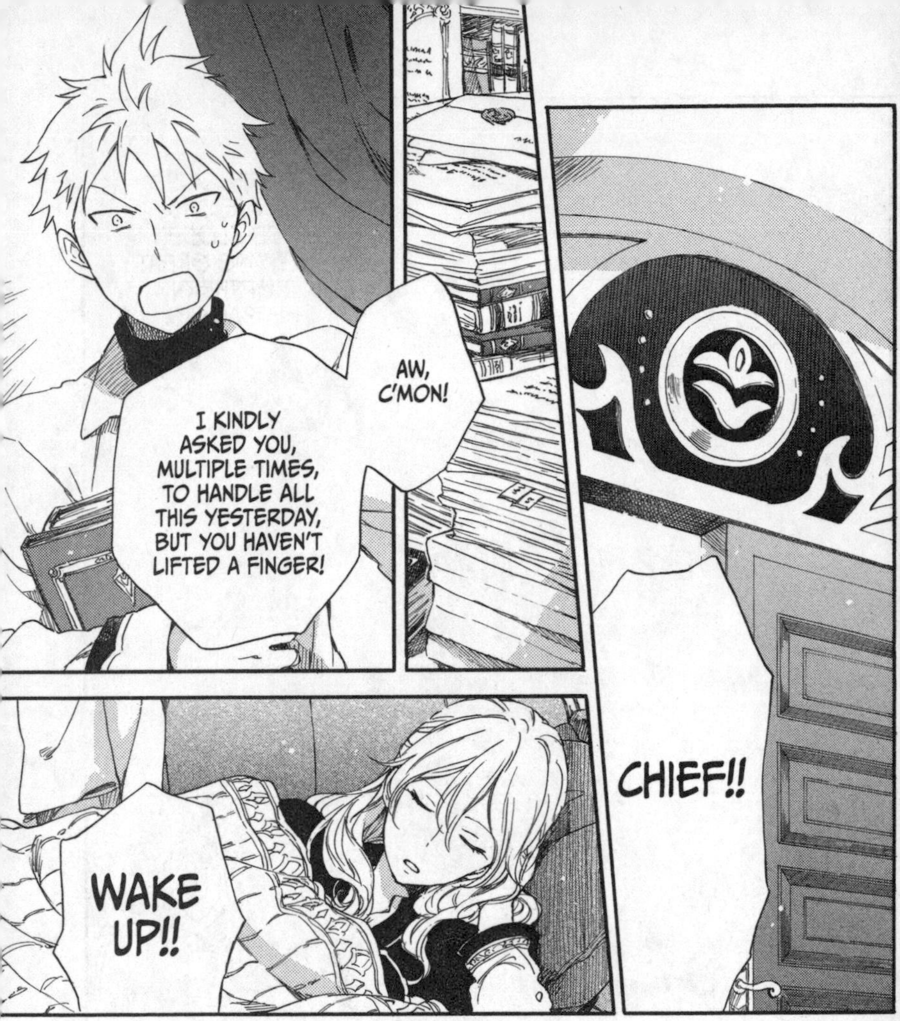
CHIEF!!
AW, C'MON!
I KINDLY ASKED YOU, MULTIPLE TIMES, TO HANDLE ALL THIS YESTERDAY, BUT YOU HAVEN'T LIFTED A FINGER!
WAKE UP!!

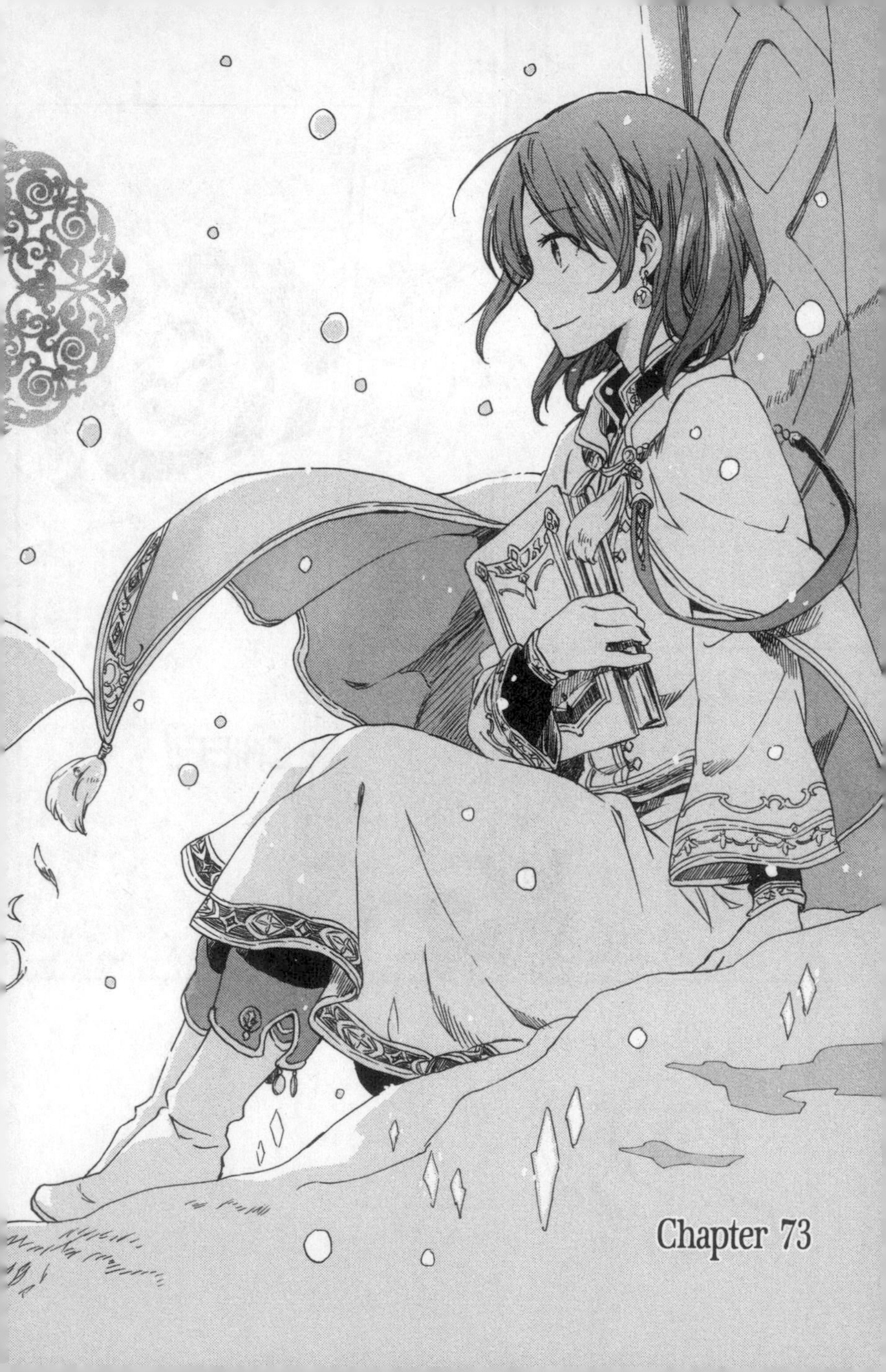

Chapter 73

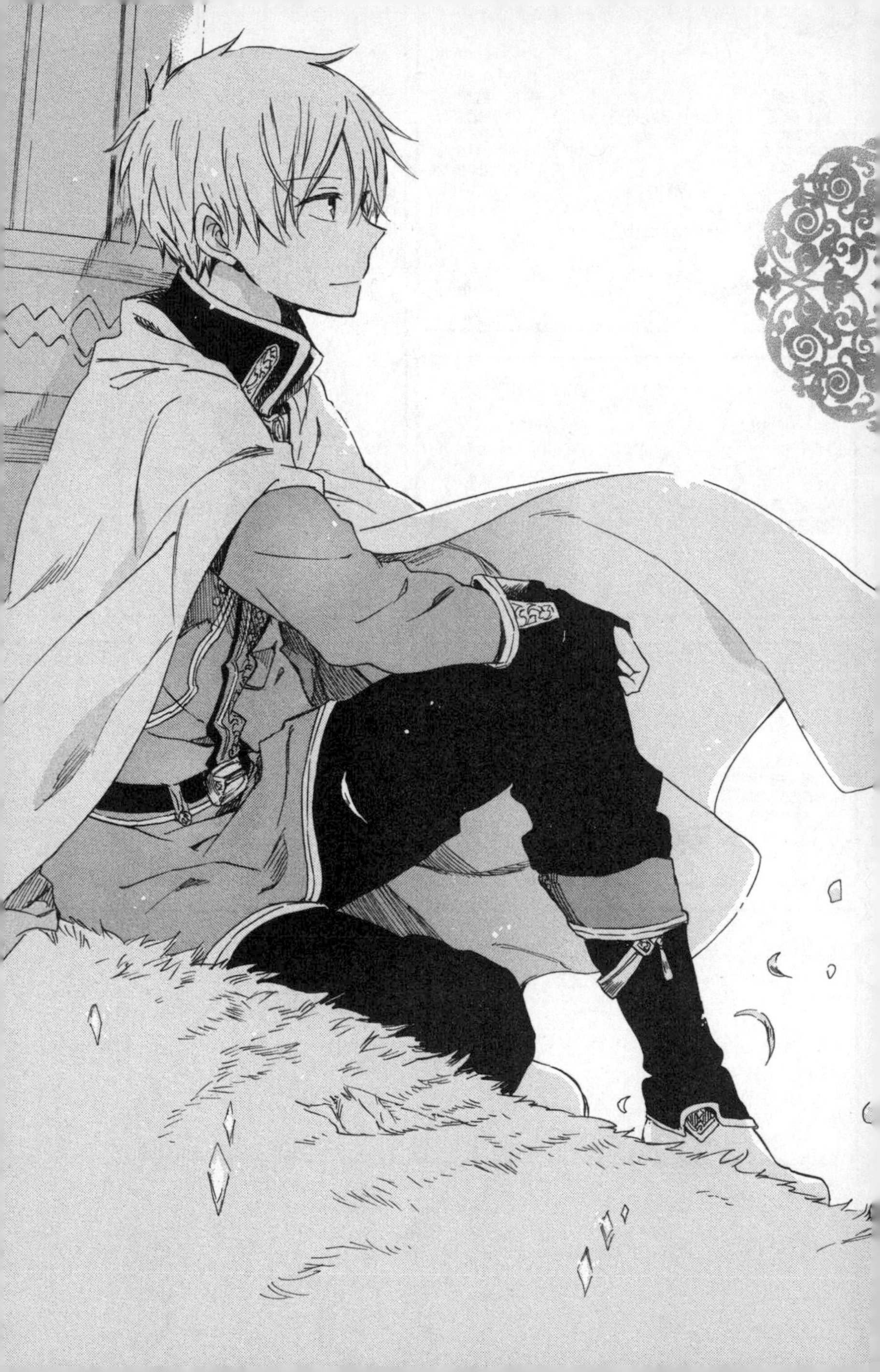

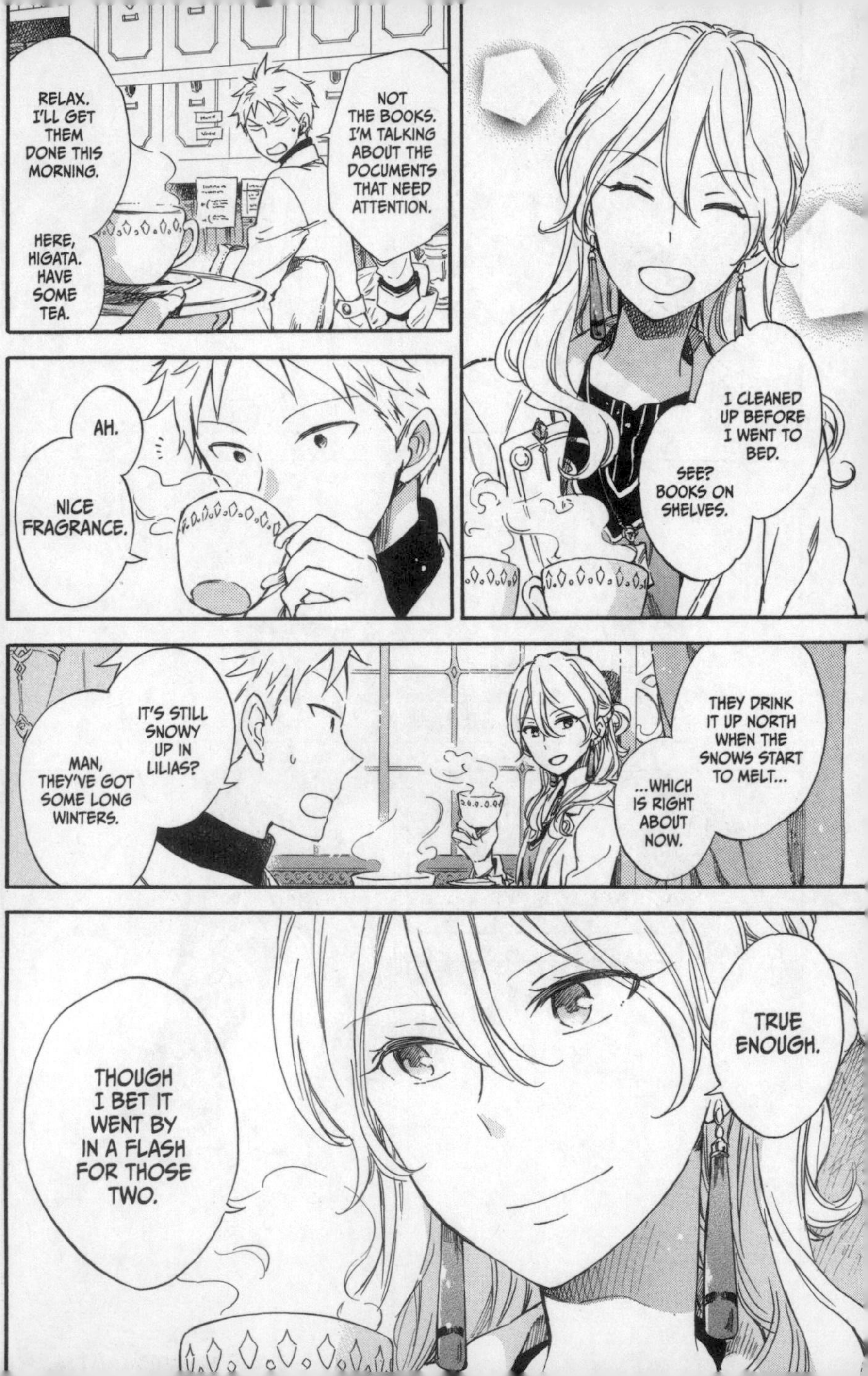
I CLEANED UP BEFORE I WENT TO BED.
SEE? BOOKS ON SHELVES.
NOT THE BOOKS. I'M TALKING ABOUT THE DOCUMENTS THAT NEED ATTENTION.
RELAX. I'LL GET THEM DONE THIS MORNING.
HERE, HIGATA. HAVE SOME TEA.
AH.
NICE FRAGRANCE.
THEY DRINK IT UP NORTH WHEN THE SNOWS START TO MELT...
...WHICH IS RIGHT ABOUT NOW.
IT'S STILL SNOWY UP IN LILIAS?
MAN, THEY'VE GOT SOME LONG WINTERS.
TRUE ENOUGH.
THOUGH I BET IT WENT BY IN A FLASH FOR THOSE TWO.

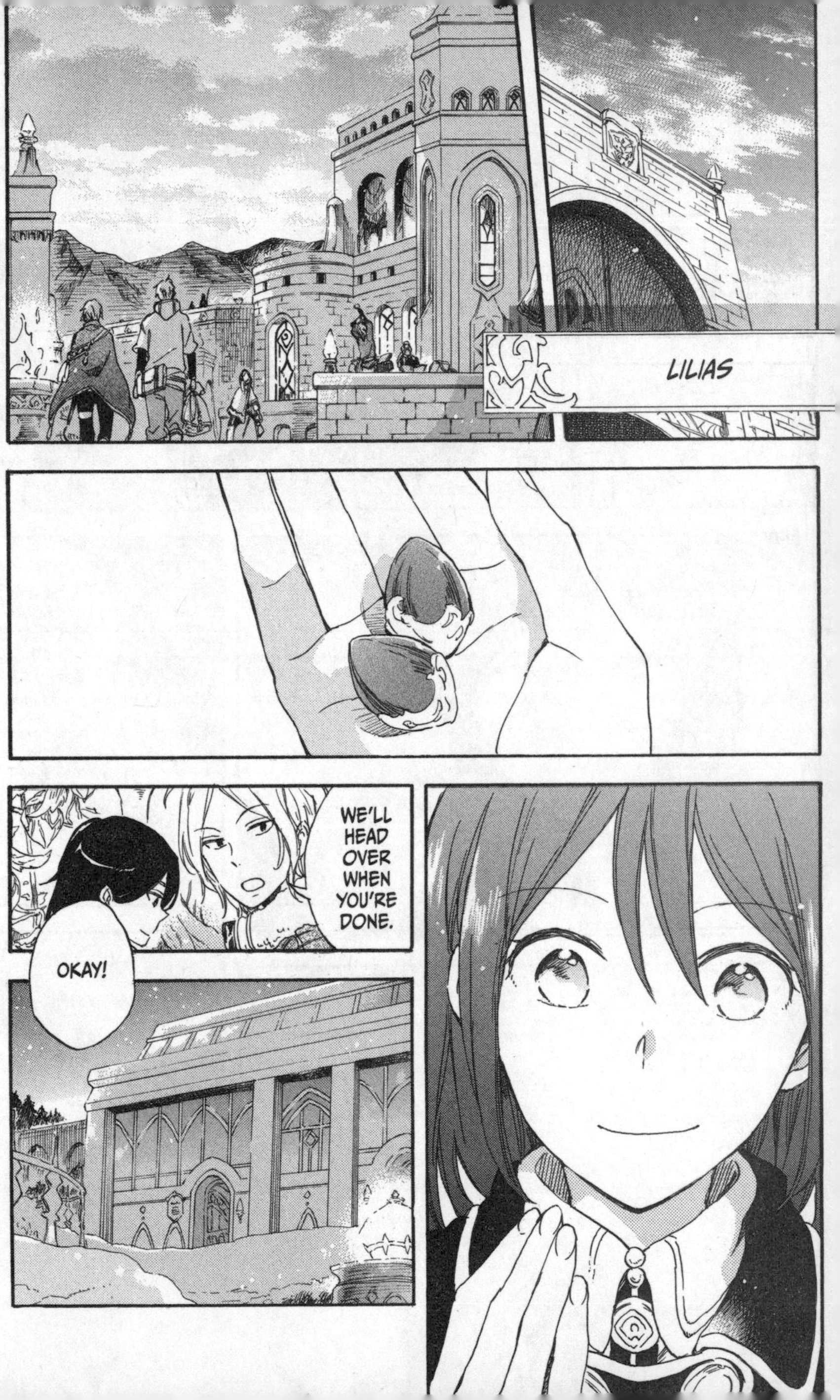
LILIAS
WE'LL HEAD OVER WHEN YOU'RE DONE.
OKAY!

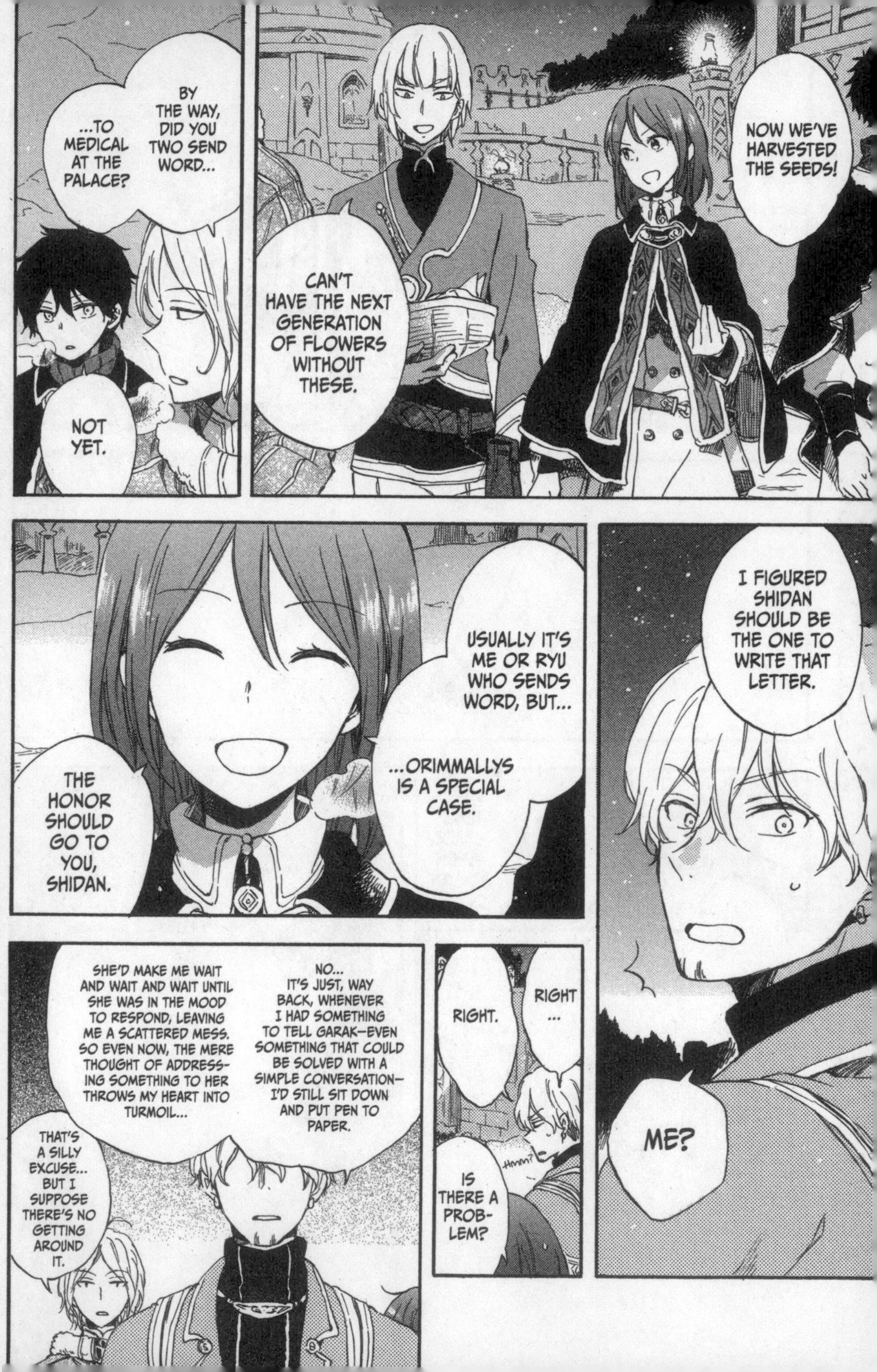
NOW WE'VE HARVESTED THE SEEDS!
CAN'T HAVE THE NEXT GENERATION OF FLOWERS WITHOUT THESE.
BY THE WAY, DID YOU TWO SEND WORD...
...TO MEDICAL AT THE PALACE?
NOT YET.
I FIGURED SHIDAN SHOULD BE THE ONE TO WRITE THAT LETTER.
ME?
USUALLY IT'S ME OR RYU WHO SENDS WORD, BUT...
...ORIMMALLYS IS A SPECIAL CASE.
THE HONOR SHOULD GO TO YOU, SHIDAN.
RIGHT...
RIGHT.
Hmm?
IS THERE A PROBLEM?
NO... IT'S JUST, WAY BACK, WHENEVER I HAD SOMETHING TO TELL GARAK—EVEN SOMETHING THAT COULD BE SOLVED WITH A SIMPLE CONVERSATION—I'D STILL SIT DOWN AND PUT PEN TO PAPER.
SHE'D MAKE ME WAIT AND WAIT AND WAIT UNTIL SHE WAS IN THE MOOD TO RESPOND, LEAVING ME A SCATTERED MESS. SO EVEN NOW, THE MERE THOUGHT OF ADDRESSING SOMETHING TO HER THROWS MY HEART INTO TURMOIL...
THAT'S A SILLY EXCUSE... BUT I SUPPOSE THERE'S NO GETTING AROUND IT.

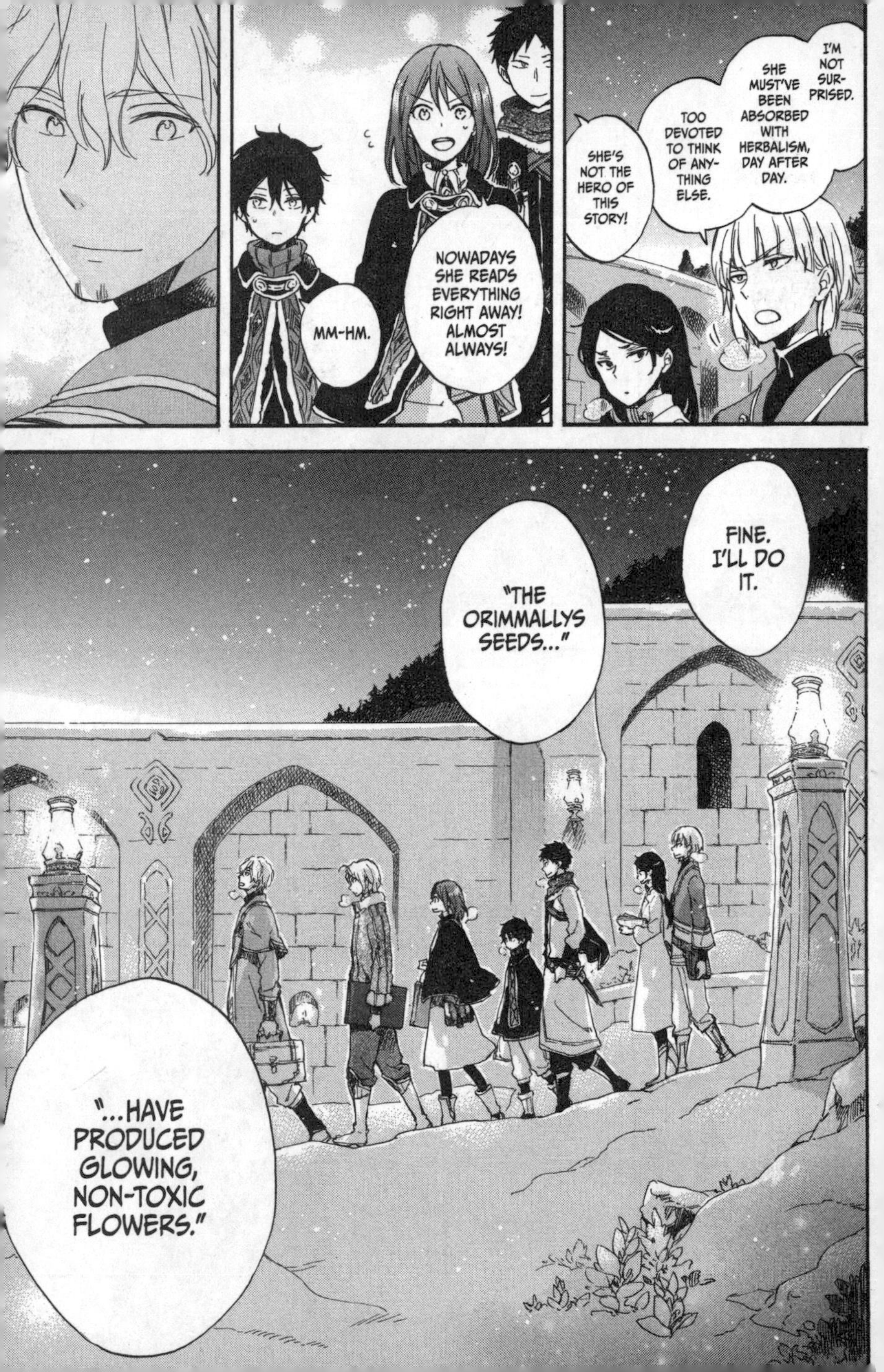
I'M NOT SURPRISED.
SHE MUST'VE BEEN ABSORBED WITH HERBALISM, DAY AFTER DAY.
TOO DEVOTED TO THINK OF ANYTHING ELSE.
SHE'S NOT THE HERO OF THIS STORY!
NOWADAYS SHE READS EVERYTHING RIGHT AWAY! ALMOST ALWAYS!
MM-HM.
FINE. I'LL DO IT.
"THE ORIMMALLYS SEEDS..."
"...HAVE PRODUCED GLOWING, NON-TOXIC FLOWERS."

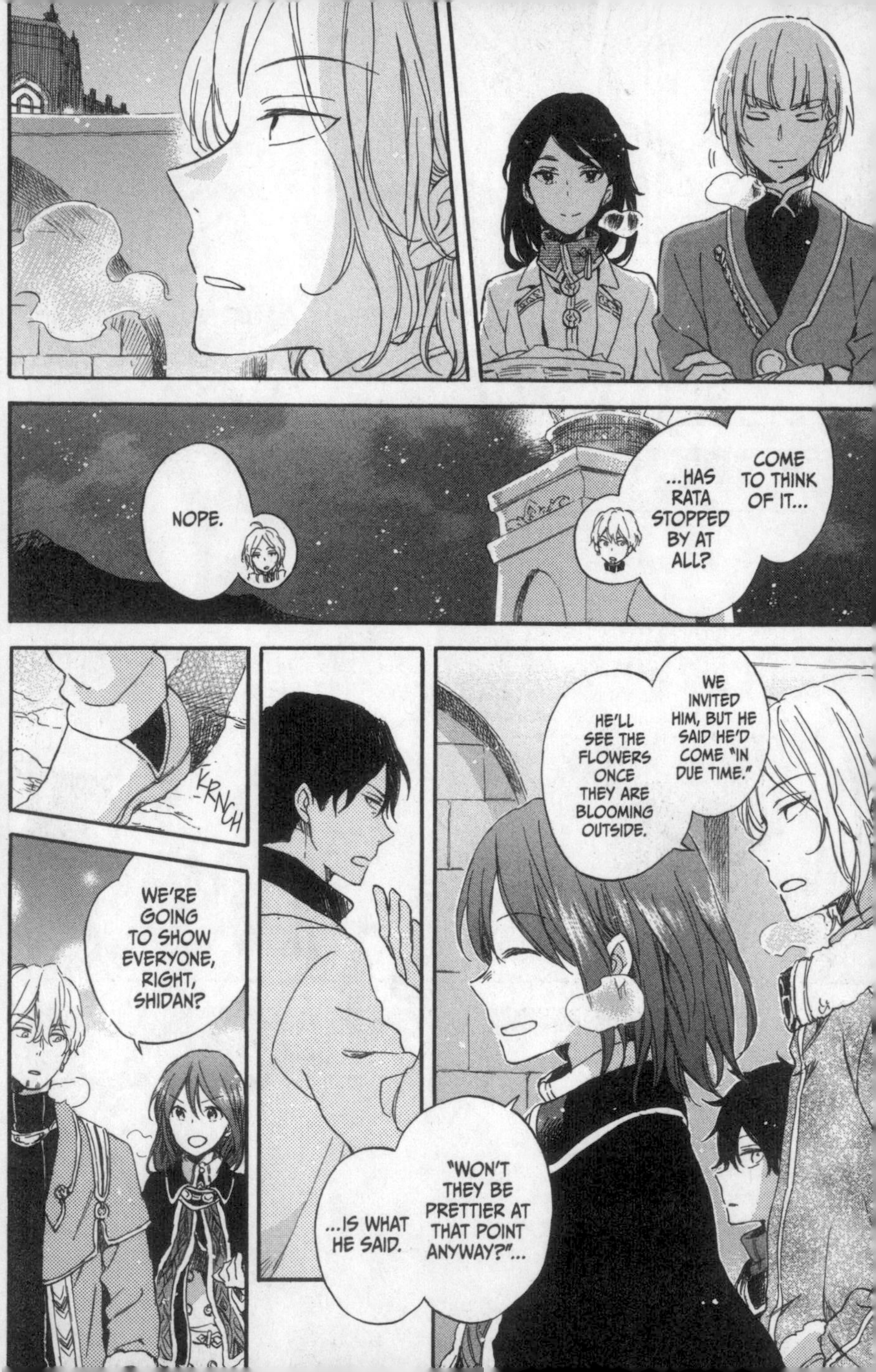
COME TO THINK OF IT...
...HAS RATA STOPPED BY AT ALL?
NOPE.
WE INVITED HIM, BUT HE SAID HE'D COME "IN DUE TIME."
HE'LL SEE THE FLOWERS ONCE THEY ARE BLOOMING OUTSIDE.
"WON'T THEY BE PRETTIER AT THAT POINT ANYWAY?"...
...IS WHAT HE SAID.
KRNCH
WE'RE GOING TO SHOW EVERYONE, RIGHT, SHIDAN?

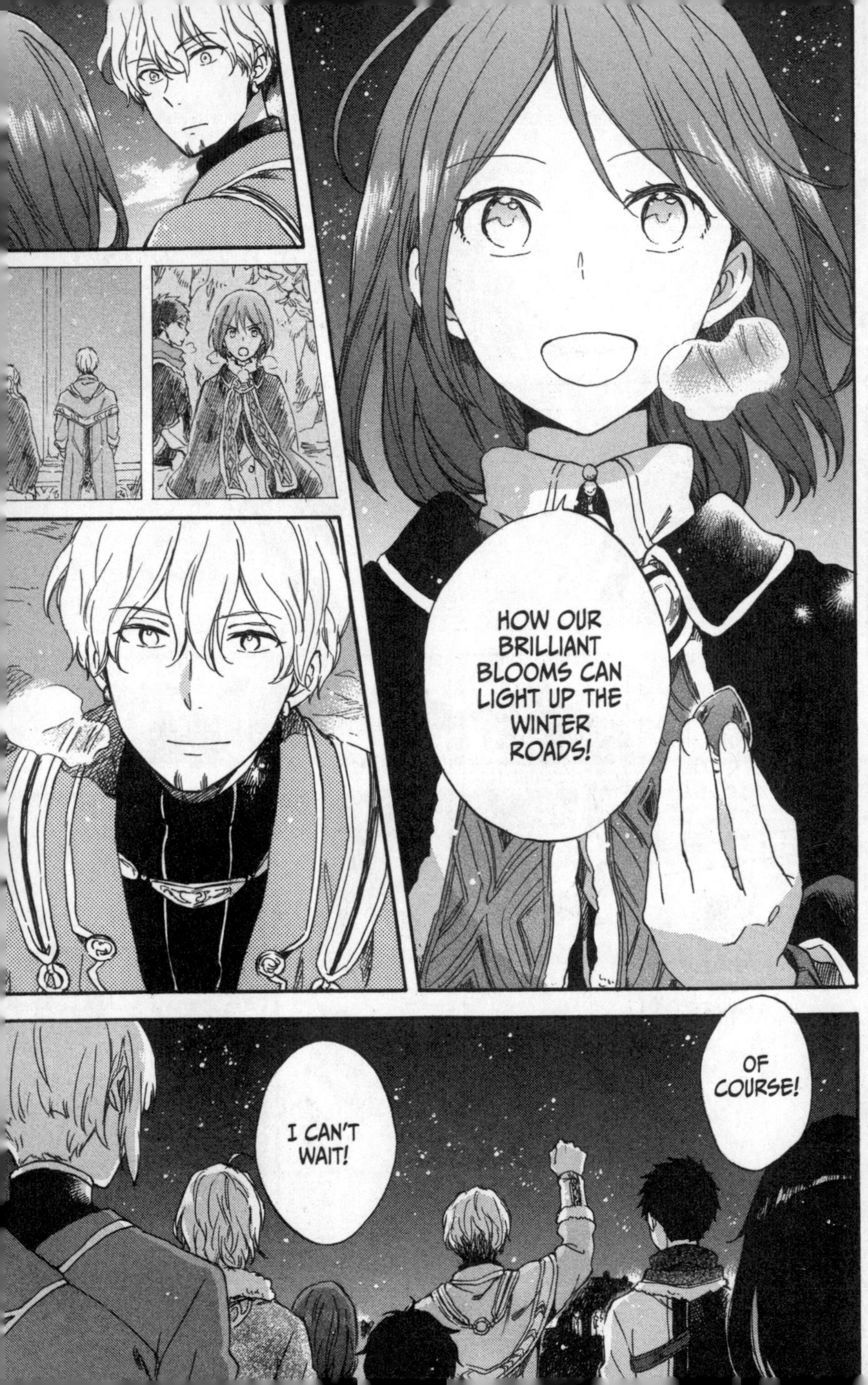
HOW OUR BRILLIANT BLOOMS CAN LIGHT UP THE WINTER ROADS!
OF COURSE!
I CAN'T WAIT!

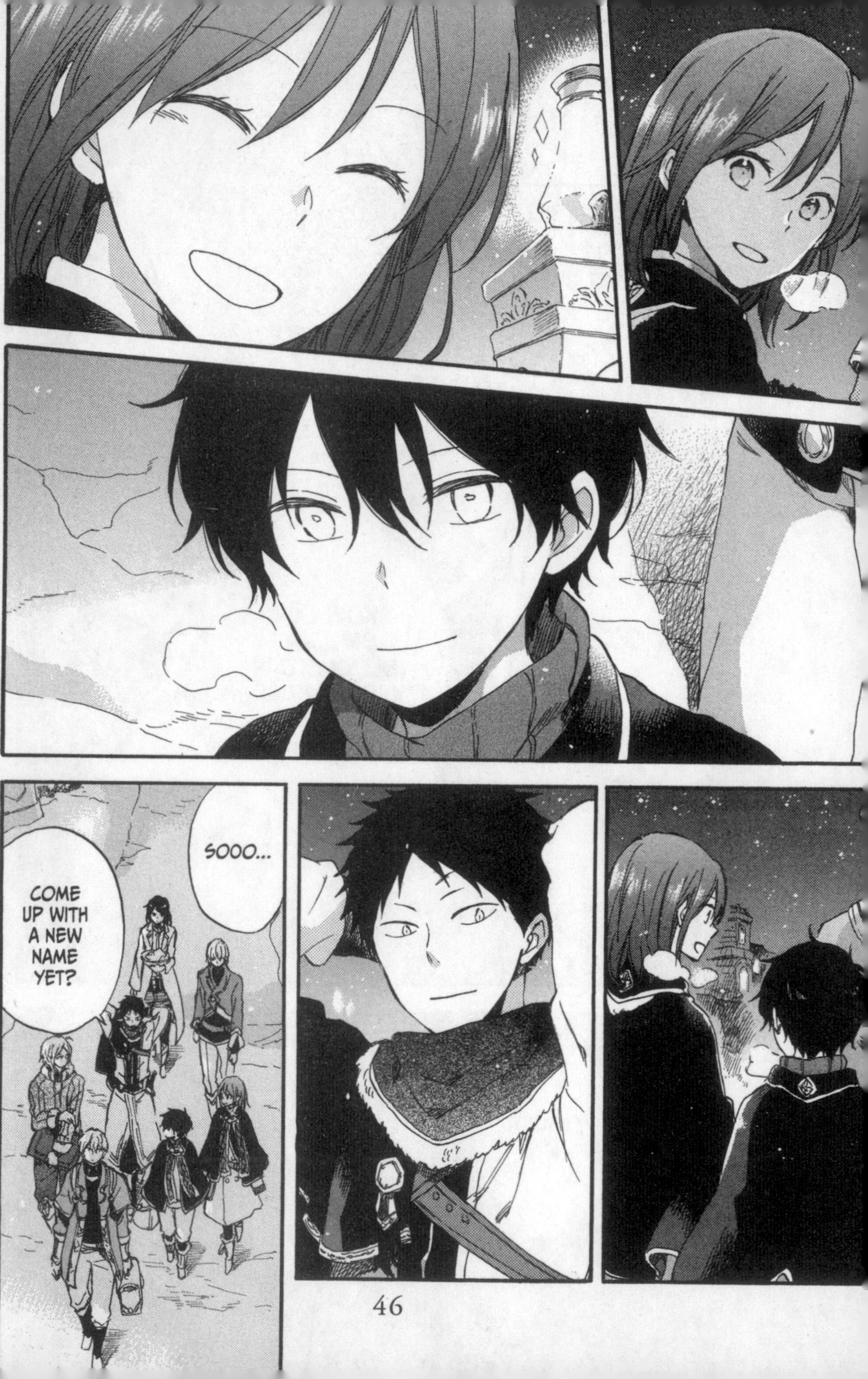
SOOO...
COME UP WITH A NEW NAME YET?

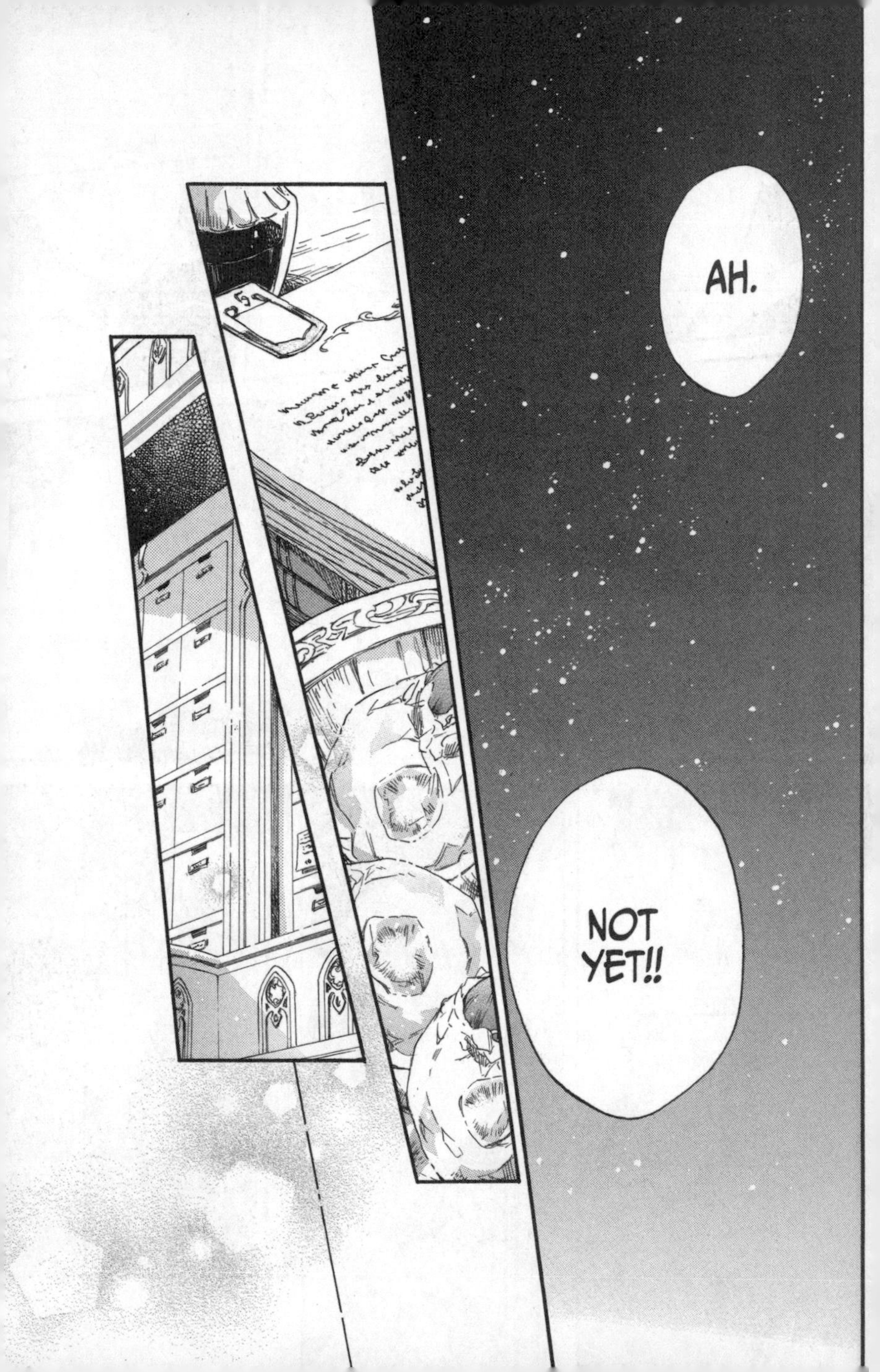
AH.
NOT YET!!

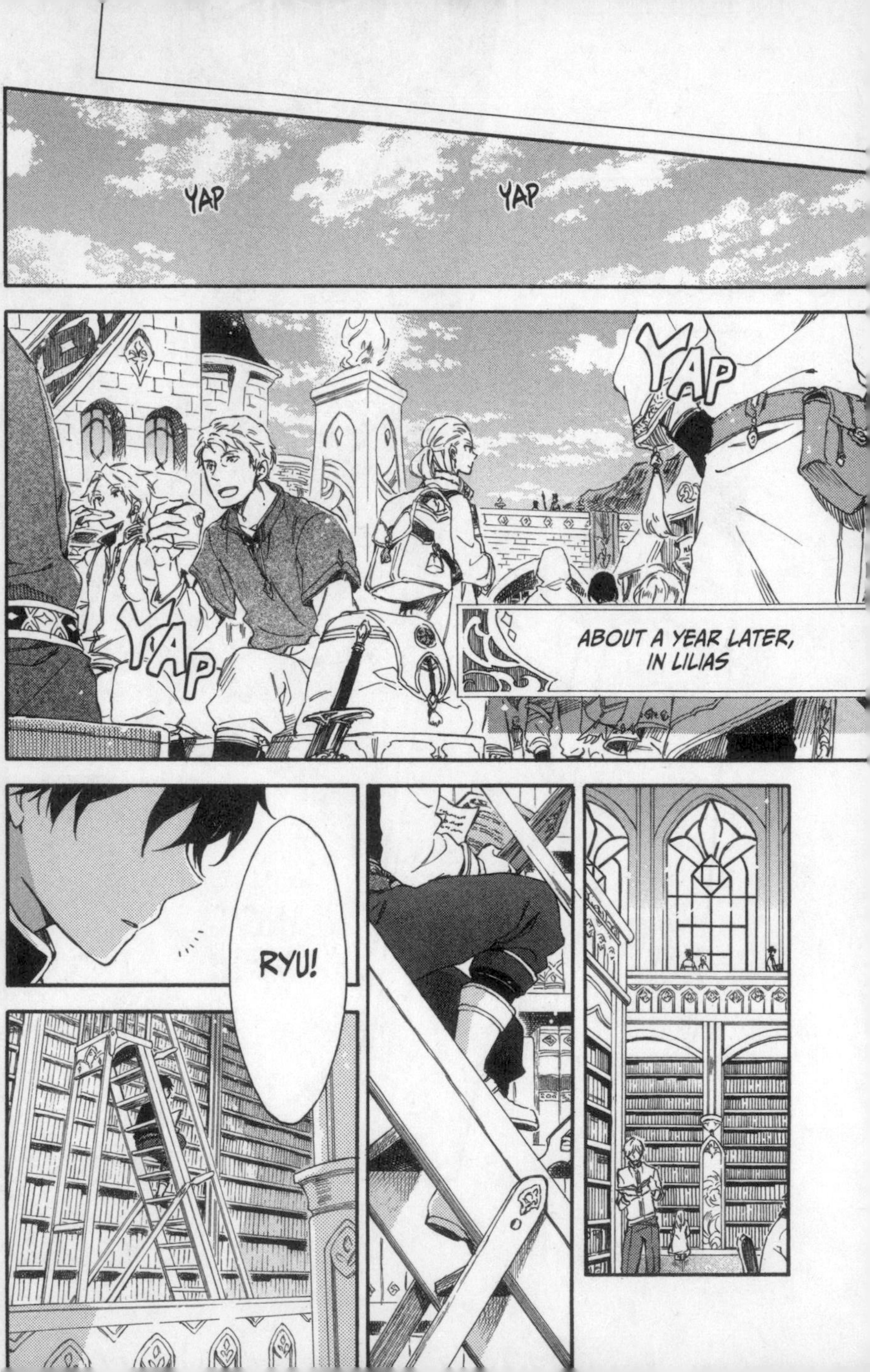
YAP
YAP
YAP
ABOUT A YEAR LATER, IN LILIAS
YAP
RYU!

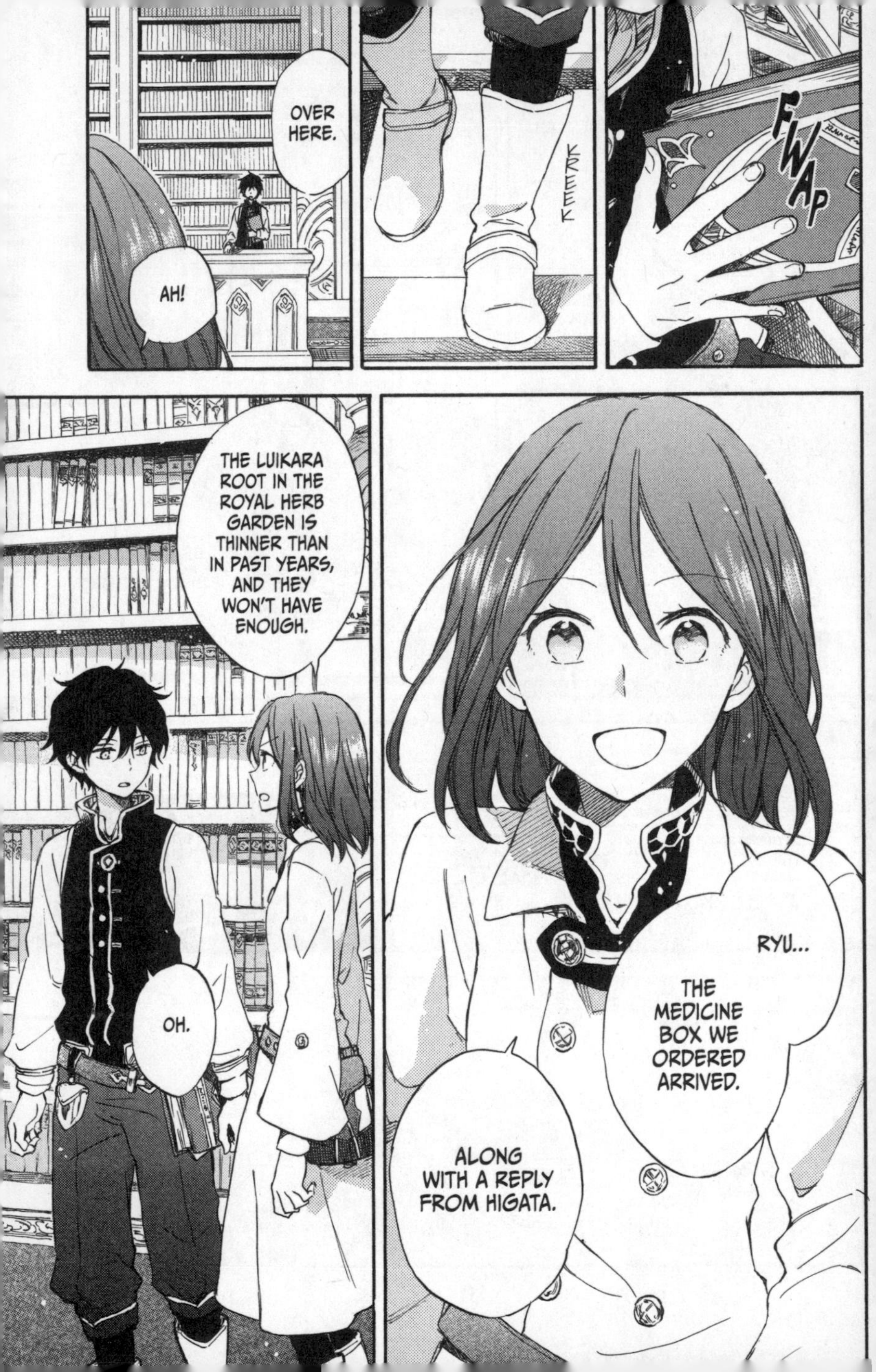
FWAP
KREEK
OVER HERE.
AH!
RYU...
THE MEDICINE BOX WE ORDERED ARRIVED.
ALONG WITH A REPLY FROM HIGATA.
THE LUIKARA ROOT IN THE ROYAL HERB GARDEN IS THINNER THAN IN PAST YEARS, AND THEY WON'T HAVE ENOUGH.
OH.

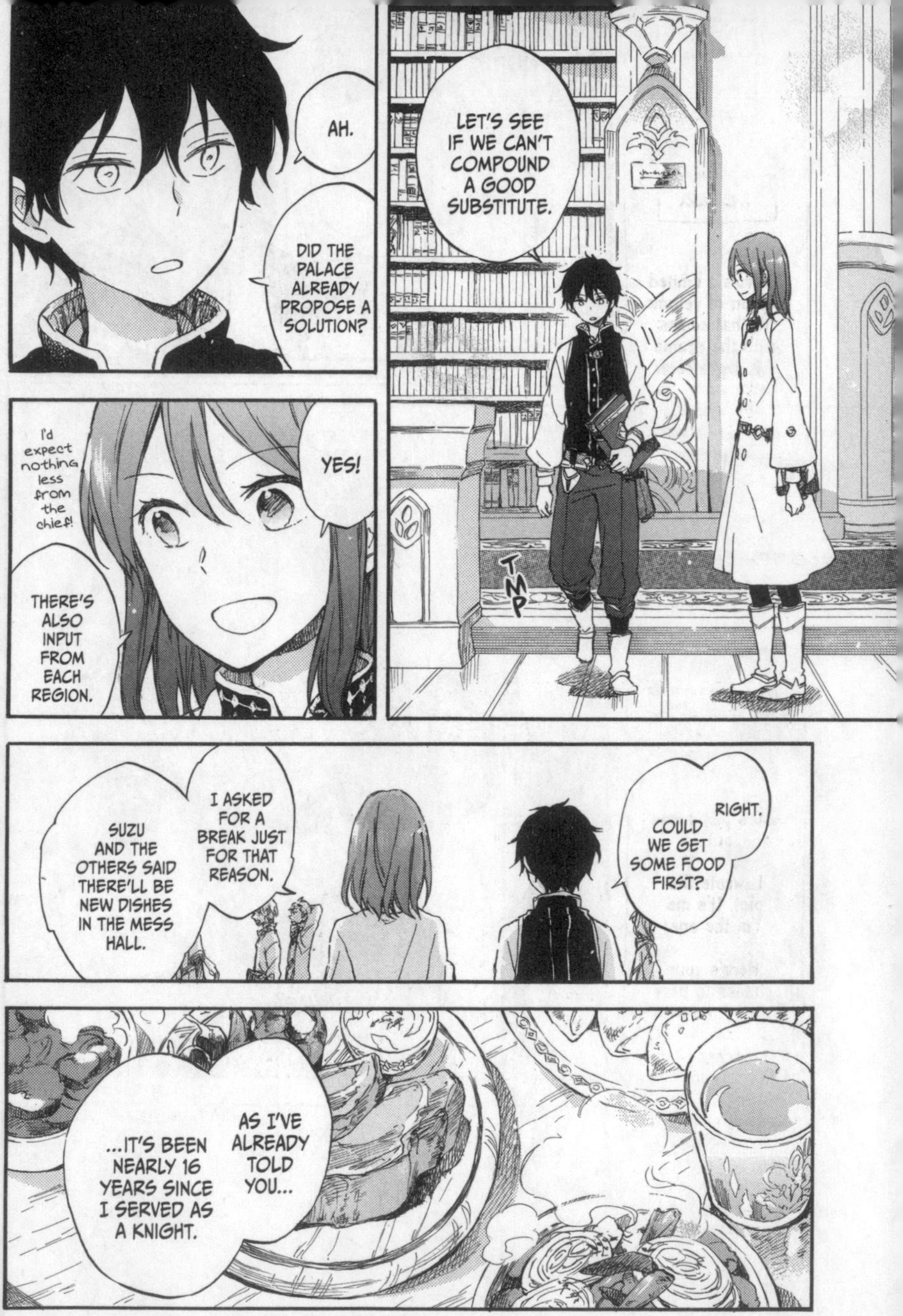
LET'S SEE IF WE CAN'T COMPOUND A GOOD SUBSTITUTE.
TMP
AH.
DID THE PALACE ALREADY PROPOSE A SOLUTION?
YES!
I'd expect nothing less from the chief!
THERE'S ALSO INPUT FROM EACH REGION.
RIGHT.
COULD WE GET SOME FOOD FIRST?
I ASKED FOR A BREAK JUST FOR THAT REASON.
SUZU AND THE OTHERS SAID THERE'LL BE NEW DISHES IN THE MESS HALL.
AS I'VE ALREADY TOLD YOU...
...IT'S BEEN NEARLY 16 YEARS SINCE I SERVED AS A KNIGHT.

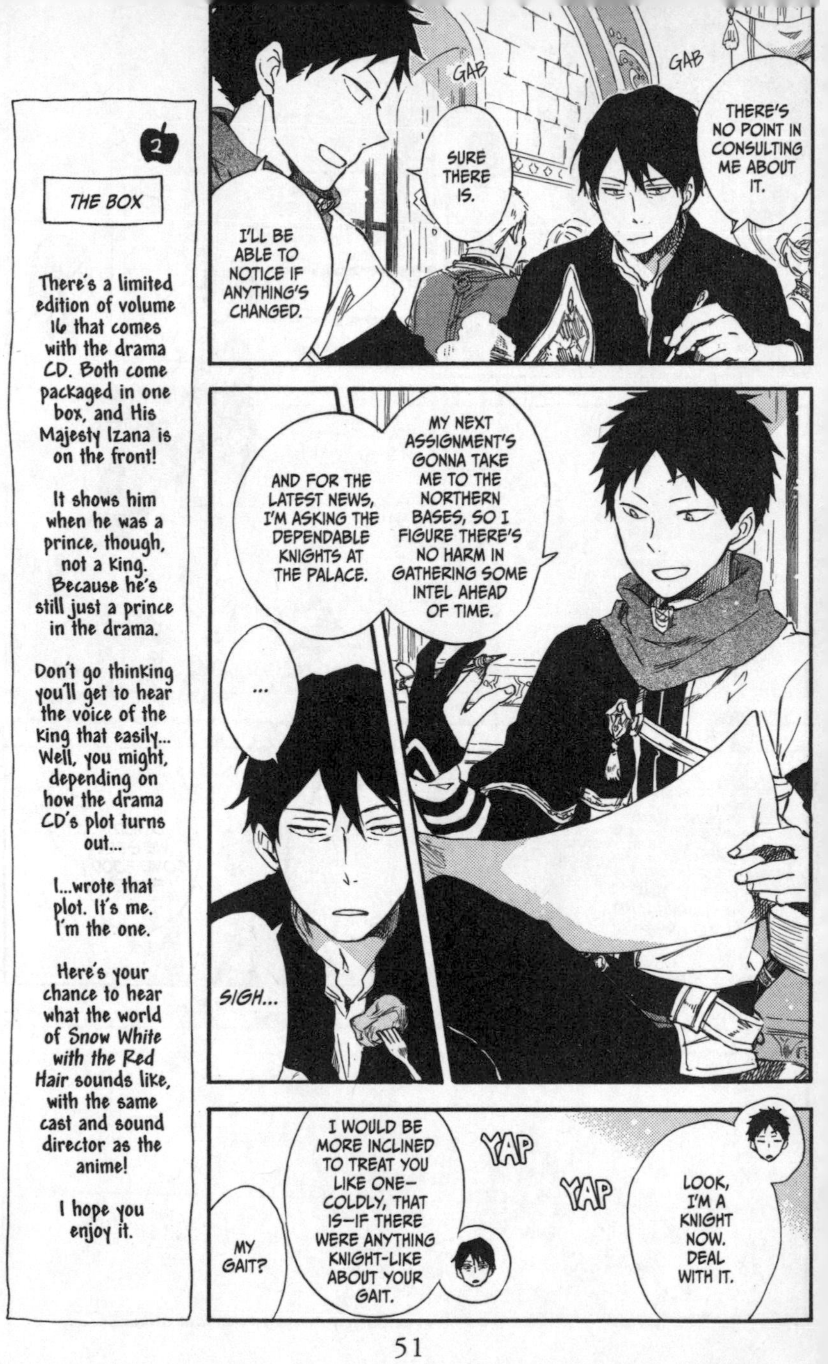
GAB
GAB
THERE'S NO POINT IN CONSULTING ME ABOUT IT.
SURE THERE IS.
I'LL BE ABLE TO NOTICE IF ANYTHING'S CHANGED.
MY NEXT ASSIGNMENT'S GONNA TAKE ME TO THE NORTHERN BASES, SO I FIGURE THERE'S NO HARM IN GATHERING SOME INTEL AHEAD OF TIME.
AND FOR THE LATEST NEWS, I'M ASKING THE DEPENDABLE KNIGHTS AT THE PALACE.
...
SIGH...
LOOK, I'M A KNIGHT NOW. DEAL WITH IT.
YAP
YAP
I WOULD BE MORE INCLINED TO TREAT YOU LIKE ONE—COLDLY, THAT IS—IF THERE WERE ANYTHING KNIGHT-LIKE ABOUT YOUR GAIT.
MY GAIT?

2

THE BOX

There's a limited edition of volume 16 that comes with the drama CD. Both come packaged in one box, and His Majesty Izana is on the front!

It shows him when he was a prince, though, not a king. Because he's still just a prince in the drama.

Don't go thinking you'll get to hear the voice of the king that easily... Well, you might, depending on how the drama CD's plot turns out...

I...wrote that plot. It's me. I'm the one.

Here's your chance to hear what the world of *Snow White with the Red Hair* sounds like, with the same cast and sound director as the anime!

I hope you enjoy it.

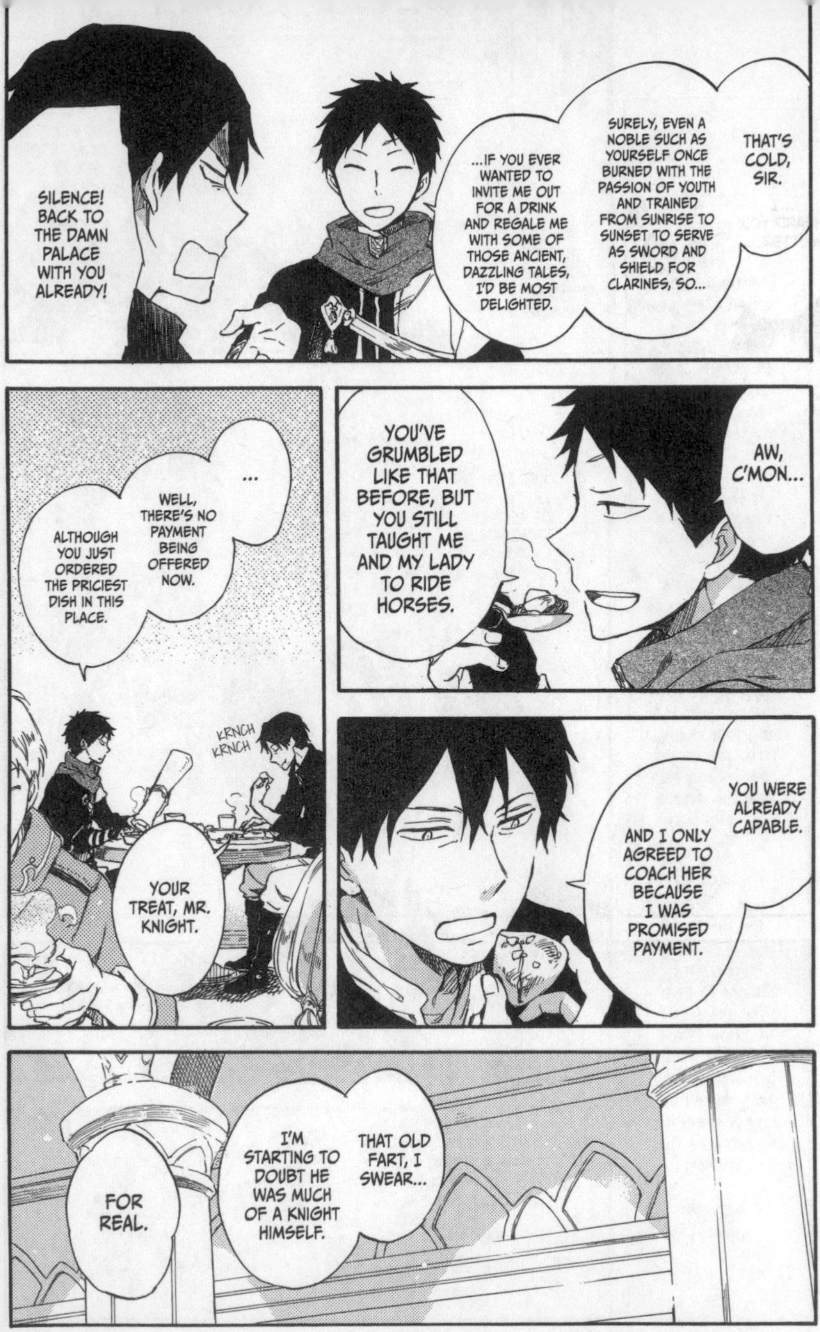
THAT'S COLD, SIR.
SURELY, EVEN A NOBLE SUCH AS YOURSELF ONCE BURNED WITH THE PASSION OF YOUTH AND TRAINED FROM SUNRISE TO SUNSET TO SERVE AS SWORD AND SHIELD FOR CLARINES, SO...
...IF YOU EVER WANTED TO INVITE ME OUT FOR A DRINK AND REGALE ME WITH SOME OF THOSE ANCIENT, DAZZLING TALES, I'D BE MOST DELIGHTED.
SILENCE! BACK TO THE DAMN PALACE WITH YOU ALREADY!
AW, C'MON...
YOU'VE GRUMBLED LIKE THAT BEFORE, BUT YOU STILL TAUGHT ME AND MY LADY TO RIDE HORSES.
YOU WERE ALREADY CAPABLE.
AND I ONLY AGREED TO COACH HER BECAUSE I WAS PROMISED PAYMENT.
...
WELL, THERE'S NO PAYMENT BEING OFFERED NOW.
ALTHOUGH YOU JUST ORDERED THE PRICIEST DISH IN THIS PLACE.
KRNCH KRNCH
YOUR TREAT, MR. KNIGHT.
THAT OLD FART, I SWEAR...
I'M STARTING TO DOUBT HE WAS MUCH OF A KNIGHT HIMSELF.
FOR REAL.

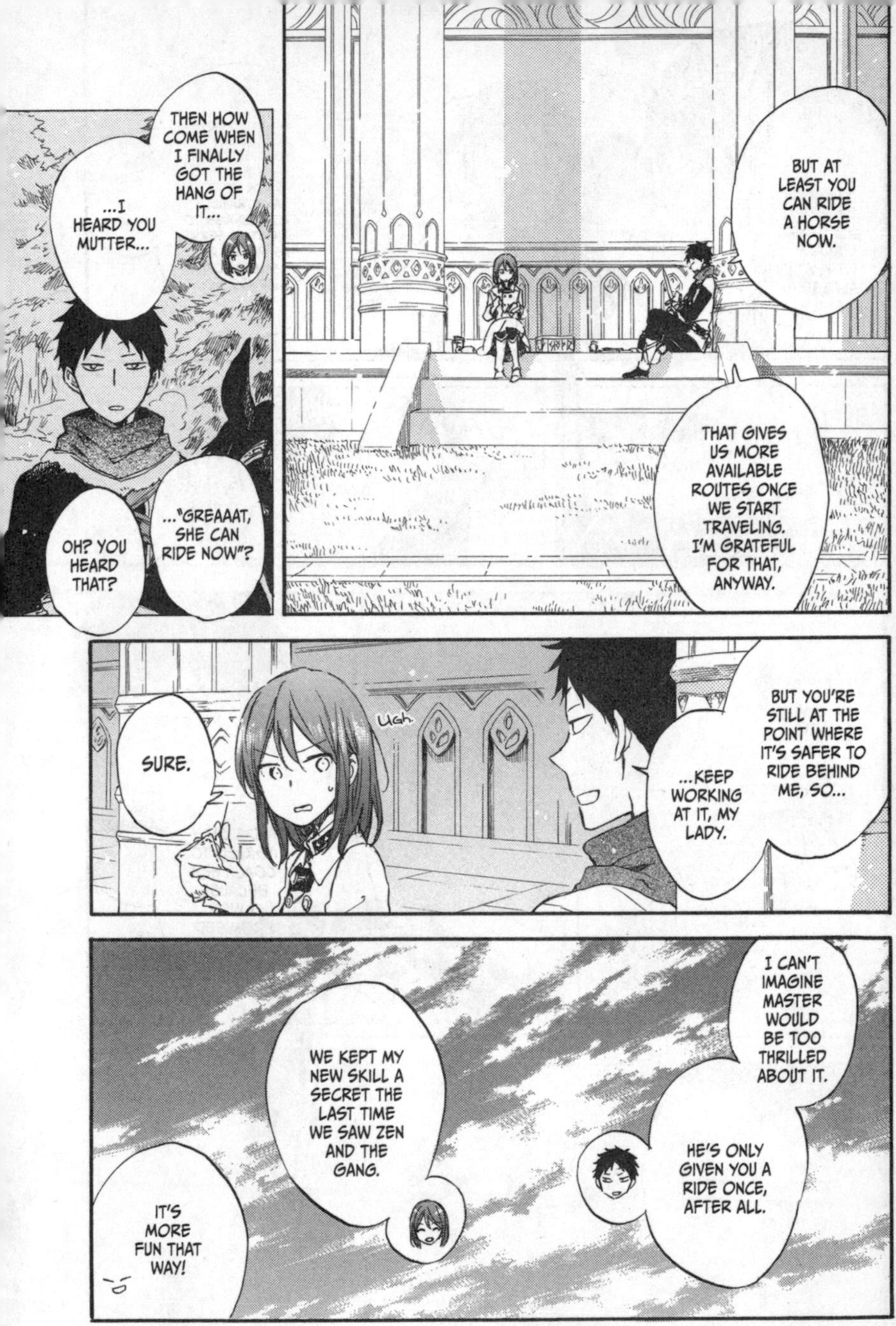
BUT AT LEAST YOU CAN RIDE A HORSE NOW.
THAT GIVES US MORE AVAILABLE ROUTES ONCE WE START TRAVELING. I'M GRATEFUL FOR THAT, ANYWAY.
THEN HOW COME WHEN I FINALLY GOT THE HANG OF IT...
...I HEARD YOU MUTTER...
..."GREAAAT, SHE CAN RIDE NOW"?
OH? YOU HEARD THAT?
BUT YOU'RE STILL AT THE POINT WHERE IT'S SAFER TO RIDE BEHIND ME, SO...
...KEEP WORKING AT IT, MY LADY.
Ugh.
SURE.
I CAN'T IMAGINE MASTER WOULD BE TOO THRILLED ABOUT IT.
HE'S ONLY GIVEN YOU A RIDE ONCE, AFTER ALL.
WE KEPT MY NEW SKILL A SECRET THE LAST TIME WE SAW ZEN AND THE GANG.
IT'S MORE FUN THAT WAY!

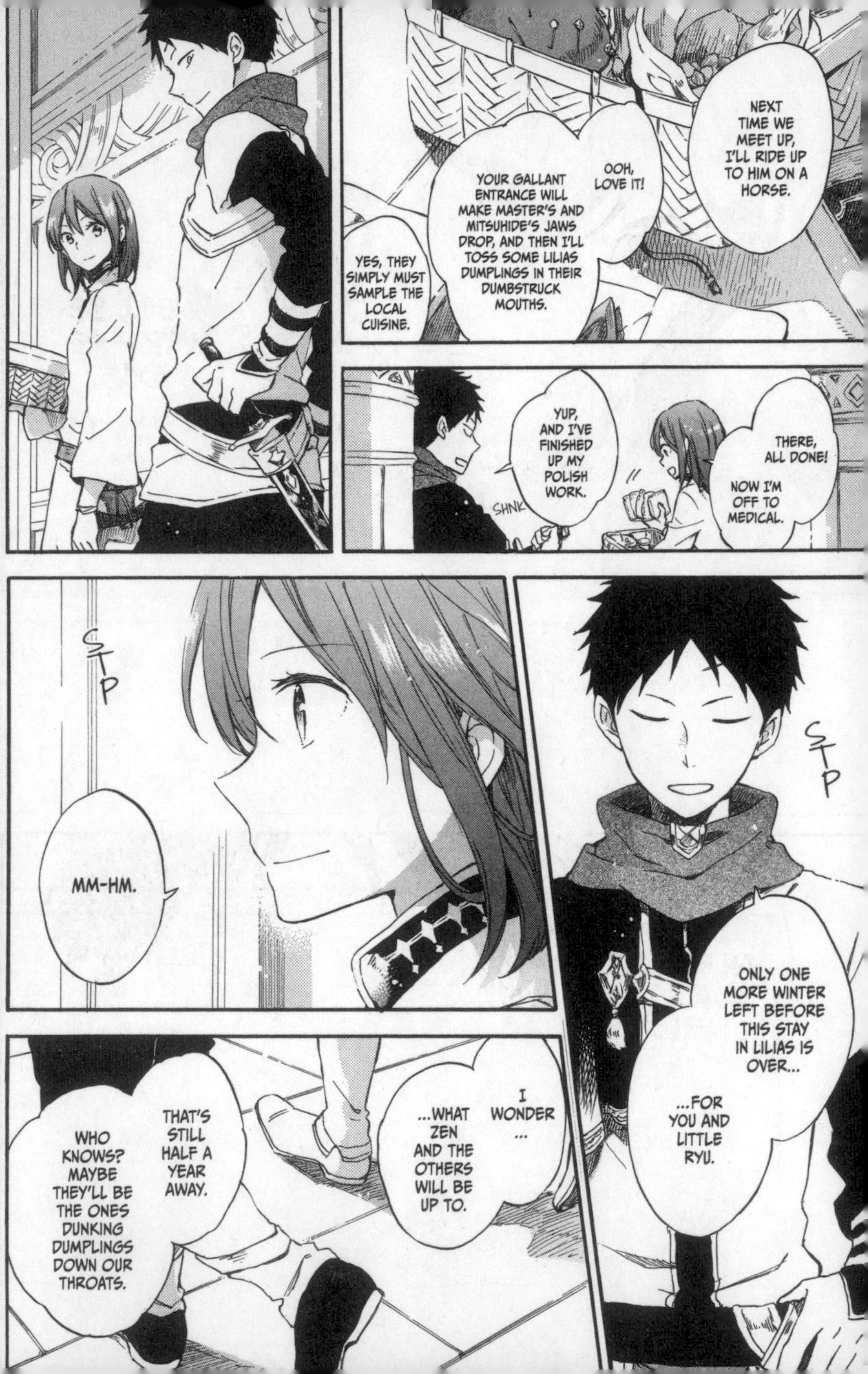
NEXT TIME WE MEET UP, I'LL RIDE UP TO HIM ON A HORSE.
OOH, LOVE IT!
YOUR GALLANT ENTRANCE WILL MAKE MASTER'S AND MITSUHIDE'S JAWS DROP, AND THEN I'LL TOSS SOME LILIAS DUMPLINGS IN THEIR DUMBSTRUCK MOUTHS.
YES, THEY SIMPLY MUST SAMPLE THE LOCAL CUISINE.
THERE, ALL DONE!
NOW I'M OFF TO MEDICAL.
YUP, AND I'VE FINISHED UP MY POLISH WORK.
SHNK
STP
ONLY ONE MORE WINTER LEFT BEFORE THIS STAY IN LILIAS IS OVER...
...FOR YOU AND LITTLE RYU.
STP
MM-HM.
I WONDER...
...WHAT ZEN AND THE OTHERS WILL BE UP TO.
THAT'S STILL HALF A YEAR AWAY.
WHO KNOWS? MAYBE THEY'LL BE THE ONES DUNKING DUMPLINGS DOWN OUR THROATS.

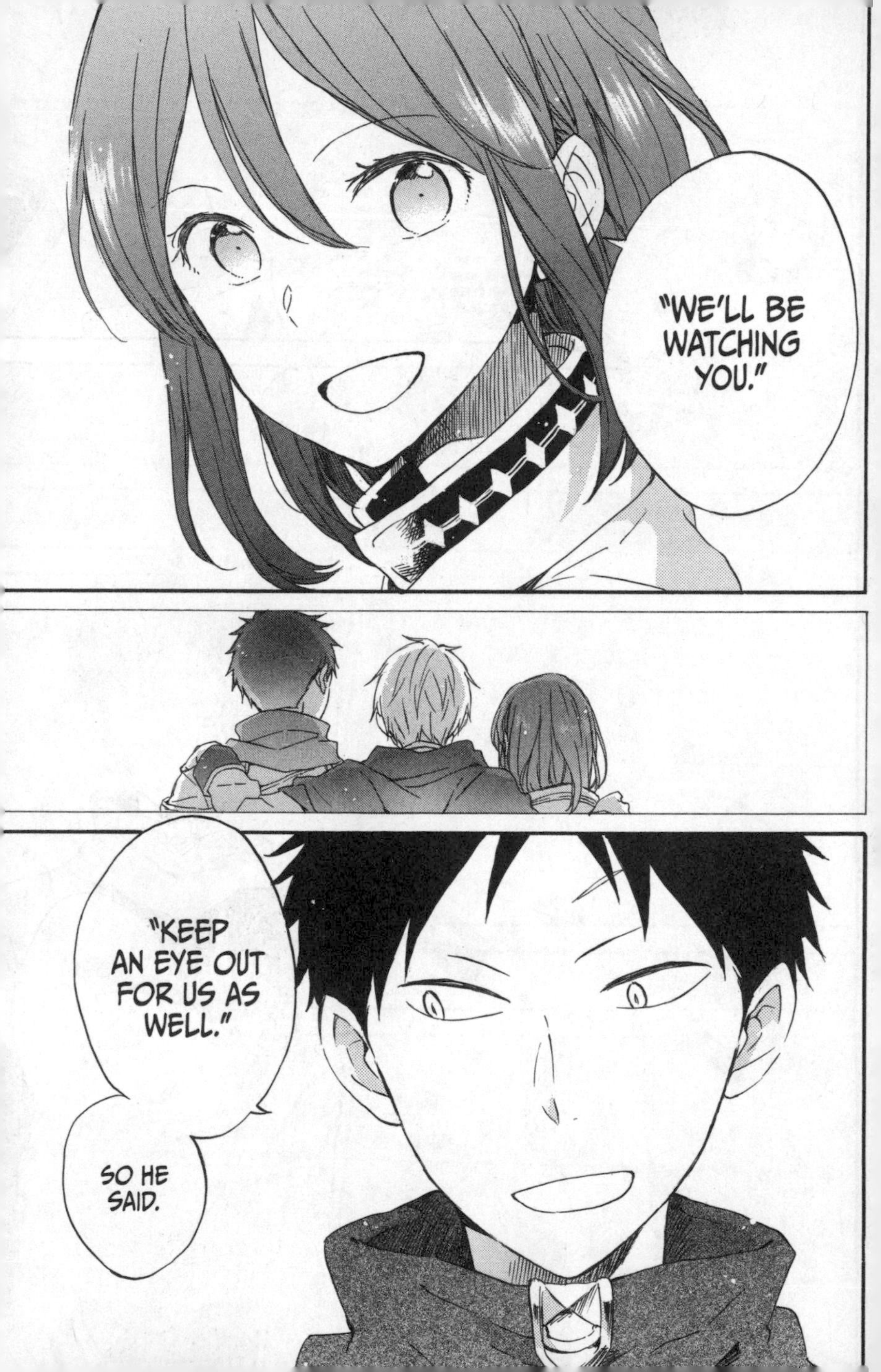
"WE'LL BE WATCHING YOU."
"KEEP AN EYE OUT FOR US AS WELL."
SO HE SAID.

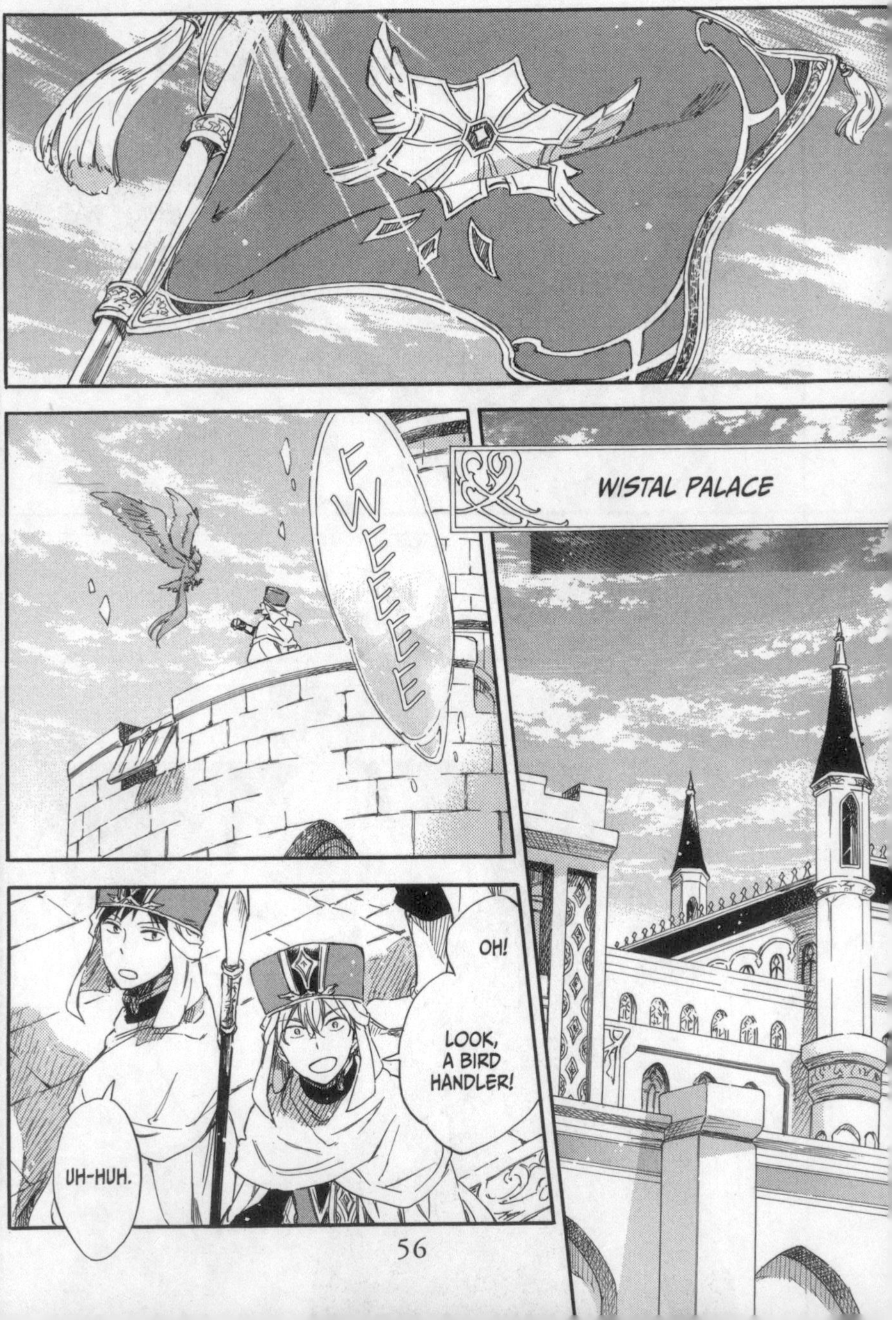
WISTAL PALACE
FWEEEEEE
OH!
LOOK, A BIRD HANDLER!
UH-HUH.

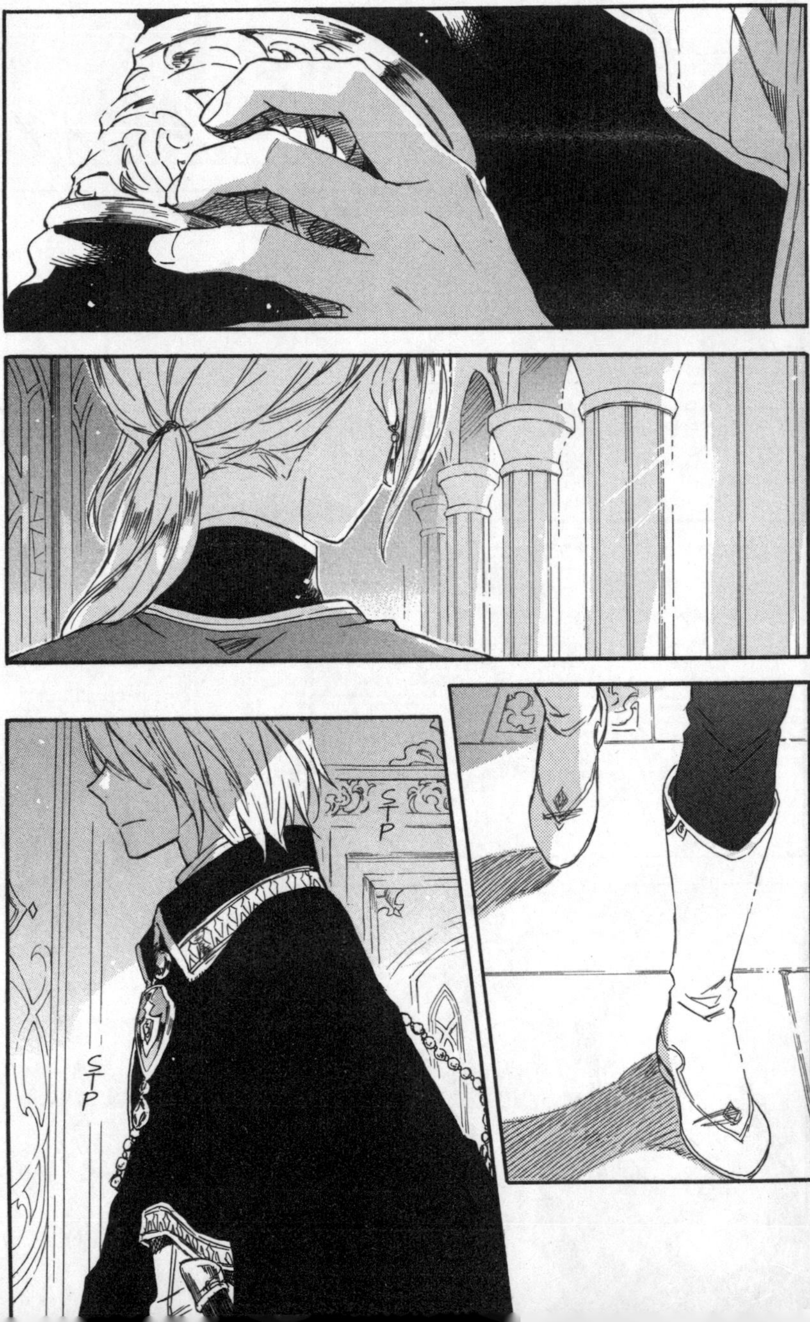
STP
STP

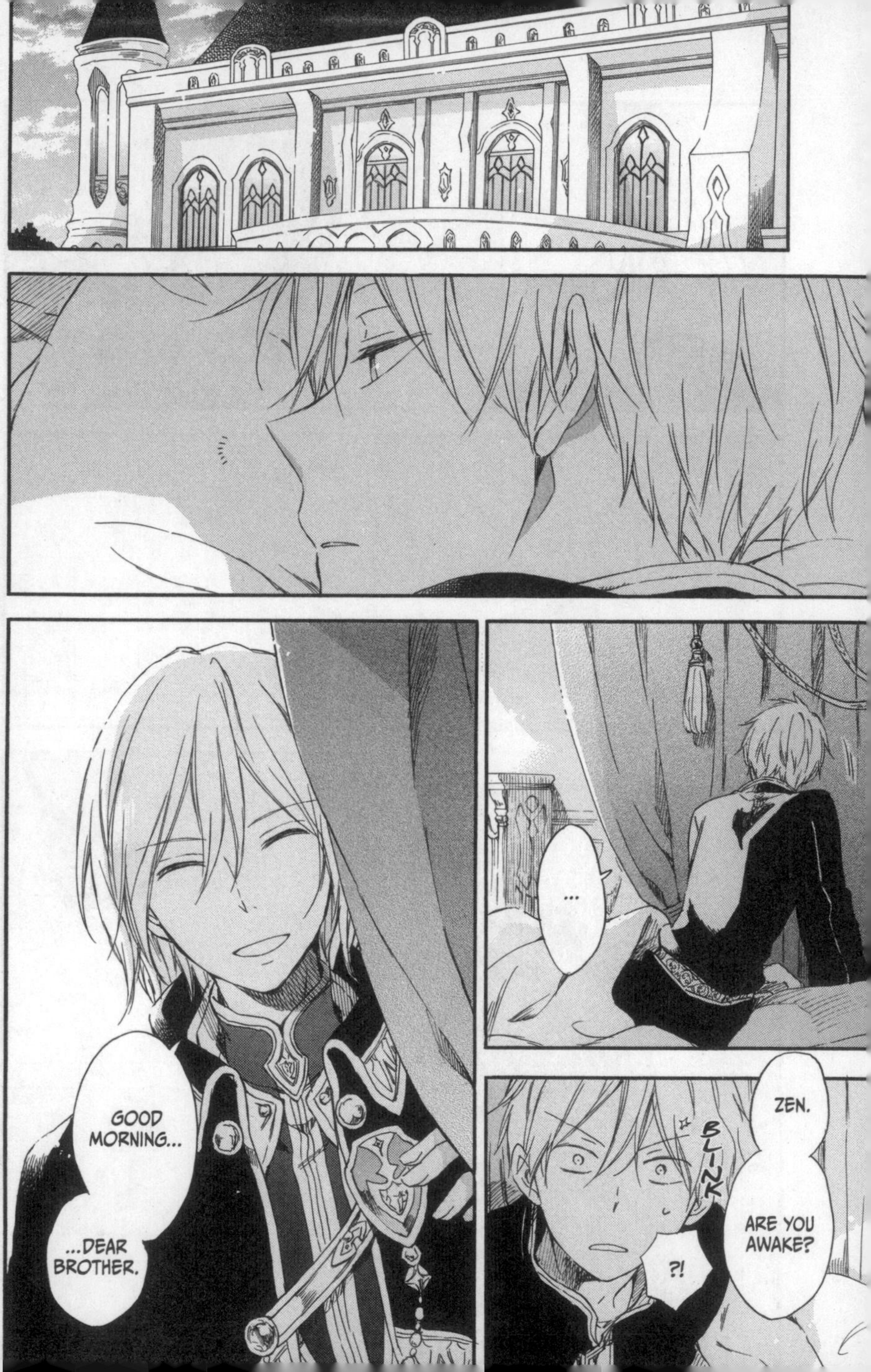
...
ZEN.
BLINK
ARE YOU AWAKE?
?!
GOOD MORNING...
...DEAR BROTHER.

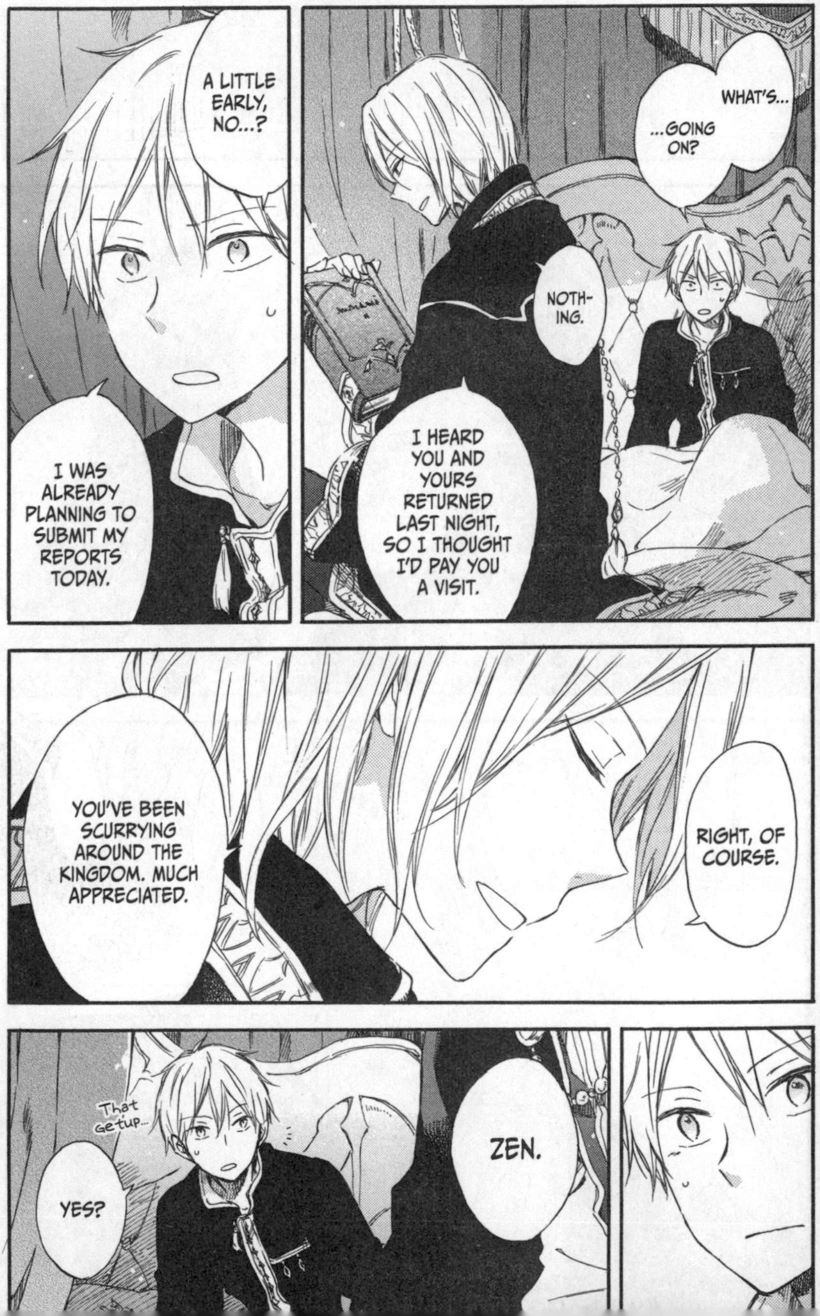
WHAT'S... ...GOING ON?
NOTH-ING.
I HEARD YOU AND YOURS RETURNED LAST NIGHT, SO I THOUGHT I'D PAY YOU A VISIT.
A LITTLE EARLY, NO...?
I WAS ALREADY PLANNING TO SUBMIT MY REPORTS TODAY.
RIGHT, OF COURSE.
YOU'VE BEEN SCURRYING AROUND THE KINGDOM. MUCH APPRECIATED.
ZEN.
That getup...
YES?

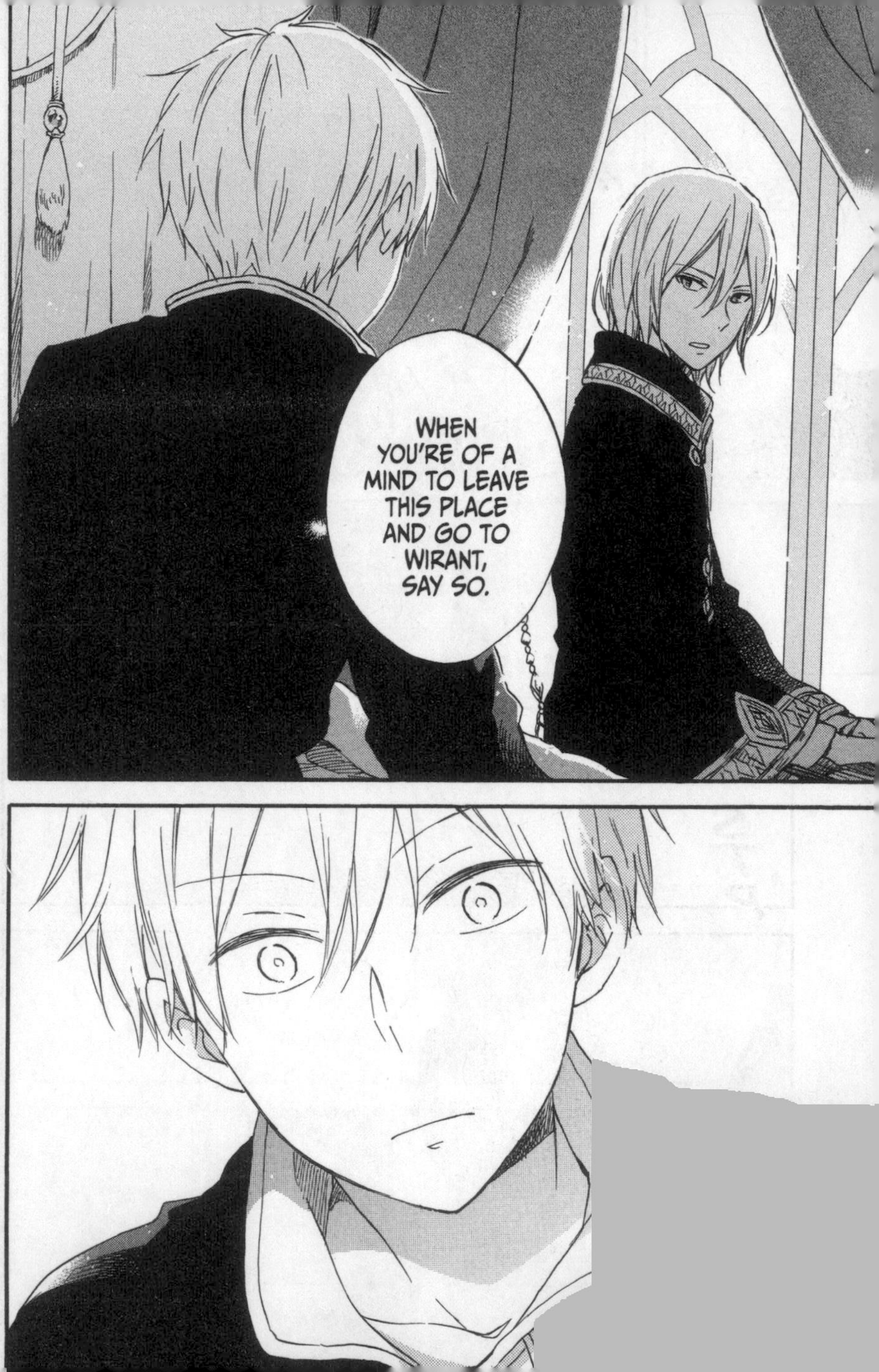
WHEN YOU'RE OF A MIND TO LEAVE THIS PLACE AND GO TO WIRANT, SAY SO.

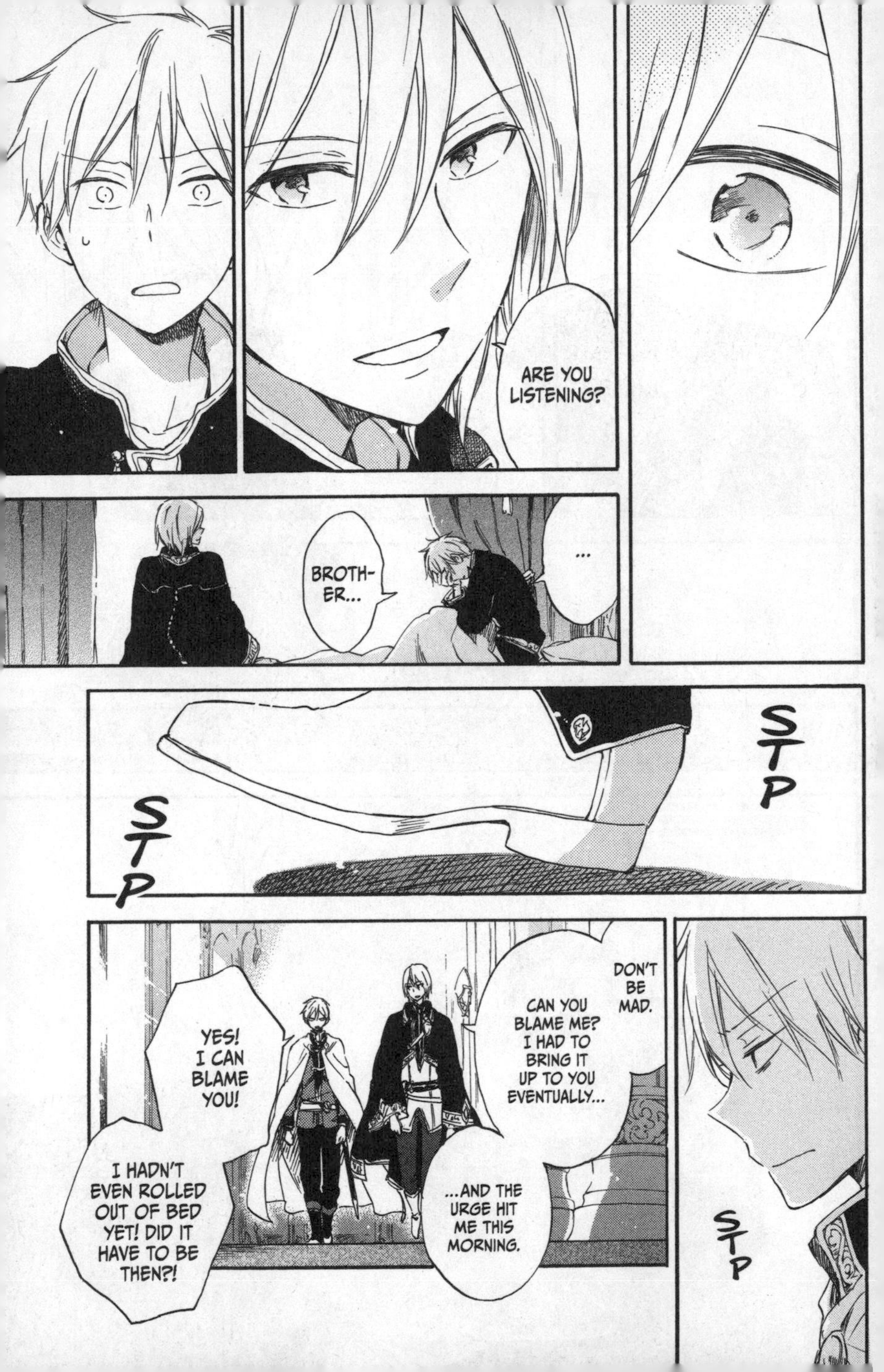
ARE YOU LISTENING?
...
BROTHER-ER...
STP
STP
STP
DON'T BE MAD.
CAN YOU BLAME ME? I HAD TO BRING IT UP TO YOU EVENTUALLY...
...AND THE URGE HIT ME THIS MORNING.
YES! I CAN BLAME YOU!
I HADN'T EVEN ROLLED OUT OF BED YET! DID IT HAVE TO BE THEN?!

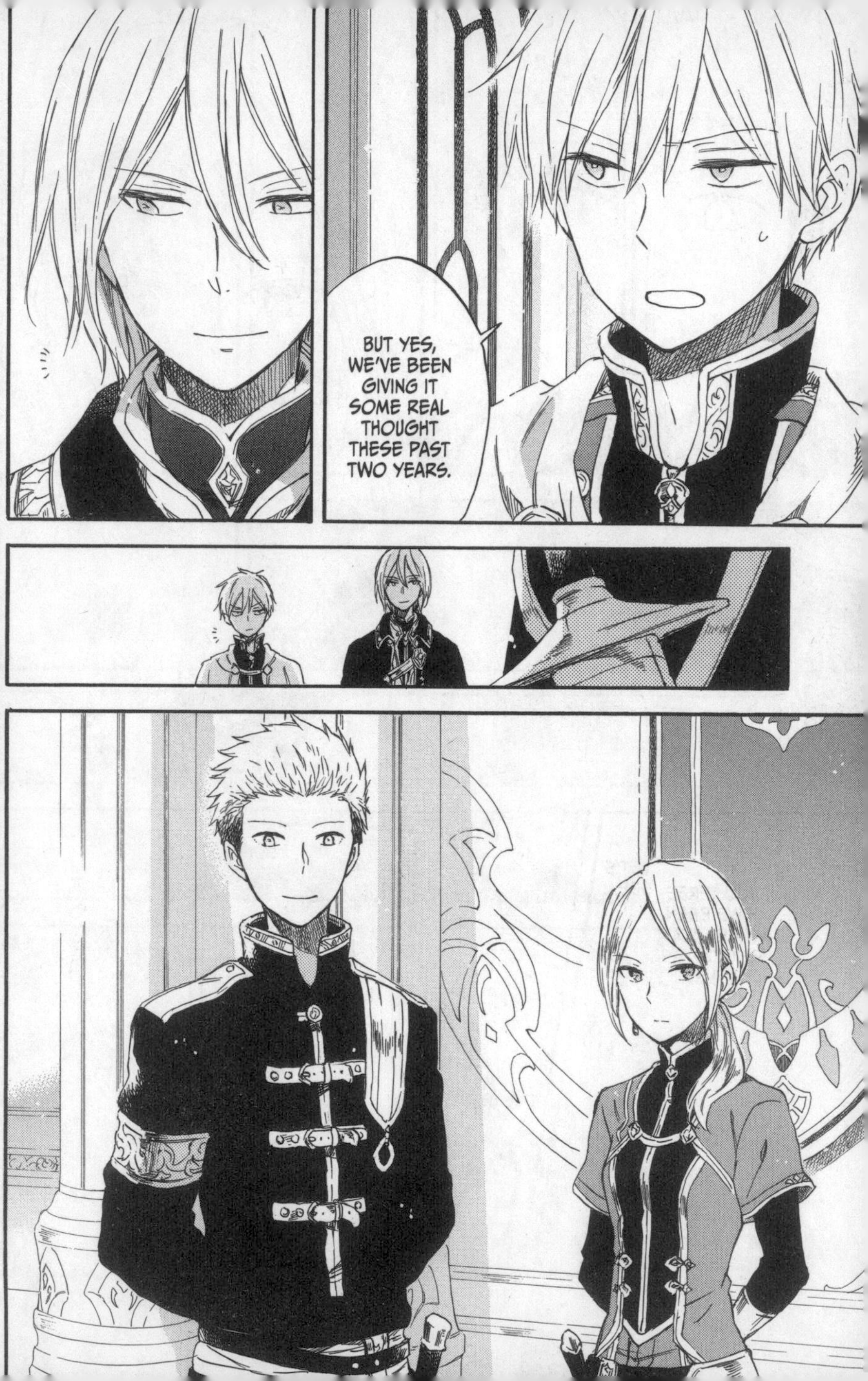
BUT YES, WE'VE BEEN GIVING IT SOME REAL THOUGHT THESE PAST TWO YEARS.

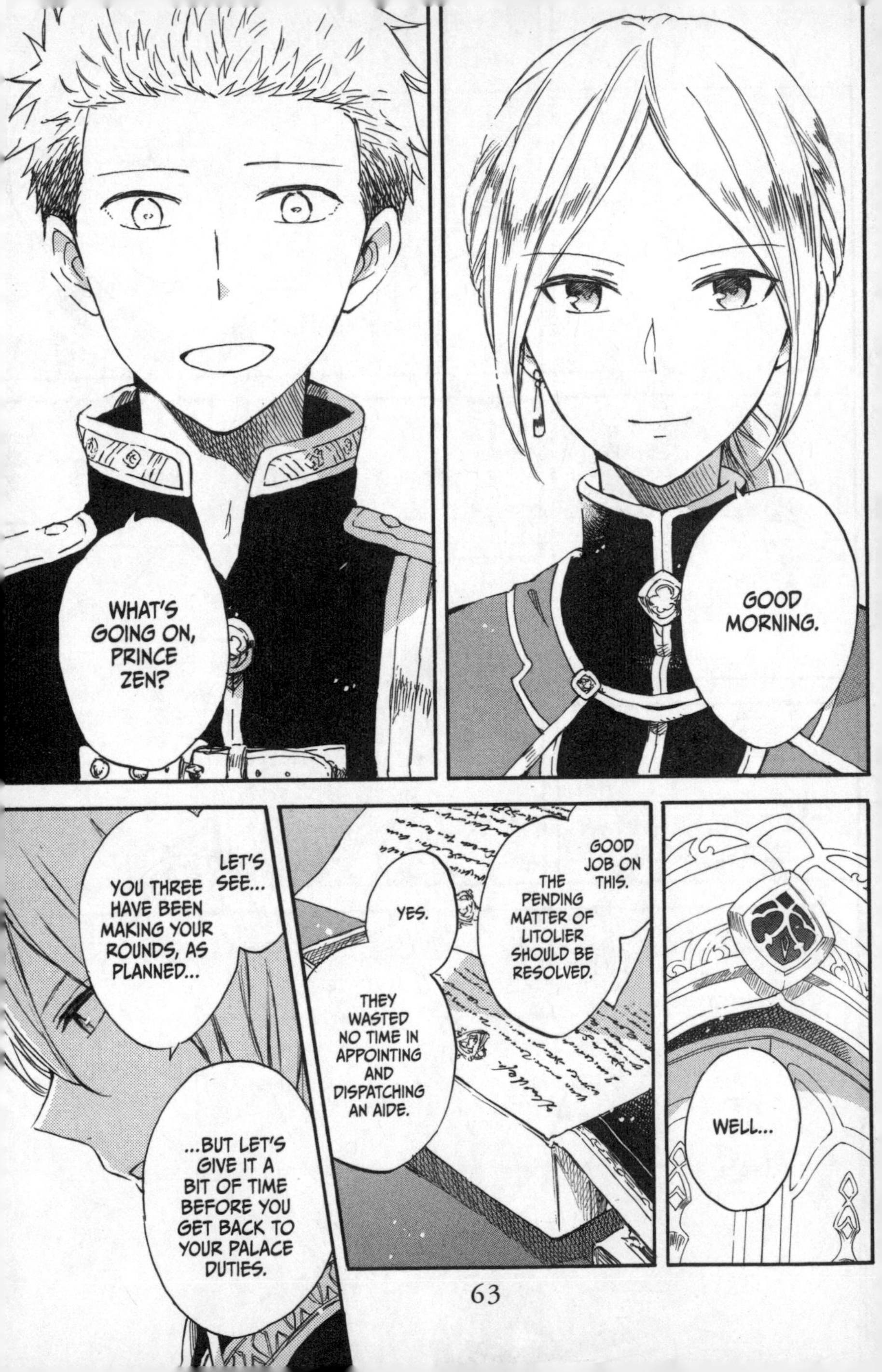
GOOD MORNING.
WHAT'S GOING ON, PRINCE ZEN?
WELL...
GOOD JOB ON THIS.
THE PENDING MATTER OF LITOLIER SHOULD BE RESOLVED.
YES.
THEY WASTED NO TIME IN APPOINTING AND DISPATCHING AN AIDE.
LET'S SEE...
YOU THREE HAVE BEEN MAKING YOUR ROUNDS, AS PLANNED...
...BUT LET'S GIVE IT A BIT OF TIME BEFORE YOU GET BACK TO YOUR PALACE DUTIES.

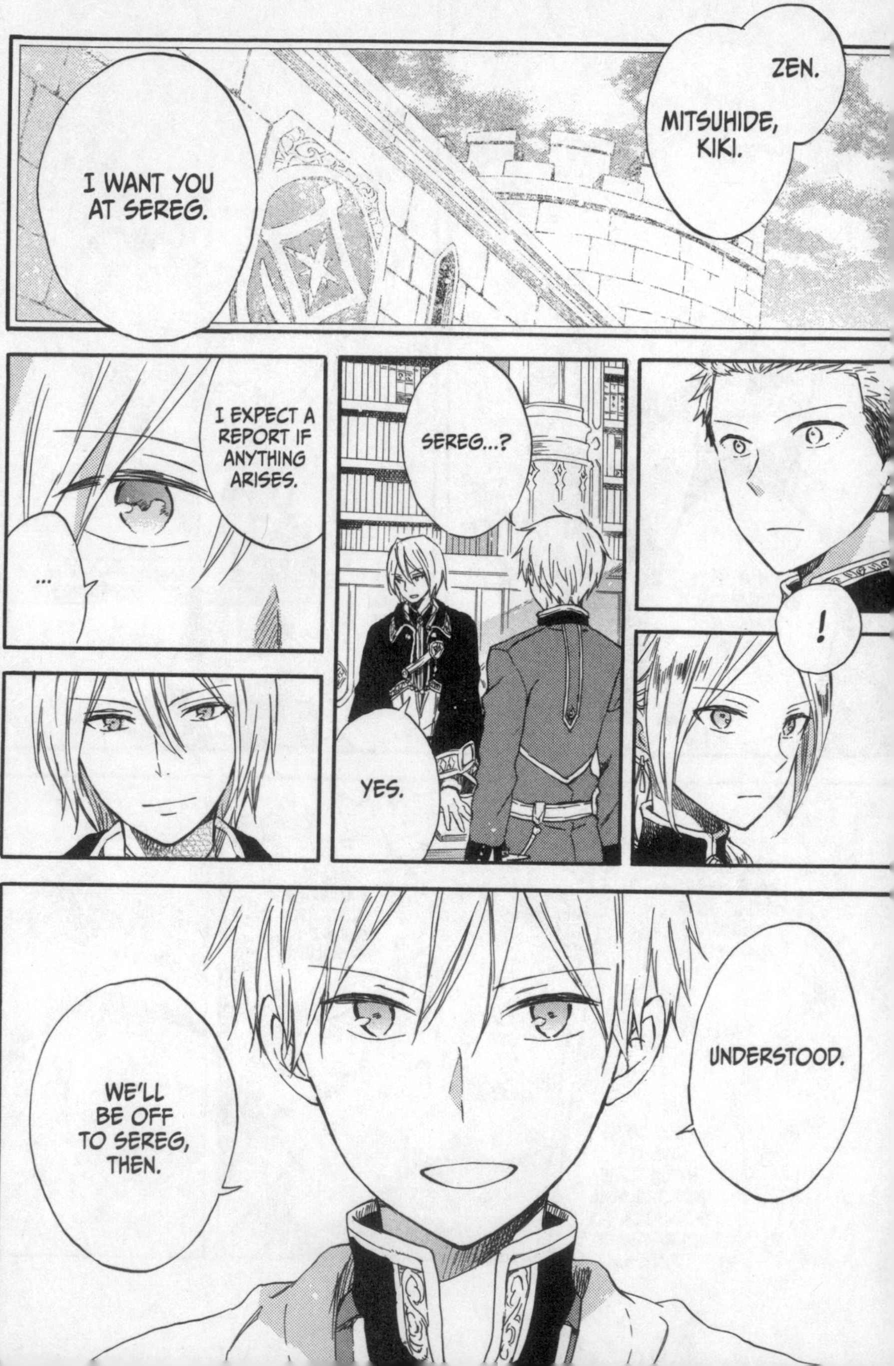
ZEN.
MITSUHIDE, KIKI.
I WANT YOU AT SEREG.
!
SEREG...?
YES.
I EXPECT A REPORT IF ANYTHING ARISES.
...
UNDERSTOOD.
WE'LL BE OFF TO SEREG, THEN.

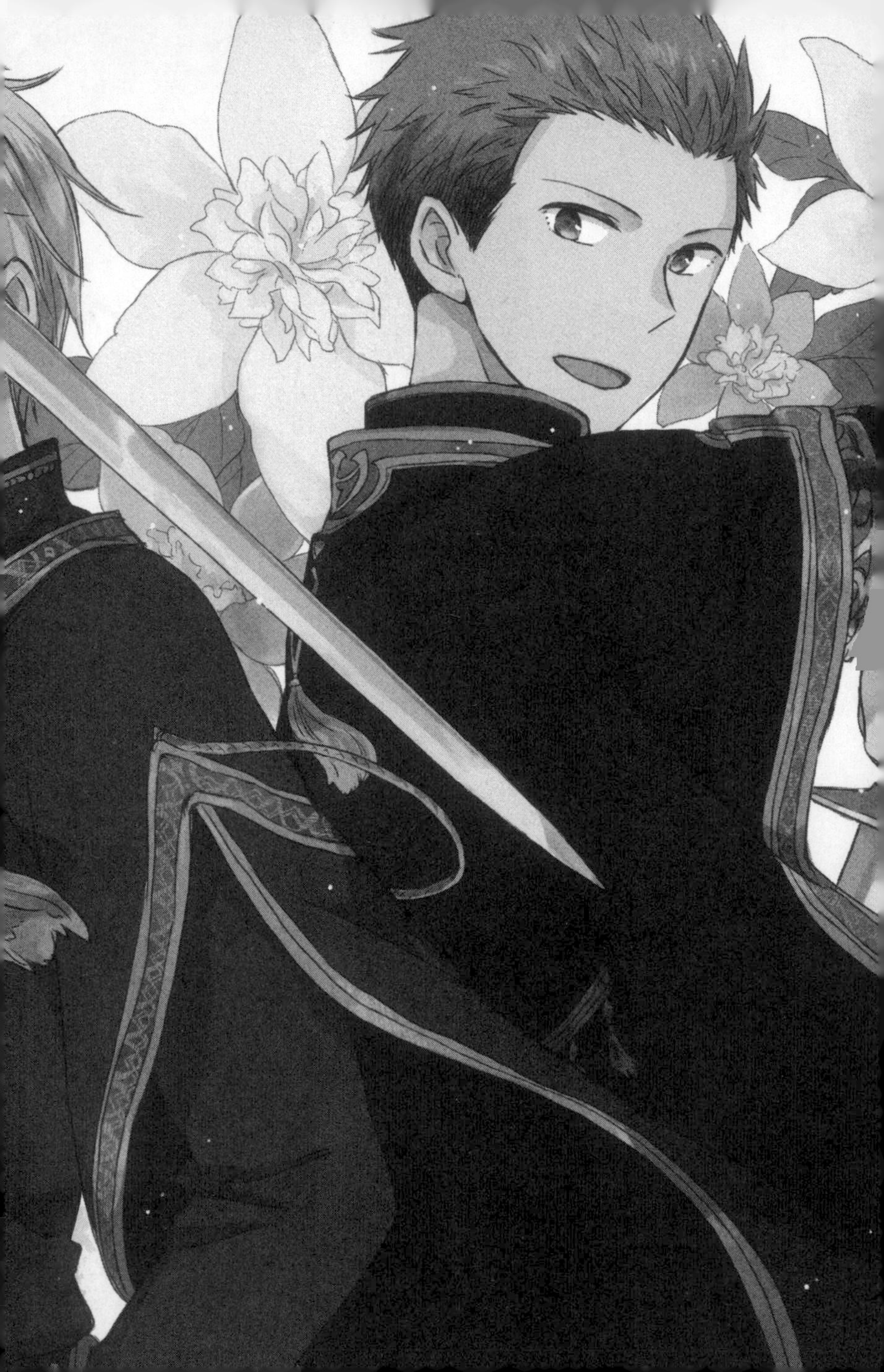

Chapter 74

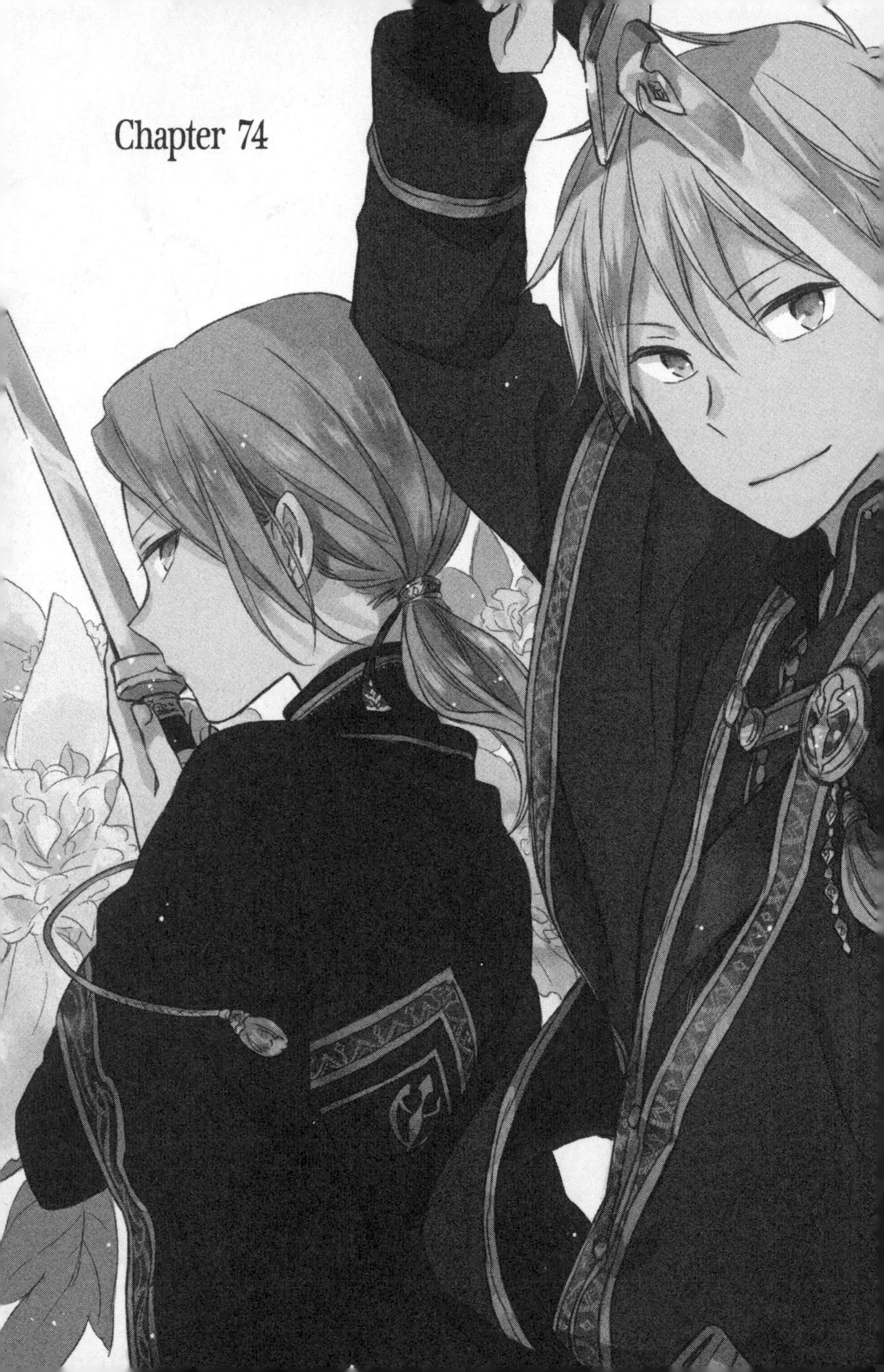

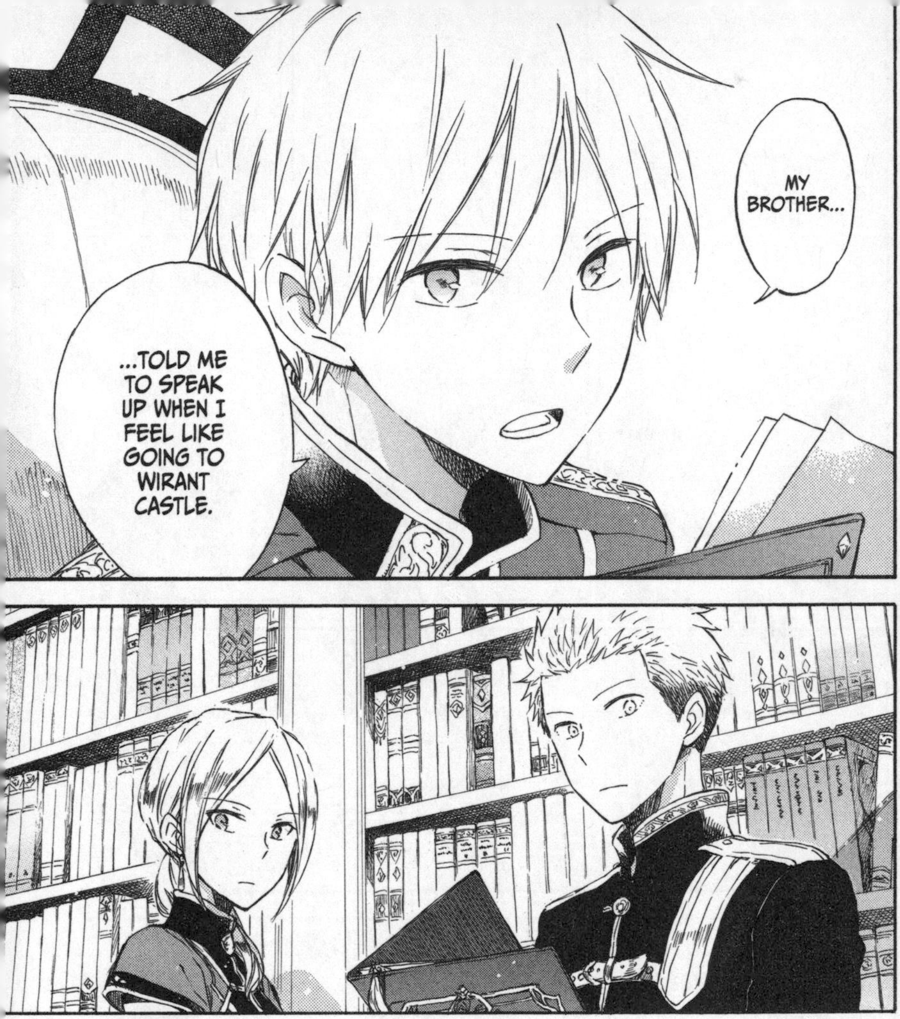
MY BROTHER...
...TOLD ME TO SPEAK UP WHEN I FEEL LIKE GOING TO WIRANT CASTLE.

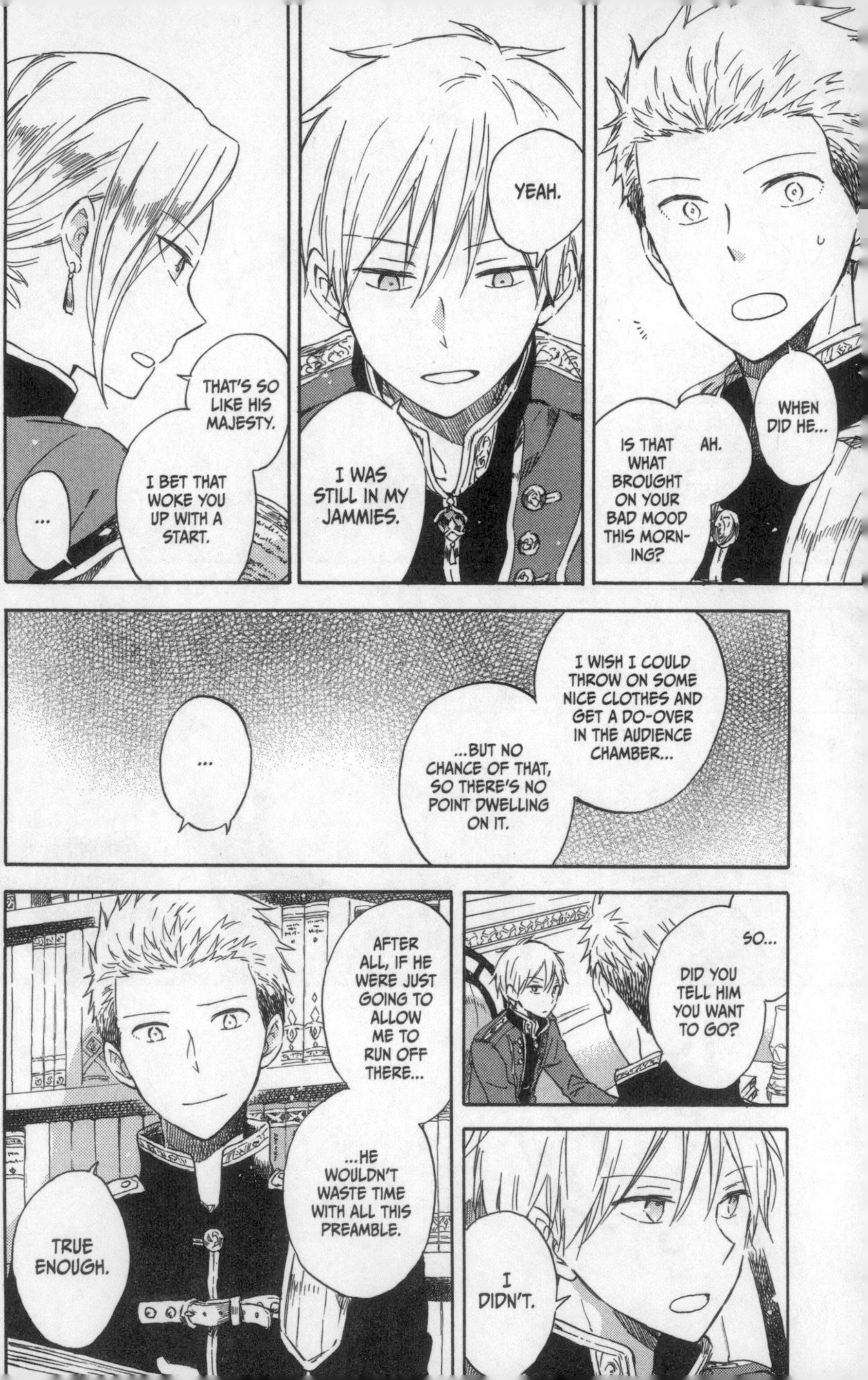
WHEN DID HE...
AH.
IS THAT WHAT BROUGHT ON YOUR BAD MOOD THIS MORNING?
YEAH.
I WAS STILL IN MY JAMMIES.
THAT'S SO LIKE HIS MAJESTY.
I BET THAT WOKE YOU UP WITH A START.
...
I WISH I COULD THROW ON SOME NICE CLOTHES AND GET A DO-OVER IN THE AUDIENCE CHAMBER...
...BUT NO CHANCE OF THAT, SO THERE'S NO POINT DWELLING ON IT.
...
SO...
DID YOU TELL HIM YOU WANT TO GO?
I DIDN'T.
AFTER ALL, IF HE WERE JUST GOING TO ALLOW ME TO RUN OFF THERE...
...HE WOULDN'T WASTE TIME WITH ALL THIS PREAMBLE.
TRUE ENOUGH.

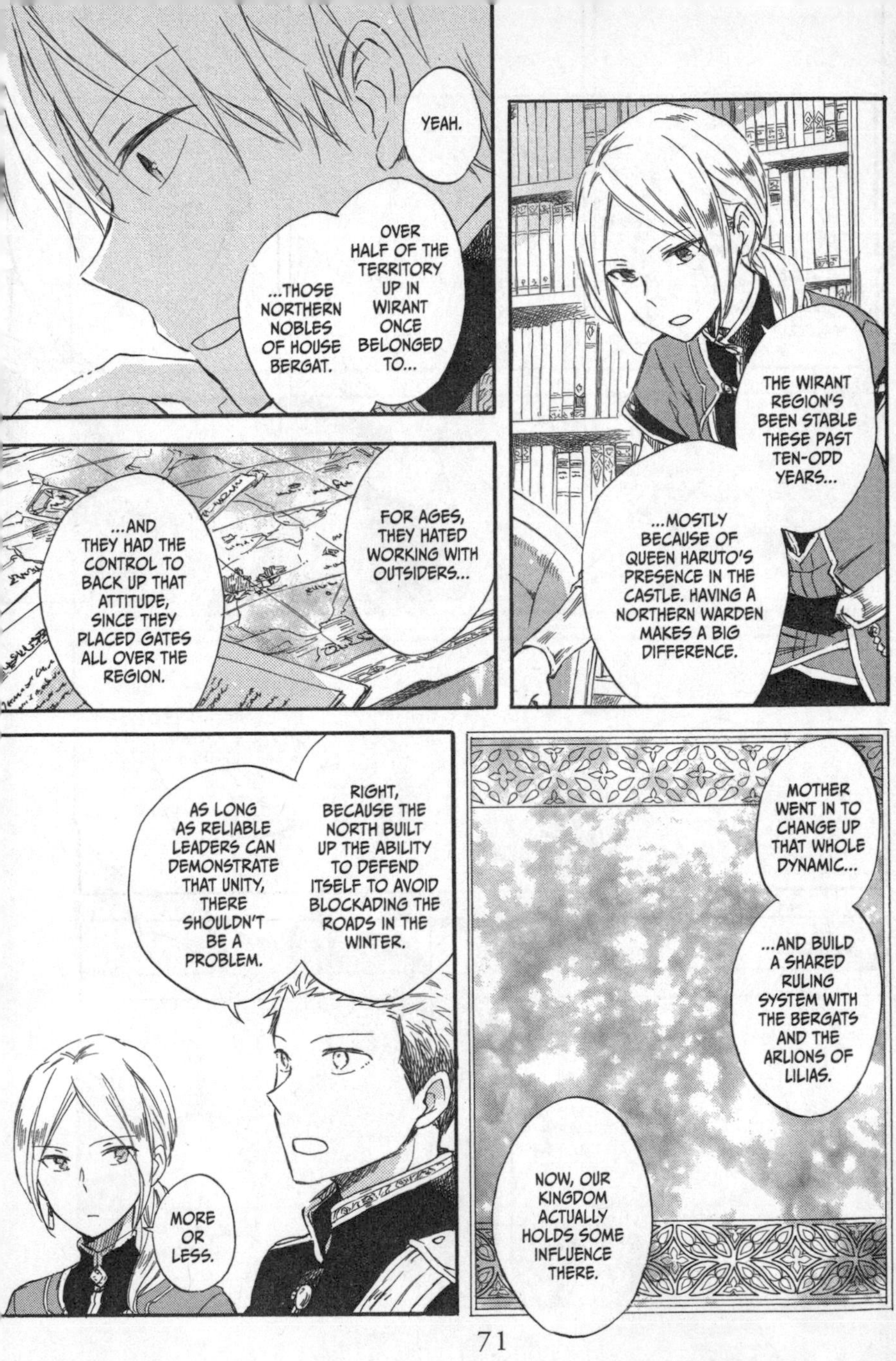
THE WIRANT REGION'S BEEN STABLE THESE PAST TEN-ODD YEARS...
...MOSTLY BECAUSE OF QUEEN HARUTO'S PRESENCE IN THE CASTLE. HAVING A NORTHERN WARDEN MAKES A BIG DIFFERENCE.
YEAH.
OVER HALF OF THE TERRITORY UP IN WIRANT ONCE BELONGED TO...
...THOSE NORTHERN NOBLES OF HOUSE BERGAT.
FOR AGES, THEY HATED WORKING WITH OUTSIDERS...
...AND THEY HAD THE CONTROL TO BACK UP THAT ATTITUDE, SINCE THEY PLACED GATES ALL OVER THE REGION.
MOTHER WENT IN TO CHANGE UP THAT WHOLE DYNAMIC...
...AND BUILD A SHARED RULING SYSTEM WITH THE BERGATS AND THE ARLIONS OF LILIAS.
NOW, OUR KINGDOM ACTUALLY HOLDS SOME INFLUENCE THERE.
RIGHT, BECAUSE THE NORTH BUILT UP THE ABILITY TO DEFEND ITSELF TO AVOID BLOCKADING THE ROADS IN THE WINTER.
AS LONG AS RELIABLE LEADERS CAN DEMONSTRATE THAT UNITY, THERE SHOULDN'T BE A PROBLEM.
MORE OR LESS.

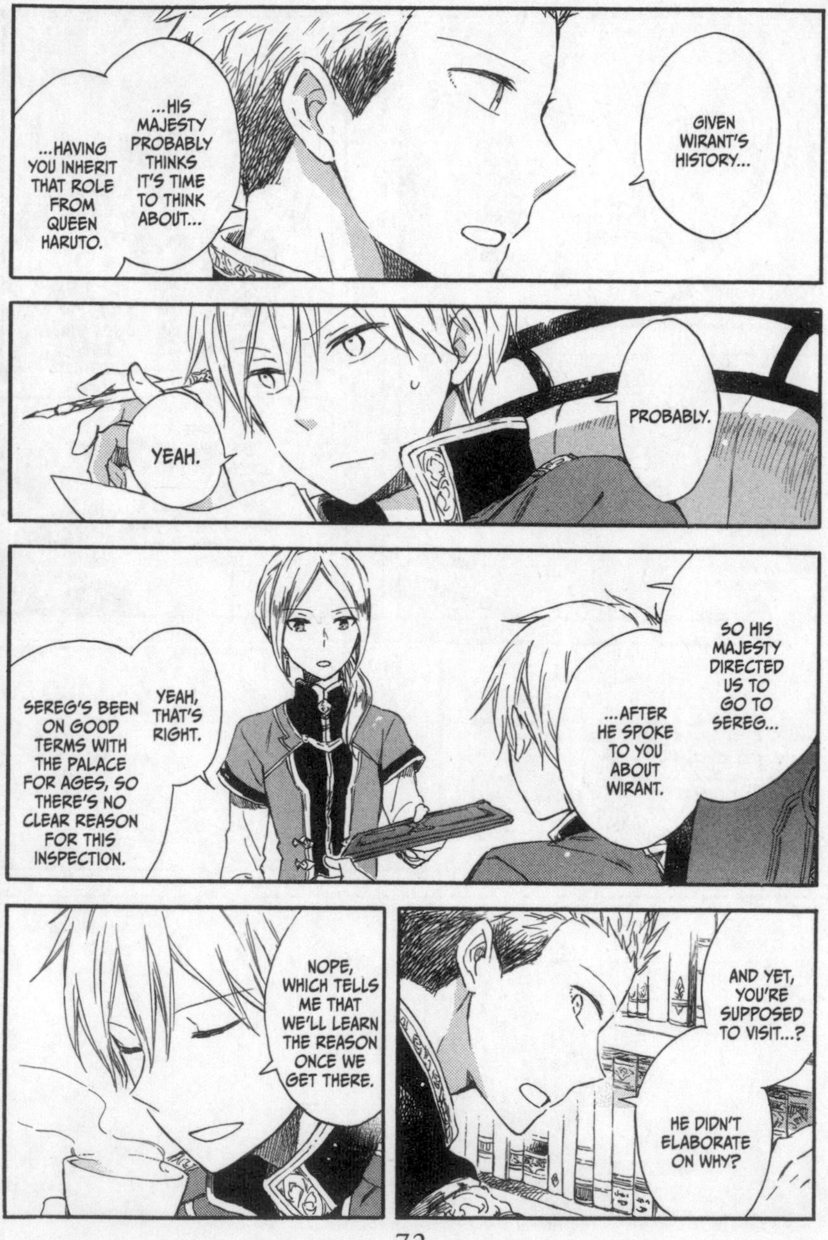
GIVEN WIRANT'S HISTORY...
...HIS MAJESTY PROBABLY THINKS IT'S TIME TO THINK ABOUT...
...HAVING YOU INHERIT THAT ROLE FROM QUEEN HARUTO.
PROBABLY.
YEAH.
SO HIS MAJESTY DIRECTED US TO GO TO SEREG...
...AFTER HE SPOKE TO YOU ABOUT WIRANT.
YEAH, THAT'S RIGHT.
SEREG'S BEEN ON GOOD TERMS WITH THE PALACE FOR AGES, SO THERE'S NO CLEAR REASON FOR THIS INSPECTION.
AND YET, YOU'RE SUPPOSED TO VISIT...?
HE DIDN'T ELABORATE ON WHY?
NOPE, WHICH TELLS ME THAT WE'LL LEARN THE REASON ONCE WE GET THERE.

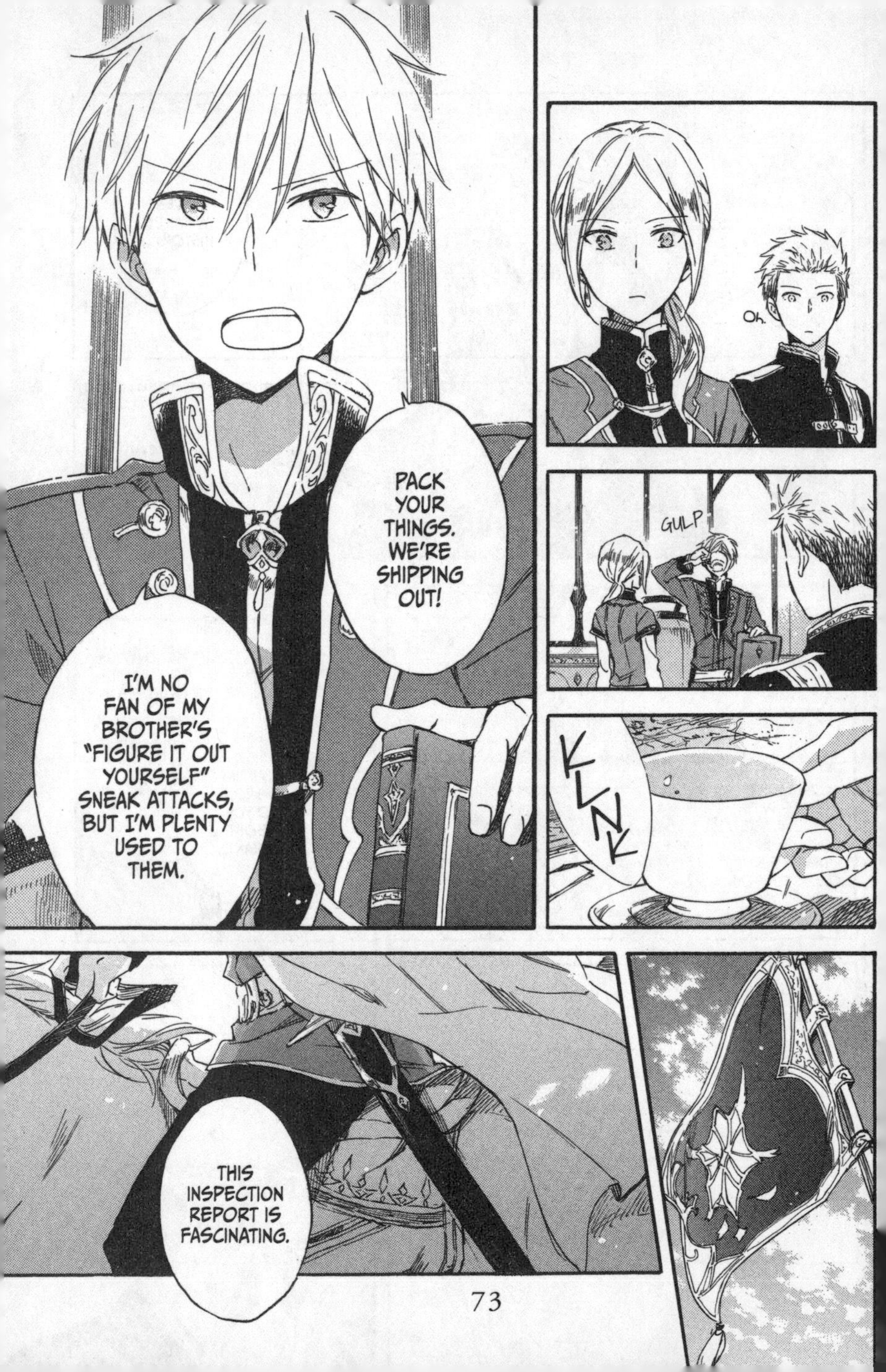
Oh.
GULP
KLNK
PACK YOUR THINGS. WE'RE SHIPPING OUT!
I'M NO FAN OF MY BROTHER'S "FIGURE IT OUT YOURSELF" SNEAK ATTACKS, BUT I'M PLENTY USED TO THEM.
THIS INSPECTION REPORT IS FASCINATING.

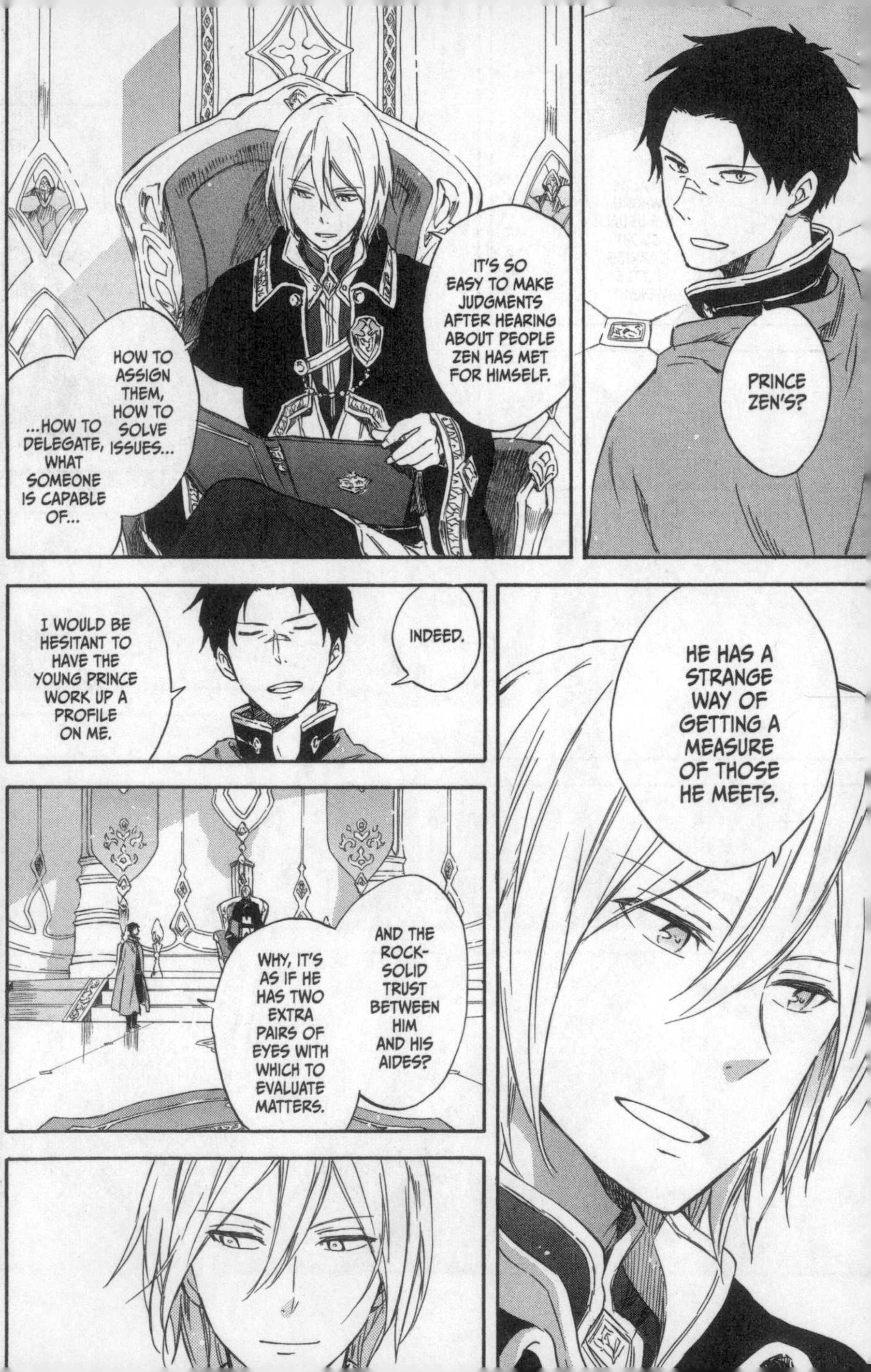
PRINCE ZEN'S?
IT'S SO EASY TO MAKE JUDGMENTS AFTER HEARING ABOUT PEOPLE ZEN HAS MET FOR HIMSELF.
HOW TO ASSIGN THEM, HOW TO SOLVE ISSUES...
...HOW TO DELEGATE, WHAT SOMEONE IS CAPABLE OF...
HE HAS A STRANGE WAY OF GETTING A MEASURE OF THOSE HE MEETS.
INDEED.
I WOULD BE HESITANT TO HAVE THE YOUNG PRINCE WORK UP A PROFILE ON ME.
AND THE ROCK-SOLID TRUST BETWEEN HIM AND HIS AIDES?
WHY, IT'S AS IF HE HAS TWO EXTRA PAIRS OF EYES WITH WHICH TO EVALUATE MATTERS.

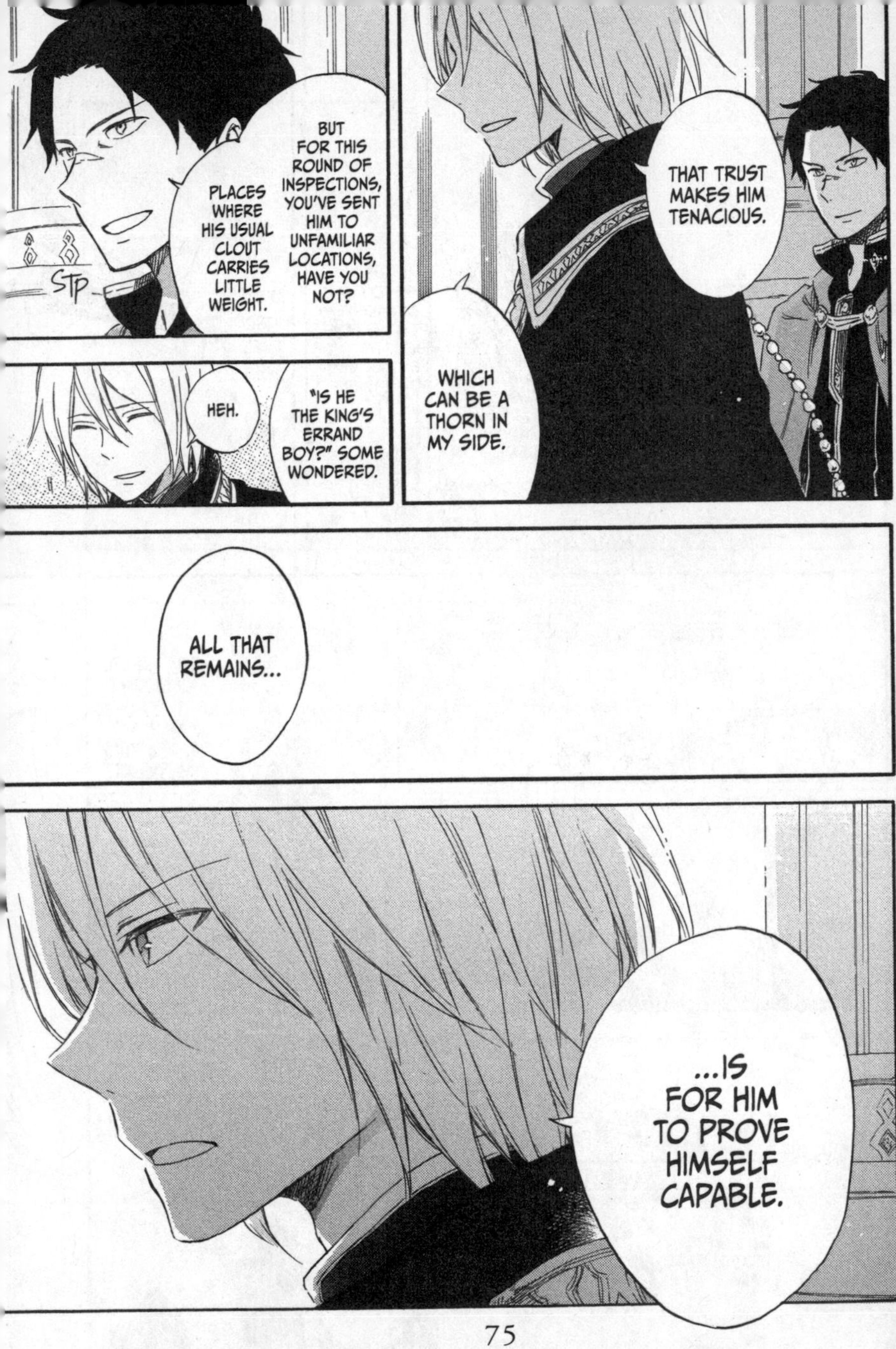
THAT TRUST MAKES HIM TENACIOUS.
WHICH CAN BE A THORN IN MY SIDE.
BUT FOR THIS ROUND OF INSPECTIONS, YOU'VE SENT HIM TO UNFAMILIAR LOCATIONS, HAVE YOU NOT?
PLACES WHERE HIS USUAL CLOUT CARRIES LITTLE WEIGHT.
STP
"IS HE THE KING'S ERRAND BOY?" SOME WONDERED.
HEH.
ALL THAT REMAINS...
...IS FOR HIM TO PROVE HIMSELF CAPABLE.

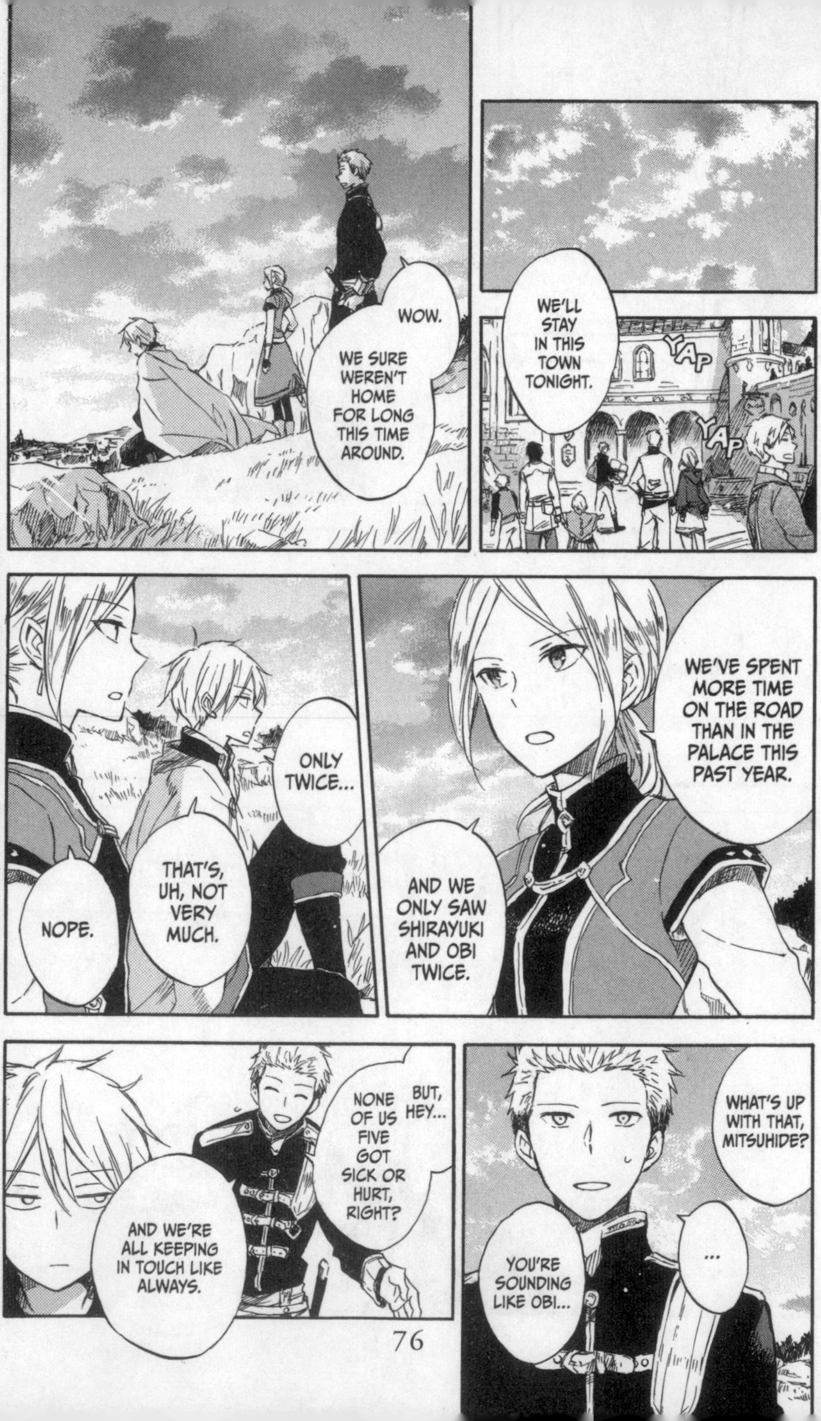

WE'LL STAY IN THIS TOWN TONIGHT.
YAP
YAP
WOW.
WE SURE WEREN'T HOME FOR LONG THIS TIME AROUND.
WE'VE SPENT MORE TIME ON THE ROAD THAN IN THE PALACE THIS PAST YEAR.
AND WE ONLY SAW SHIRAYUKI AND OBI TWICE.
ONLY TWICE...
THAT'S, UH, NOT VERY MUCH.
NOPE.
WHAT'S UP WITH THAT, MITSUHIDE?
...
YOU'RE SOUNDING LIKE OBI...
BUT, HEY...
NONE OF US FIVE GOT SICK OR HURT, RIGHT?
AND WE'RE ALL KEEPING IN TOUCH LIKE ALWAYS.

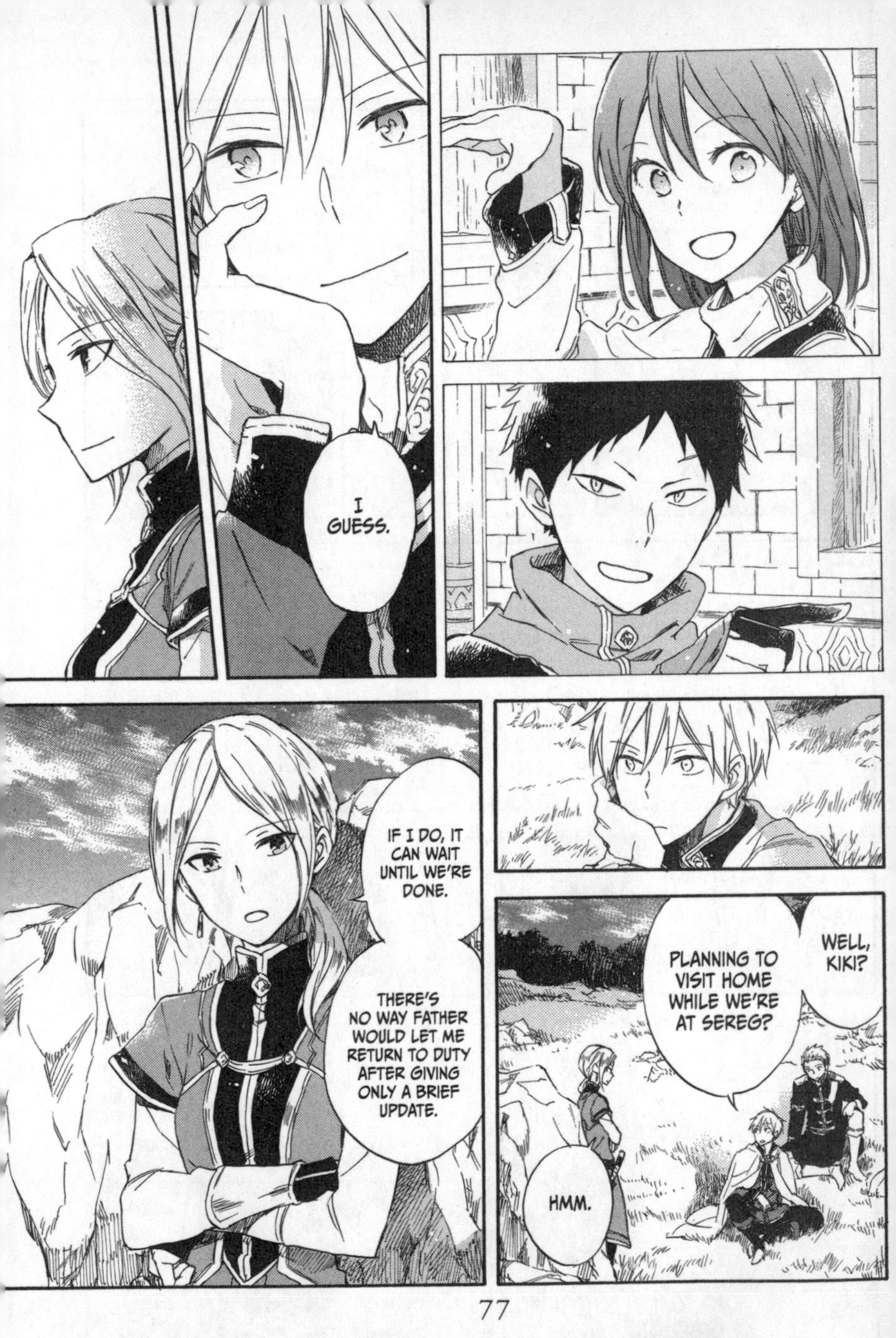
I GUESS.
WELL, KIKI?
PLANNING TO VISIT HOME WHILE WE'RE AT SEREG?
HMM.
IF I DO, IT CAN WAIT UNTIL WE'RE DONE.
THERE'S NO WAY FATHER WOULD LET ME RETURN TO DUTY AFTER GIVING ONLY A BRIEF UPDATE.

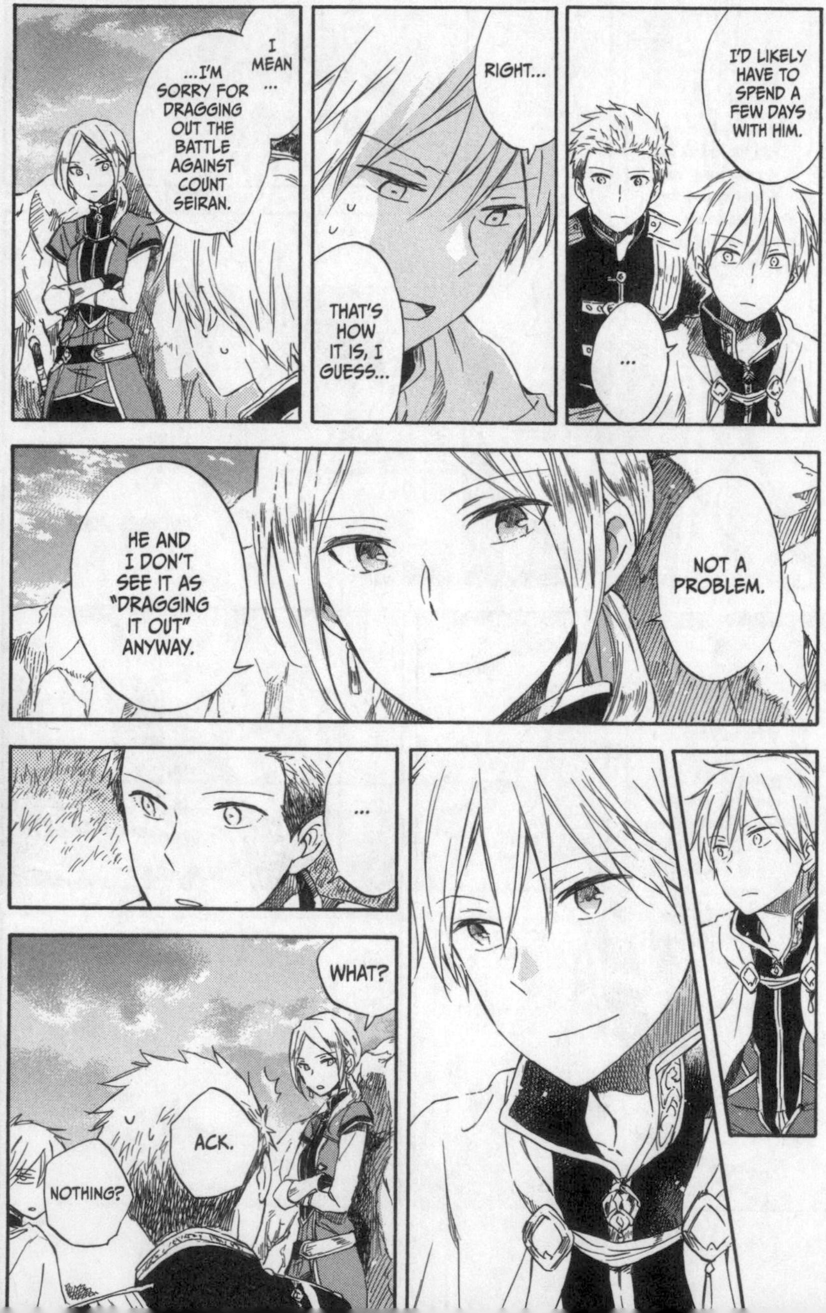
I'D LIKELY HAVE TO SPEND A FEW DAYS WITH HIM.
...
RIGHT...
THAT'S HOW IT IS, I GUESS...
I MEAN ...
...I'M SORRY FOR DRAGGING OUT THE BATTLE AGAINST COUNT SEIRAN.
NOT A PROBLEM.
HE AND I DON'T SEE IT AS "DRAGGING IT OUT" ANYWAY.
...
WHAT?
ACK.
NOTHING?

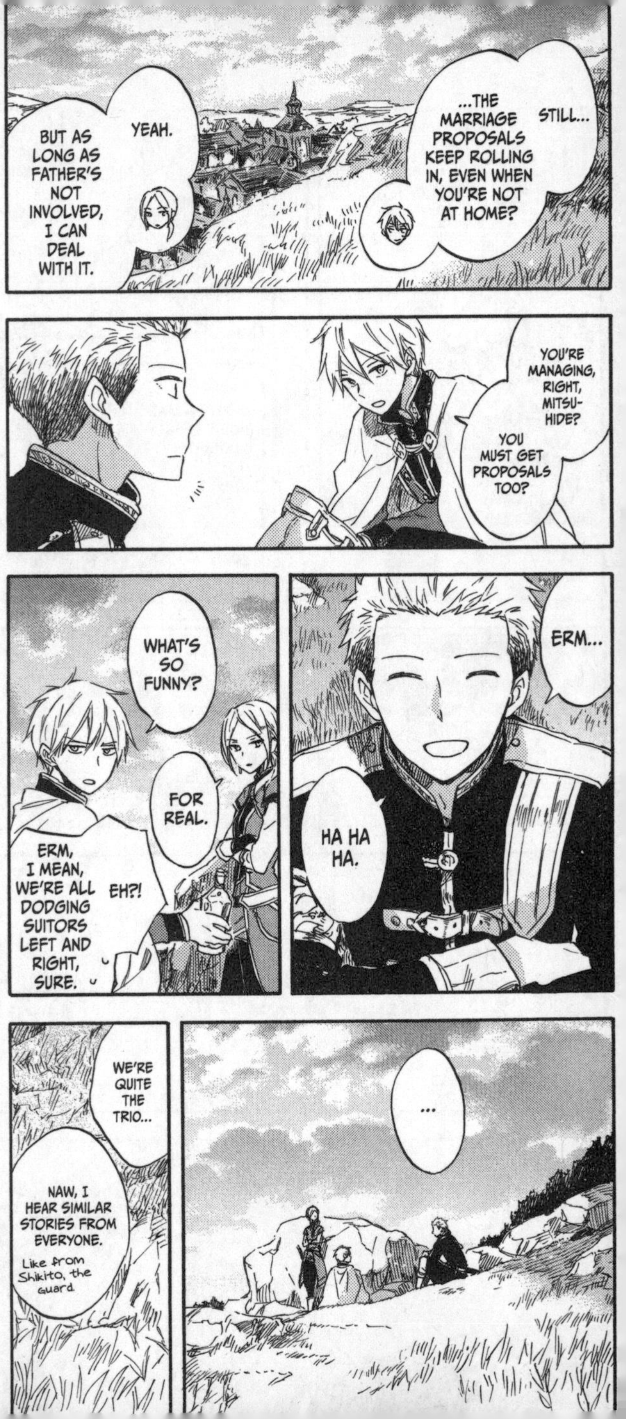
STILL...
...THE MARRIAGE PROPOSALS KEEP ROLLING IN, EVEN WHEN YOU'RE NOT AT HOME?
YEAH.
BUT AS LONG AS FATHER'S NOT INVOLVED, I CAN DEAL WITH IT.
YOU'RE MANAGING, RIGHT, MITSU-HIDE?
YOU MUST GET PROPOSALS TOO?
ERM...
HA HA HA.
WHAT'S SO FUNNY?
FOR REAL.
EH?!
ERM, I MEAN, WE'RE ALL DODGING SUITORS LEFT AND RIGHT, SURE.
...
WE'RE QUITE THE TRIO...
NAW, I HEAR SIMILAR STORIES FROM EVERYONE.
Like from Shikito, the guard.

3

RECORDING STUDIO (PART 1)

I wasn't involved with the drama CD I mentioned, but I have visited the recording studio a few times for the Snow White anime.

Just like with seeing the characters animated, hearing their voices makes them start to really come to life. It's exciting.

Once, the whole cast stood in front of a row of mics to produce the background chatter sound effects seen in the manga, like when the characters are out and about in town. It was amazing!

We're talking about lines that aren't even written in the script, mind you, but when they all start yapping at once it's like WOW! All of a sudden, I found myself transported to a harbor town in Clarines.

Another time, they performed an elegant soiree scene in the palace—which is nothing at all like the harbor town. Then, too, I felt like I was really at the soiree...

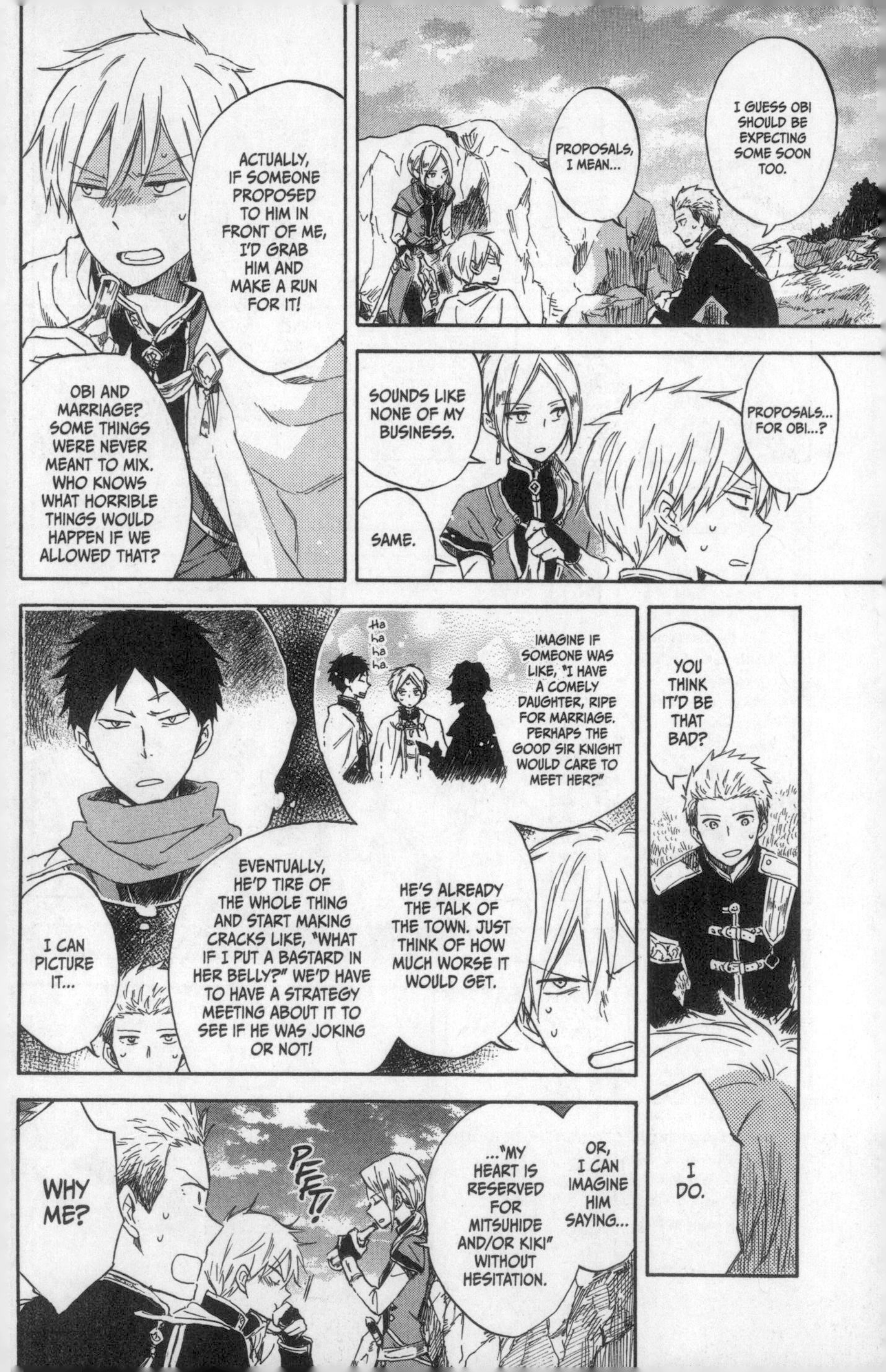
I GUESS OBI SHOULD BE EXPECTING SOME SOON TOO.
PROPOSALS, I MEAN...
PROPOSALS... FOR OBI...?
SOUNDS LIKE NONE OF MY BUSINESS.
SAME.
ACTUALLY, IF SOMEONE PROPOSED TO HIM IN FRONT OF ME, I'D GRAB HIM AND MAKE A RUN FOR IT!
OBI AND MARRIAGE? SOME THINGS WERE NEVER MEANT TO MIX. WHO KNOWS WHAT HORRIBLE THINGS WOULD HAPPEN IF WE ALLOWED THAT?
YOU THINK IT'D BE THAT BAD?
I DO.
IMAGINE IF SOMEONE WAS LIKE, "I HAVE A COMELY DAUGHTER, RIPE FOR MARRIAGE. PERHAPS THE GOOD SIR KNIGHT WOULD CARE TO MEET HER?"
Ha ha ha ha.
HE'S ALREADY THE TALK OF THE TOWN. JUST THINK OF HOW MUCH WORSE IT WOULD GET.
EVENTUALLY, HE'D TIRE OF THE WHOLE THING AND START MAKING CRACKS LIKE, "WHAT IF I PUT A BASTARD IN HER BELLY?" WE'D HAVE TO HAVE A STRATEGY MEETING ABOUT IT TO SEE IF HE WAS JOKING OR NOT!
I CAN PICTURE IT...
OR, I CAN IMAGINE HIM SAYING...
..."MY HEART IS RESERVED FOR MITSUHIDE AND/OR KIKI" WITHOUT HESITATION.
PFFT!
WHY ME?

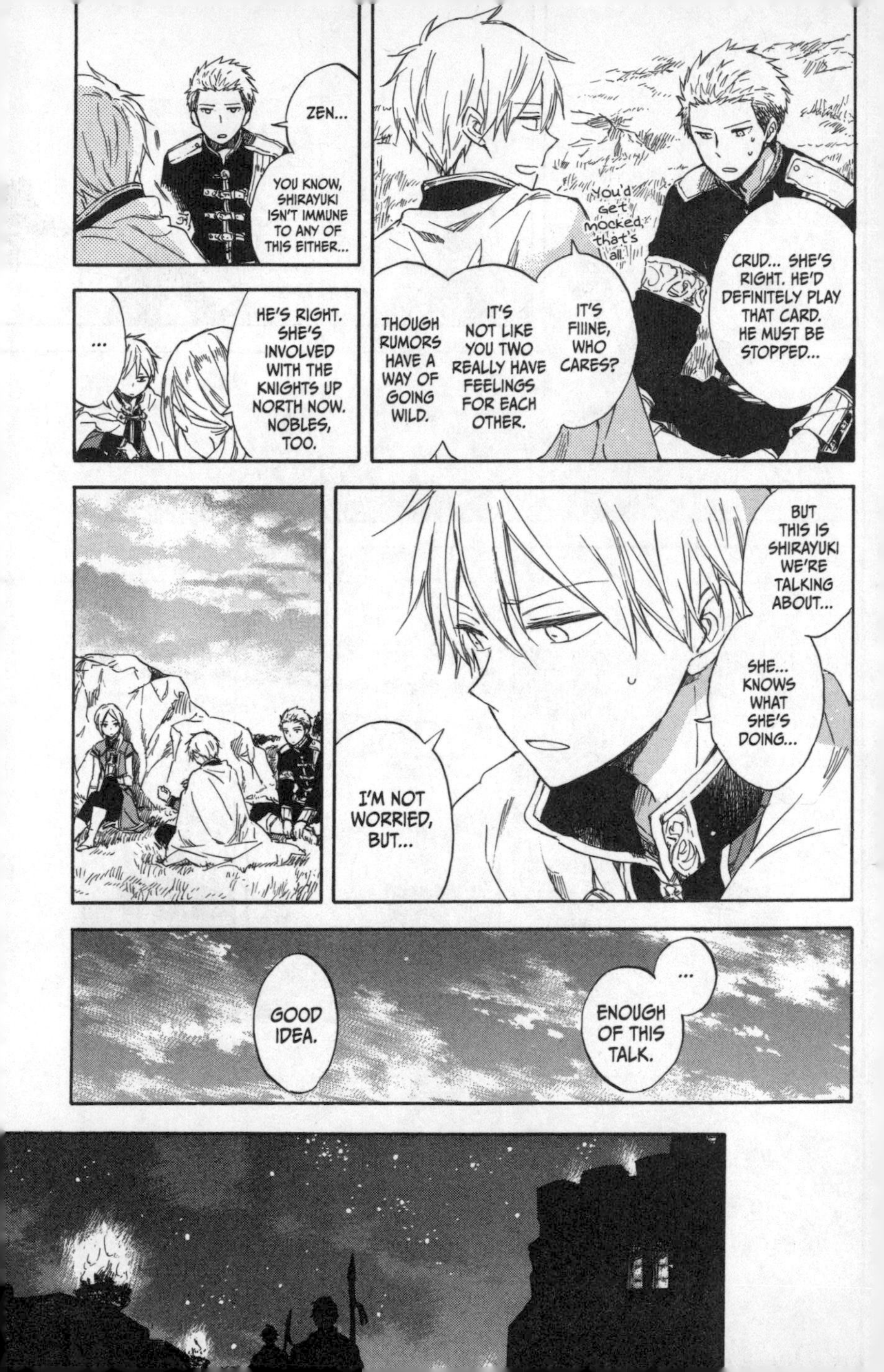
IT'S FIIINE, WHO CARES?
IT'S NOT LIKE YOU TWO REALLY HAVE FEELINGS FOR EACH OTHER.
THOUGH RUMORS HAVE A WAY OF GOING WILD.
You'd get mocked, that's all.
CRUD... SHE'S RIGHT. HE'D DEFINITELY PLAY THAT CARD. HE MUST BE STOPPED...
ZEN...
YOU KNOW, SHIRAYUKI ISN'T IMMUNE TO ANY OF THIS EITHER...
HE'S RIGHT. SHE'S INVOLVED WITH THE KNIGHTS UP NORTH NOW. NOBLES, TOO.
...
BUT THIS IS SHIRAYUKI WE'RE TALKING ABOUT...
SHE... KNOWS WHAT SHE'S DOING...
I'M NOT WORRIED, BUT...
...
ENOUGH OF THIS TALK.
GOOD IDEA.

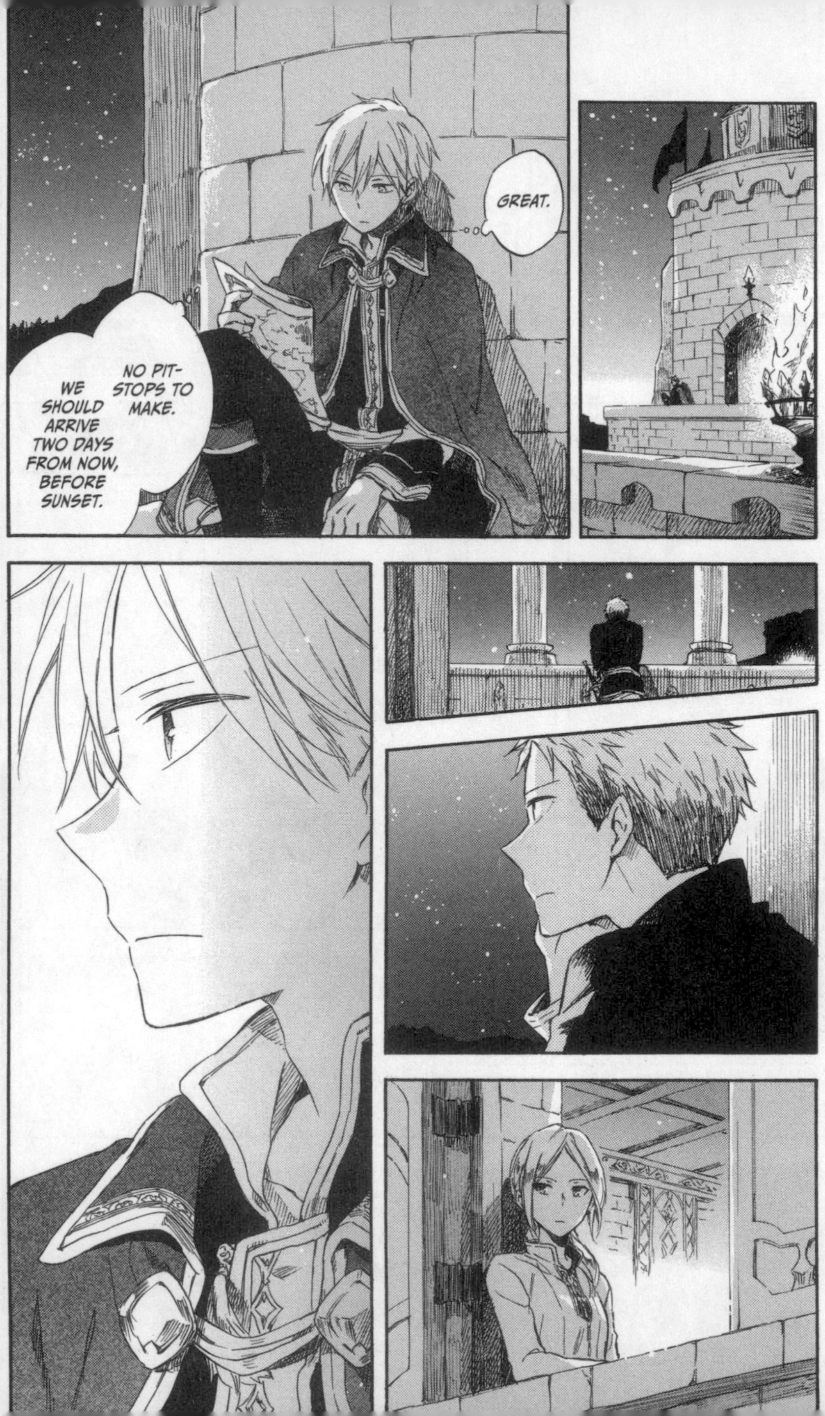
GREAT.
NO PIT-STOPS TO MAKE. WE SHOULD ARRIVE TWO DAYS FROM NOW, BEFORE SUNSET.

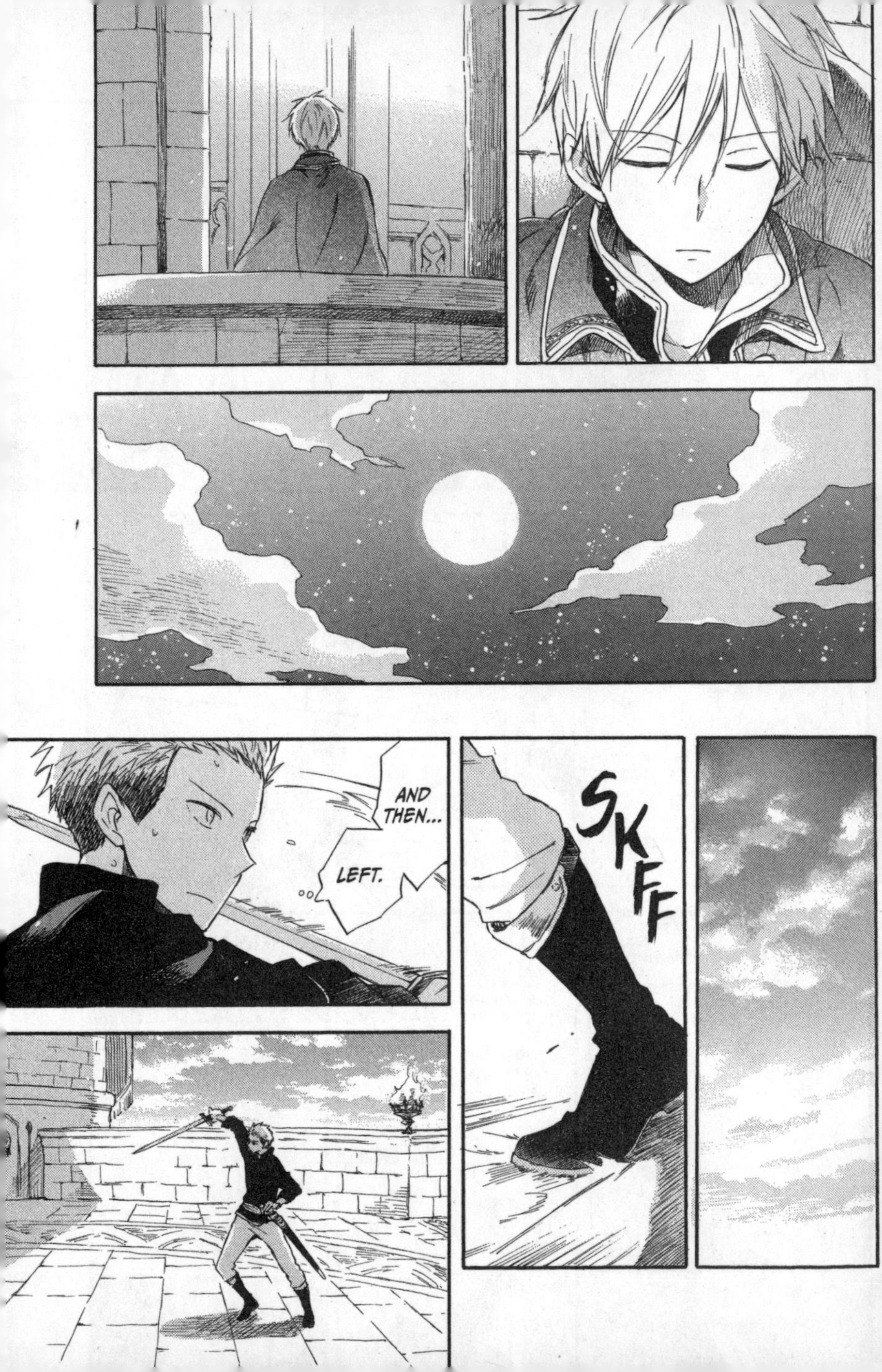
SKFF
AND THEN...
LEFT.

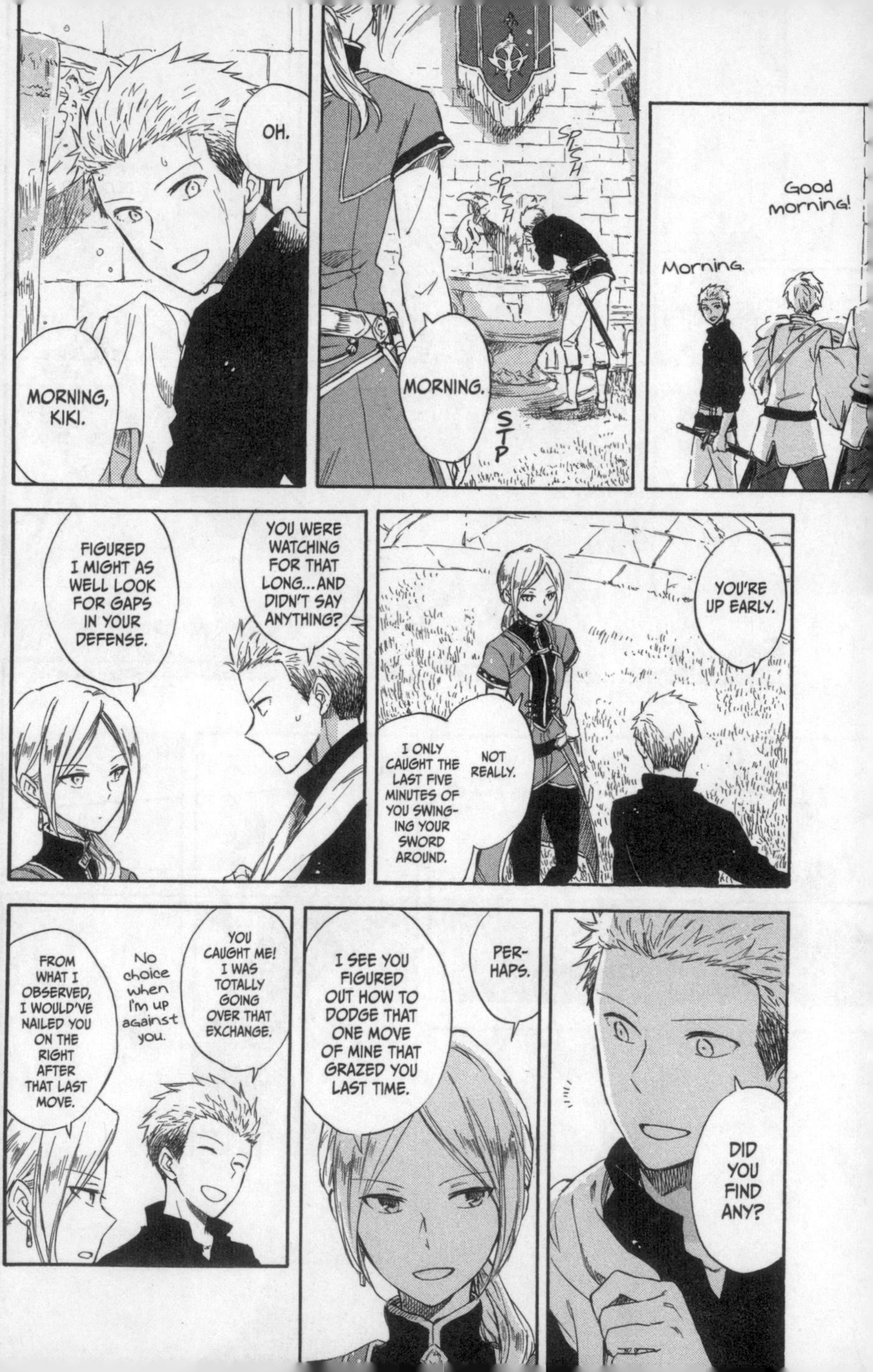
Good morning!
Morning.
SPLSH
SPLSH
MORNING.
STP
OH.
MORNING, KIKI.
YOU'RE UP EARLY.
NOT REALLY.
I ONLY CAUGHT THE LAST FIVE MINUTES OF YOU SWING-ING YOUR SWORD AROUND.
YOU WERE WATCHING FOR THAT LONG...AND DIDN'T SAY ANYTHING?
FIGURED I MIGHT AS WELL LOOK FOR GAPS IN YOUR DEFENSE.
DID YOU FIND ANY?
PER-HAPS.
I SEE YOU FIGURED OUT HOW TO DODGE THAT ONE MOVE OF MINE THAT GRAZED YOU LAST TIME.
YOU CAUGHT ME! I WAS TOTALLY GOING OVER THAT EXCHANGE.
No choice when I'm up against you.
FROM WHAT I OBSERVED, I WOULD'VE NAILED YOU ON THE RIGHT AFTER THAT LAST MOVE.

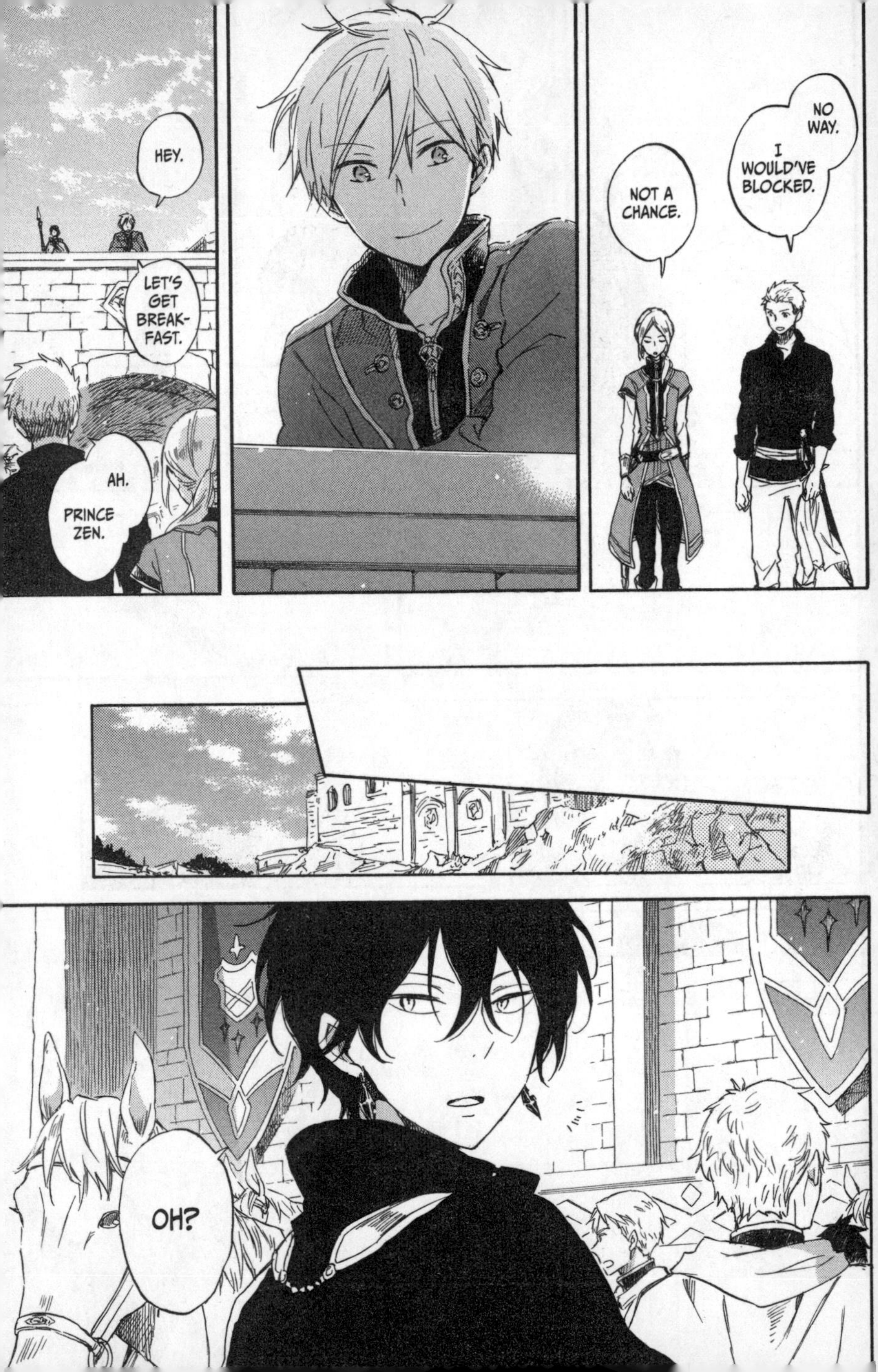
NO WAY.
I WOULD'VE BLOCKED.
NOT A CHANCE.
HEY.
LET'S GET BREAK-FAST.
AH.
PRINCE ZEN.
OH?

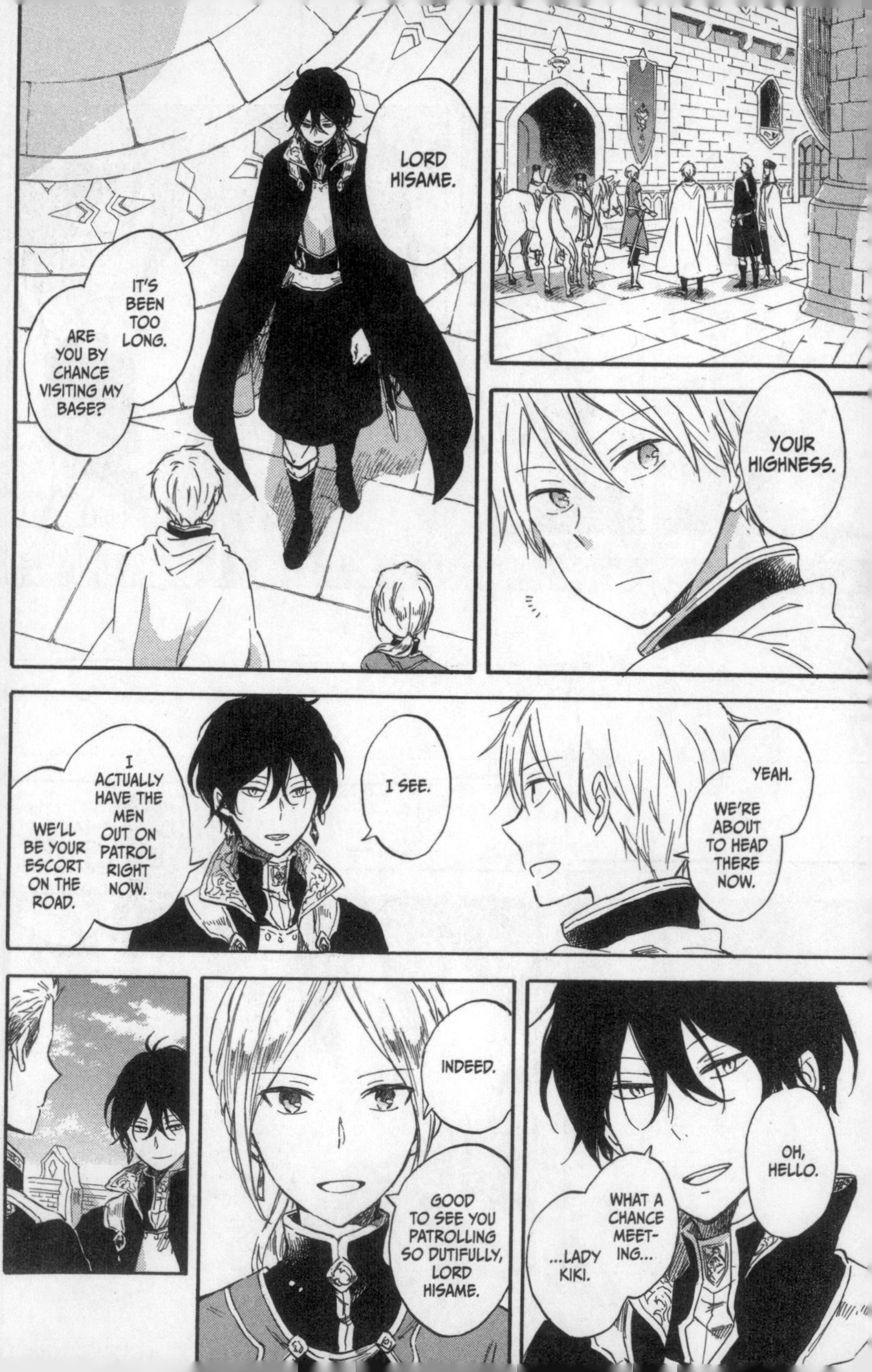
YOUR HIGHNESS.
LORD HISAME.
IT'S BEEN TOO LONG.
ARE YOU BY CHANCE VISITING MY BASE?
YEAH.
WE'RE ABOUT TO HEAD THERE NOW.
I SEE.
I ACTUALLY HAVE THE MEN OUT ON PATROL RIGHT NOW.
WE'LL BE YOUR ESCORT ON THE ROAD.
OH, HELLO.
WHAT A CHANCE MEET-ING...
...LADY KIKI.
INDEED.
GOOD TO SEE YOU PATROLLING SO DUTIFULLY, LORD HISAME.

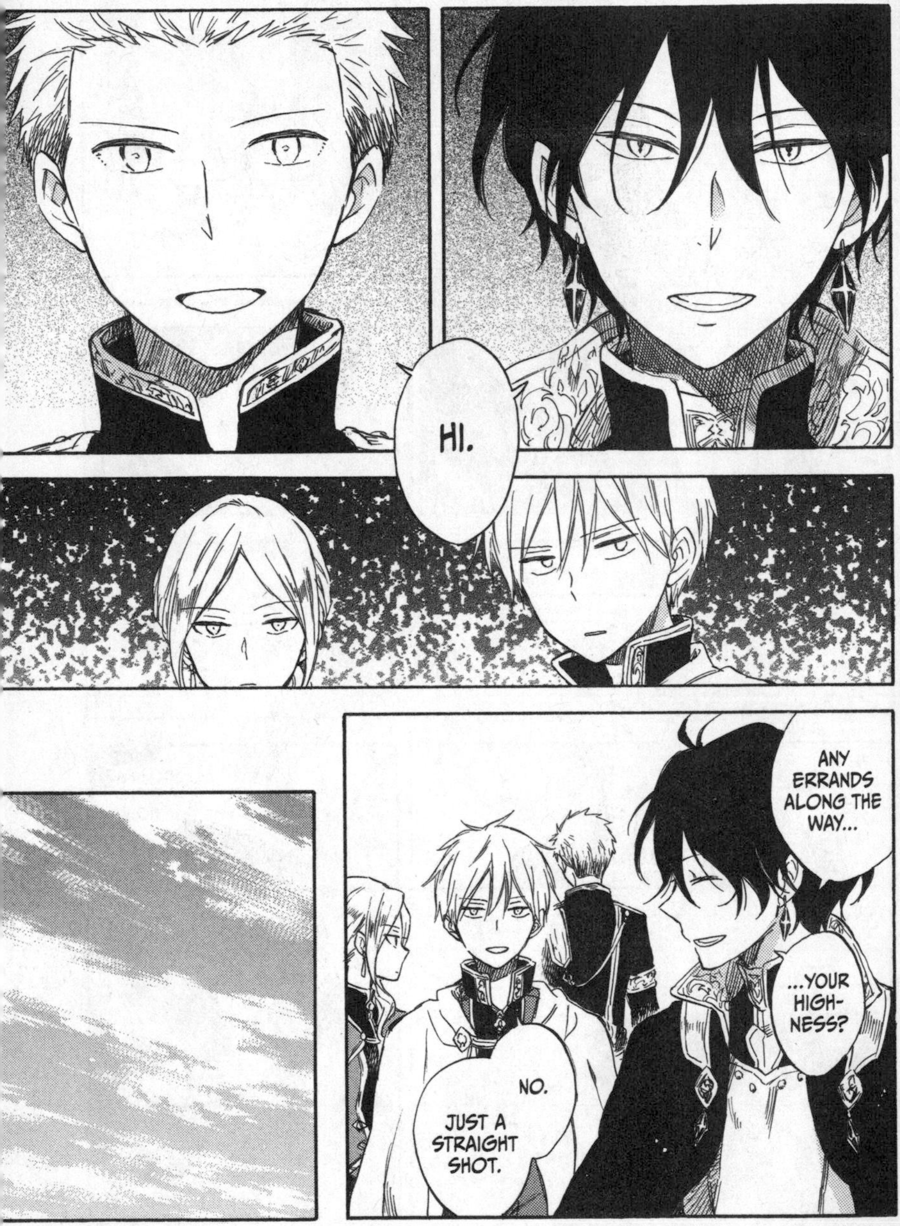
HI.
ANY ERRANDS ALONG THE WAY...
...YOUR HIGH-NESS?
NO.
JUST A STRAIGHT SHOT.

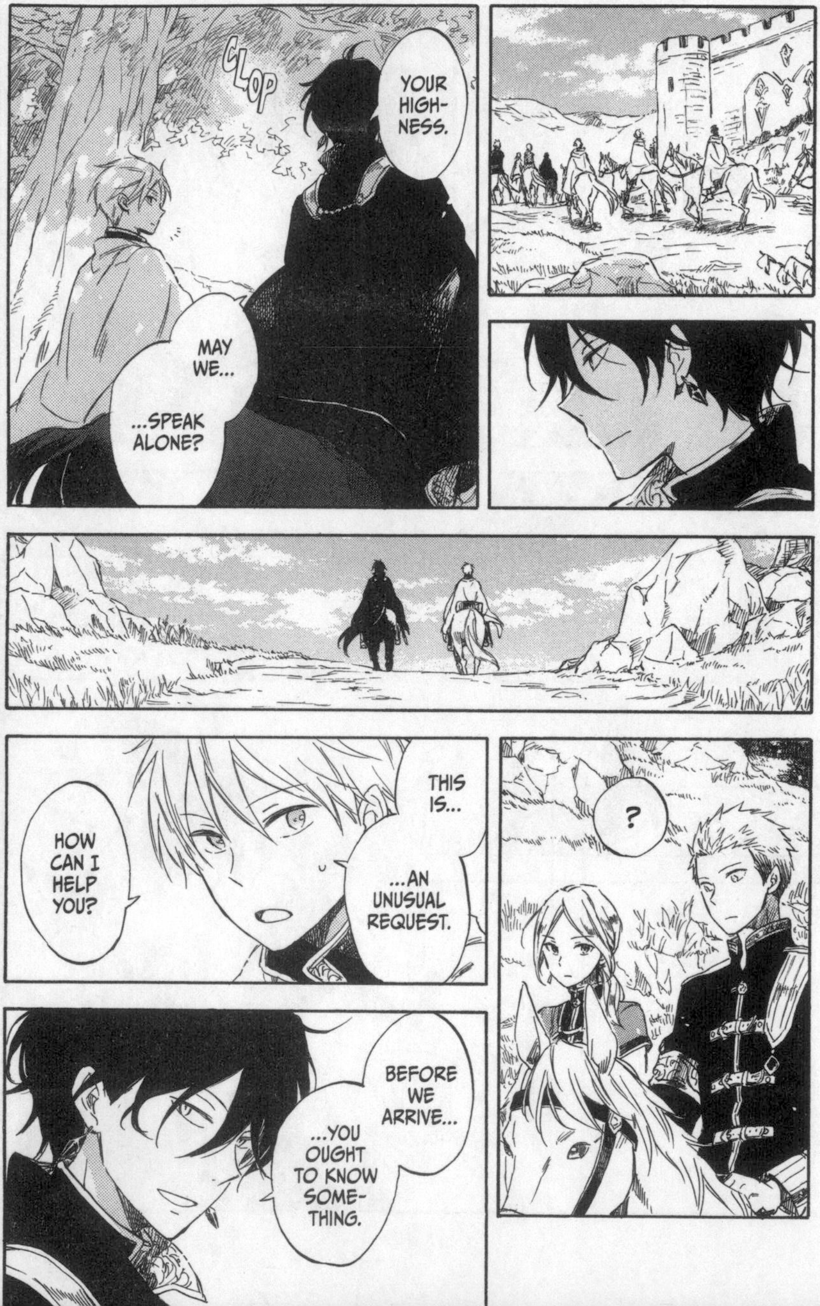
CLOP
YOUR HIGH-NESS.
MAY WE...
...SPEAK ALONE?
?
THIS IS...
...AN UNUSUAL REQUEST.
HOW CAN I HELP YOU?
BEFORE WE ARRIVE...
...YOU OUGHT TO KNOW SOME-THING.

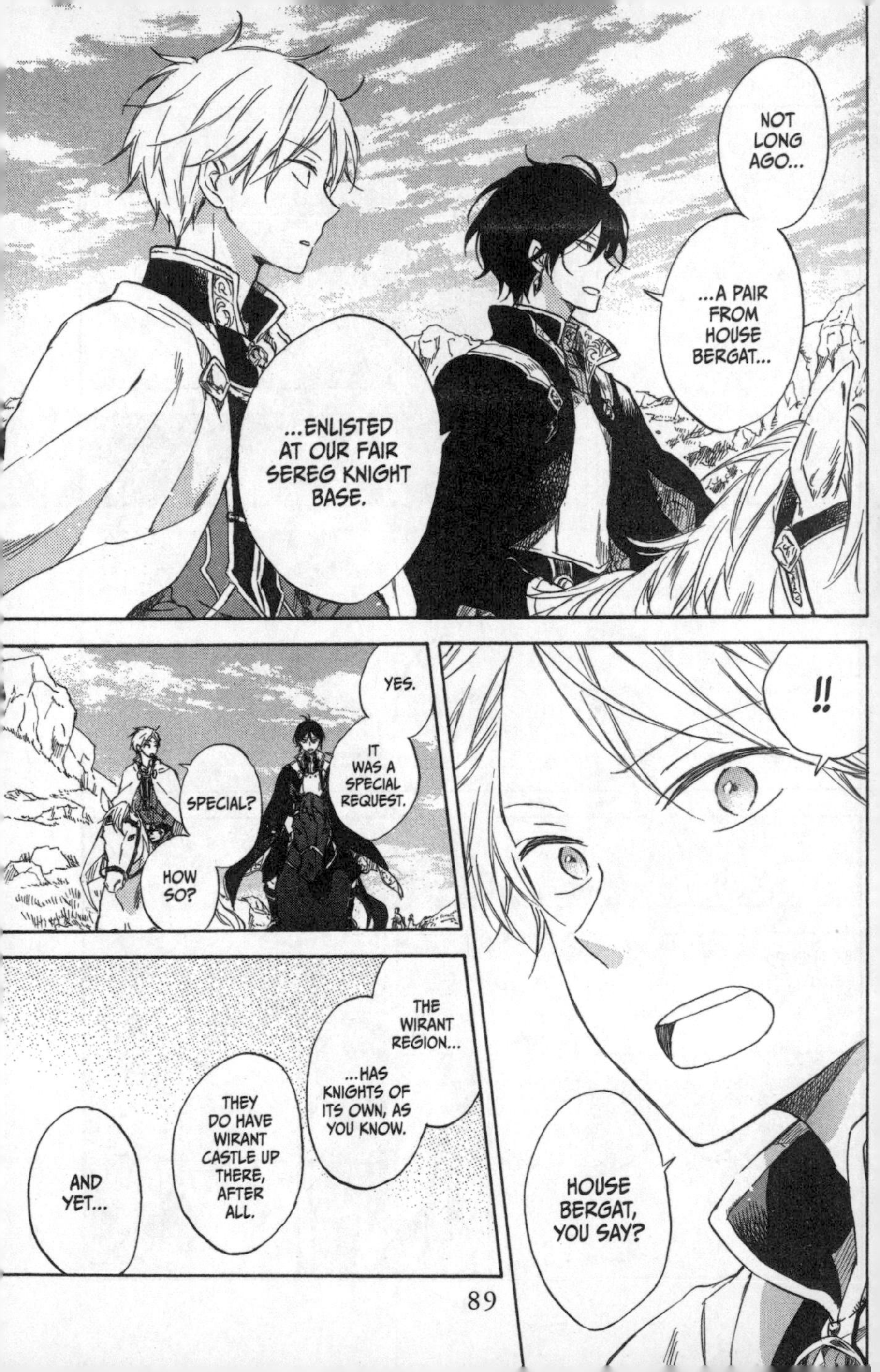

NOT LONG AGO...
...A PAIR FROM HOUSE BERGAT...
...ENLISTED AT OUR FAIR SEREG KNIGHT BASE.
!!
HOUSE BERGAT, YOU SAY?
YES.
IT WAS A SPECIAL REQUEST.
SPECIAL?
HOW SO?
THE WIRANT REGION...
...HAS KNIGHTS OF ITS OWN, AS YOU KNOW.
THEY DO HAVE WIRANT CASTLE UP THERE, AFTER ALL.
AND YET...

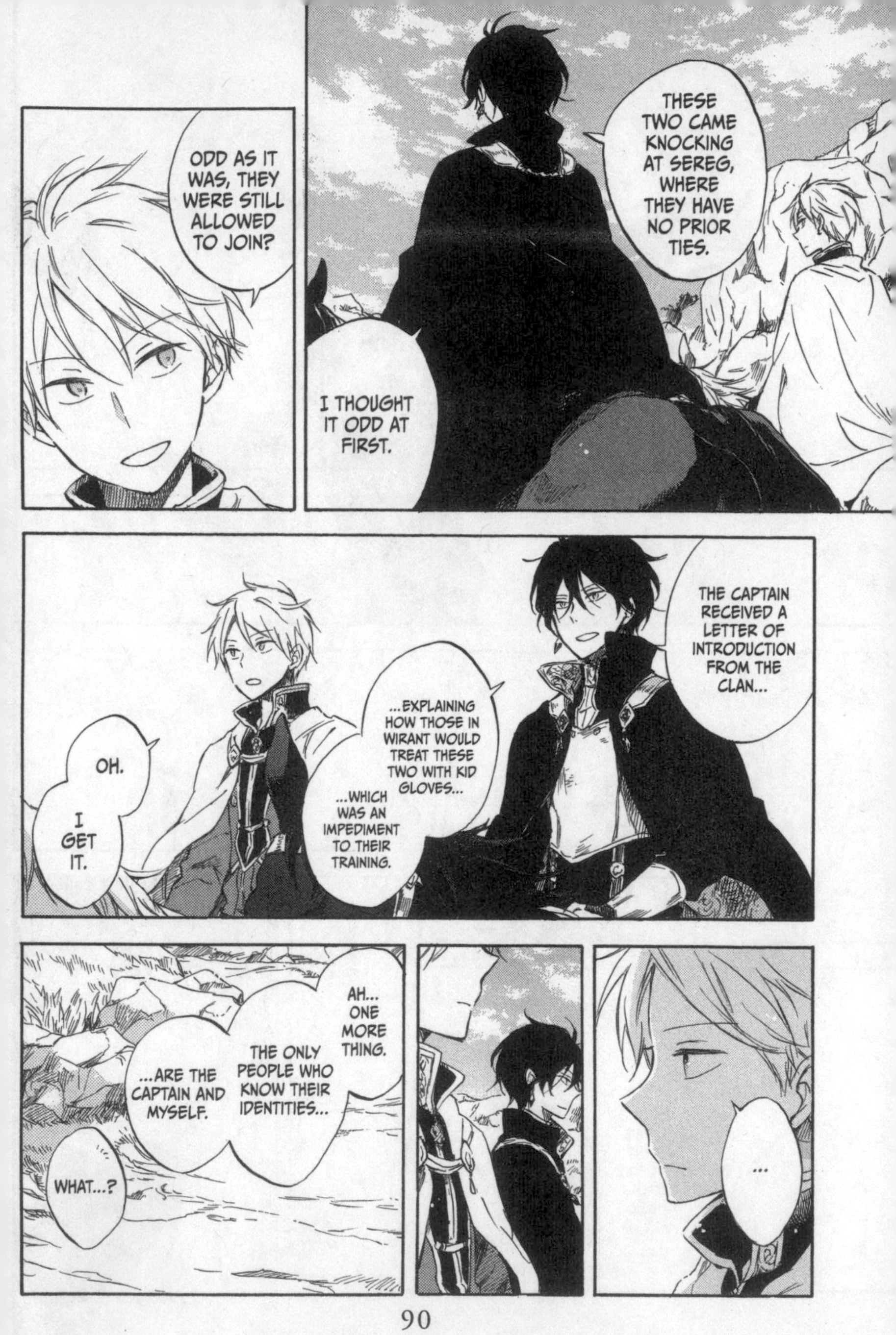
THESE TWO CAME KNOCKING AT SEREG, WHERE THEY HAVE NO PRIOR TIES.
I THOUGHT IT ODD AT FIRST.
ODD AS IT WAS, THEY WERE STILL ALLOWED TO JOIN?
THE CAPTAIN RECEIVED A LETTER OF INTRODUCTION FROM THE CLAN...
...EXPLAINING HOW THOSE IN WIRANT WOULD TREAT THESE TWO WITH KID GLOVES...
...WHICH WAS AN IMPEDIMENT TO THEIR TRAINING.
OH.
I GET IT.
...
AH... ONE MORE THING.
THE ONLY PEOPLE WHO KNOW THEIR IDENTITIES...
...ARE THE CAPTAIN AND MYSELF.
WHAT...?

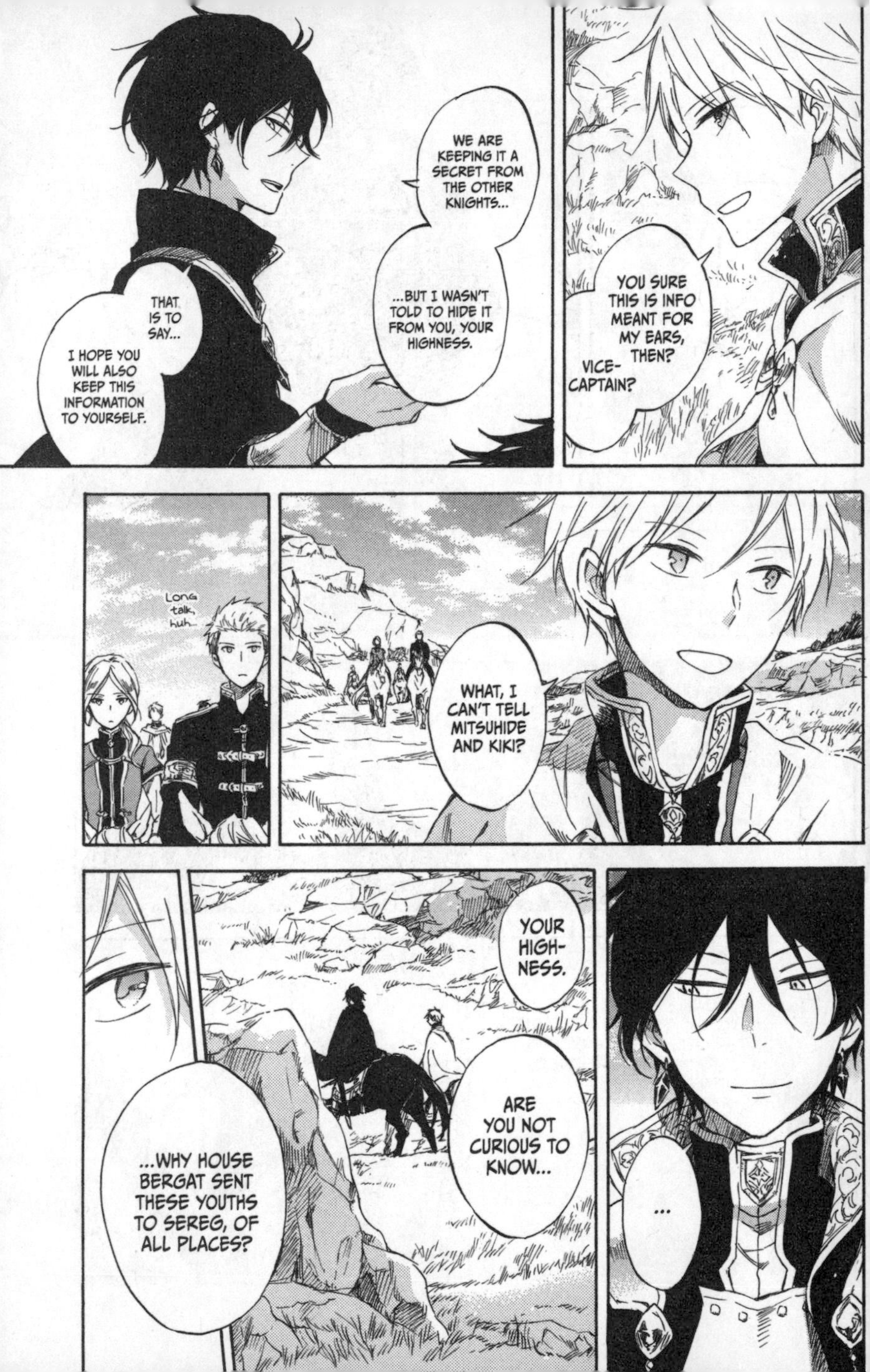

YOU SURE THIS IS INFO MEANT FOR MY EARS, THEN?
VICE-CAPTAIN?
WE ARE KEEPING IT A SECRET FROM THE OTHER KNIGHTS...
...BUT I WASN'T TOLD TO HIDE IT FROM YOU, YOUR HIGHNESS.
THAT IS TO SAY...
I HOPE YOU WILL ALSO KEEP THIS INFORMATION TO YOURSELF.
WHAT, I CAN'T TELL MITSUHIDE AND KIKI?
Long talk, huh.
YOUR HIGHNESS.
ARE YOU NOT CURIOUS TO KNOW...
...WHY HOUSE BERGAT SENT THESE YOUTHS TO SEREG, OF ALL PLACES?
...

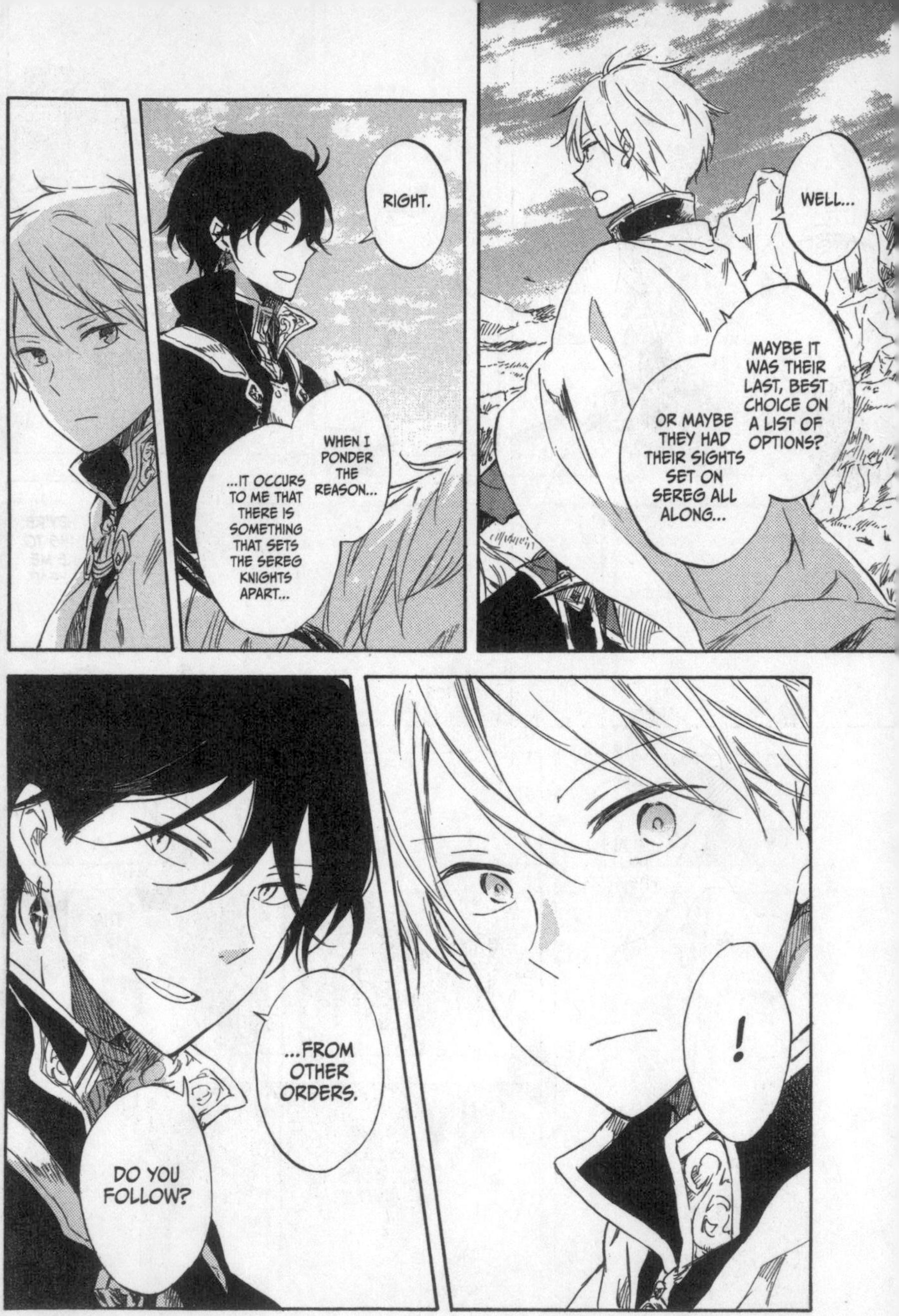

WELL...
MAYBE IT WAS THEIR LAST, BEST CHOICE ON A LIST OF OPTIONS?
OR MAYBE THEY HAD THEIR SIGHTS SET ON SEREG ALL ALONG...
RIGHT.
WHEN I PONDER THE REASON...
...IT OCCURS TO ME THAT THERE IS SOMETHING THAT SETS THE SEREG KNIGHTS APART...
!
...FROM OTHER ORDERS.
DO YOU FOLLOW?

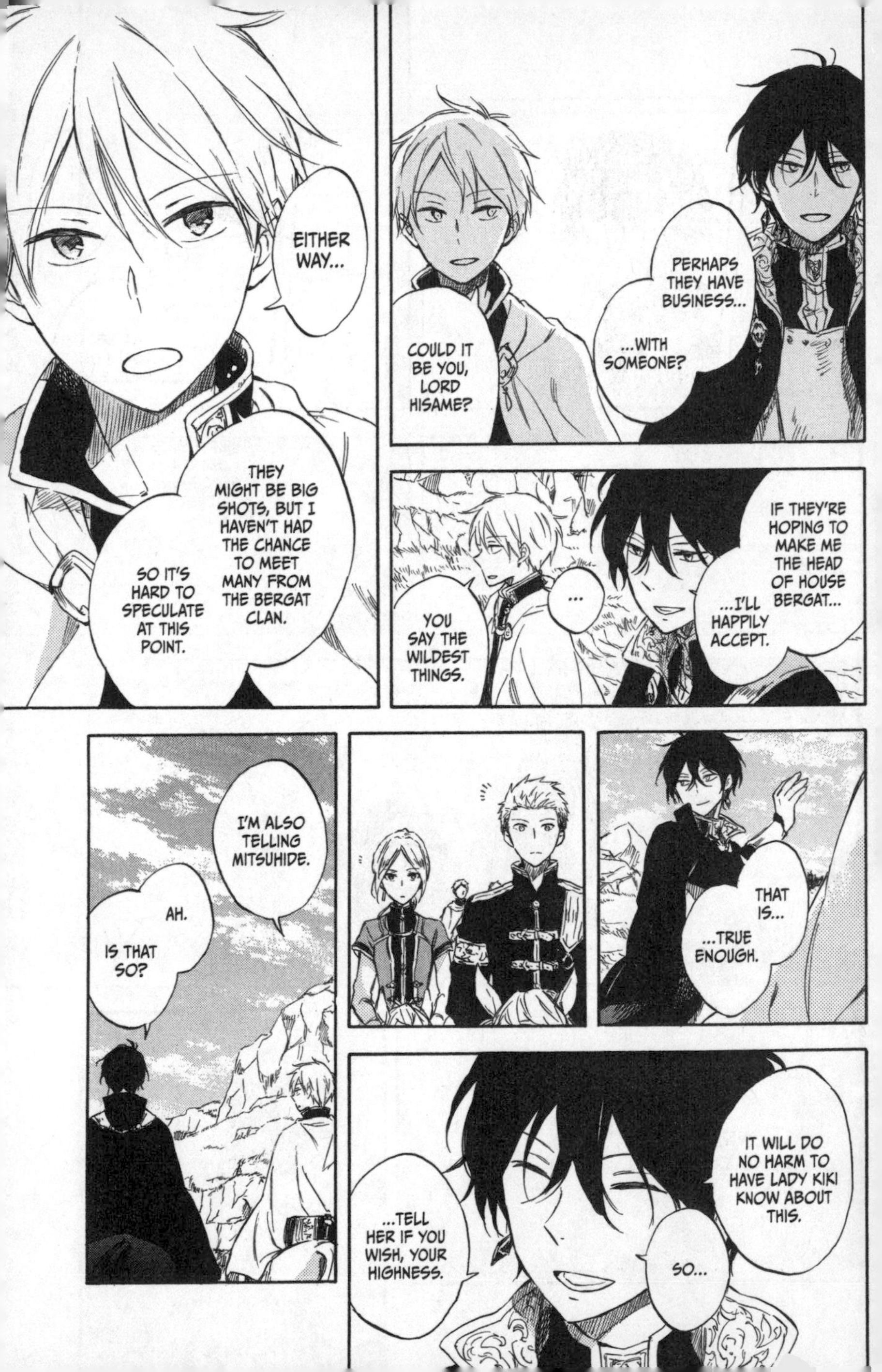
PERHAPS THEY HAVE BUSINESS...
...WITH SOMEONE?
COULD IT BE YOU, LORD HISAME?
IF THEY'RE HOPING TO MAKE ME THE HEAD OF HOUSE BERGAT...
...I'LL HAPPILY ACCEPT.
...
YOU SAY THE WILDEST THINGS.
EITHER WAY...
THEY MIGHT BE BIG SHOTS, BUT I HAVEN'T HAD THE CHANCE TO MEET MANY FROM THE BERGAT CLAN.
SO IT'S HARD TO SPECULATE AT THIS POINT.
THAT IS...
...TRUE ENOUGH.
IT WILL DO NO HARM TO HAVE LADY KIKI KNOW ABOUT THIS.
SO...
...TELL HER IF YOU WISH, YOUR HIGHNESS.
I'M ALSO TELLING MITSUHIDE.
AH.
IS THAT SO?

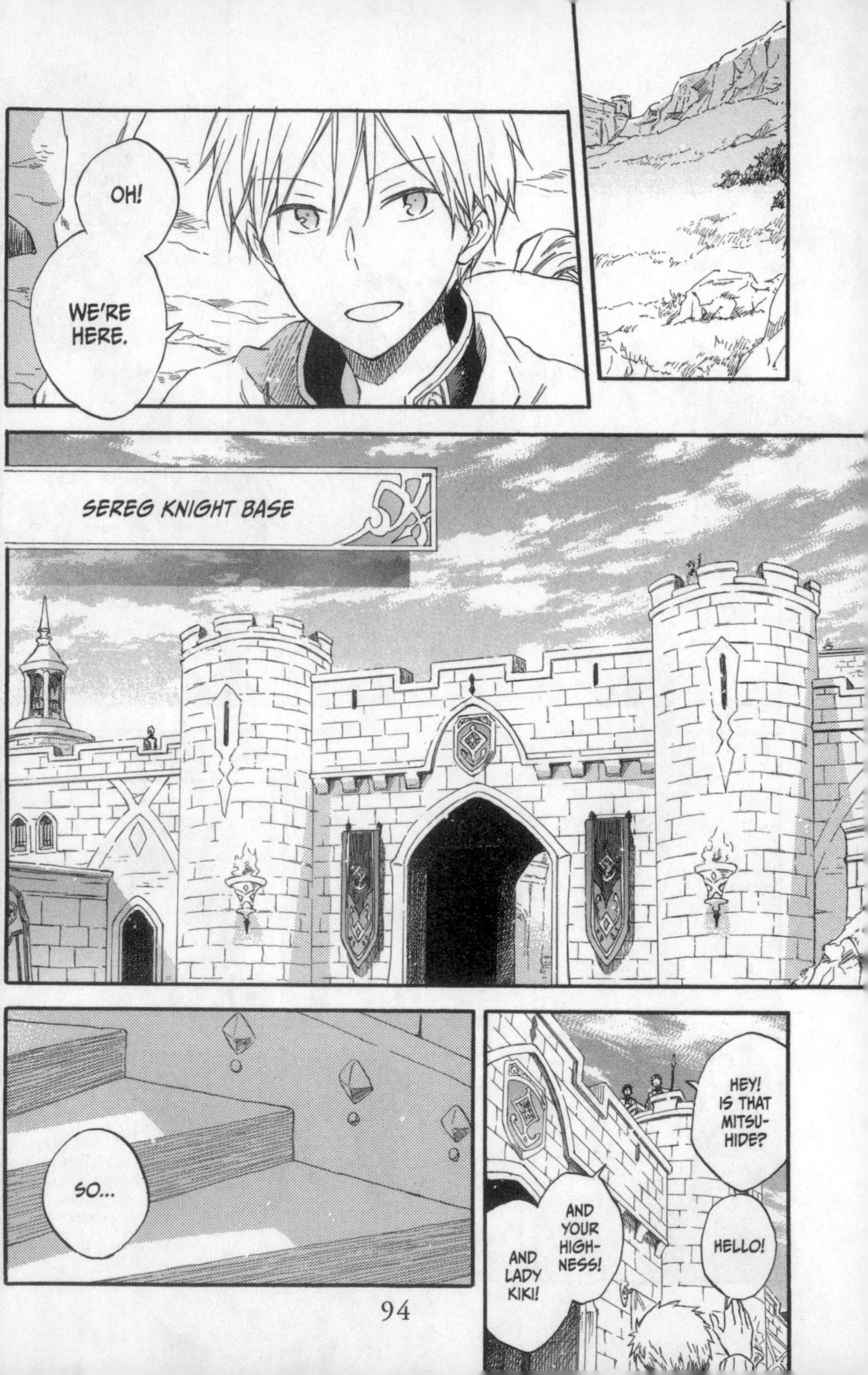
OH!
WE'RE HERE.
SEREG KNIGHT BASE
HEY! IS THAT MITSU-HIDE?
HELLO!
AND YOUR HIGH-NESS!
AND LADY KIKI!
SO...

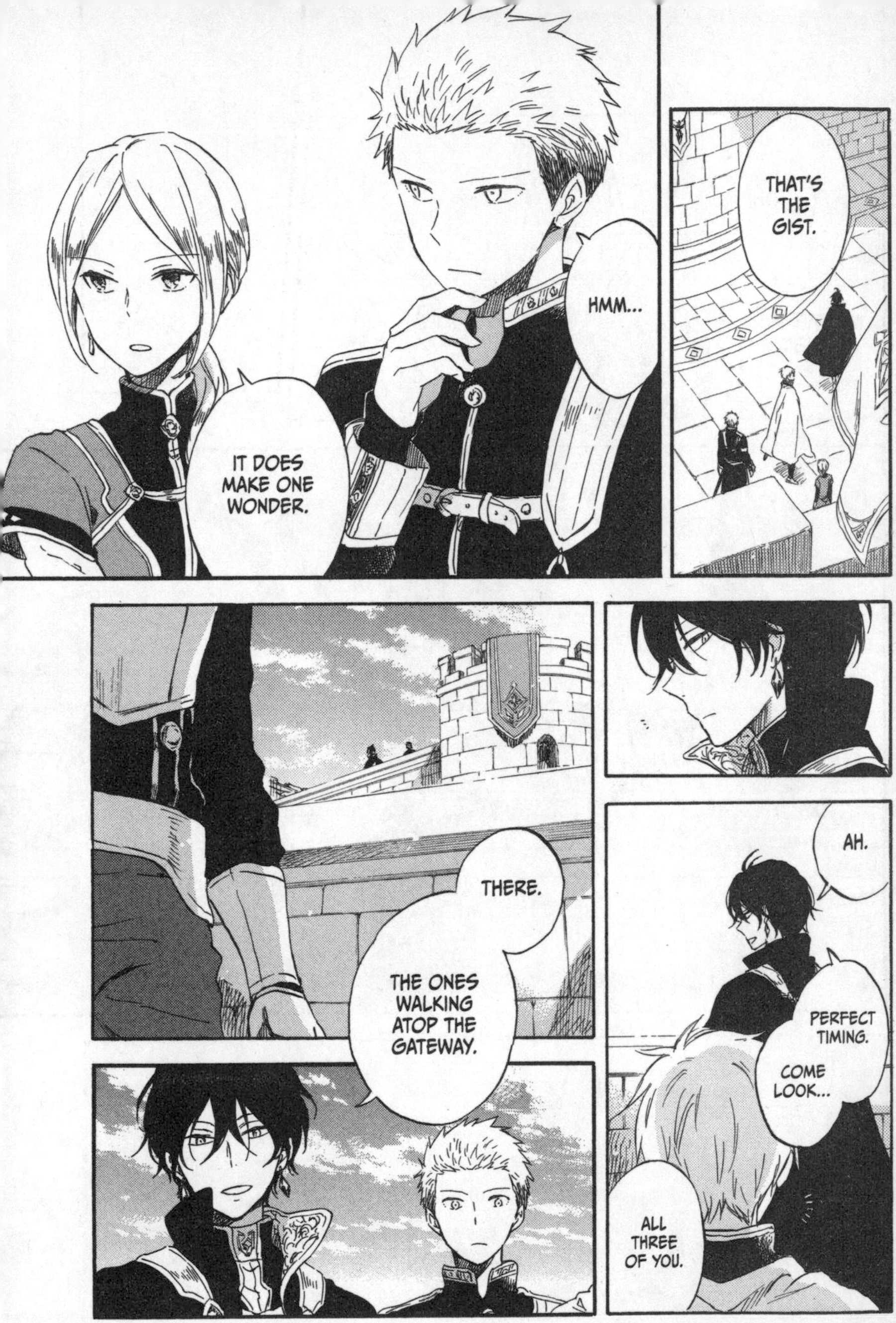
THAT'S THE GIST.
HMM...
IT DOES MAKE ONE WONDER.
...
AH.
PERFECT TIMING.
COME LOOK...
ALL THREE OF YOU.
THERE.
THE ONES WALKING ATOP THE GATEWAY.

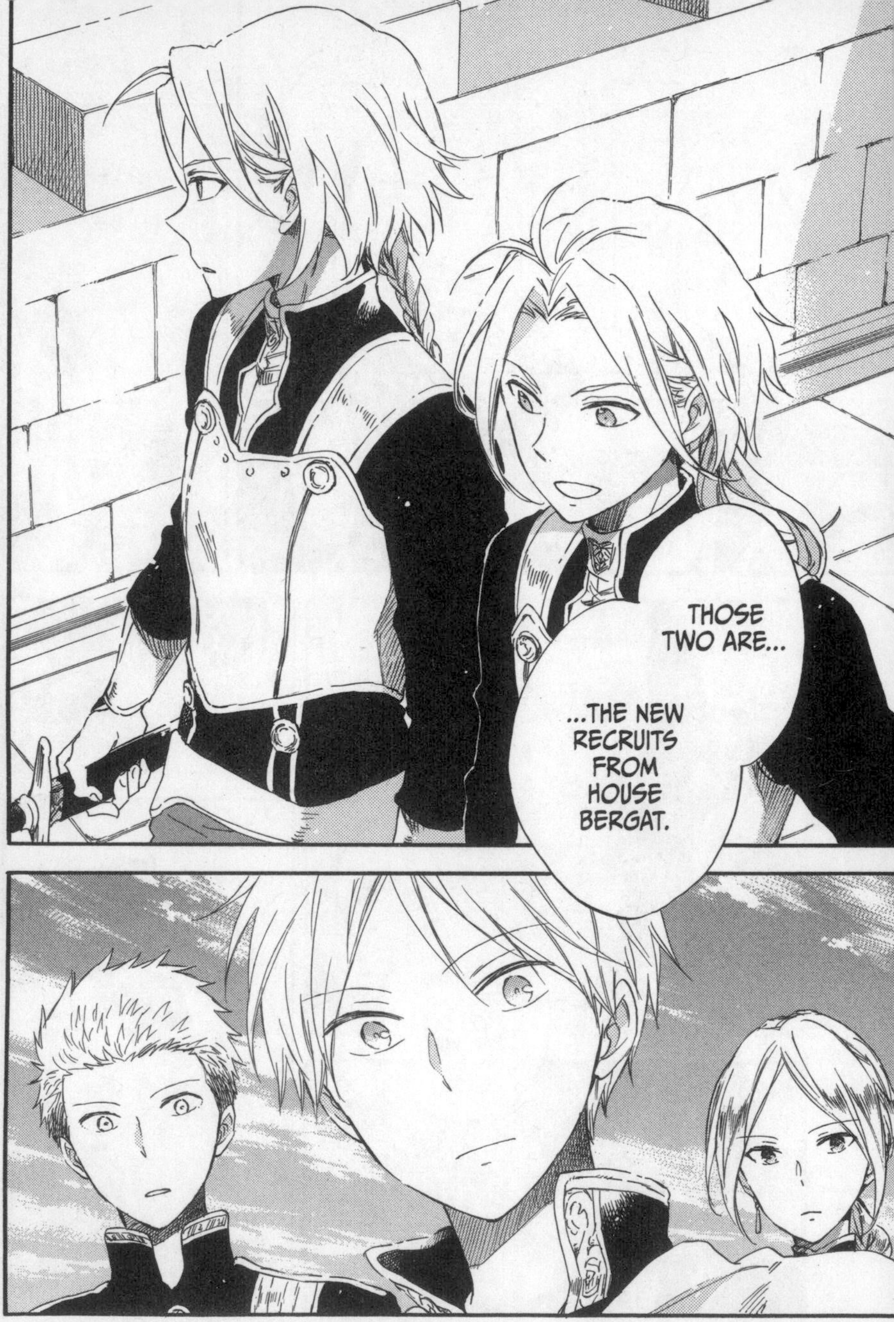
THOSE TWO ARE...
...THE NEW RECRUITS FROM HOUSE BERGAT.

Chapter 75

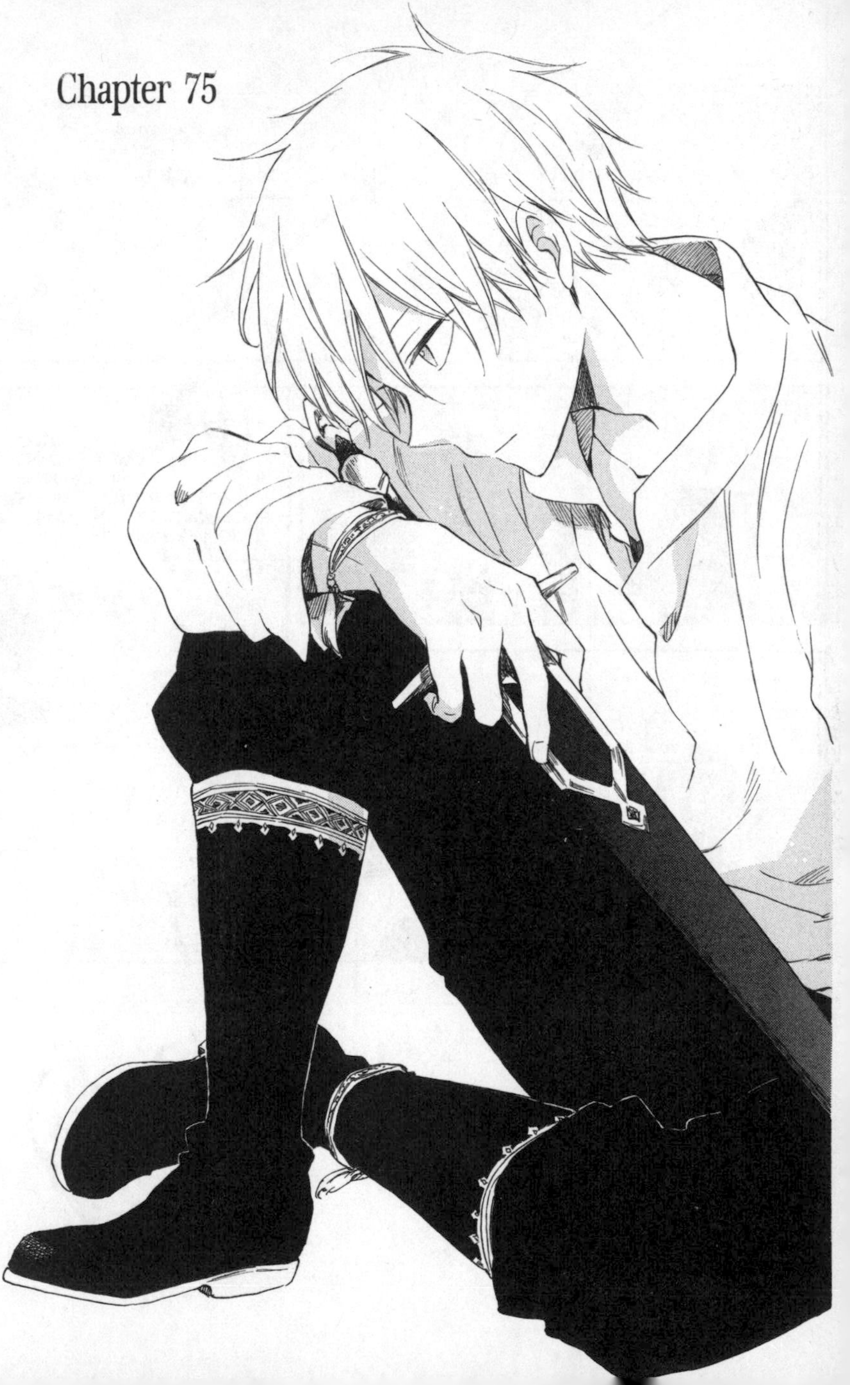

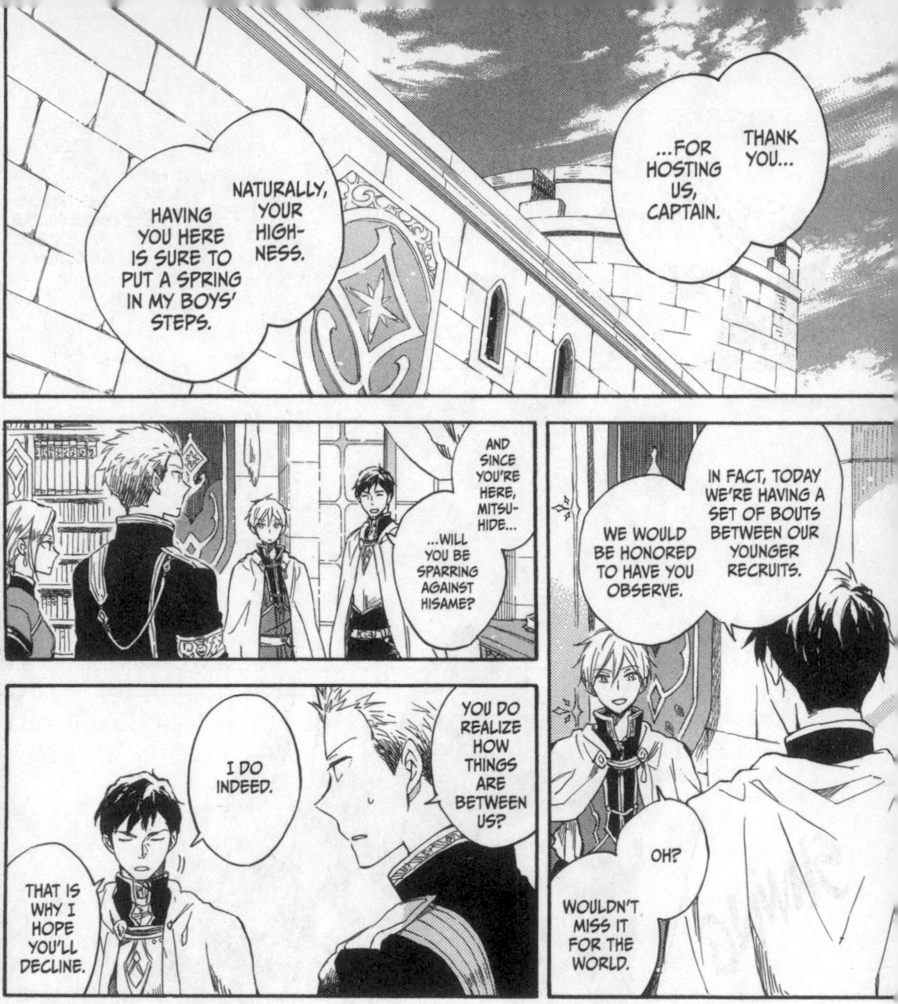
THANK YOU...
...FOR HOSTING US, CAPTAIN.
NATURALLY, YOUR HIGHNESS.
HAVING YOU HERE IS SURE TO PUT A SPRING IN MY BOYS' STEPS.
IN FACT, TODAY WE'RE HAVING A SET OF BOUTS BETWEEN OUR YOUNGER RECRUITS.
WE WOULD BE HONORED TO HAVE YOU OBSERVE.
OH?
WOULDN'T MISS IT FOR THE WORLD.
AND SINCE YOU'RE HERE, MITSU-HIDE...
...WILL YOU BE SPARRING AGAINST HISAME?
YOU DO REALIZE HOW THINGS ARE BETWEEN US?
I DO INDEED.
THAT IS WHY I HOPE YOU'LL DECLINE.

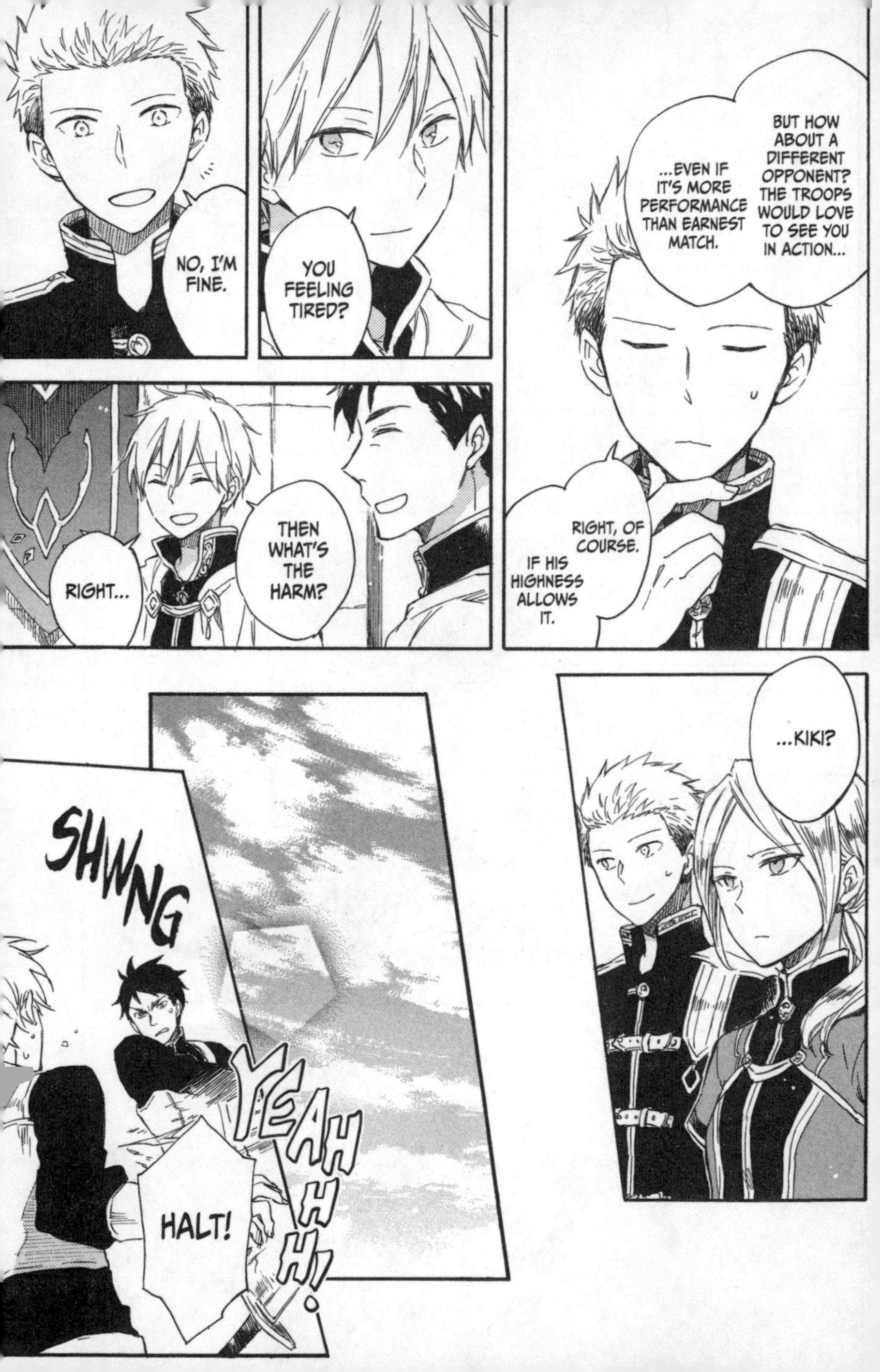
BUT HOW ABOUT A DIFFERENT OPPONENT? THE TROOPS WOULD LOVE TO SEE YOU IN ACTION...
...EVEN IF IT'S MORE PERFORMANCE THAN EARNEST MATCH.
RIGHT, OF COURSE.
IF HIS HIGHNESS ALLOWS IT.
YOU FEELING TIRED?
NO, I'M FINE.
THEN WHAT'S THE HARM?
RIGHT...
...KIKI?
SHWNG
YEAHHHH!
HALT!

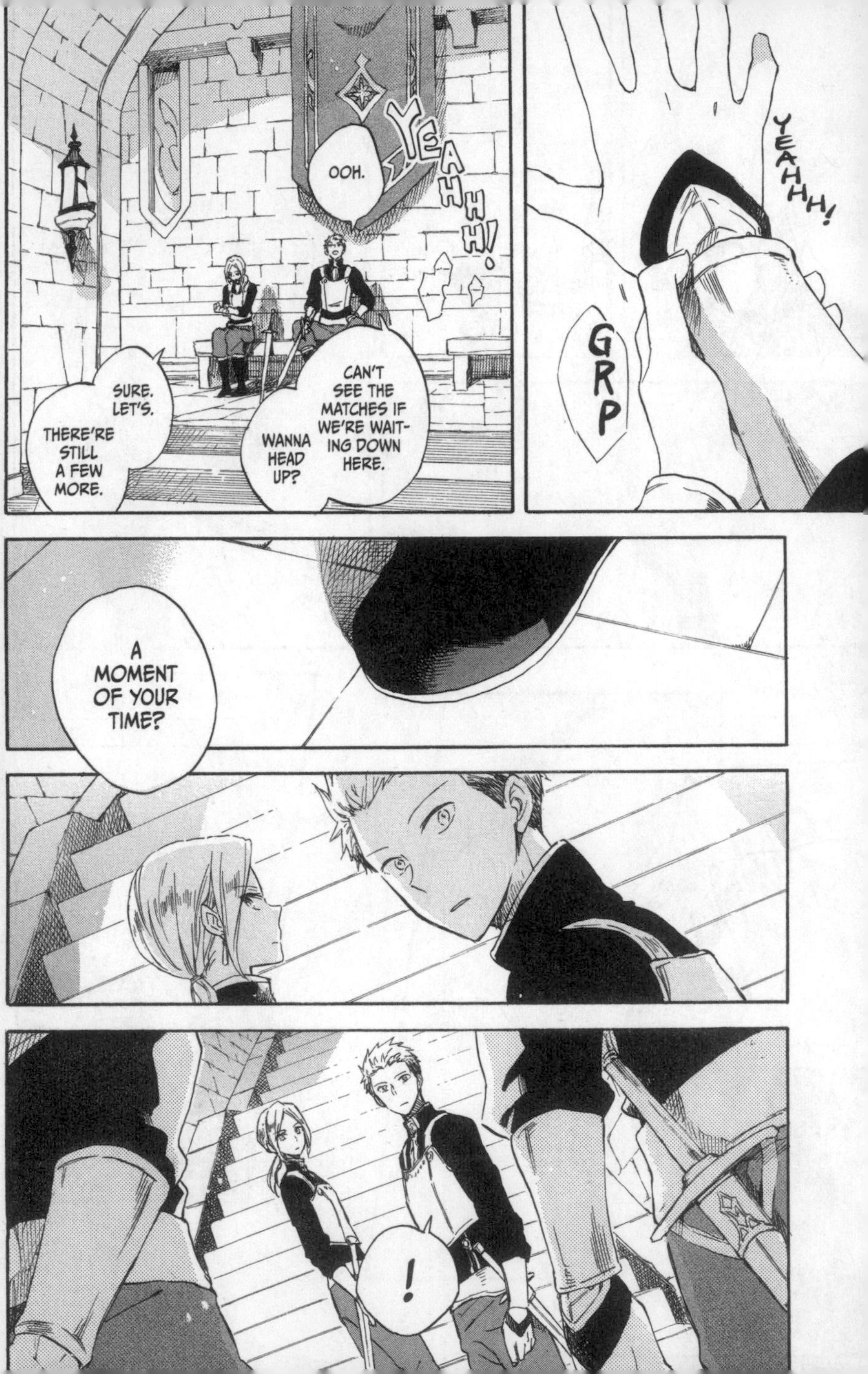
YEAHHH!
GRP
OOH.
YEAHHH!
CAN'T SEE THE MATCHES IF WE'RE WAITING DOWN HERE.
WANNA HEAD UP?
SURE. LET'S.
THERE'RE STILL A FEW MORE.
A MOMENT OF YOUR TIME?
!

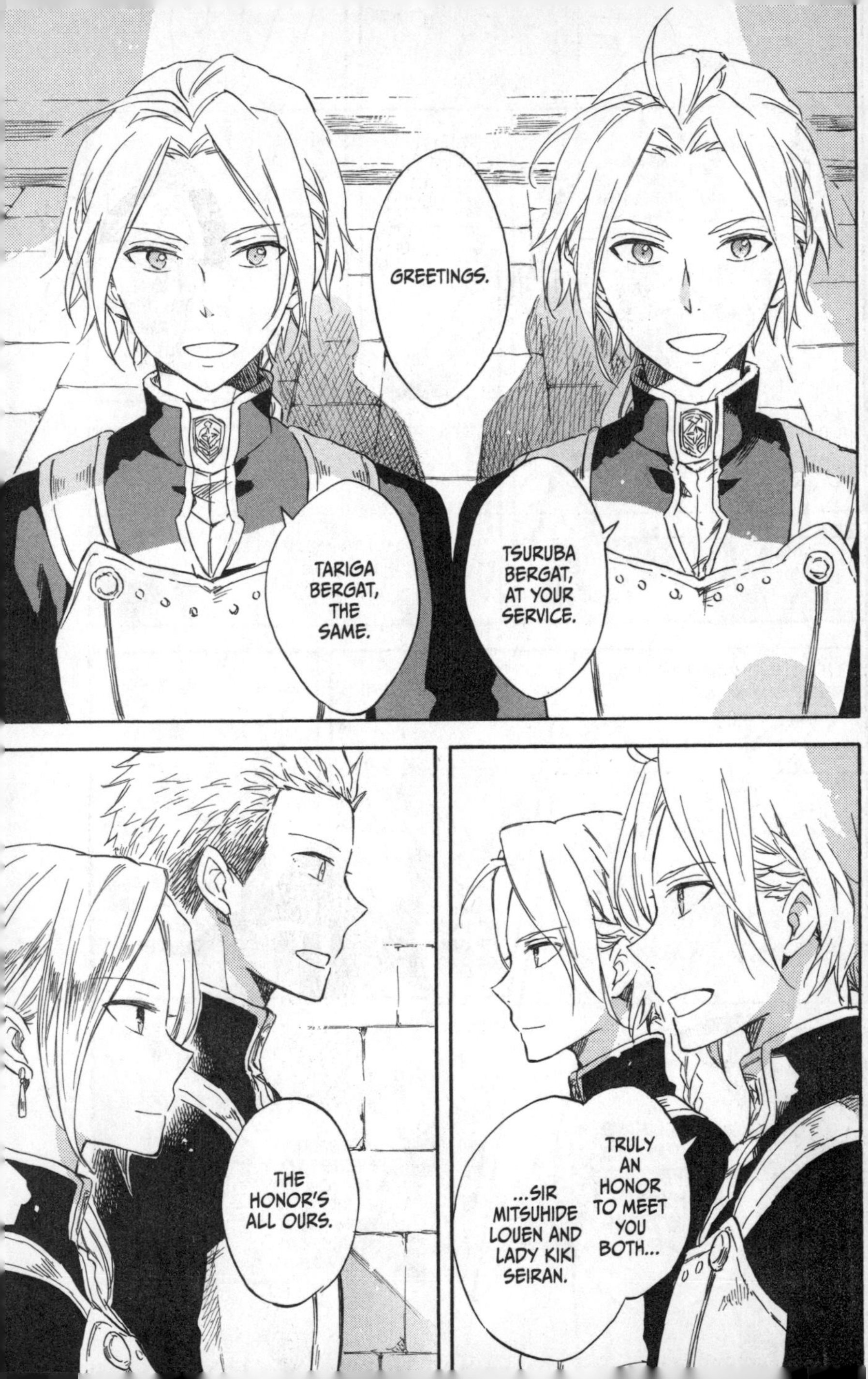
GREETINGS.
TSURUBA BERGAT, AT YOUR SERVICE.
TARIGA BERGAT, THE SAME.
TRULY AN HONOR TO MEET YOU BOTH...
...SIR MITSUHIDE LOUEN AND LADY KIKI SEIRAN.
THE HONOR'S ALL OURS.

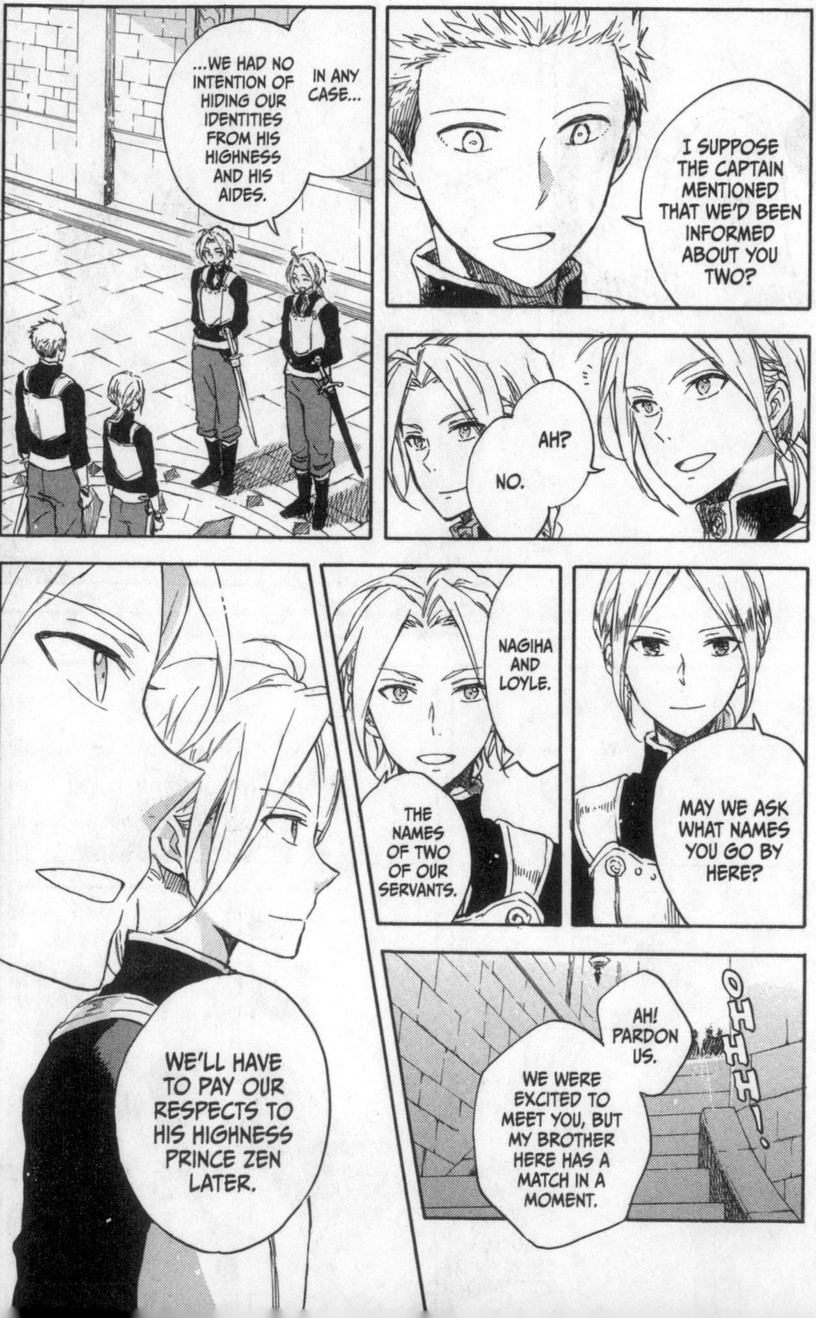

I SUPPOSE THE CAPTAIN MENTIONED THAT WE'D BEEN INFORMED ABOUT YOU TWO?
AH?
NO.
IN ANY CASE...
...WE HAD NO INTENTION OF HIDING OUR IDENTITIES FROM HIS HIGHNESS AND HIS AIDES.
MAY WE ASK WHAT NAMES YOU GO BY HERE?
NAGIHA AND LOYLE.
THE NAMES OF TWO OF OUR SERVANTS.
OHHH!
AH! PARDON US.
WE WERE EXCITED TO MEET YOU, BUT MY BROTHER HERE HAS A MATCH IN A MOMENT.
WE'LL HAVE TO PAY OUR RESPECTS TO HIS HIGHNESS PRINCE ZEN LATER.

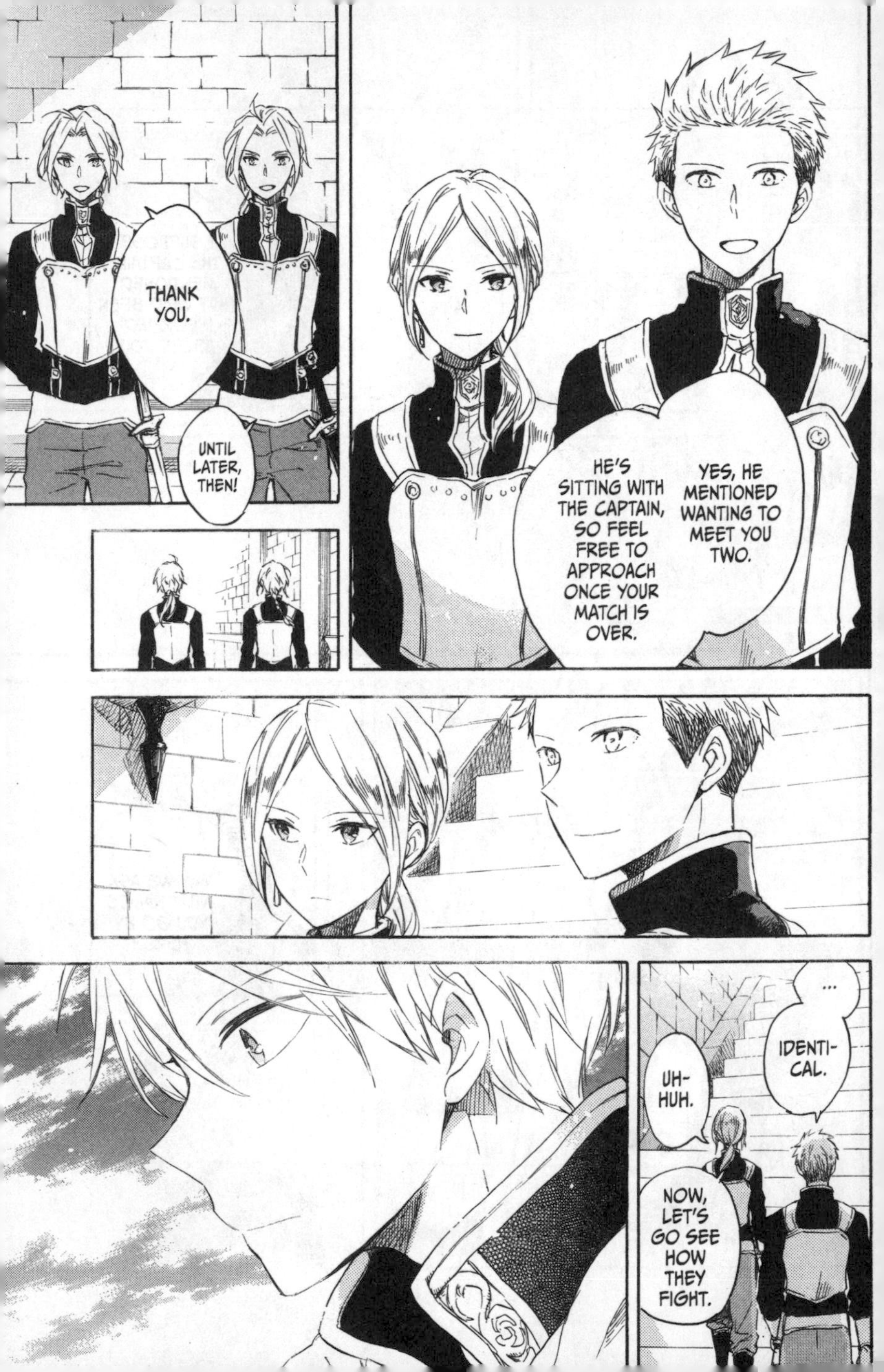
YES, HE MENTIONED WANTING TO MEET YOU TWO.
HE'S SITTING WITH THE CAPTAIN, SO FEEL FREE TO APPROACH ONCE YOUR MATCH IS OVER.
THANK YOU.
UNTIL LATER, THEN!
...
IDENTICAL.
UH-HUH.
NOW, LET'S GO SEE HOW THEY FIGHT.

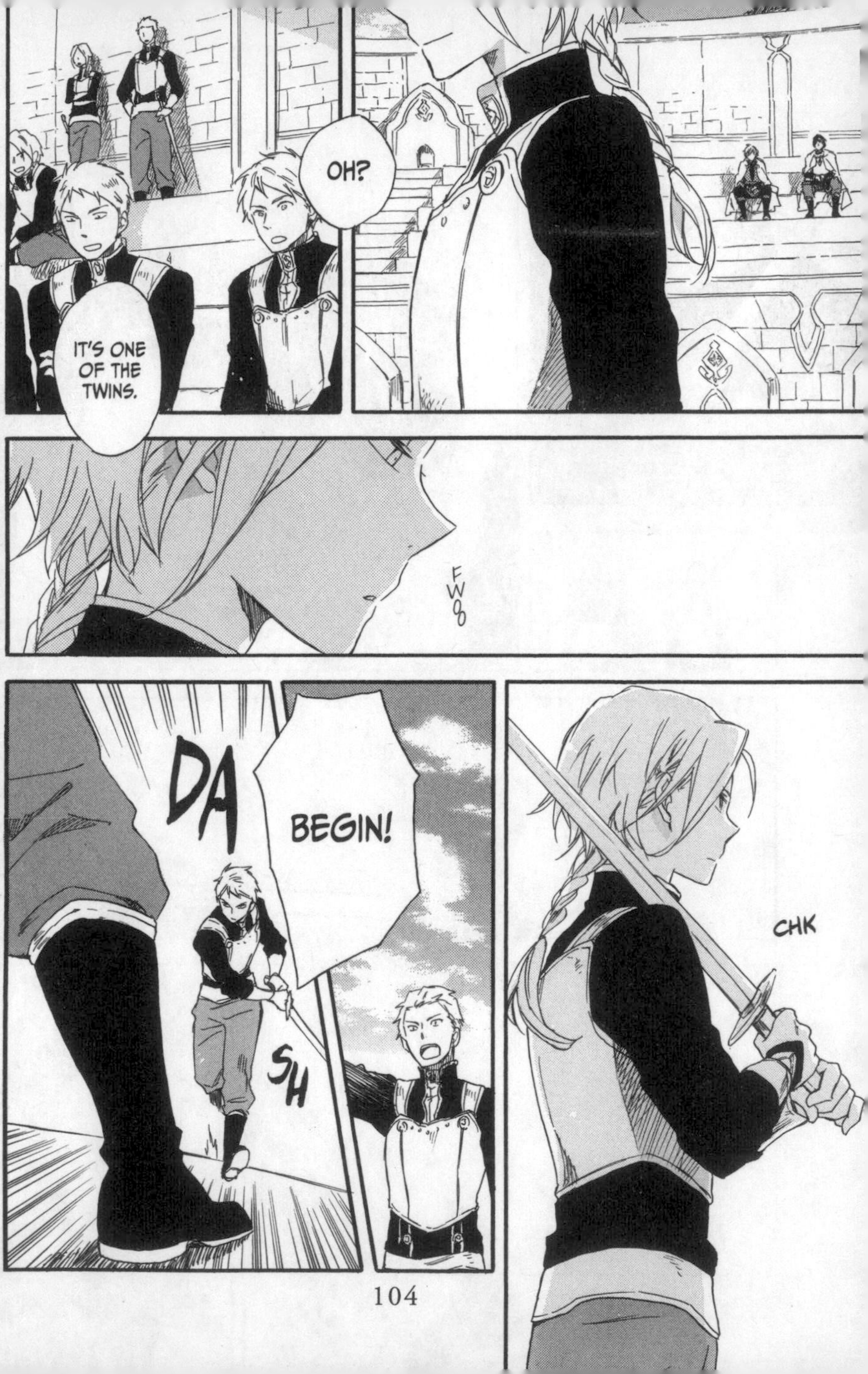
OH?
IT'S ONE OF THE TWINS.
FWOO
CHK
BEGIN!
SH
DA

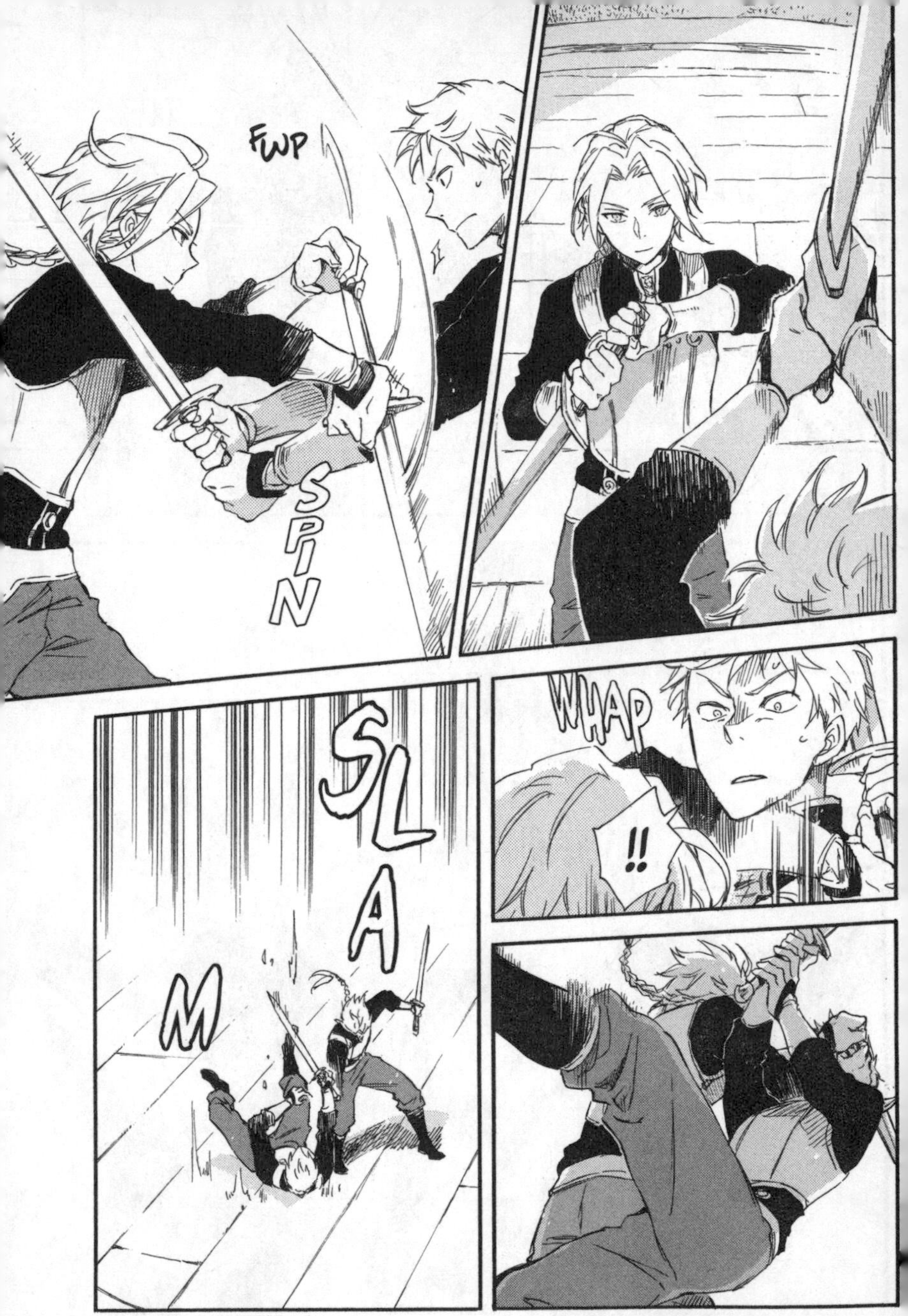
FWP
SPIN
WHAP
!!
SLAM

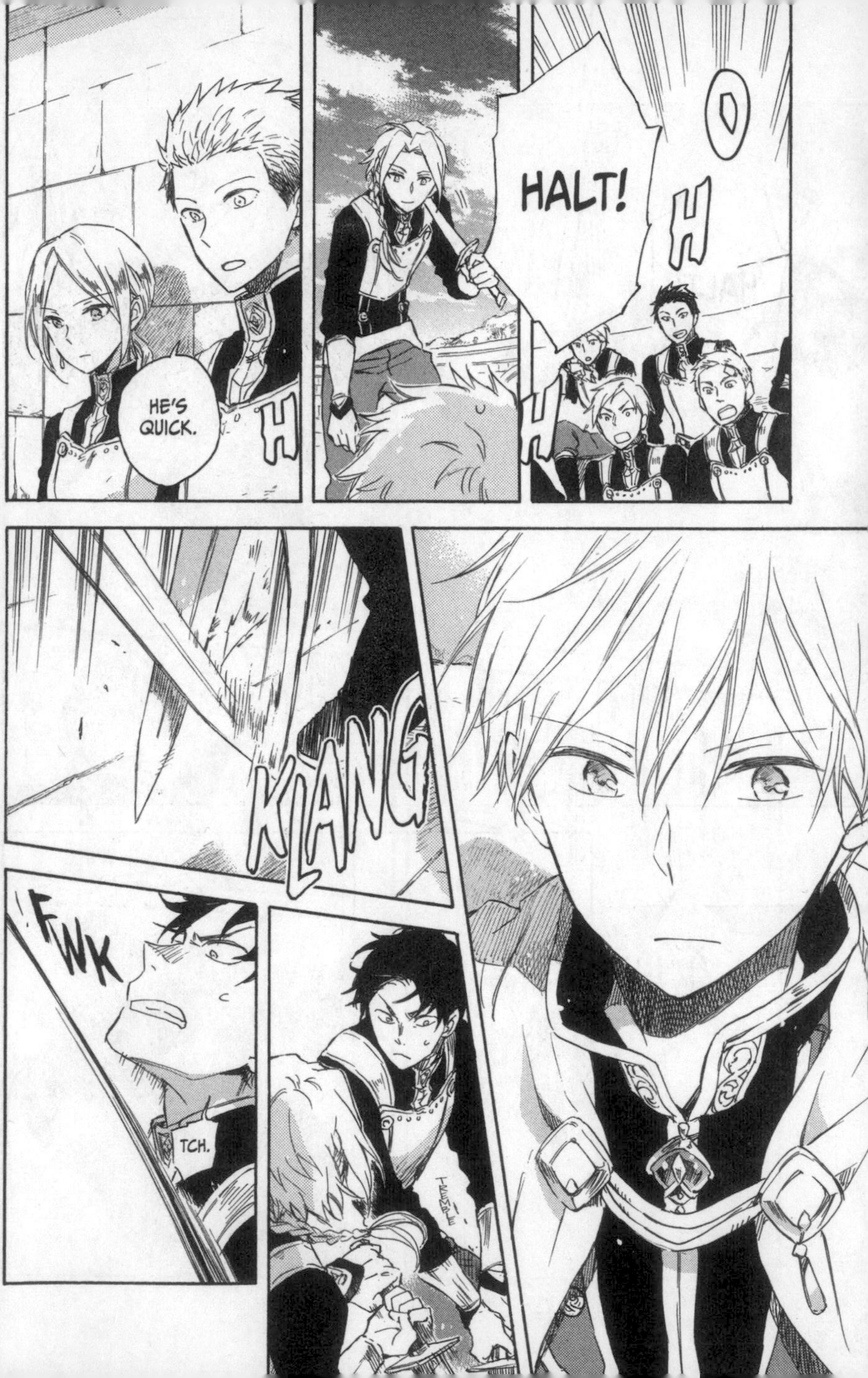

HALT!
HE'S QUICK.
KLANG
TREMBLE
FWK
TCH.

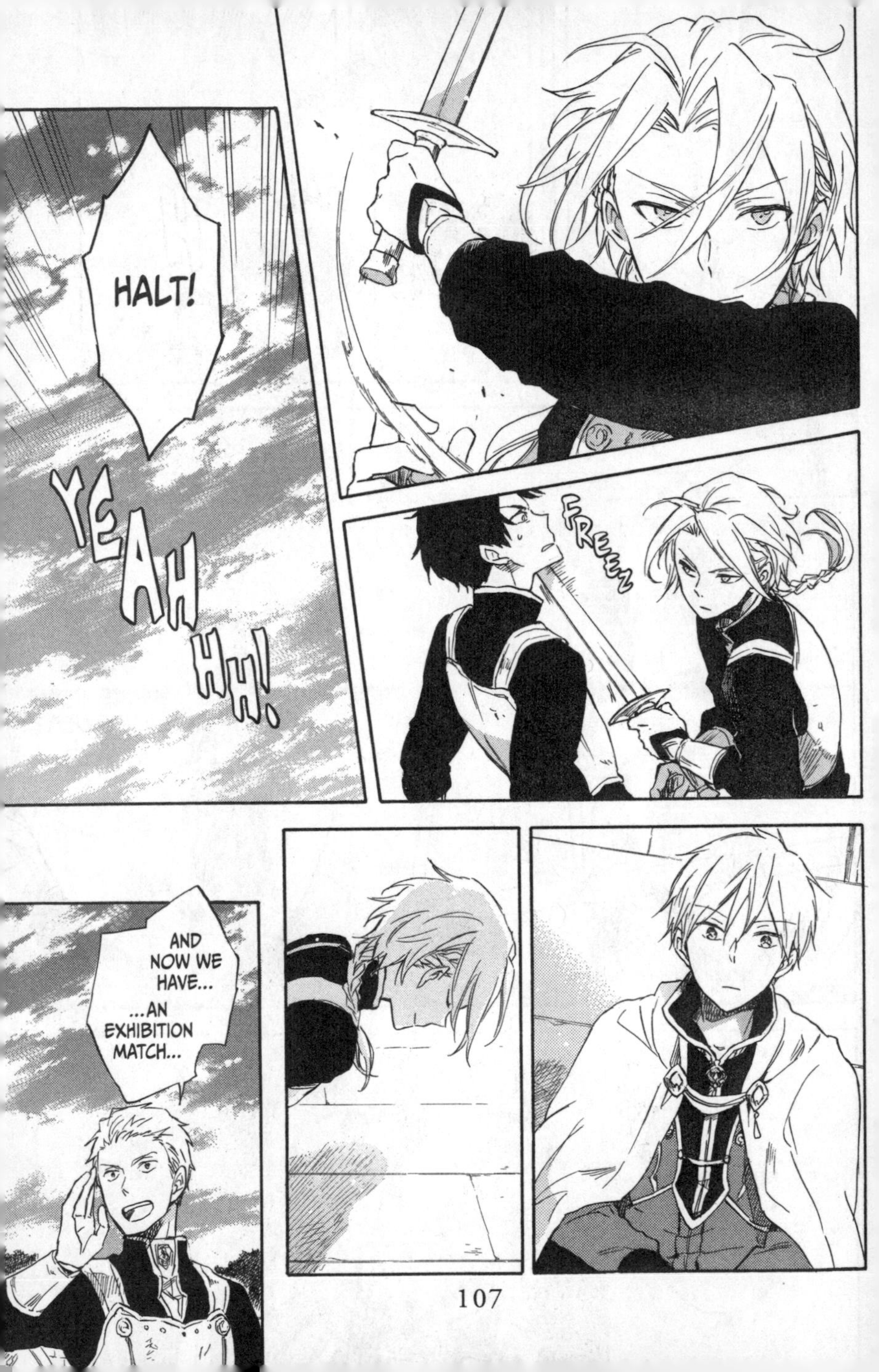
FREEZ
HALT!
YEAHHH!
AND NOW WE HAVE...
...AN EXHIBITION MATCH...

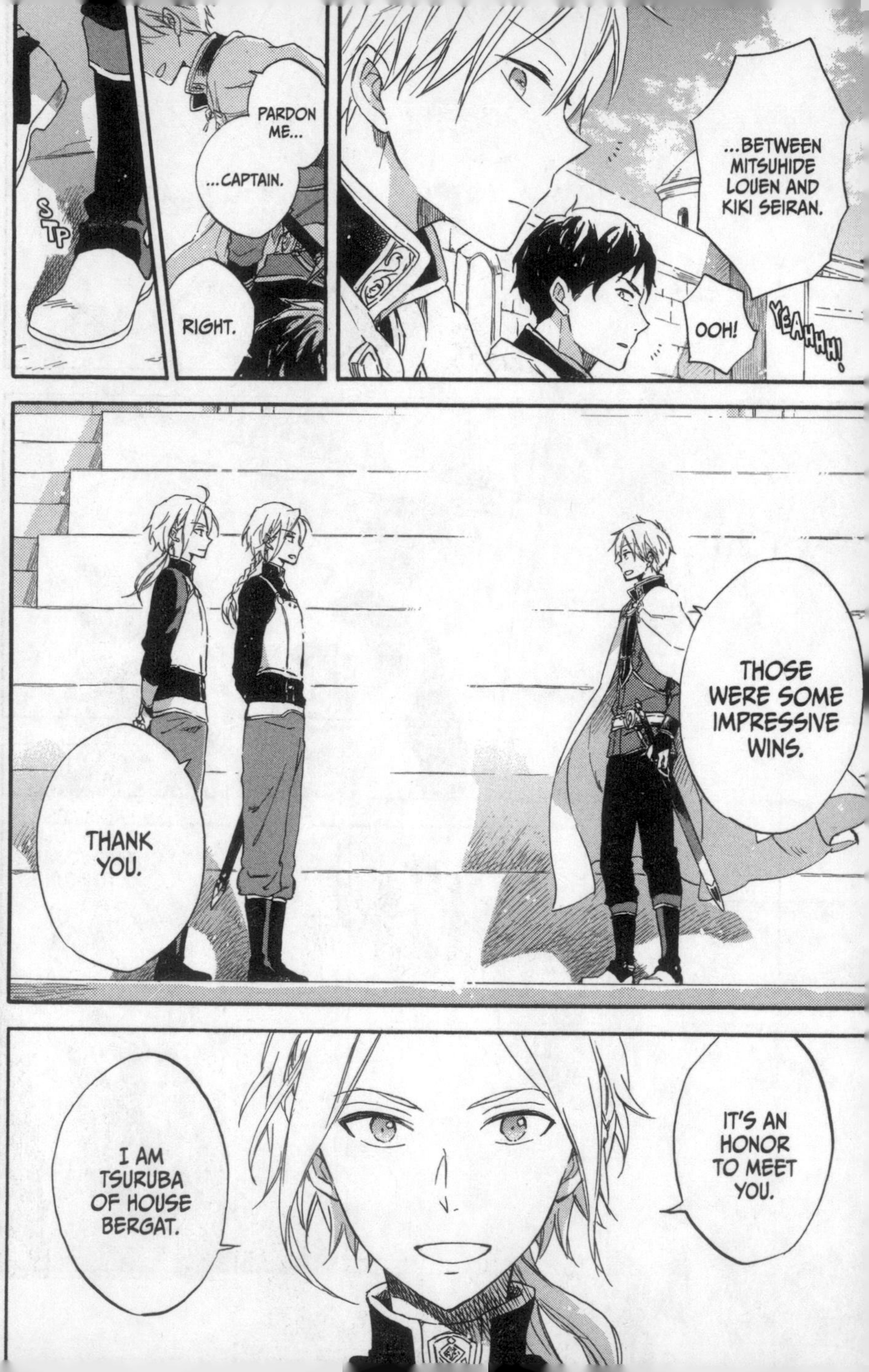
...BETWEEN MITSUHIDE LOUEN AND KIKI SEIRAN.
OOH!
YEAHHH!
PARDON ME...
...CAPTAIN.
RIGHT.
STP
THOSE WERE SOME IMPRESSIVE WINS.
THANK YOU.
IT'S AN HONOR TO MEET YOU.
I AM TSURUBA OF HOUSE BERGAT.

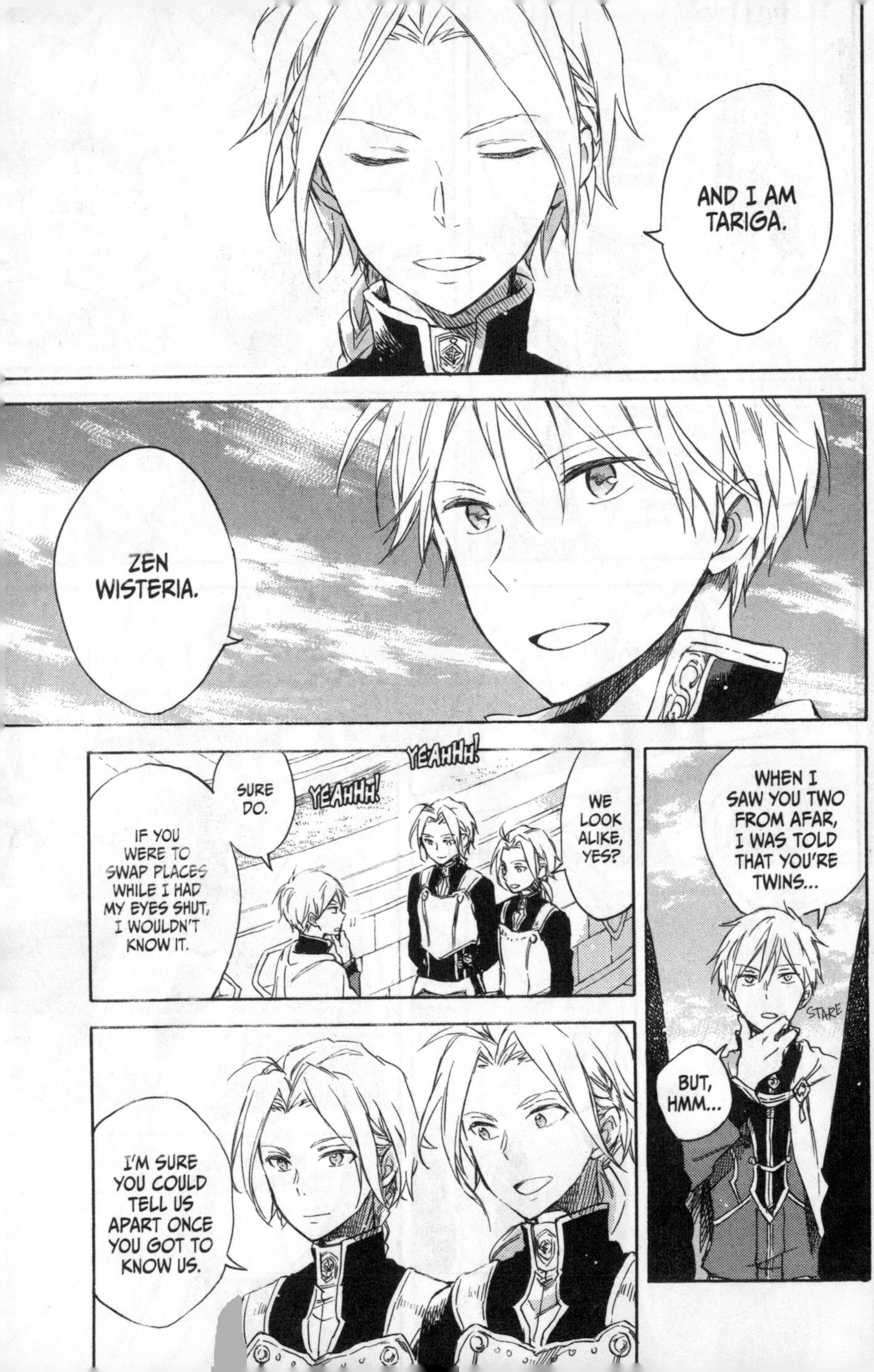
AND I AM TARIGA.
ZEN WISTERIA.
WHEN I SAW YOU TWO FROM AFAR, I WAS TOLD THAT YOU'RE TWINS...
STARE
BUT, HMM...
YEAHHH!
WE LOOK ALIKE, YES?
YEAHHH!
SURE DO.
IF YOU WERE TO SWAP PLACES WHILE I HAD MY EYES SHUT, I WOULDN'T KNOW IT.
I'M SURE YOU COULD TELL US APART ONCE YOU GOT TO KNOW US.

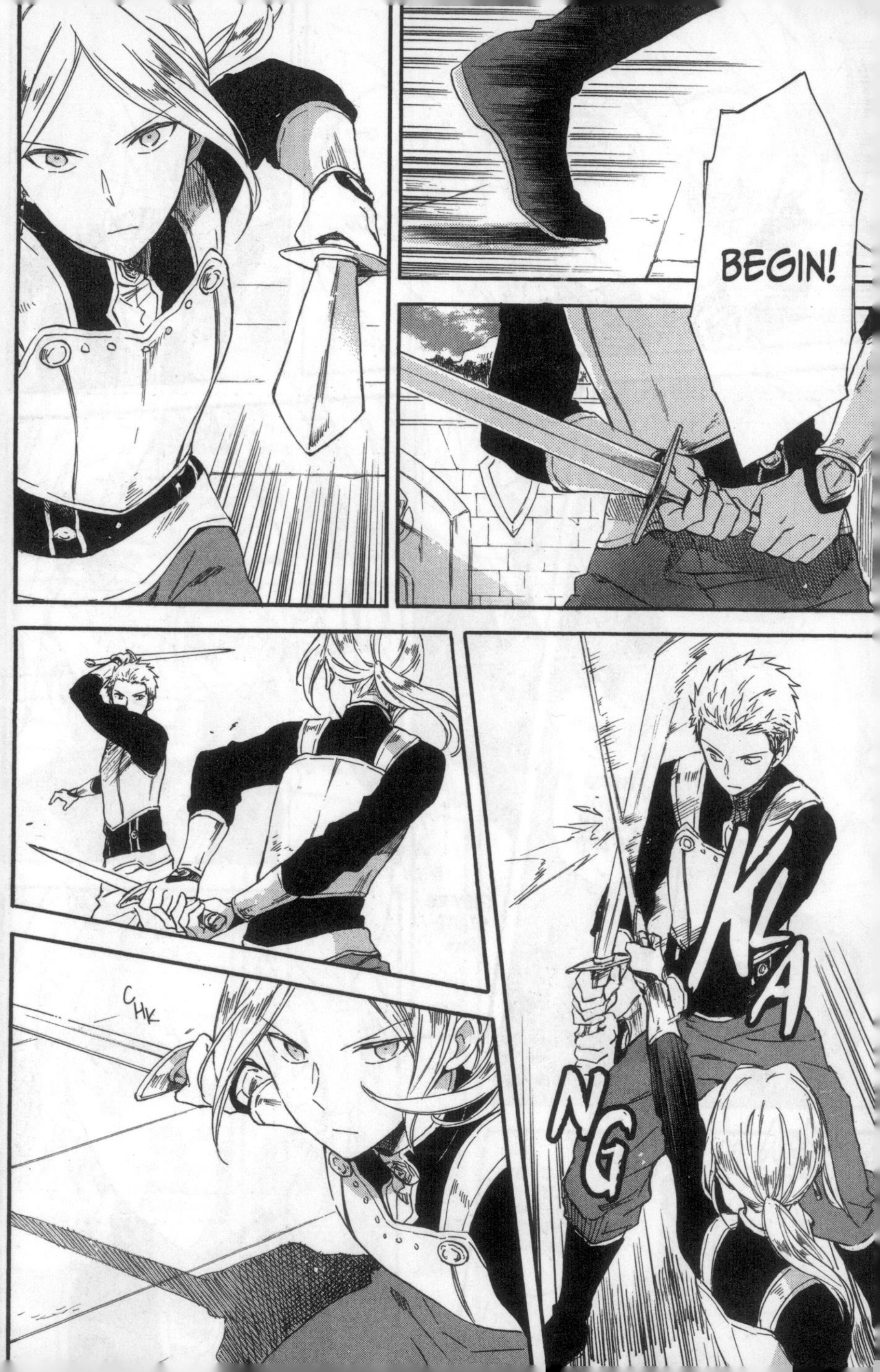
BEGIN!
KLANG
CHK

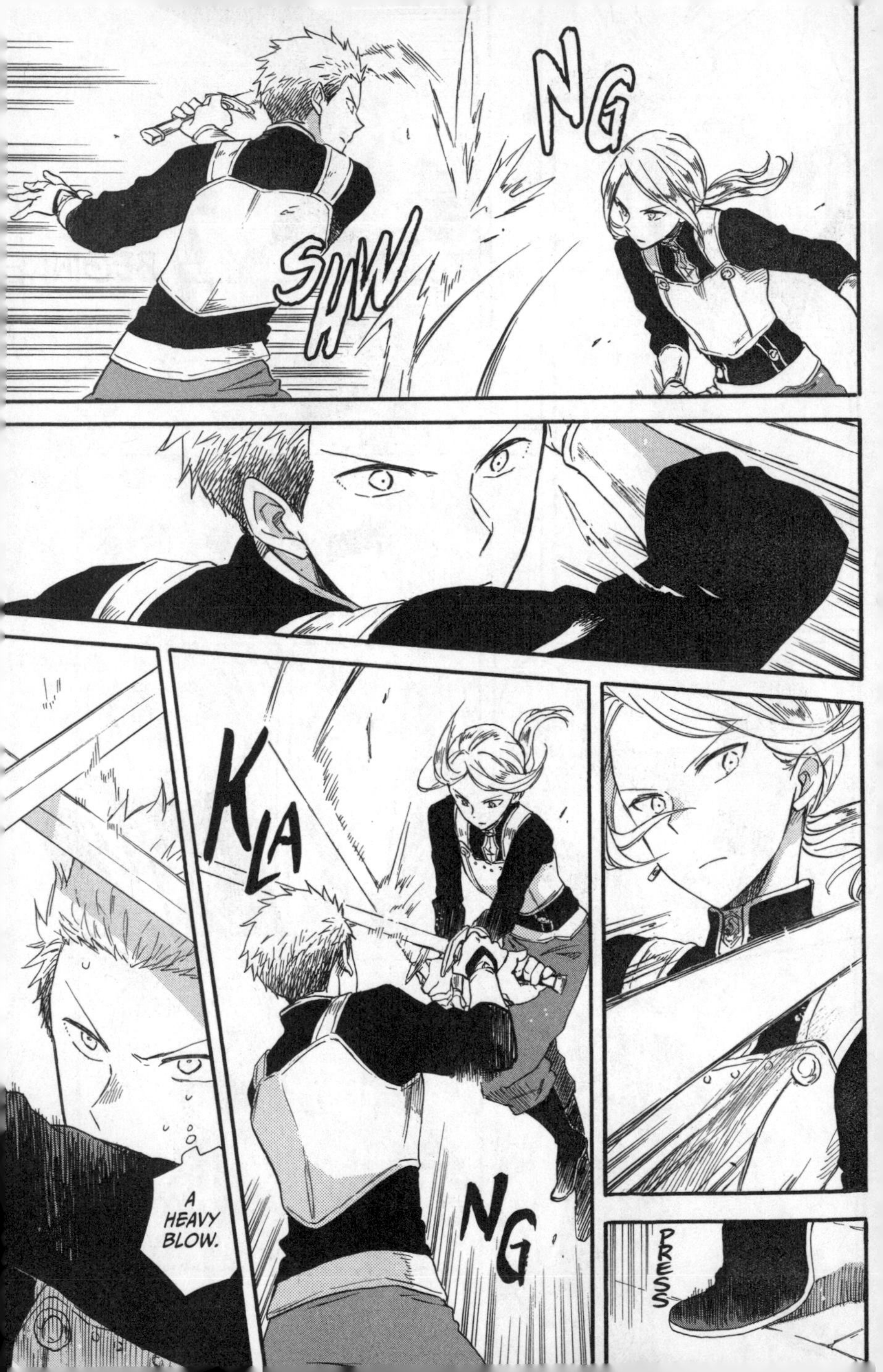
SHW
NG
PRESS
KLA
NG
A HEAVY BLOW.

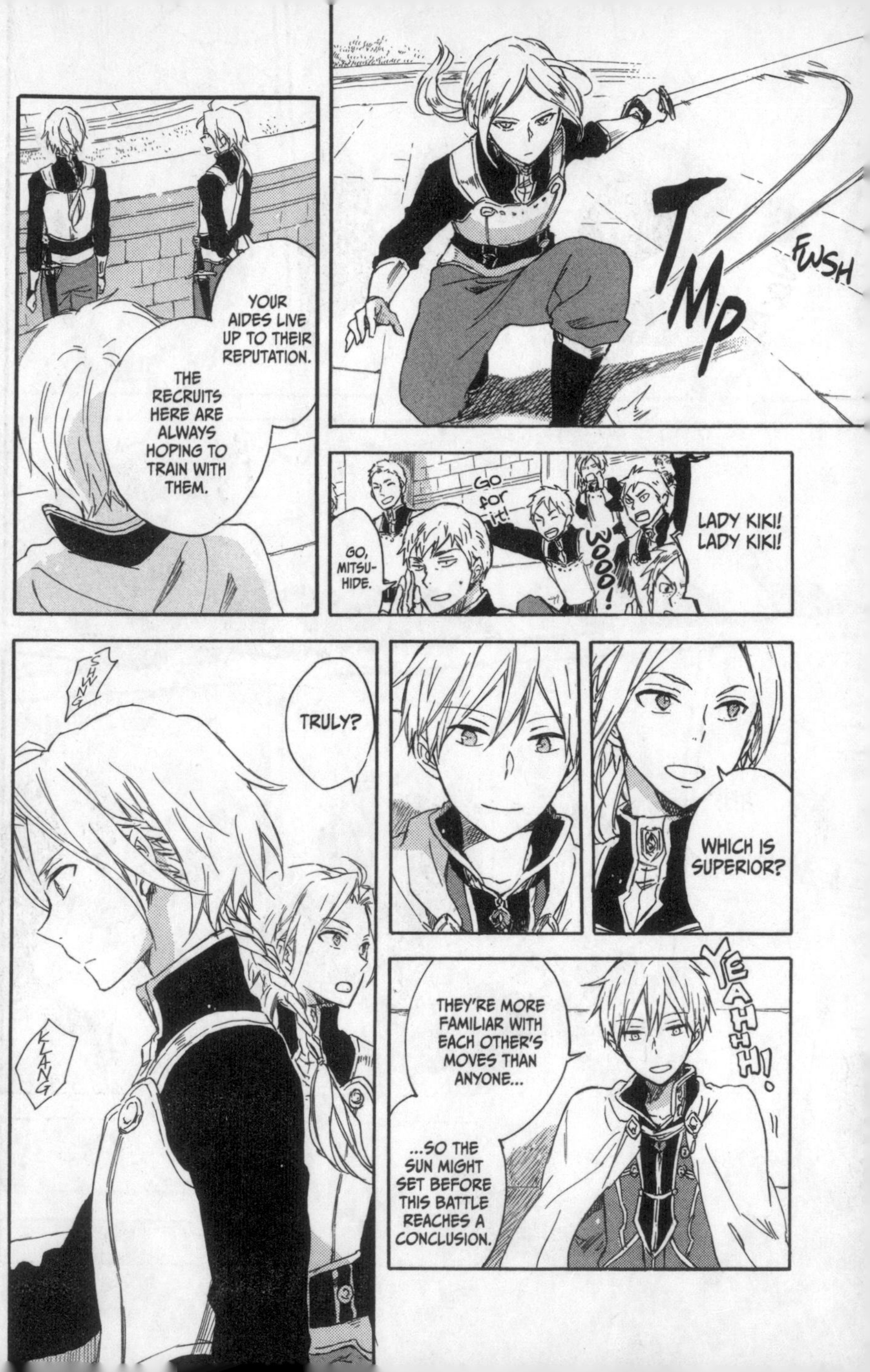
FWSH
TMP
LADY KIKI! LADY KIKI!
WOOO!
Go for it!
GO, MITSU-HIDE.
YOUR AIDES LIVE UP TO THEIR REPUTATION.
THE RECRUITS HERE ARE ALWAYS HOPING TO TRAIN WITH THEM.
WHICH IS SUPERIOR?
YEAHHH!
THEY'RE MORE FAMILIAR WITH EACH OTHER'S MOVES THAN ANYONE...
...SO THE SUN MIGHT SET BEFORE THIS BATTLE REACHES A CONCLUSION.
TRULY?
SHNG
KLANG

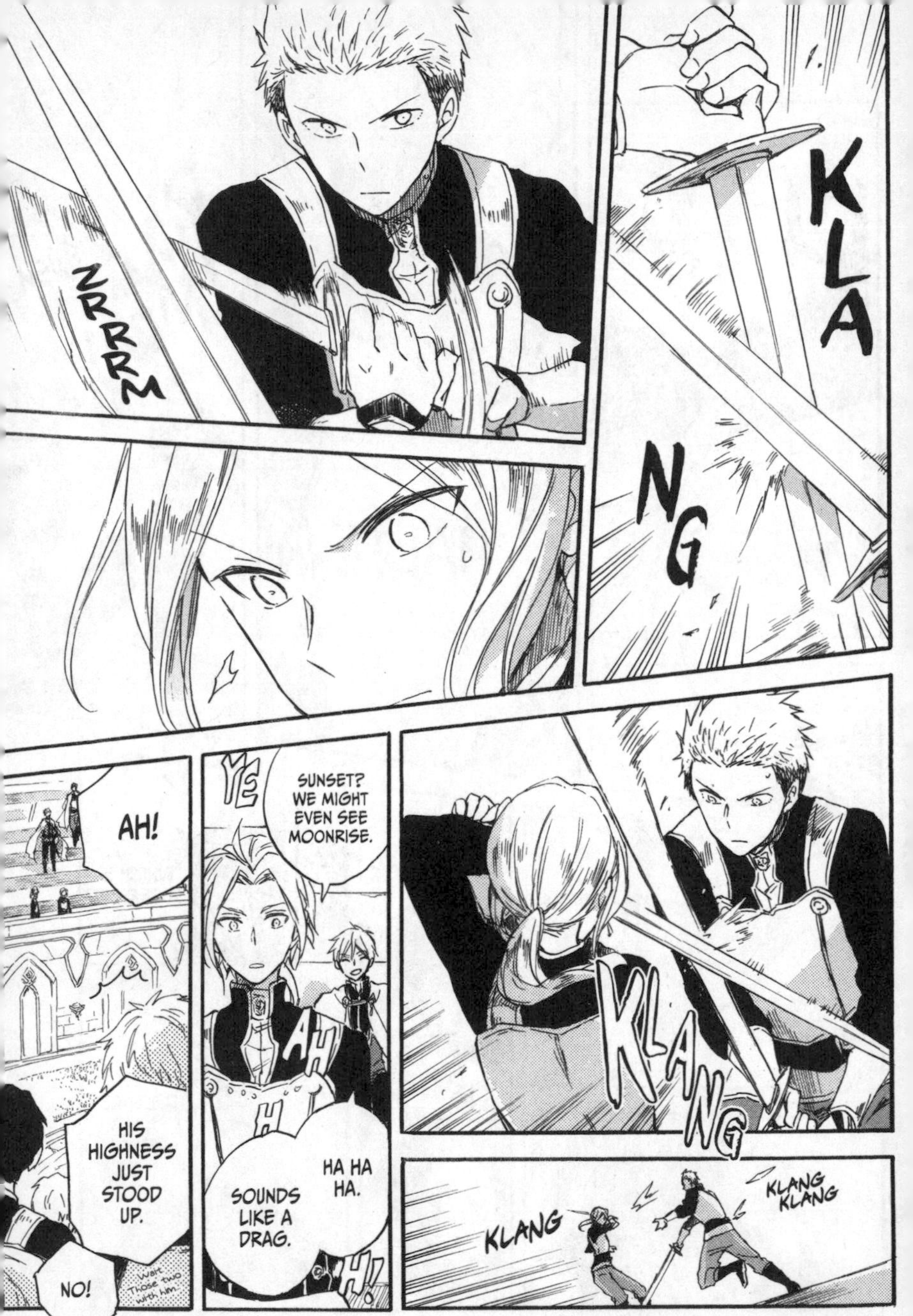
KLANG
ZRRRM
KLANG
KLANG
KLANG KLANG
YE
SUNSET? WE MIGHT EVEN SEE MOONRISE.
AHHH!
HA HA HA.
SOUNDS LIKE A DRAG.
AH!
HIS HIGHNESS JUST STOOD UP.
Wait. Those two with him...
NO!

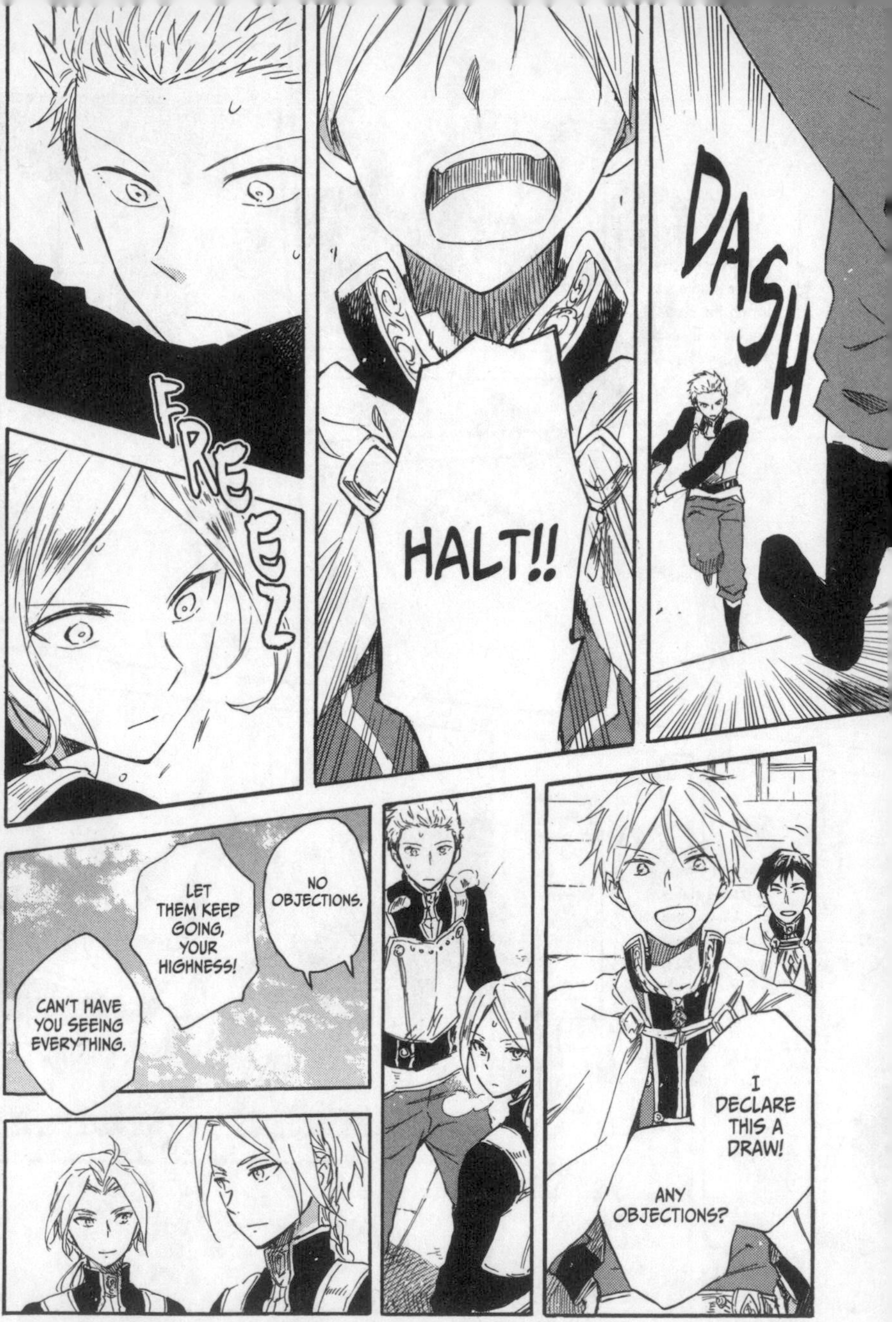
DASH
HALT!!
FREEZ
I DECLARE THIS A DRAW!
ANY OBJECTIONS?
NO OBJECTIONS.
LET THEM KEEP GOING, YOUR HIGHNESS!
CAN'T HAVE YOU SEEING EVERYTHING.

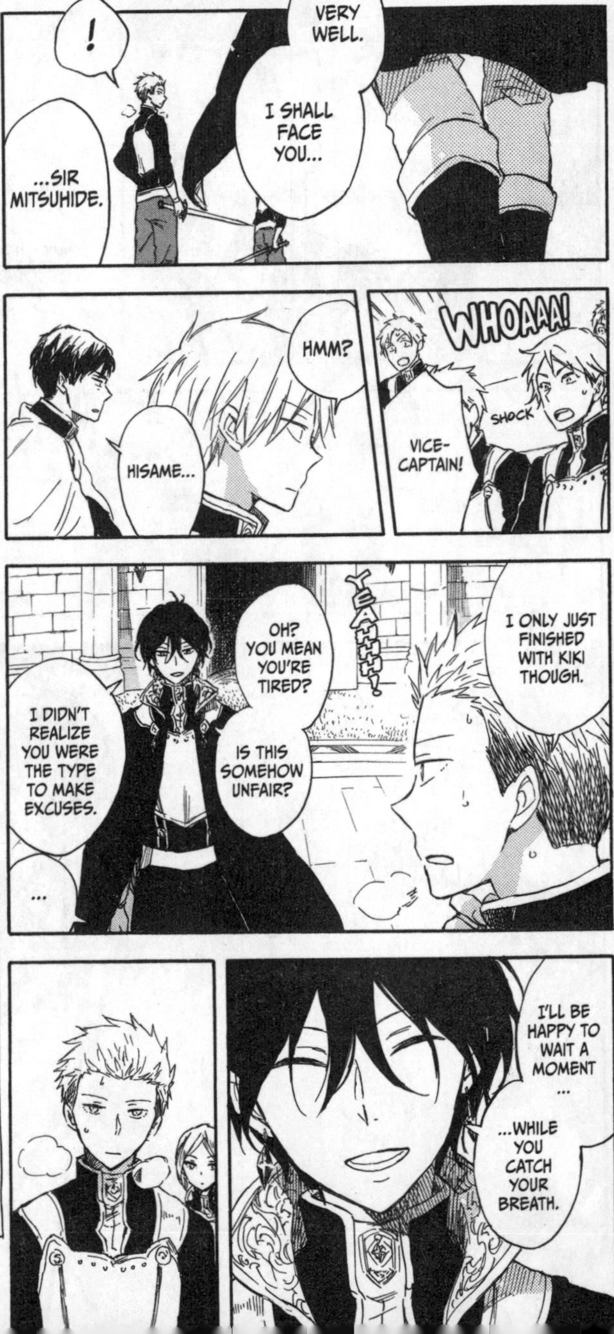
VERY WELL.
I SHALL FACE YOU...
!
...SIR MITSUHIDE.
WHOAAA!
SHOCK
VICE-CAPTAIN!
HMM?
HISAME...
I ONLY JUST FINISHED WITH KIKI THOUGH.
YEAHHH!
OH? YOU MEAN YOU'RE TIRED?
IS THIS SOMEHOW UNFAIR?
I DIDN'T REALIZE YOU WERE THE TYPE TO MAKE EXCUSES.
...
I'LL BE HAPPY TO WAIT A MOMENT ...
...WHILE YOU CATCH YOUR BREATH.

4

RECORDING STUDIO (PART 2)

My first visit to the studio was during the recording for episode 2. Mihaya's episode!

As the author of this series, I tried to imagine the characters' voices, but never really got a solid grasp on what they would sound like, so when I heard their voices recorded for the first time, it was bizarre. It felt like I was spying on my characters from behind a pillar in the shadows.

Then, the sound director would give amazingly specific direction, like, "Right now, this character is feeling this way, so..." I loved hearing them interpret and break down scenes, so I made a point to listen each time.

By explaining those nuances, the director helped the cast to modify their acting right on the spot.

Amazing things happen when an anime world is being created.

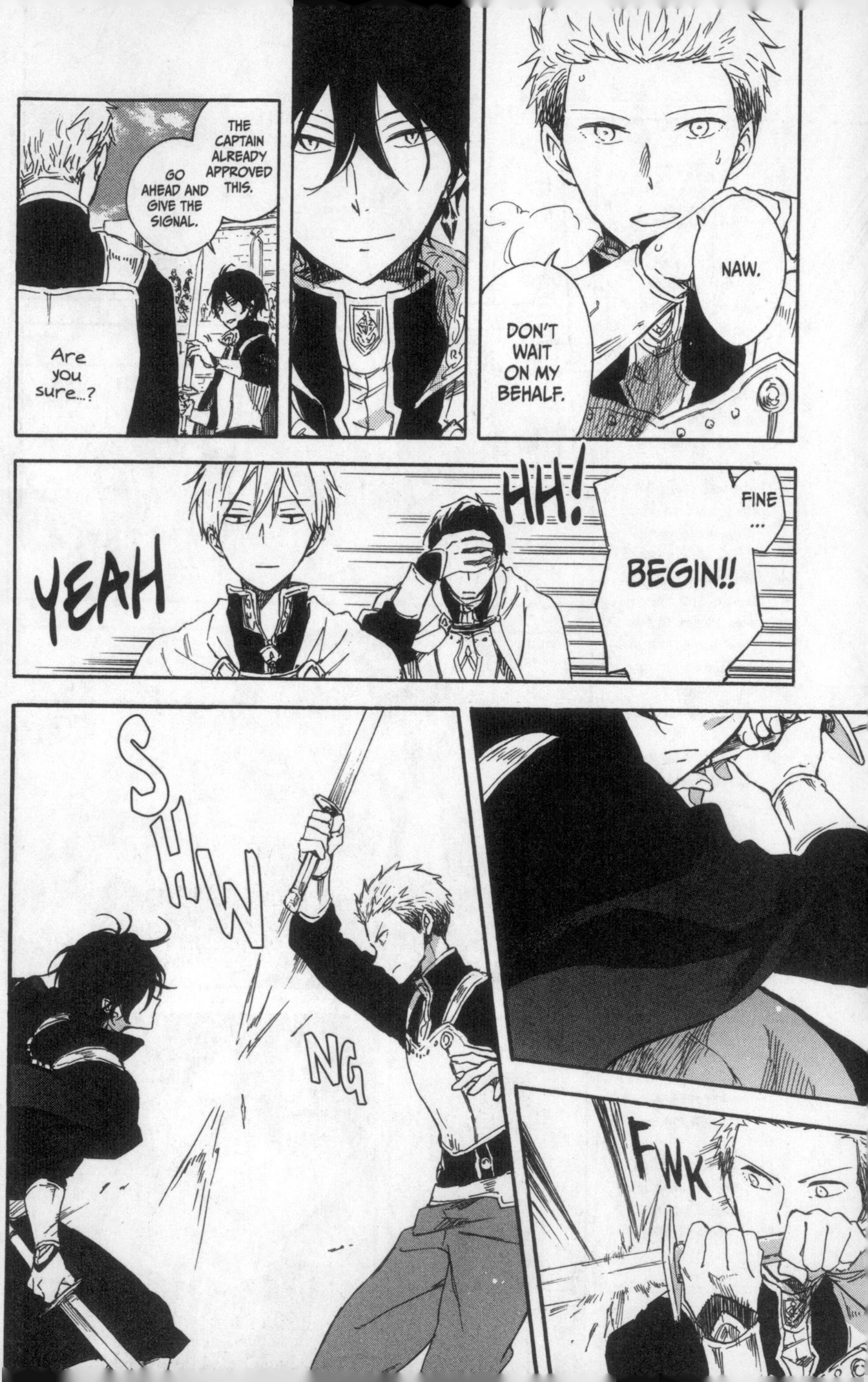
NAW.
DON'T WAIT ON MY BEHALF.
THE CAPTAIN ALREADY APPROVED THIS.
GO AHEAD AND GIVE THE SIGNAL.
Are you sure...?
FINE ...
BEGIN!!
HH!
YEAH
FWK
SHWNG

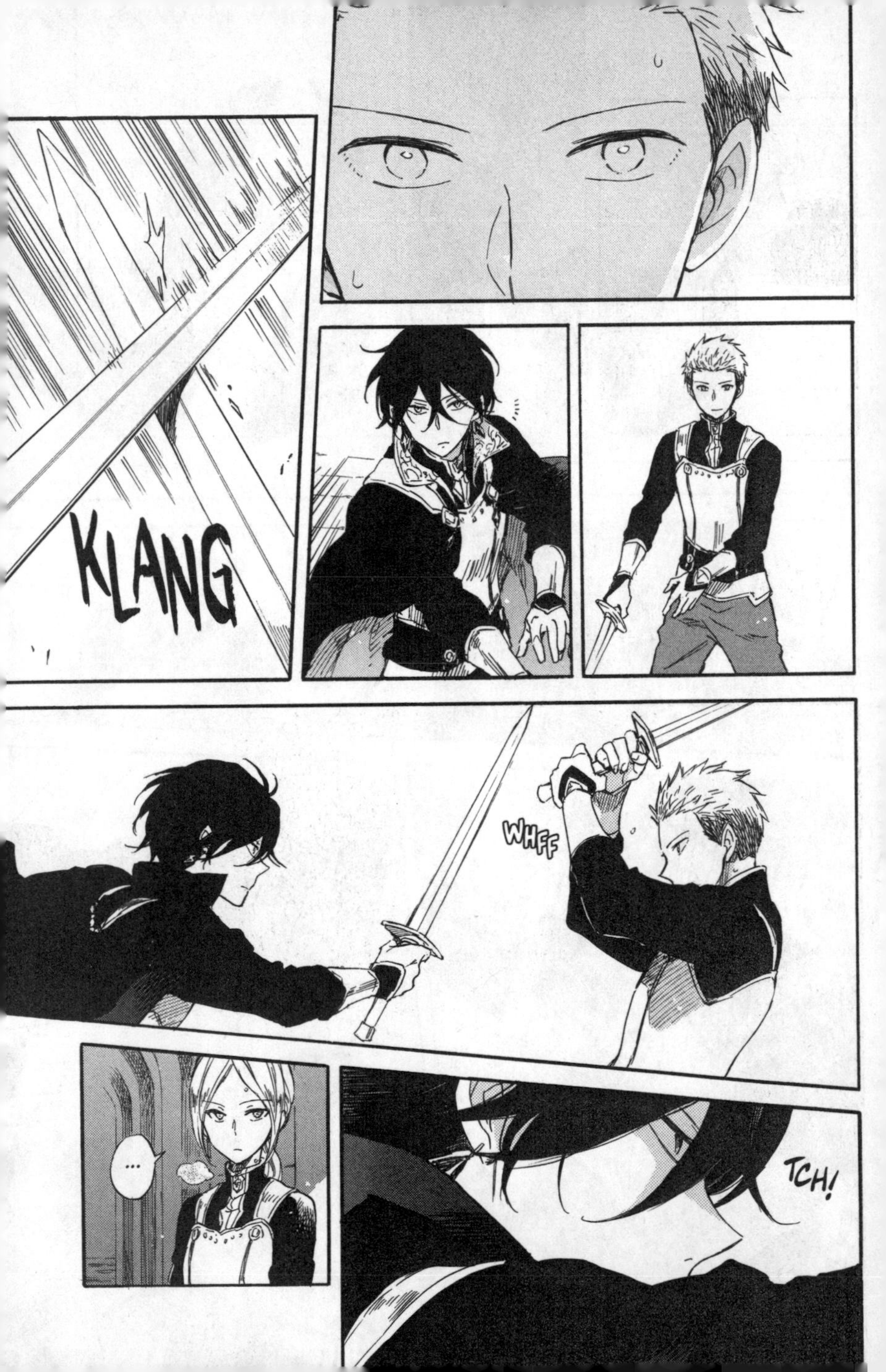
KLANG
WHFF
TCH!
...

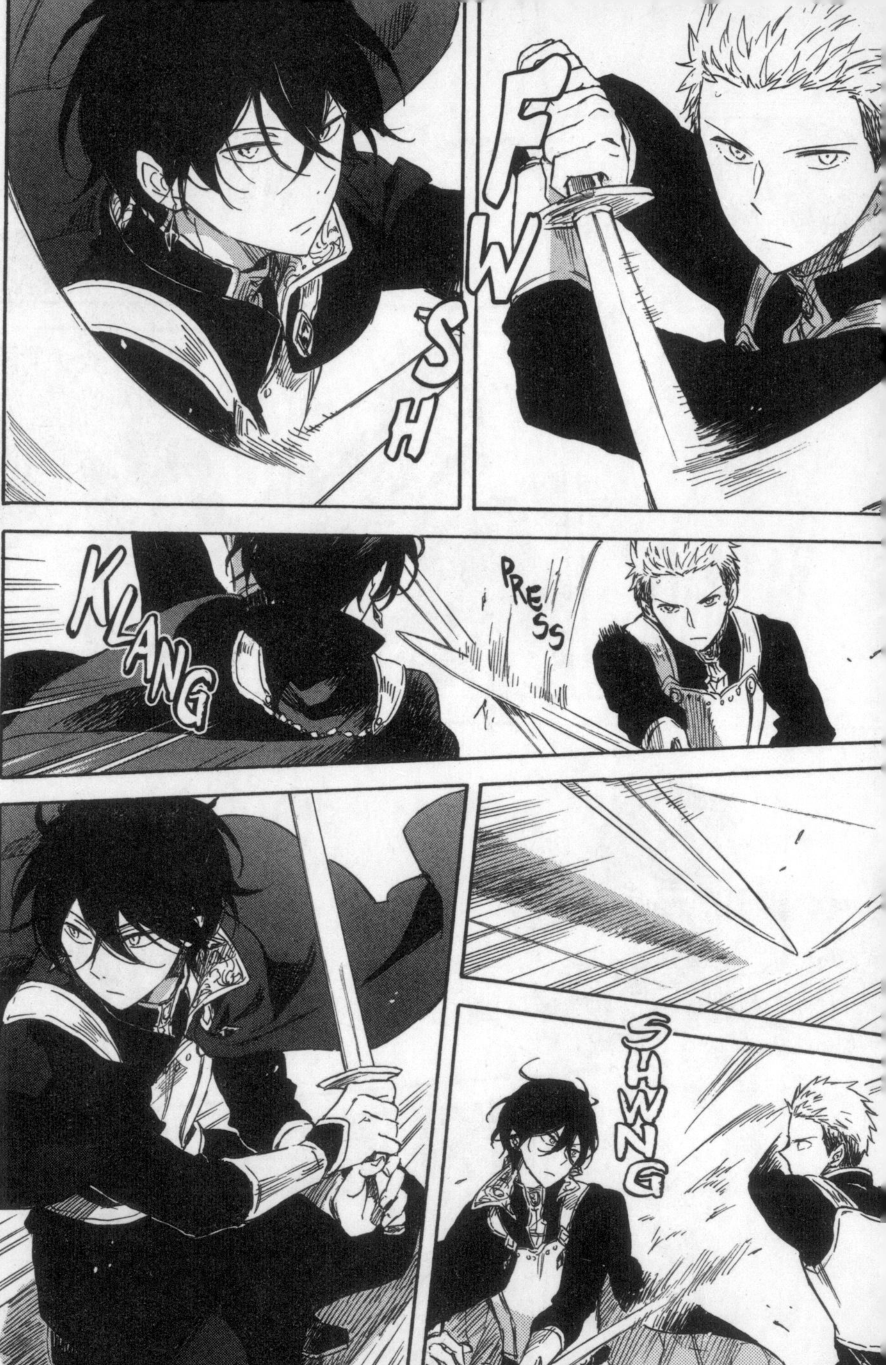
FWSH
PRESS
KLANG
SHWNG

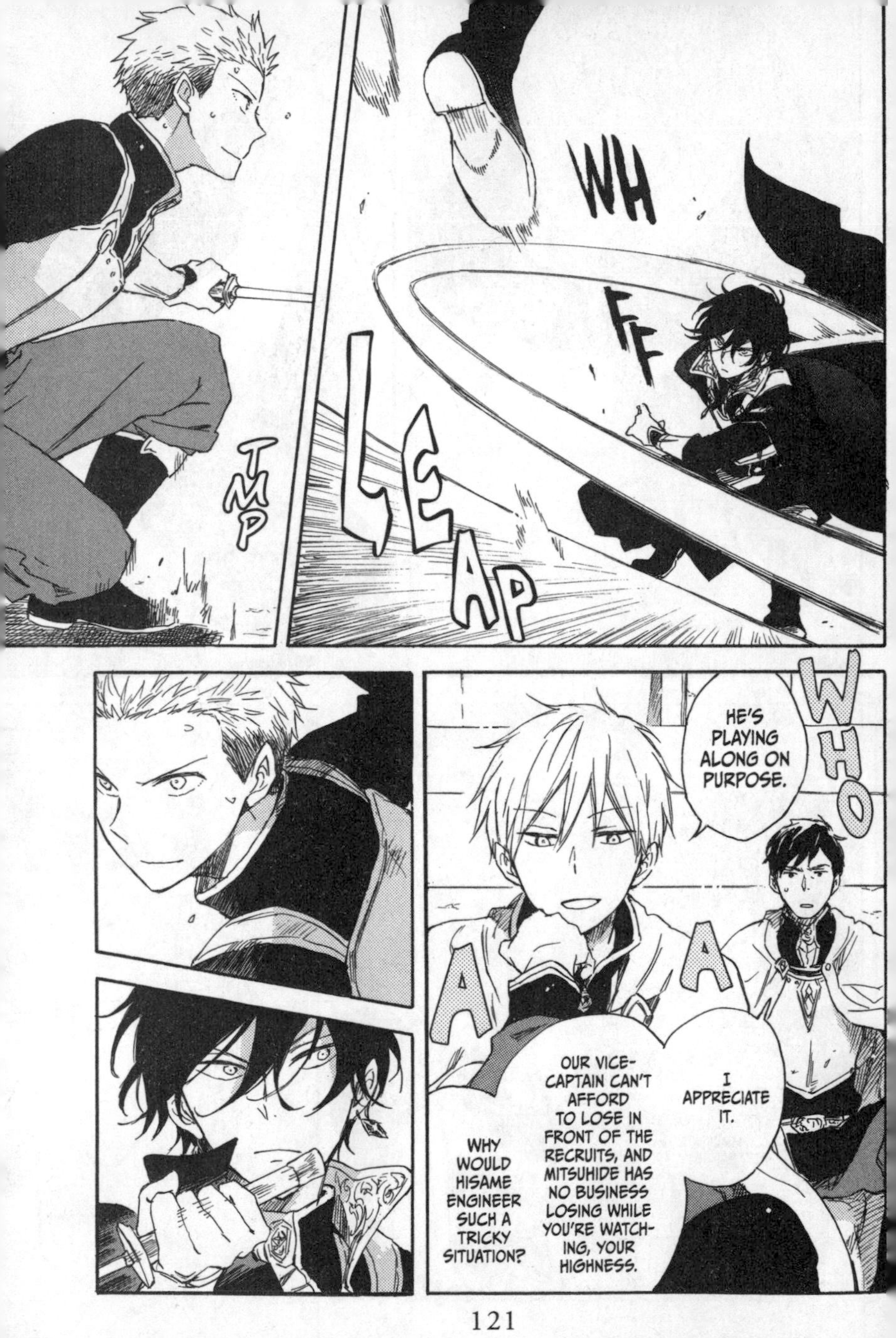
WHFF
LEAP
TMP
WHOA
HE'S PLAYING ALONG ON PURPOSE.
AA
I APPRECIATE IT.
OUR VICE-CAPTAIN CAN'T AFFORD TO LOSE IN FRONT OF THE RECRUITS, AND MITSUHIDE HAS NO BUSINESS LOSING WHILE YOU'RE WATCHING, YOUR HIGHNESS.
WHY WOULD HISAME ENGINEER SUCH A TRICKY SITUATION?

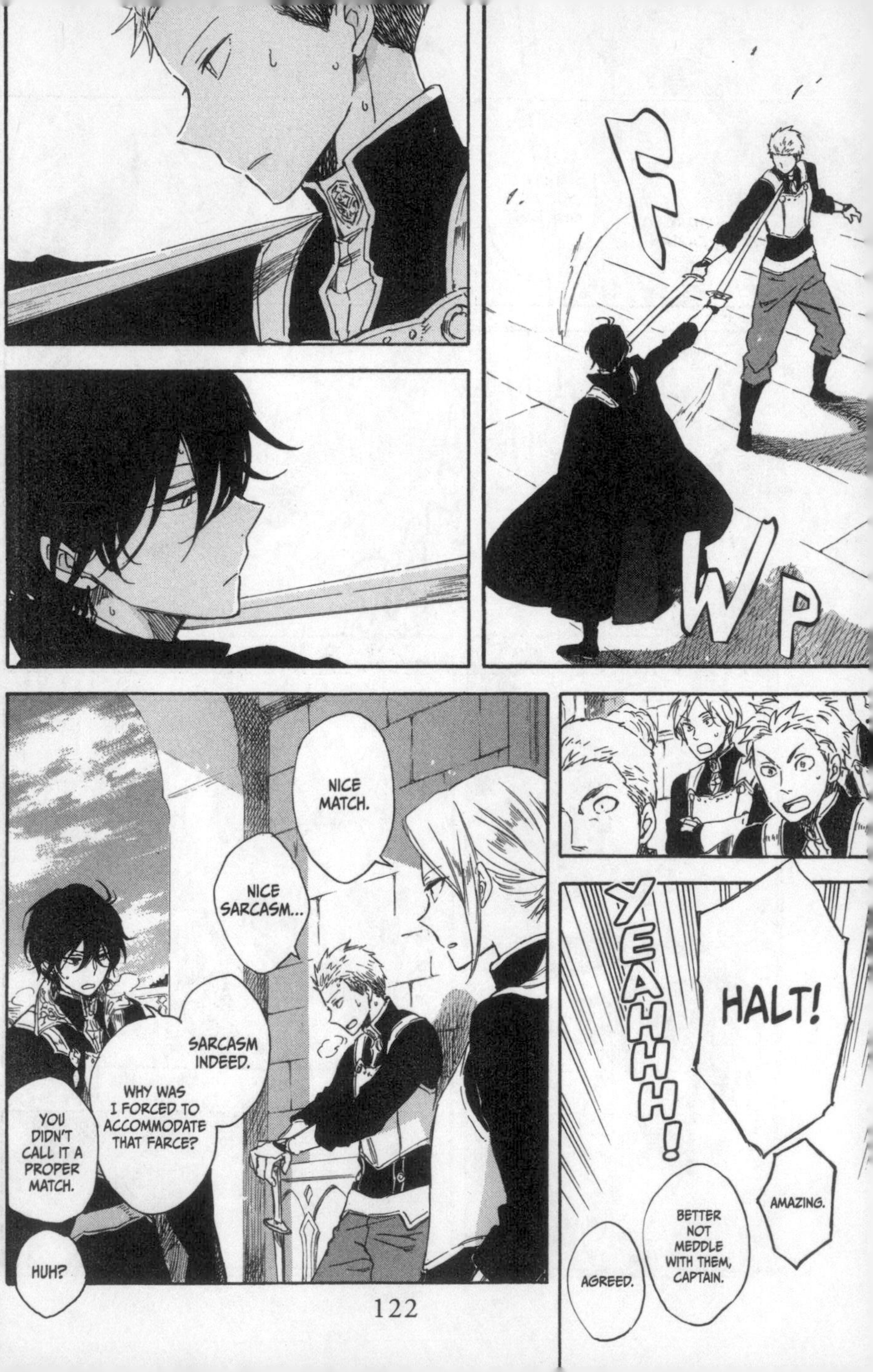
F
WP
YEAHHHH!
HALT!
AMAZING.
BETTER NOT MEDDLE WITH THEM, CAPTAIN.
AGREED.
NICE MATCH.
NICE SARCASM...
SARCASM INDEED.
WHY WAS I FORCED TO ACCOMMODATE THAT FARCE?
YOU DIDN'T CALL IT A PROPER MATCH.
HUH?

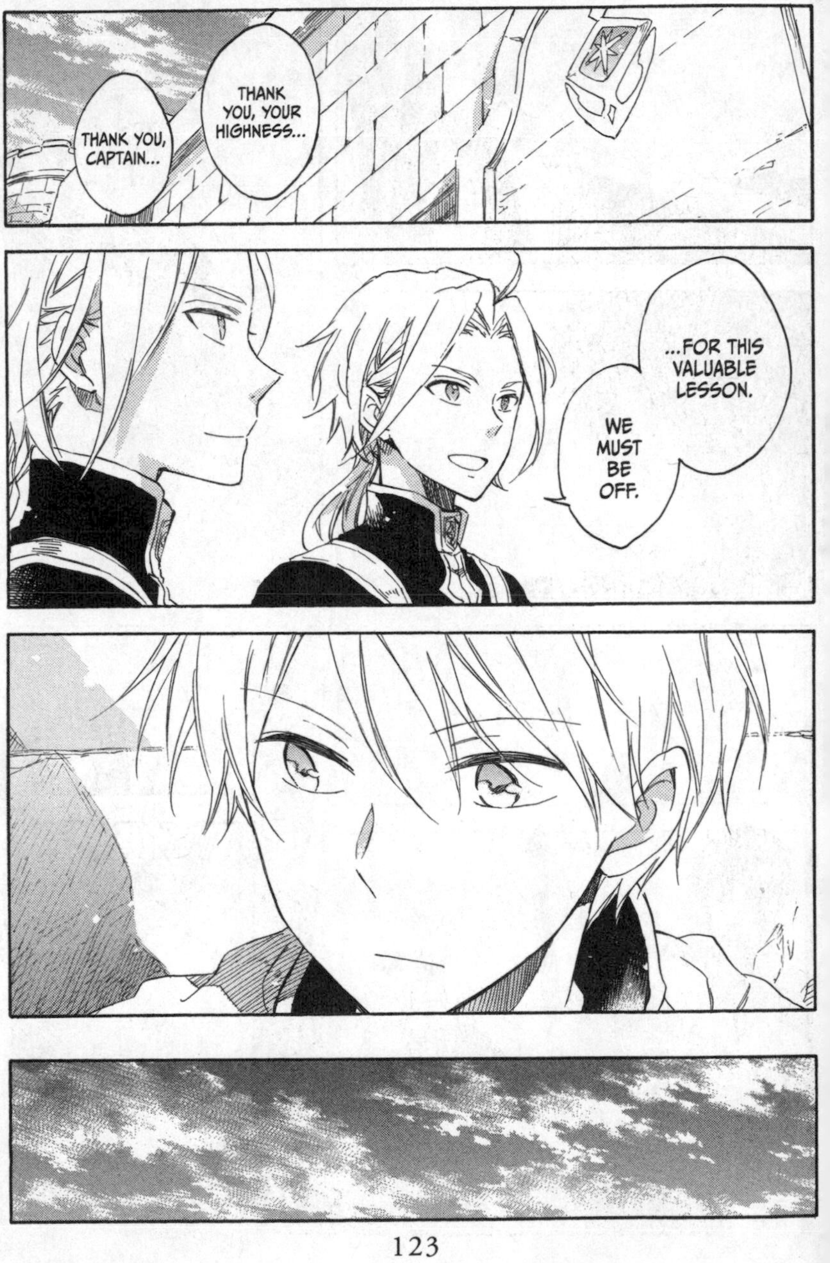
THANK YOU, YOUR HIGHNESS...
THANK YOU, CAPTAIN...
...FOR THIS VALUABLE LESSON.
WE MUST BE OFF.

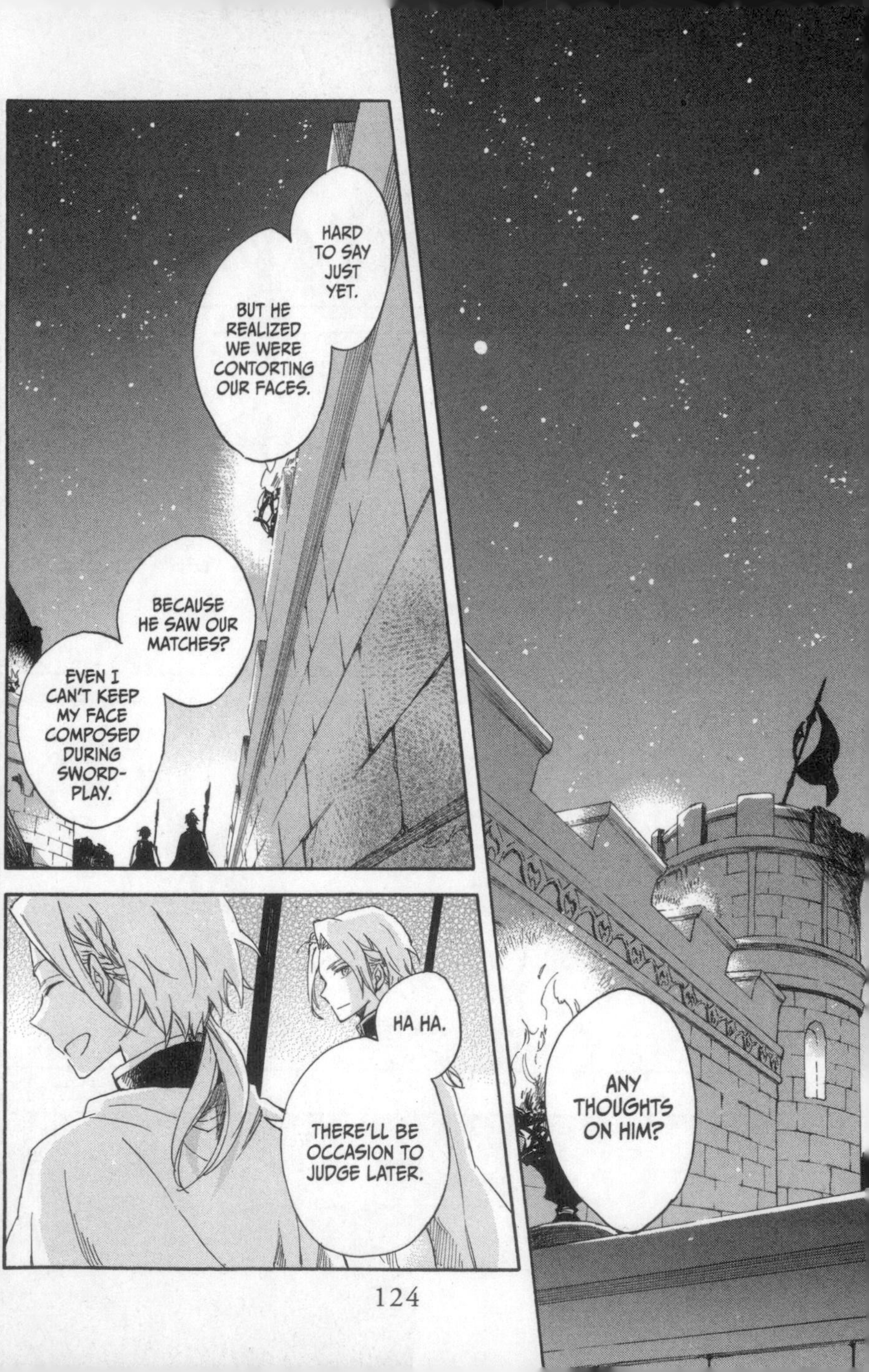
ANY THOUGHTS ON HIM?
HARD TO SAY JUST YET.
BUT HE REALIZED WE WERE CONTORTING OUR FACES.
BECAUSE HE SAW OUR MATCHES?
EVEN I CAN'T KEEP MY FACE COMPOSED DURING SWORD-PLAY.
HA HA.
THERE'LL BE OCCASION TO JUDGE LATER.

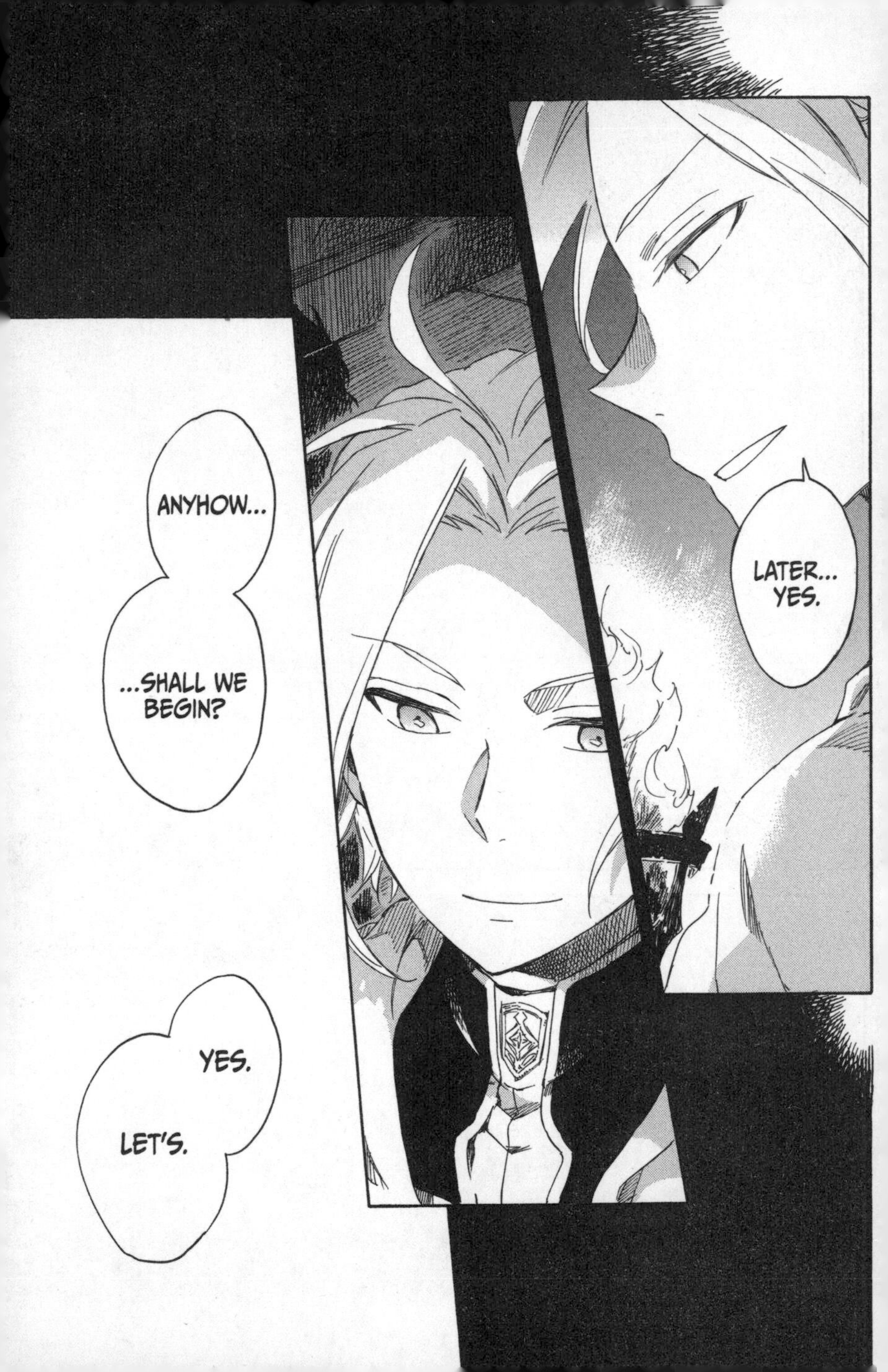
LATER... YES.
ANYHOW...
...SHALL WE BEGIN?
YES.
LET'S.

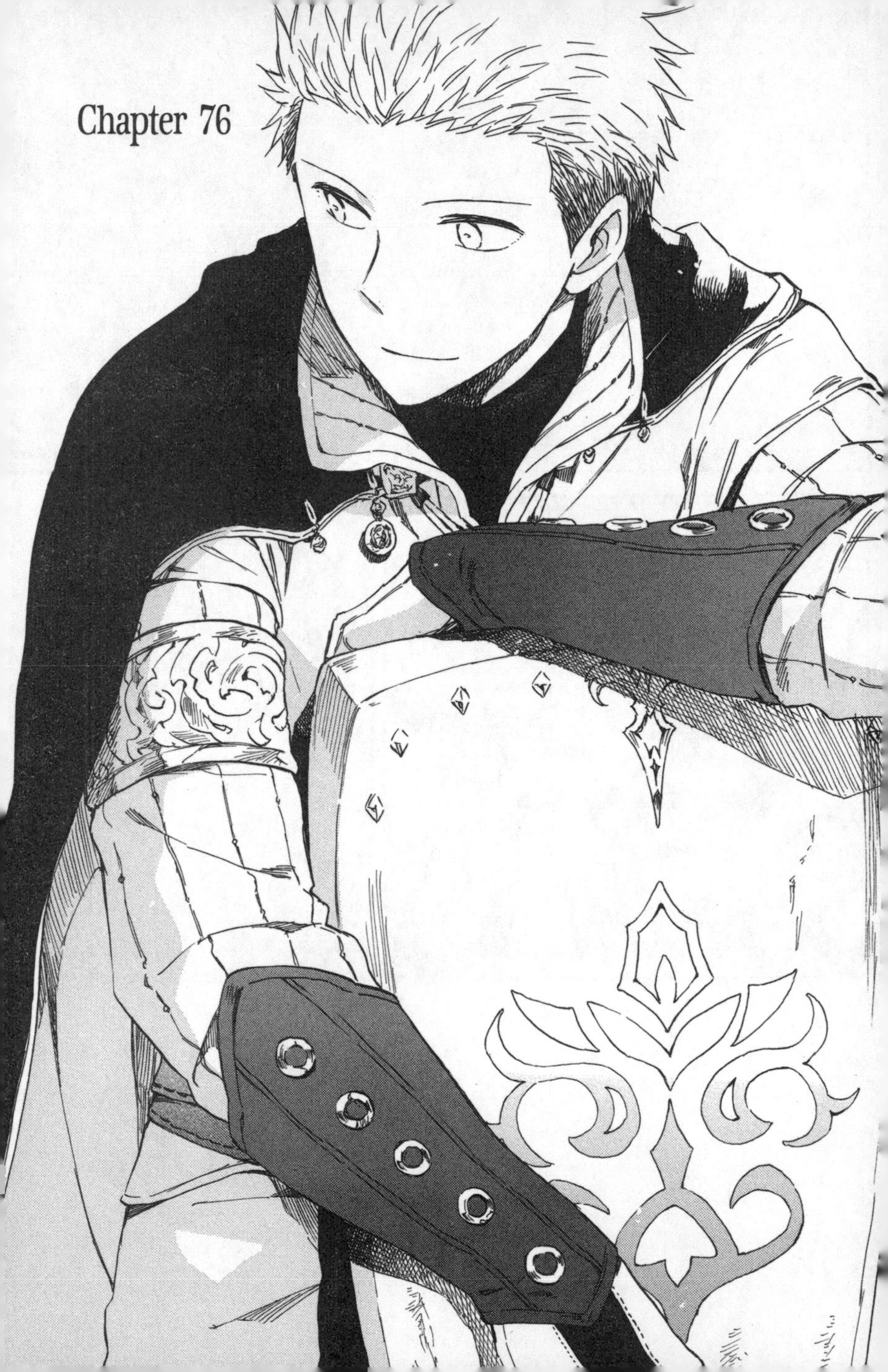
Chapter 76

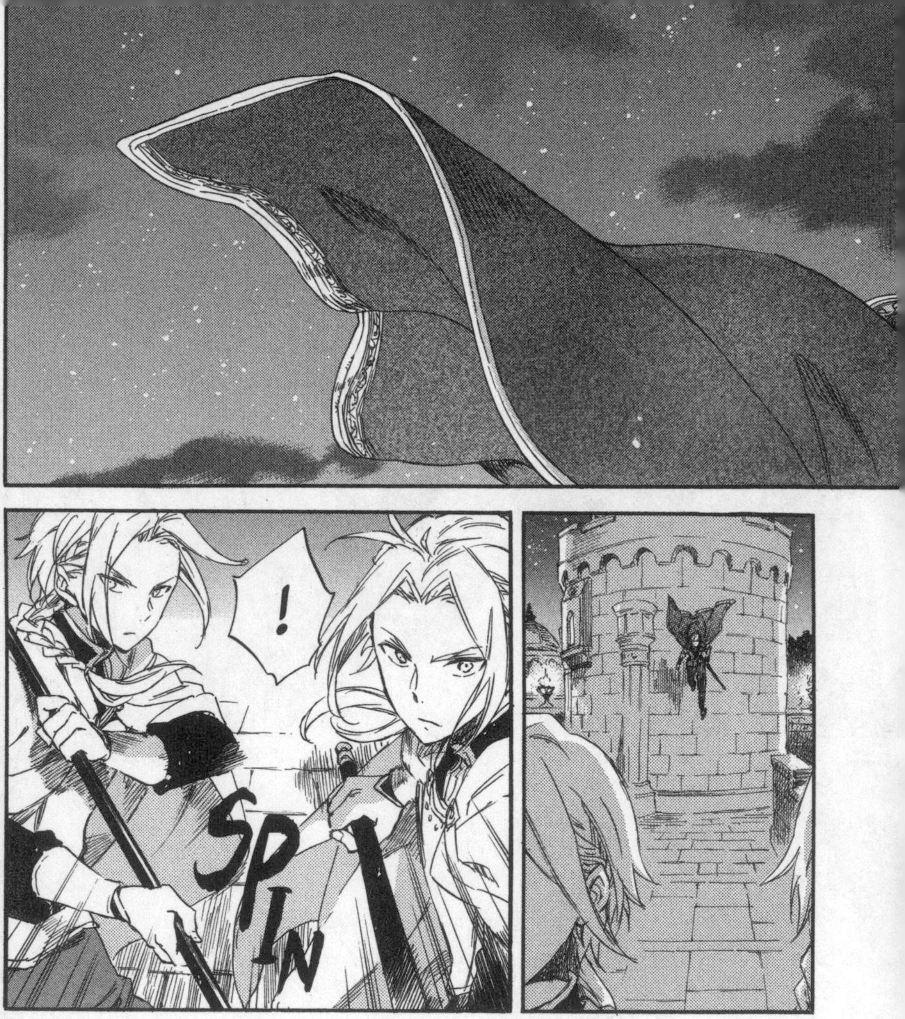
!
SPIN

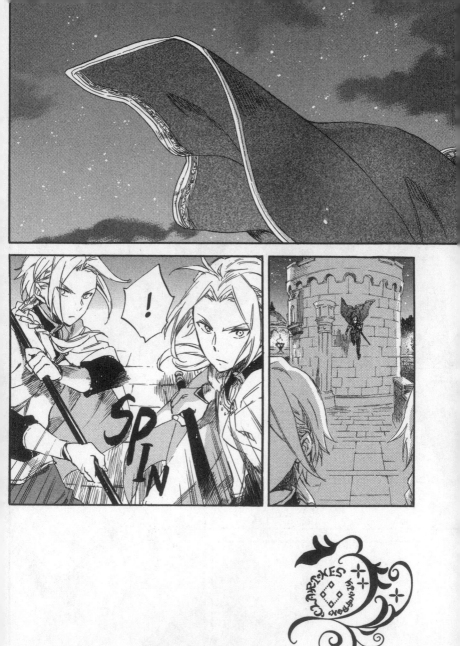

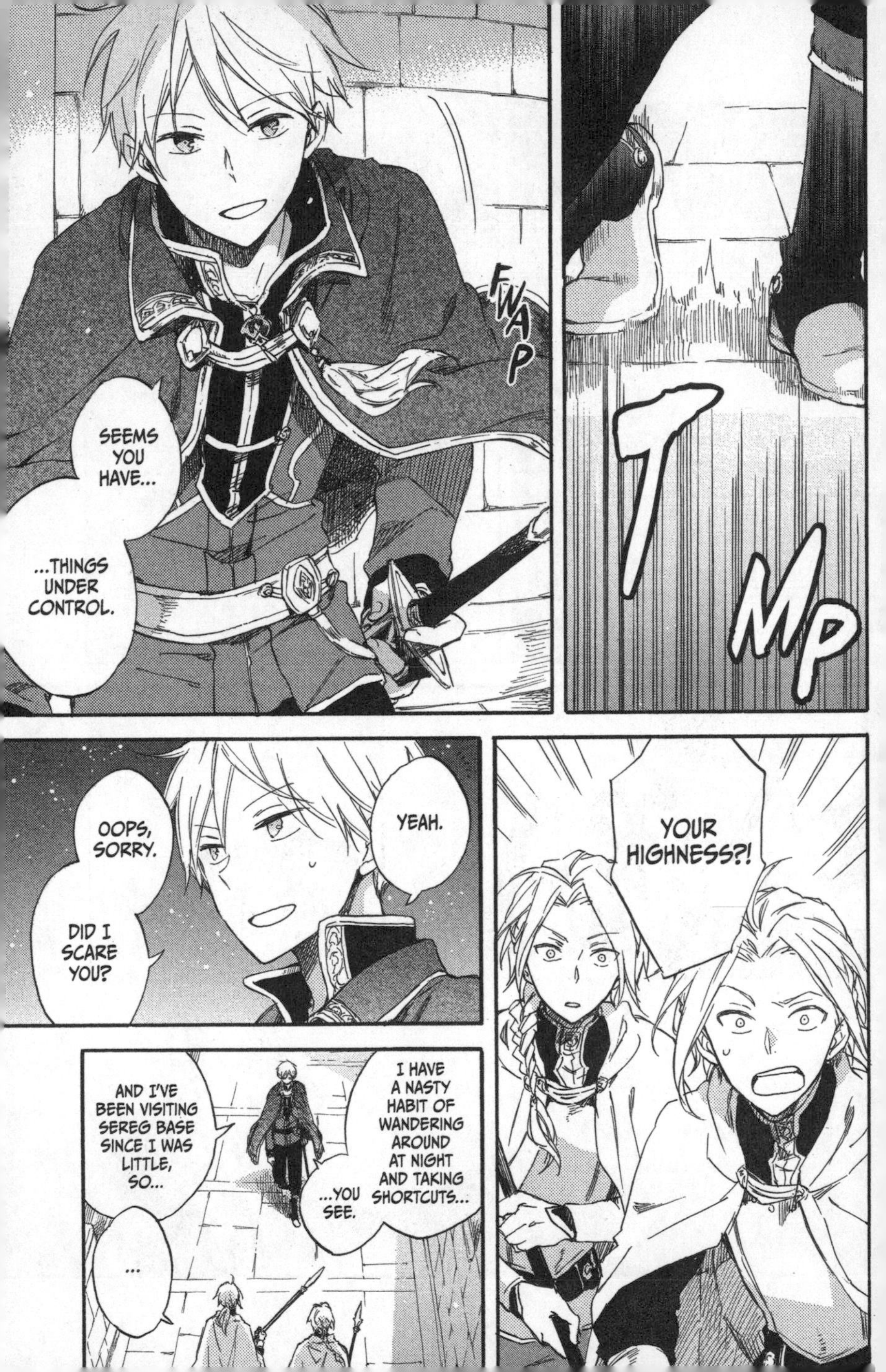
TMP
FWAP
SEEMS YOU HAVE...
...THINGS UNDER CONTROL.
YOUR HIGHNESS?!
YEAH.
OOPS, SORRY.
DID I SCARE YOU?
I HAVE A NASTY HABIT OF WANDERING AROUND AT NIGHT AND TAKING SHORTCUTS...
...YOU SEE.
AND I'VE BEEN VISITING SEREG BASE SINCE I WAS LITTLE, SO...
...

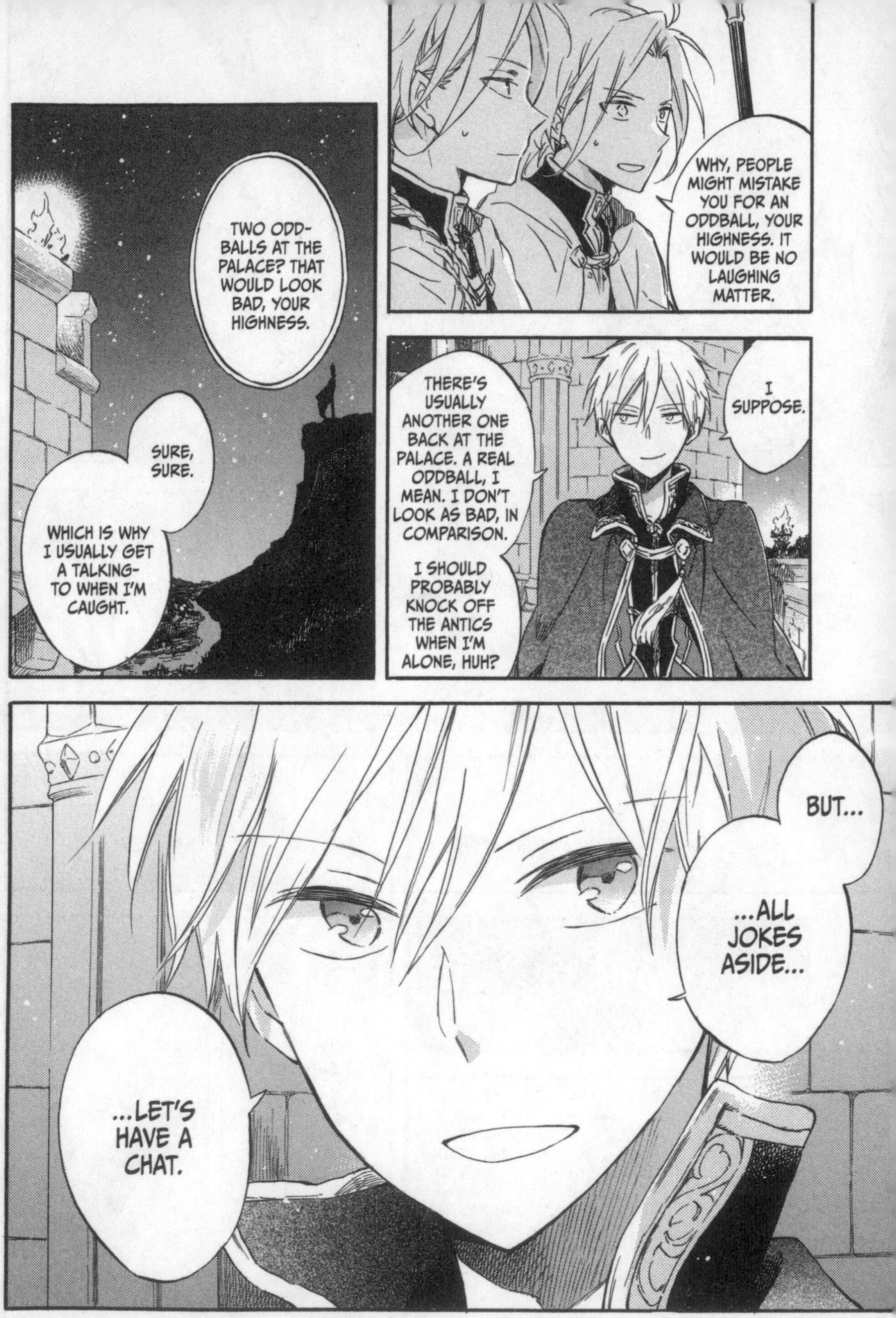
WHY, PEOPLE MIGHT MISTAKE YOU FOR AN ODDBALL, YOUR HIGHNESS. IT WOULD BE NO LAUGHING MATTER.
I SUPPOSE.
THERE'S USUALLY ANOTHER ONE BACK AT THE PALACE. A REAL ODDBALL, I MEAN. I DON'T LOOK AS BAD, IN COMPARISON.
I SHOULD PROBABLY KNOCK OFF THE ANTICS WHEN I'M ALONE, HUH?
TWO ODD-BALLS AT THE PALACE? THAT WOULD LOOK BAD, YOUR HIGHNESS.
SURE, SURE.
WHICH IS WHY I USUALLY GET A TALKING-TO WHEN I'M CAUGHT.
BUT...
...ALL JOKES ASIDE...
...LET'S HAVE A CHAT.

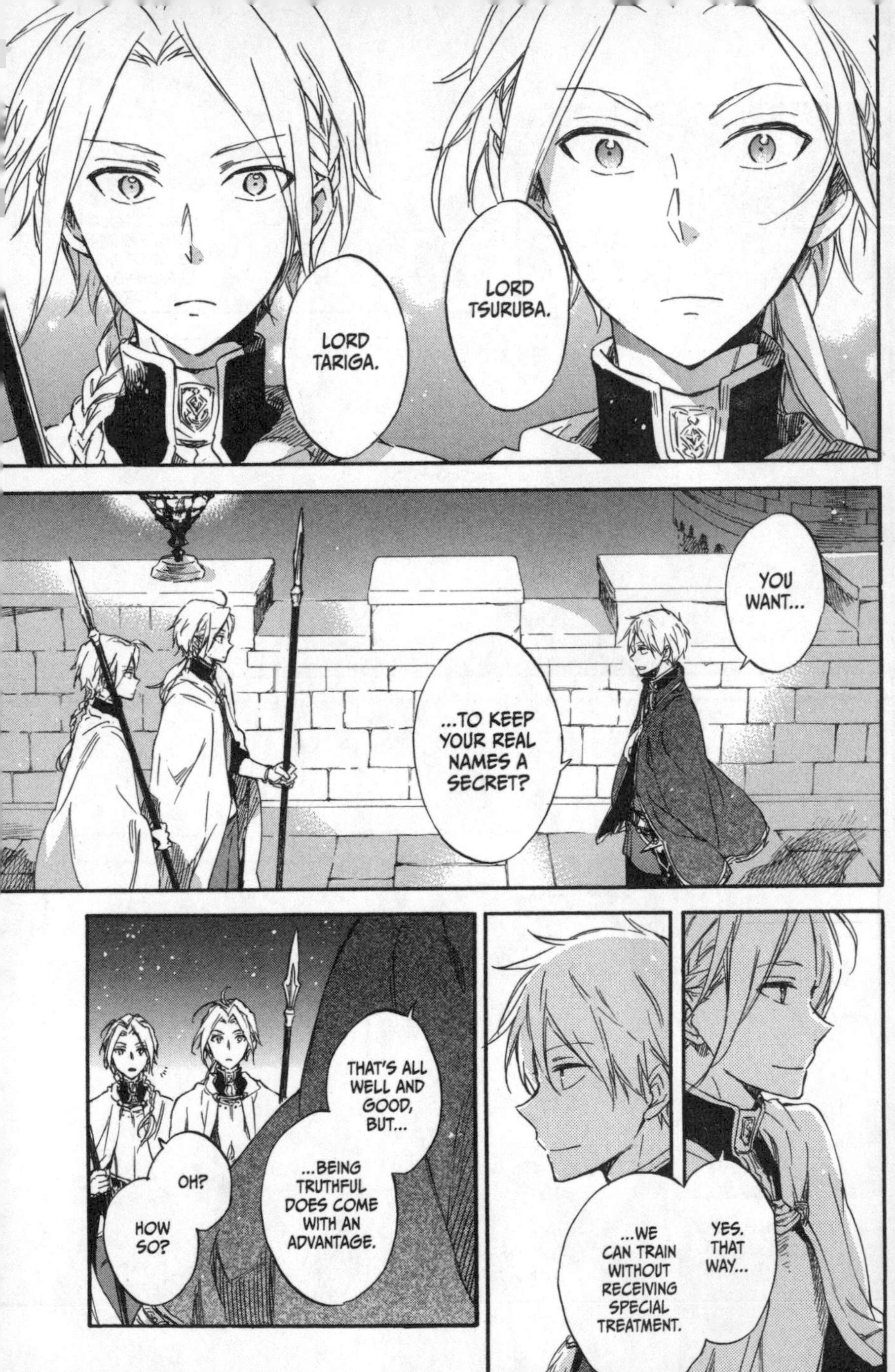
LORD TSURUBA.
LORD TARIGA.
YOU WANT...
...TO KEEP YOUR REAL NAMES A SECRET?
YES. THAT WAY...
...WE CAN TRAIN WITHOUT RECEIVING SPECIAL TREATMENT.
THAT'S ALL WELL AND GOOD, BUT...
...BEING TRUTHFUL DOES COME WITH AN ADVANTAGE.
OH?
HOW SO?

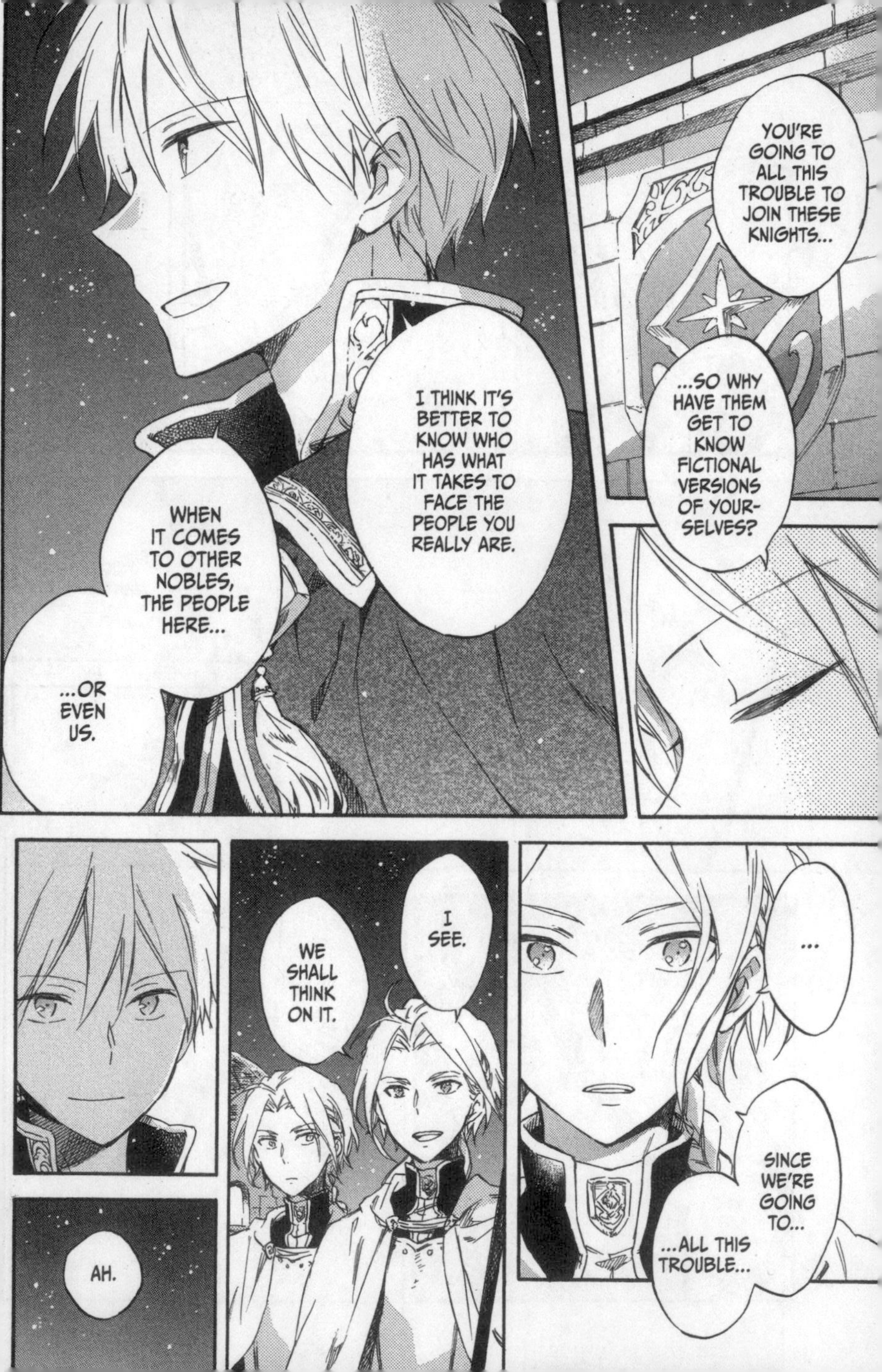
YOU'RE GOING TO ALL THIS TROUBLE TO JOIN THESE KNIGHTS...
...SO WHY HAVE THEM GET TO KNOW FICTIONAL VERSIONS OF YOUR-SELVES?
I THINK IT'S BETTER TO KNOW WHO HAS WHAT IT TAKES TO FACE THE PEOPLE YOU REALLY ARE.
WHEN IT COMES TO OTHER NOBLES, THE PEOPLE HERE...
...OR EVEN US.
...
SINCE WE'RE GOING TO...
...ALL THIS TROUBLE...
I SEE.
WE SHALL THINK ON IT.
AH.

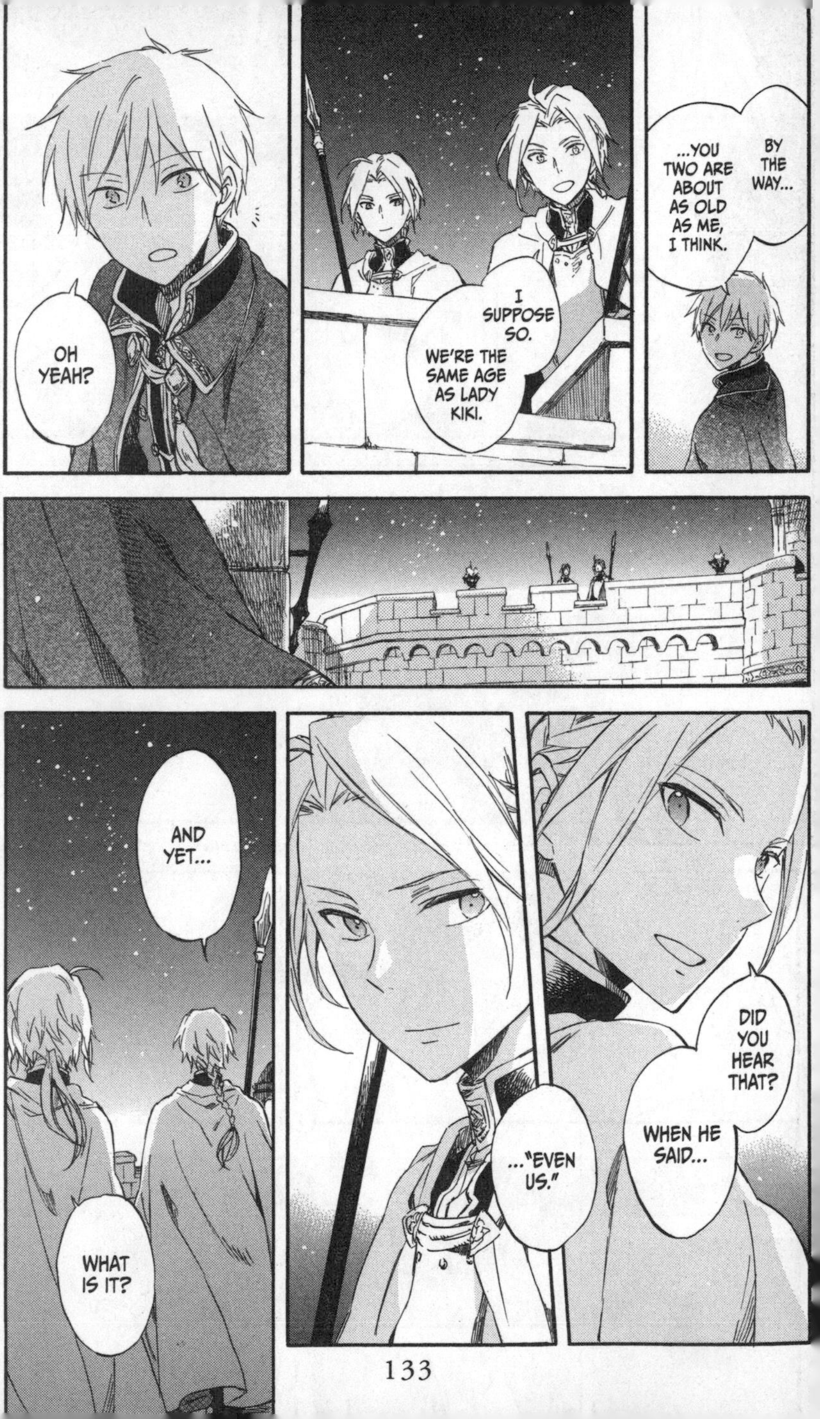
BY THE WAY...
...YOU TWO ARE ABOUT AS OLD AS ME, I THINK.
I SUPPOSE SO.
WE'RE THE SAME AGE AS LADY KIKI.
OH YEAH?
DID YOU HEAR THAT?
WHEN HE SAID...
..."EVEN US."
AND YET...
WHAT IS IT?

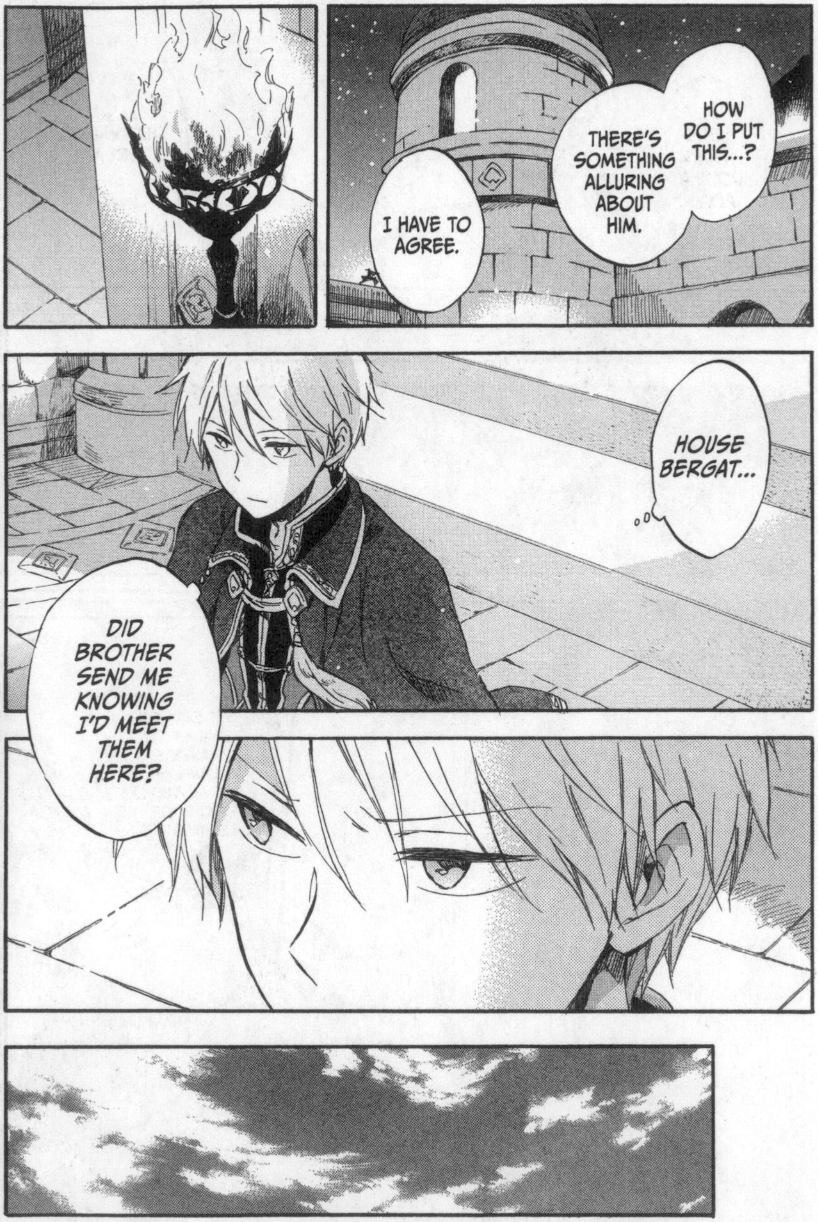
HOW DO I PUT THIS...?
THERE'S SOMETHING ALLURING ABOUT HIM.
I HAVE TO AGREE.
HOUSE BERGAT...
DID BROTHER SEND ME KNOWING I'D MEET THEM HERE?

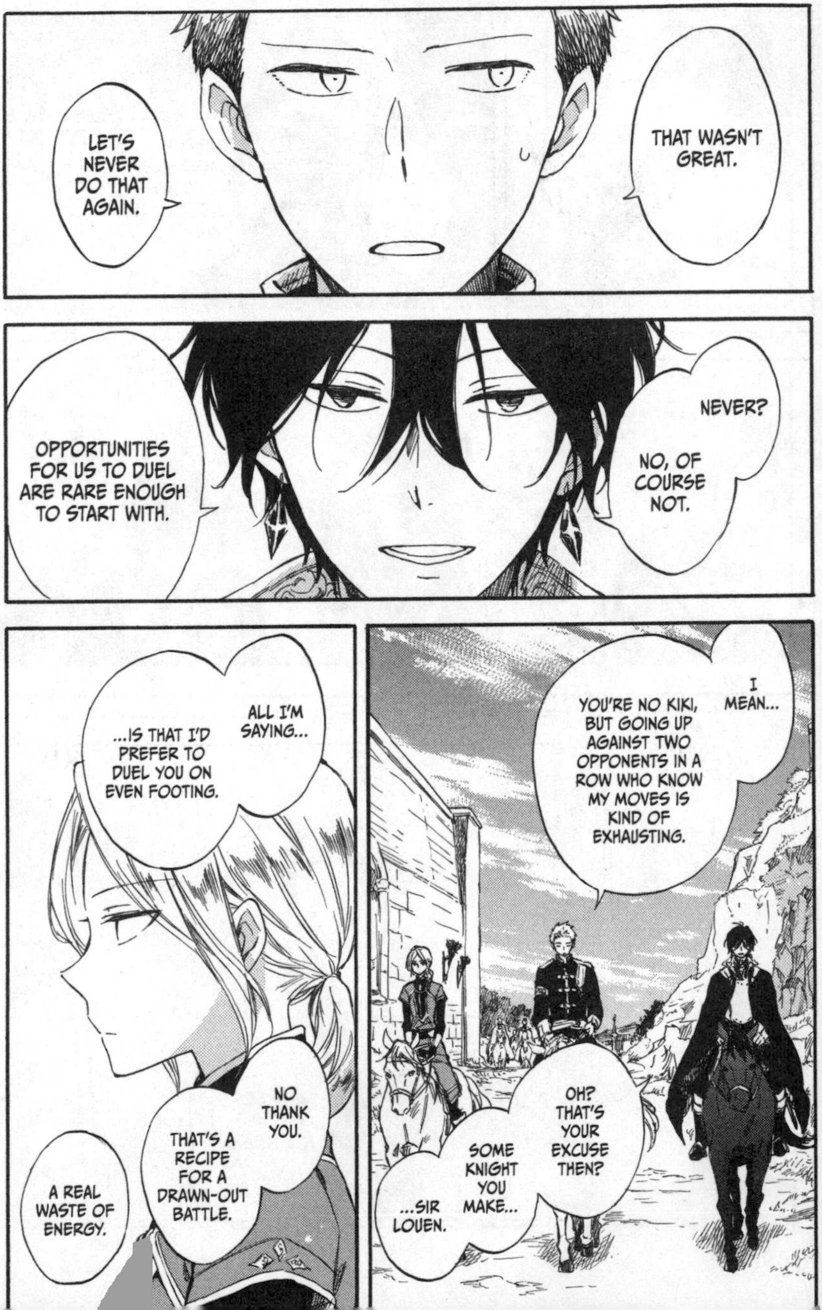
THAT WASN'T GREAT.
LET'S NEVER DO THAT AGAIN.
NEVER?
NO, OF COURSE NOT.
OPPORTUNITIES FOR US TO DUEL ARE RARE ENOUGH TO START WITH.
I MEAN...
YOU'RE NO KIKI, BUT GOING UP AGAINST TWO OPPONENTS IN A ROW WHO KNOW MY MOVES IS KIND OF EXHAUSTING.
OH? THAT'S YOUR EXCUSE THEN?
SOME KNIGHT YOU MAKE...
...SIR LOUEN.
ALL I'M SAYING...
...IS THAT I'D PREFER TO DUEL YOU ON EVEN FOOTING.
NO THANK YOU.
THAT'S A RECIPE FOR A DRAWN-OUT BATTLE.
A REAL WASTE OF ENERGY.

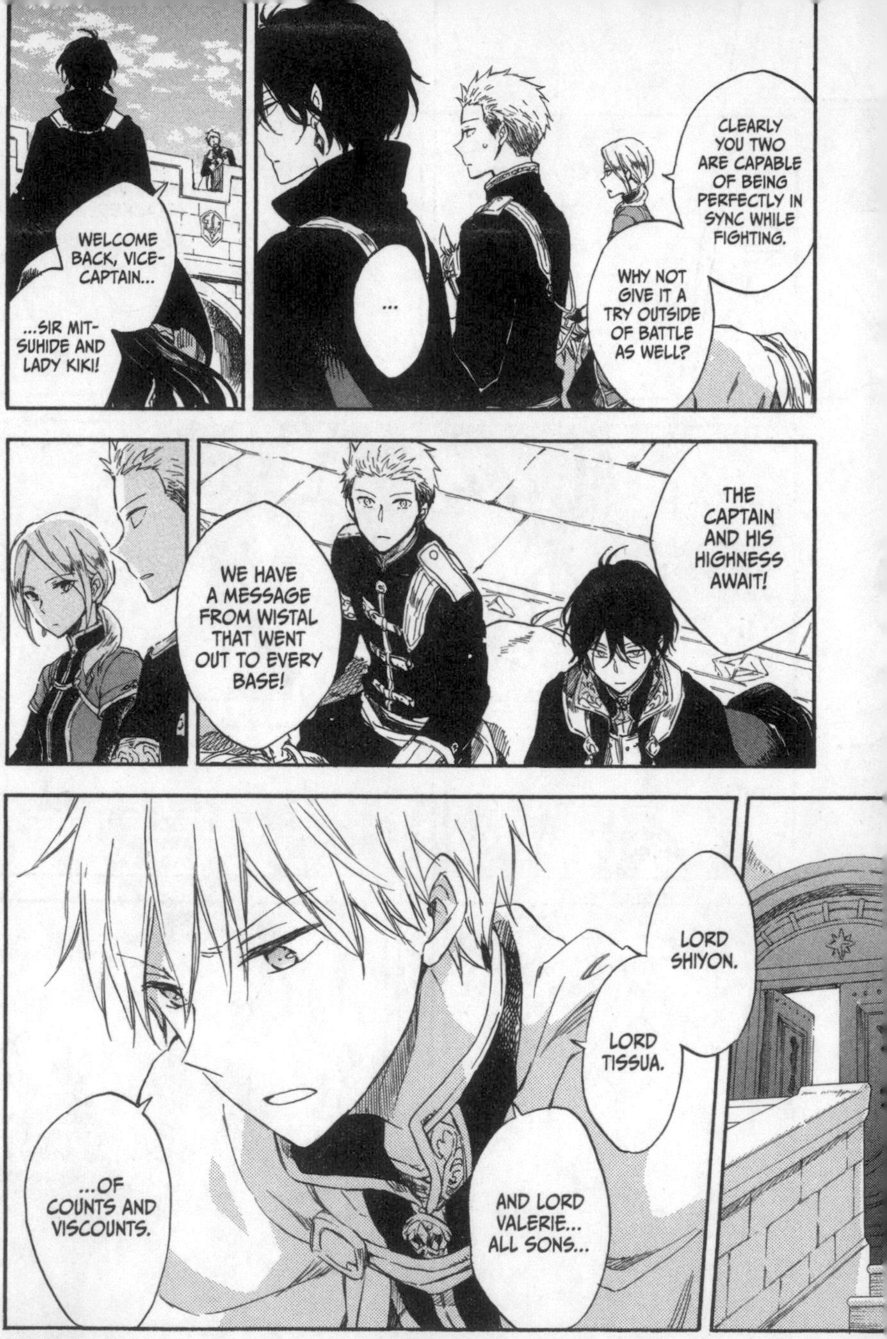
CLEARLY YOU TWO ARE CAPABLE OF BEING PERFECTLY IN SYNC WHILE FIGHTING.
WHY NOT GIVE IT A TRY OUTSIDE OF BATTLE AS WELL?
...
WELCOME BACK, VICE-CAPTAIN...
...SIR MIT-SUHIDE AND LADY KIKI!
THE CAPTAIN AND HIS HIGHNESS AWAIT!
WE HAVE A MESSAGE FROM WISTAL THAT WENT OUT TO EVERY BASE!
LORD SHIYON.
LORD TISSUA.
AND LORD VALERIE... ALL SONS...
...OF COUNTS AND VISCOUNTS.

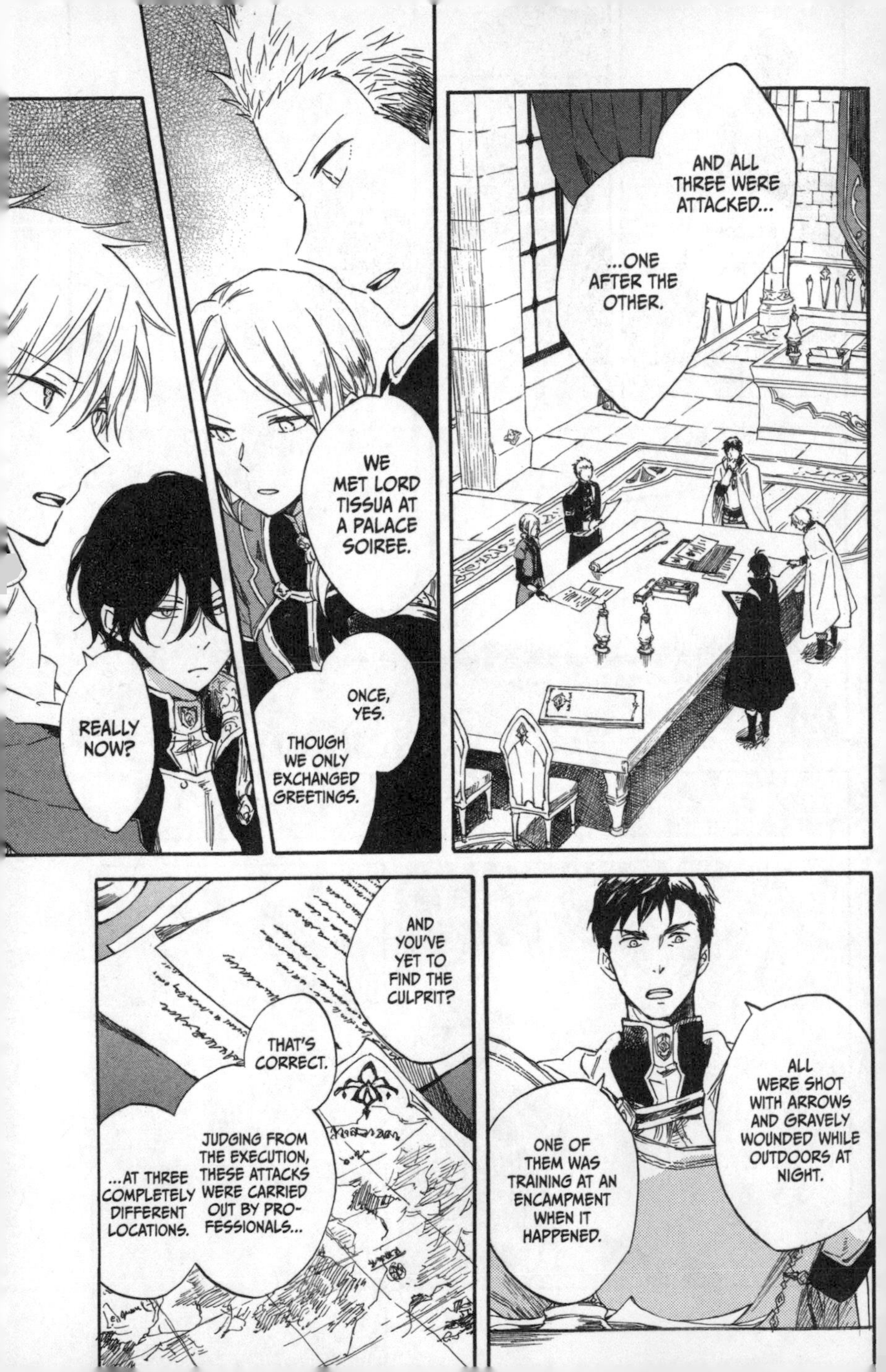
AND ALL THREE WERE ATTACKED...
...ONE AFTER THE OTHER.
WE MET LORD TISSUA AT A PALACE SOIREE.
ONCE, YES.
THOUGH WE ONLY EXCHANGED GREETINGS.
REALLY NOW?
ALL WERE SHOT WITH ARROWS AND GRAVELY WOUNDED WHILE OUTDOORS AT NIGHT.
ONE OF THEM WAS TRAINING AT AN ENCAMPMENT WHEN IT HAPPENED.
AND YOU'VE YET TO FIND THE CULPRIT?
THAT'S CORRECT.
JUDGING FROM THE EXECUTION, THESE ATTACKS WERE CARRIED OUT BY PRO-FESSIONALS...
...AT THREE COMPLETELY DIFFERENT LOCATIONS.

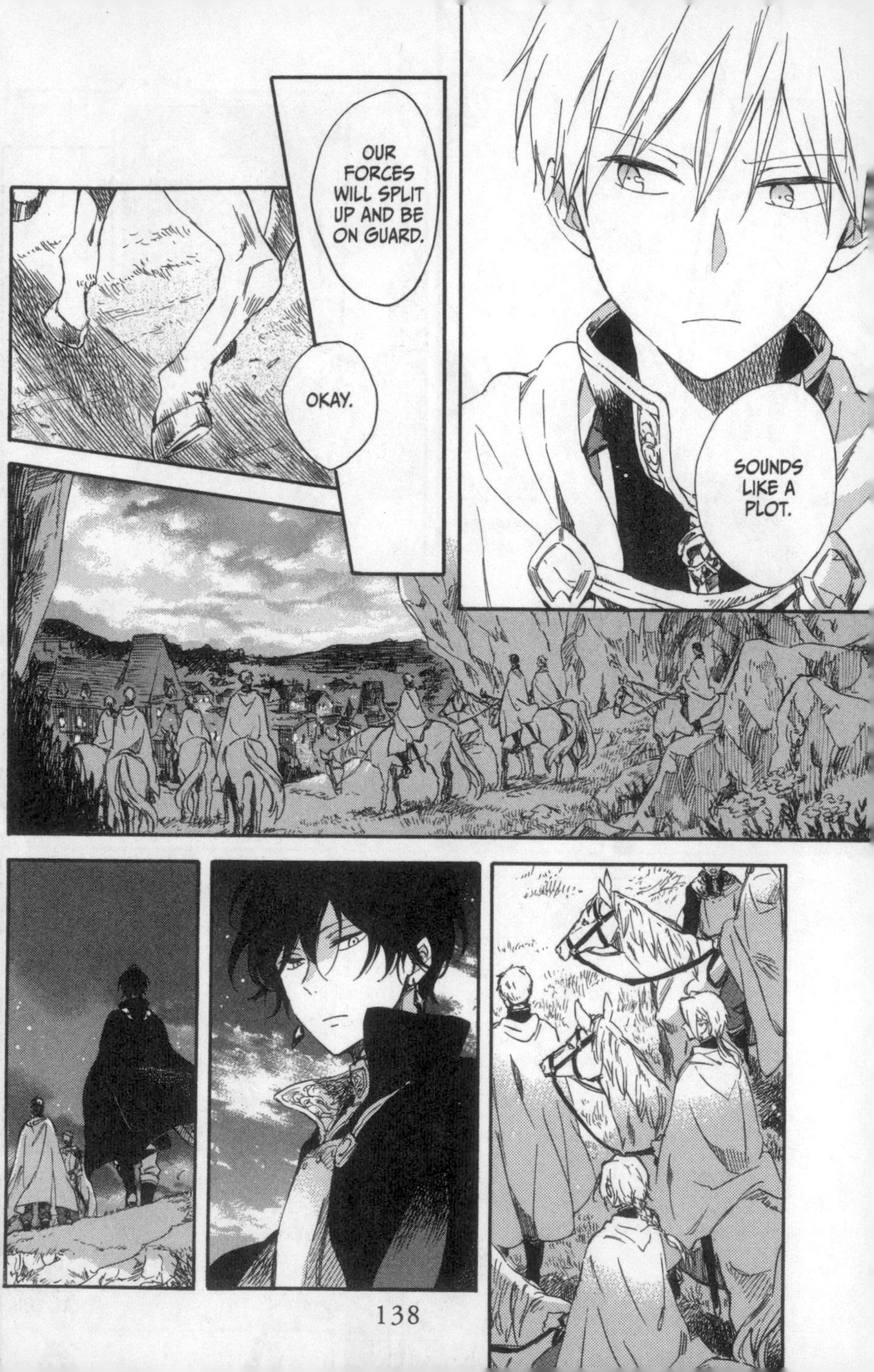
SOUNDS LIKE A PLOT.
OUR FORCES WILL SPLIT UP AND BE ON GUARD.
OKAY.

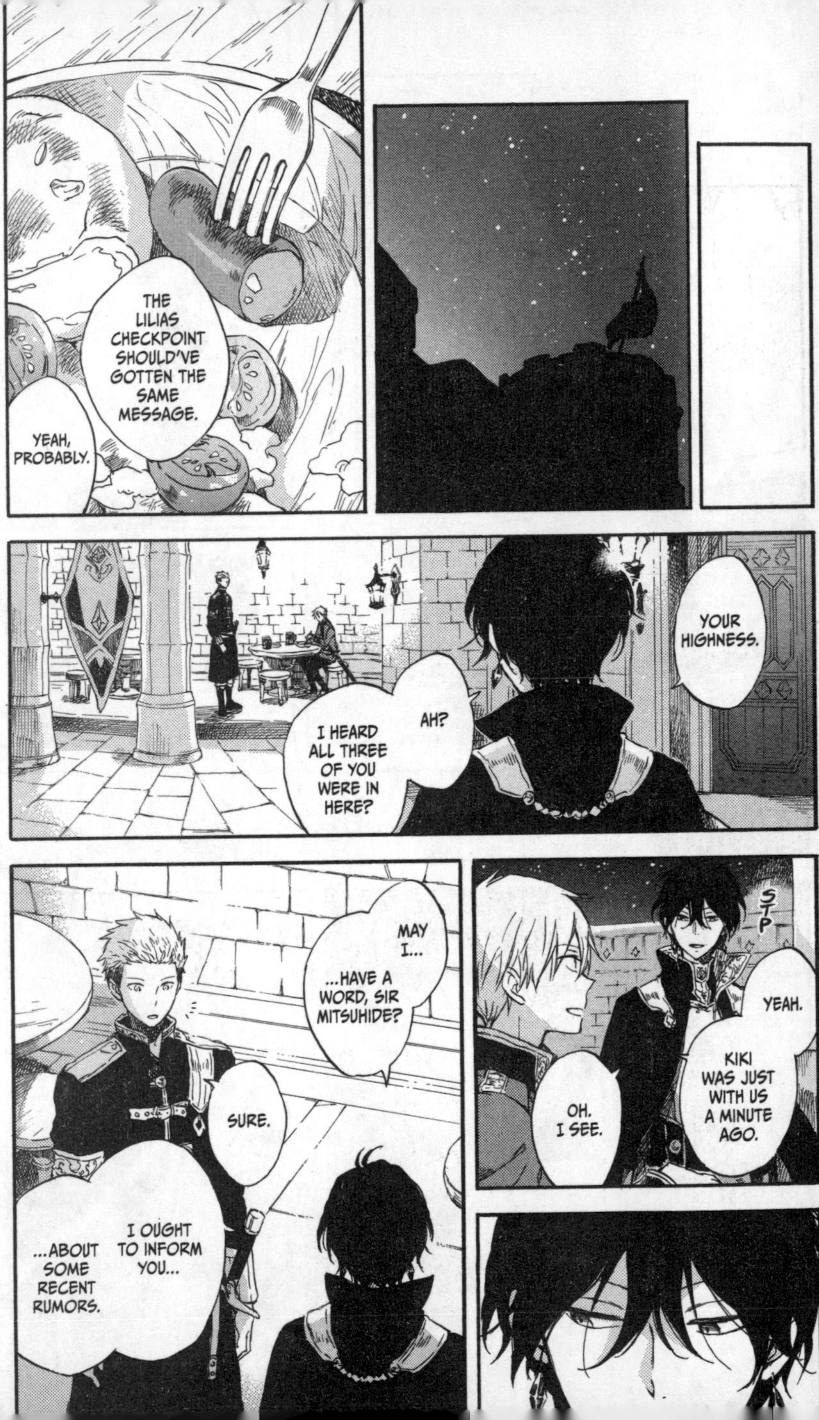
THE LILIAS CHECKPOINT SHOULD'VE GOTTEN THE SAME MESSAGE.
YEAH, PROBABLY.
YOUR HIGHNESS.
AH?
I HEARD ALL THREE OF YOU WERE IN HERE?
STP
YEAH.
KIKI WAS JUST WITH US A MINUTE AGO.
OH. I SEE.
MAY I...
...HAVE A WORD, SIR MITSUHIDE?
SURE.
I OUGHT TO INFORM YOU...
...ABOUT SOME RECENT RUMORS.

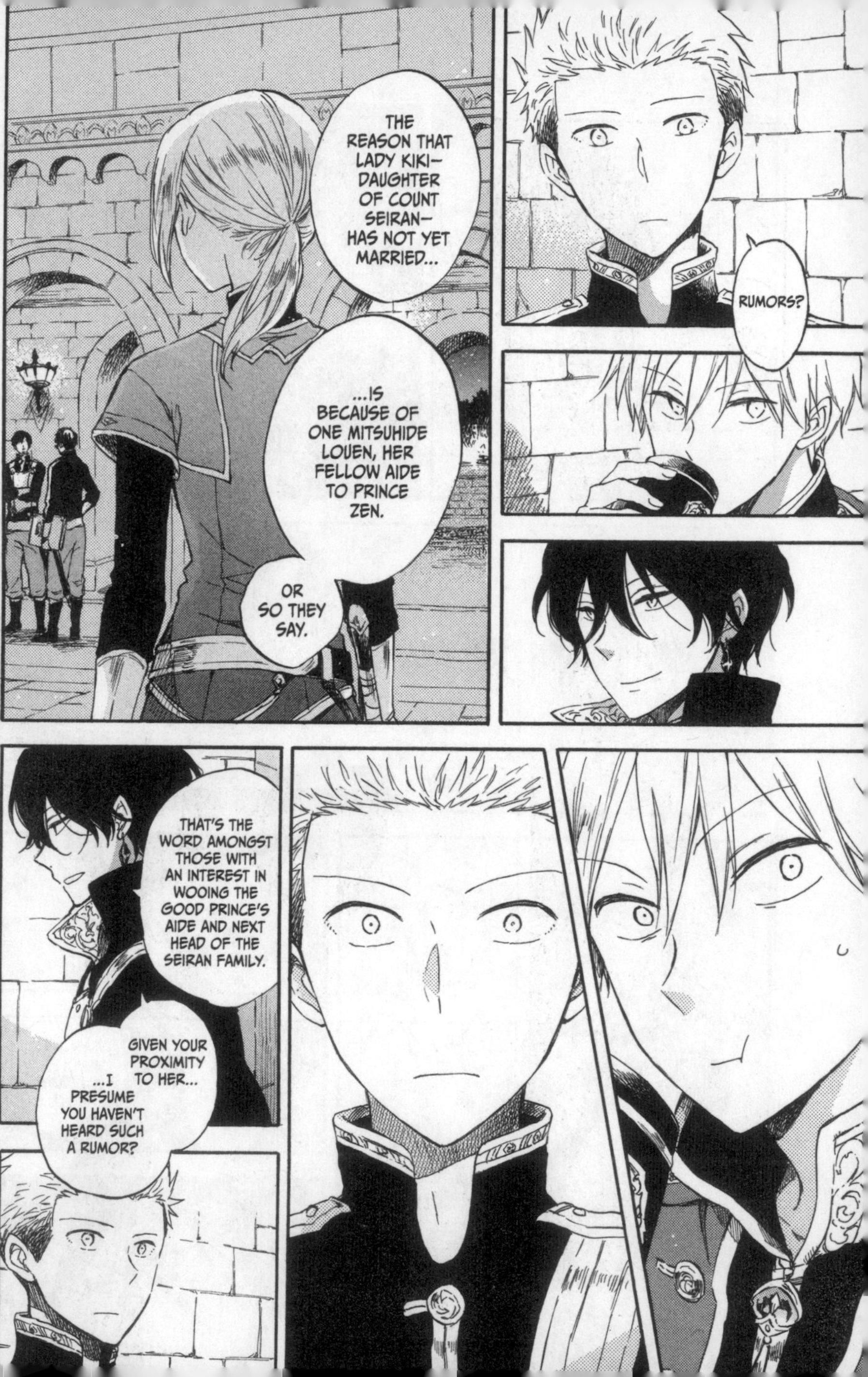
RUMORS?
THE REASON THAT LADY KIKI—DAUGHTER OF COUNT SEIRAN—HAS NOT YET MARRIED...
...IS BECAUSE OF ONE MITSUHIDE LOUEN, HER FELLOW AIDE TO PRINCE ZEN.
OR SO THEY SAY.
THAT'S THE WORD AMONGST THOSE WITH AN INTEREST IN WOOING THE GOOD PRINCE'S AIDE AND NEXT HEAD OF THE SEIRAN FAMILY.
GIVEN YOUR PROXIMITY TO HER...
...I PRESUME YOU HAVEN'T HEARD SUCH A RUMOR?

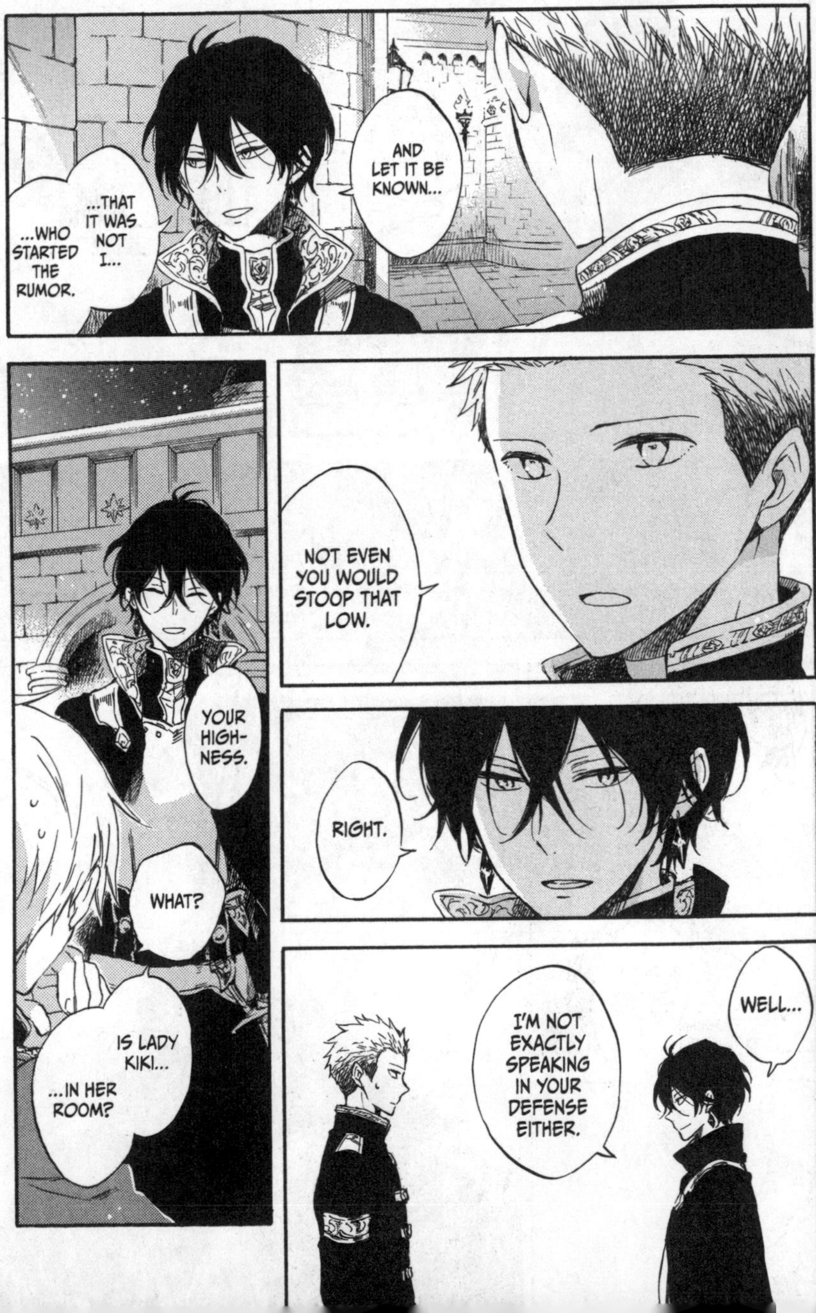
AND LET IT BE KNOWN...
...THAT IT WAS NOT I...
...WHO STARTED THE RUMOR.
NOT EVEN YOU WOULD STOOP THAT LOW.
RIGHT.
WELL...
I'M NOT EXACTLY SPEAKING IN YOUR DEFENSE EITHER.
YOUR HIGHNESS.
WHAT?
IS LADY KIKI...
...IN HER ROOM?

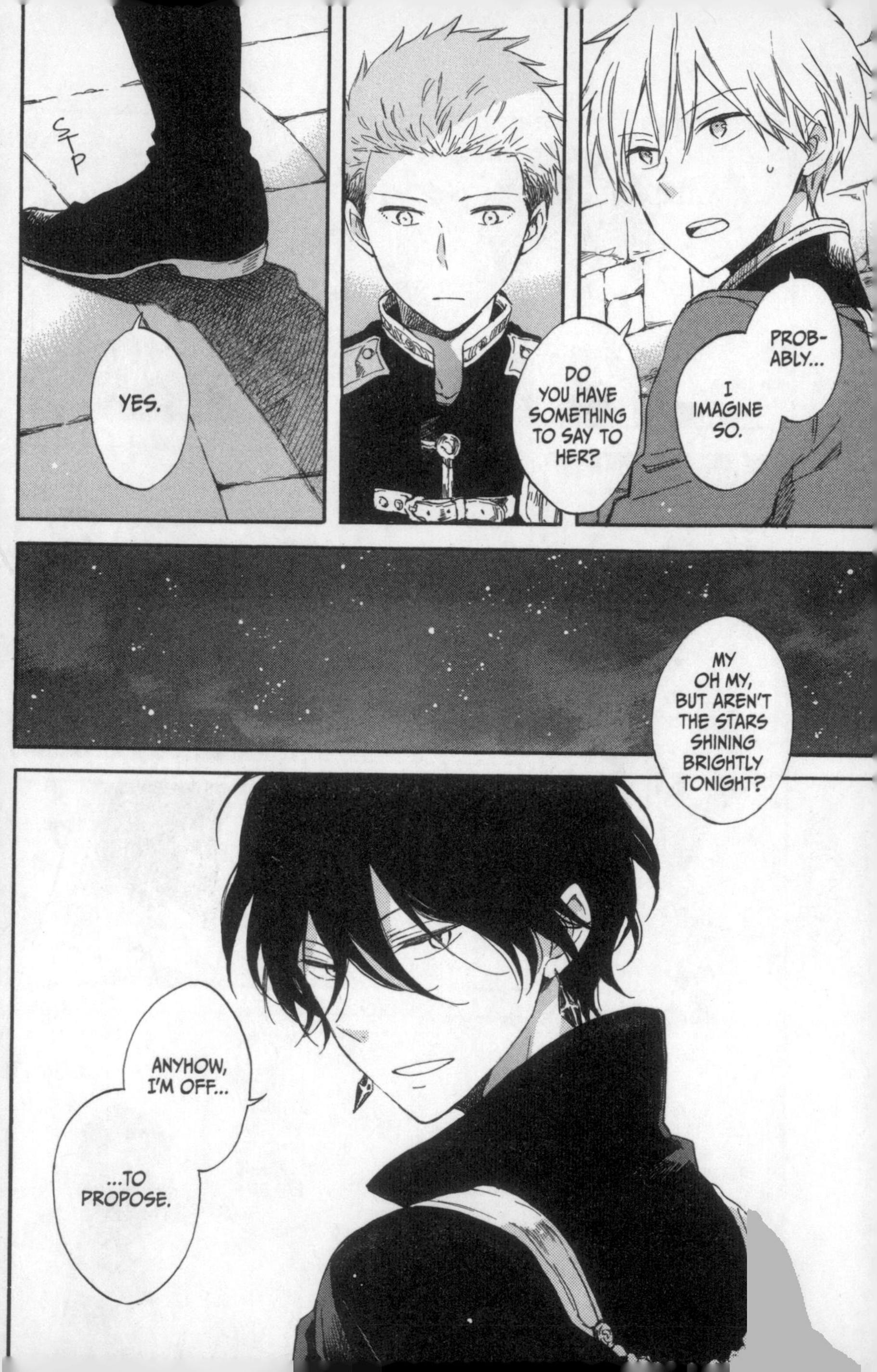
PROB-ABLY...
I IMAGINE SO.
DO YOU HAVE SOMETHING TO SAY TO HER?
STP
YES.
MY OH MY, BUT AREN'T THE STARS SHINING BRIGHTLY TONIGHT?
ANYHOW, I'M OFF...
...TO PROPOSE.

Chapter 77

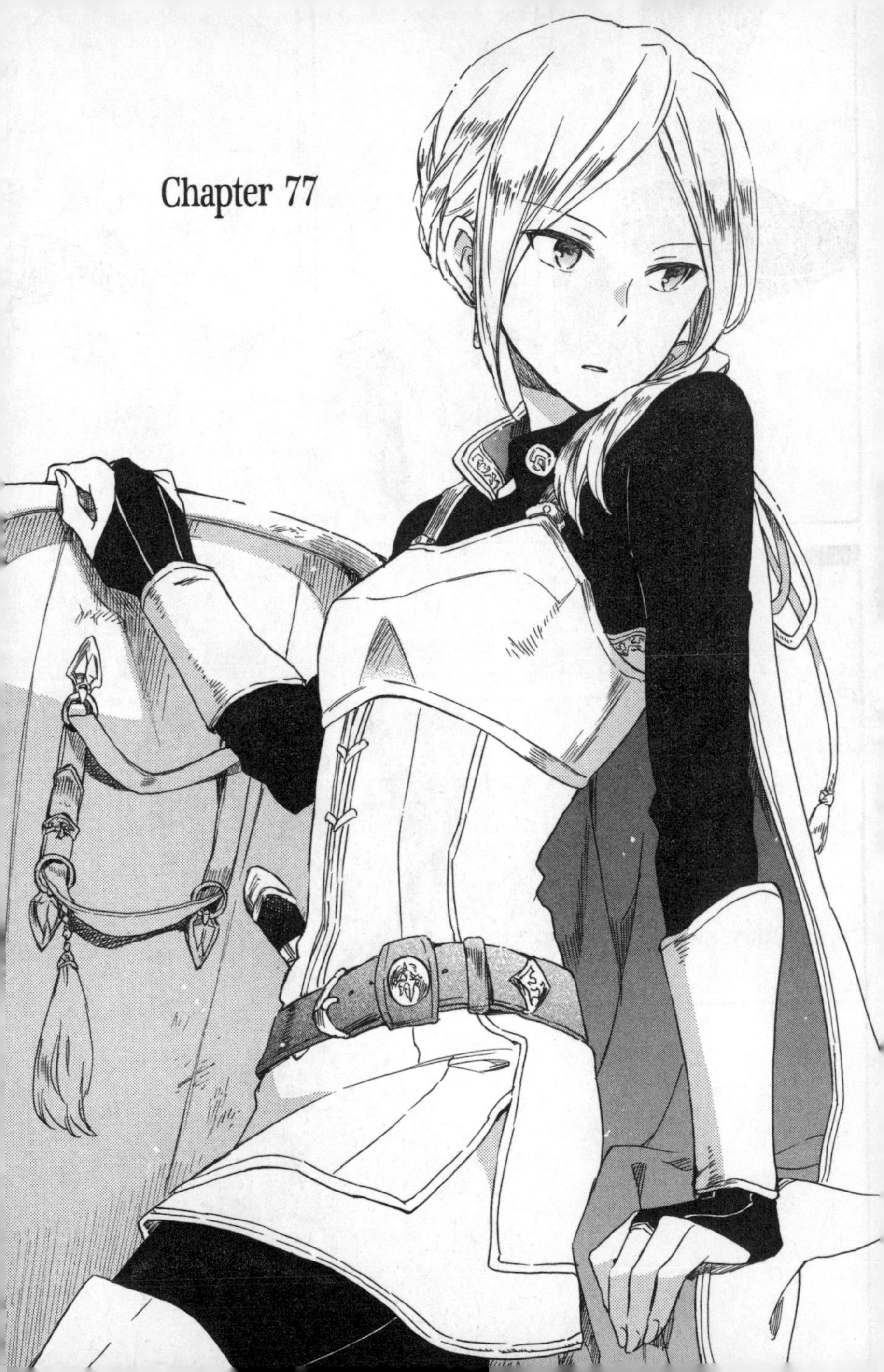

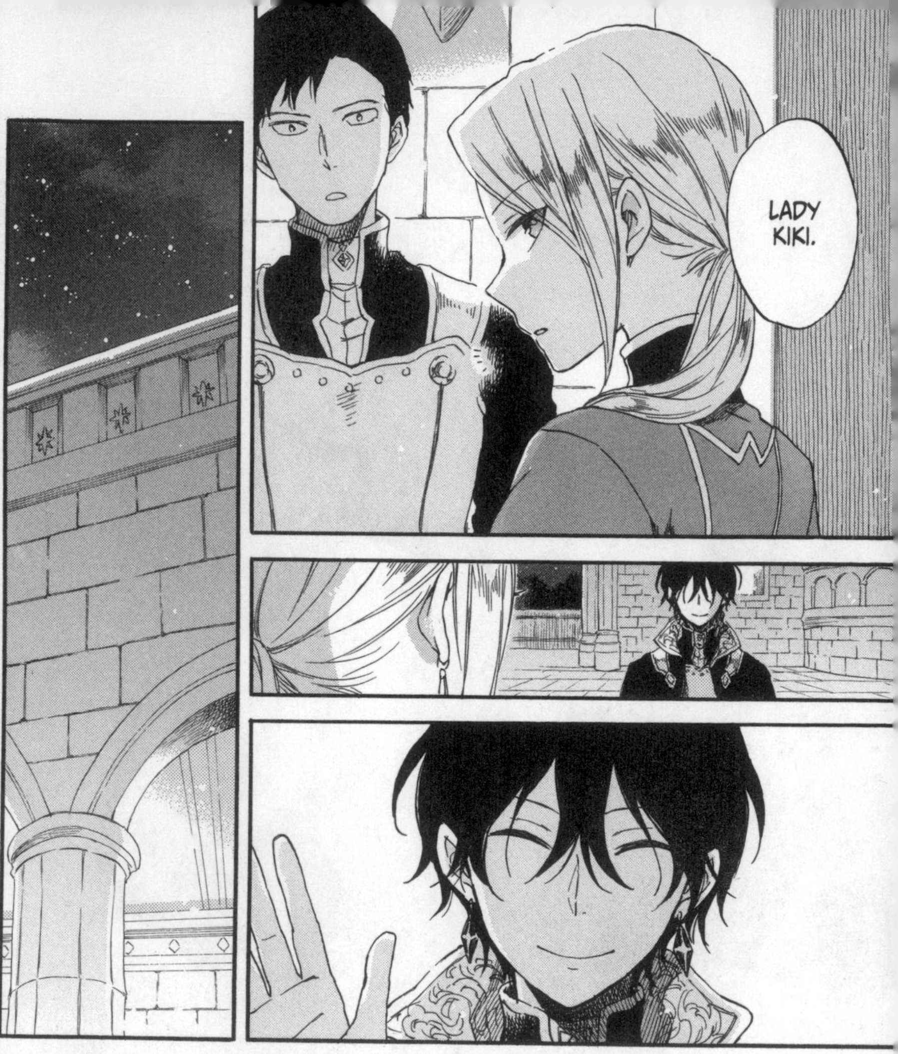
LADY KIKI.

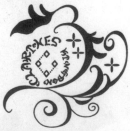

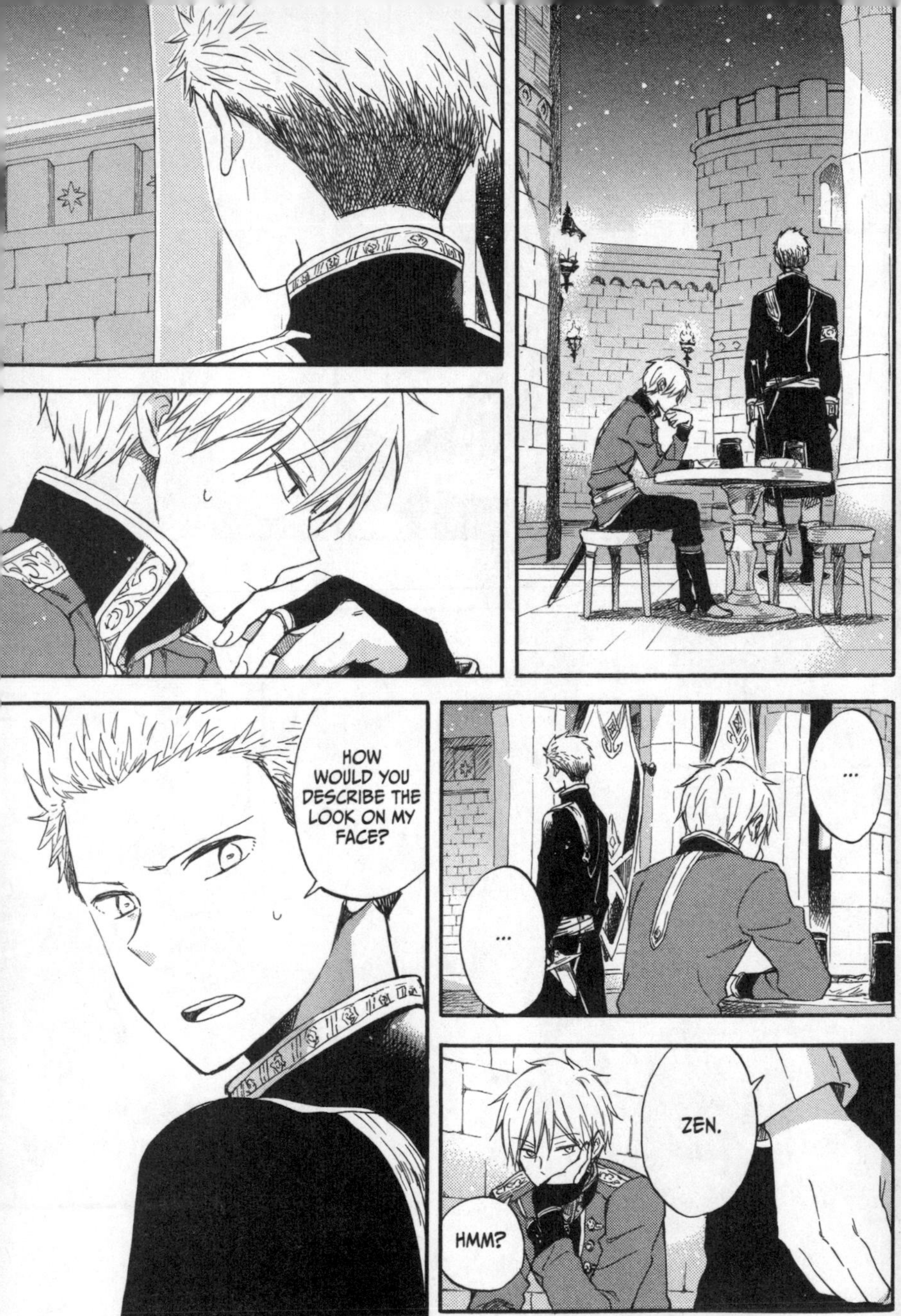
...
...
ZEN.
HMM?
HOW WOULD YOU DESCRIBE THE LOOK ON MY FACE?

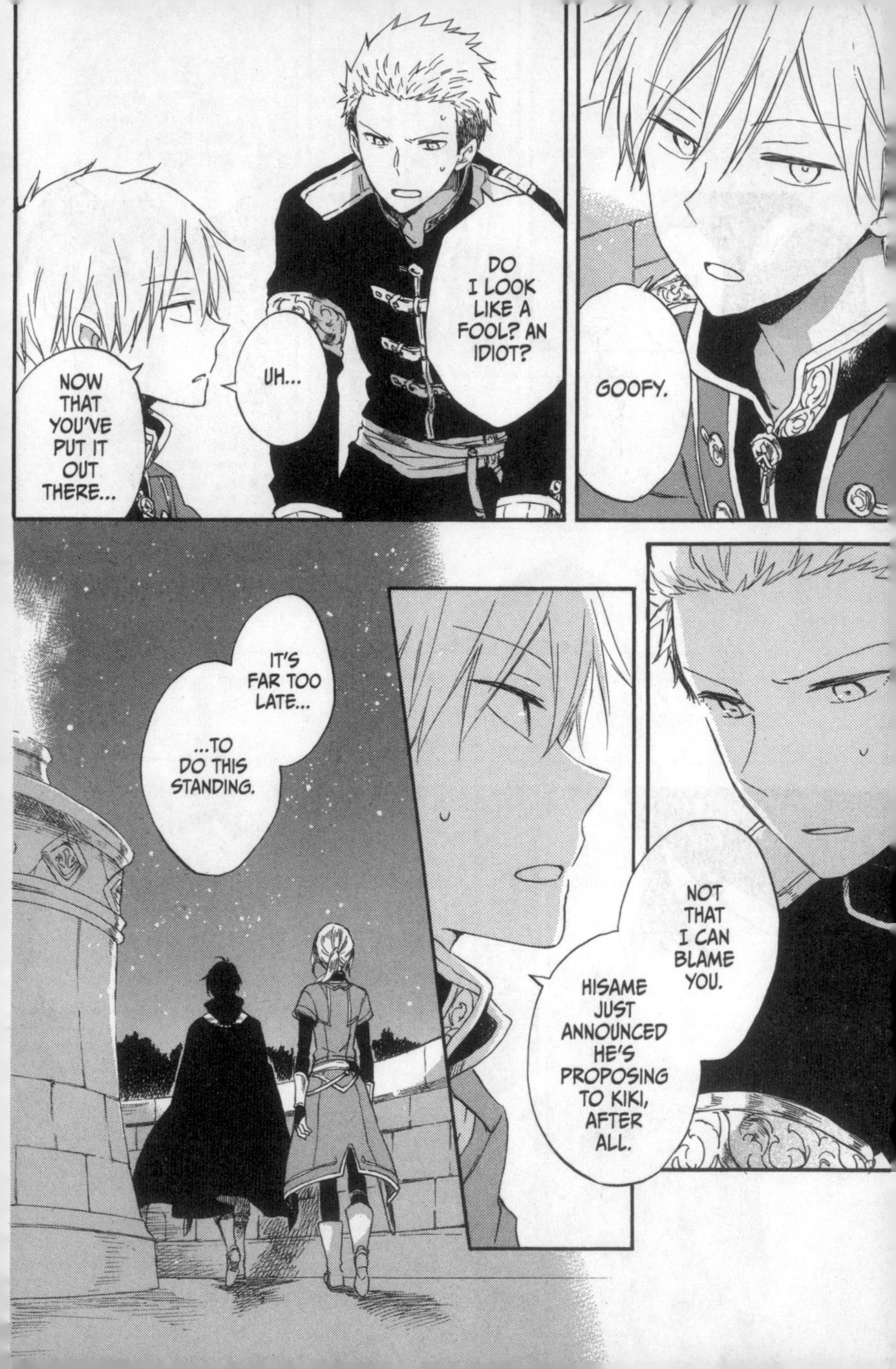
GOOFY.
DO I LOOK LIKE A FOOL? AN IDIOT?
UH...
NOW THAT YOU'VE PUT IT OUT THERE...
NOT THAT I CAN BLAME YOU.
HISAME JUST ANNOUNCED HE'S PROPOSING TO KIKI, AFTER ALL.
IT'S FAR TOO LATE...
...TO DO THIS STANDING.

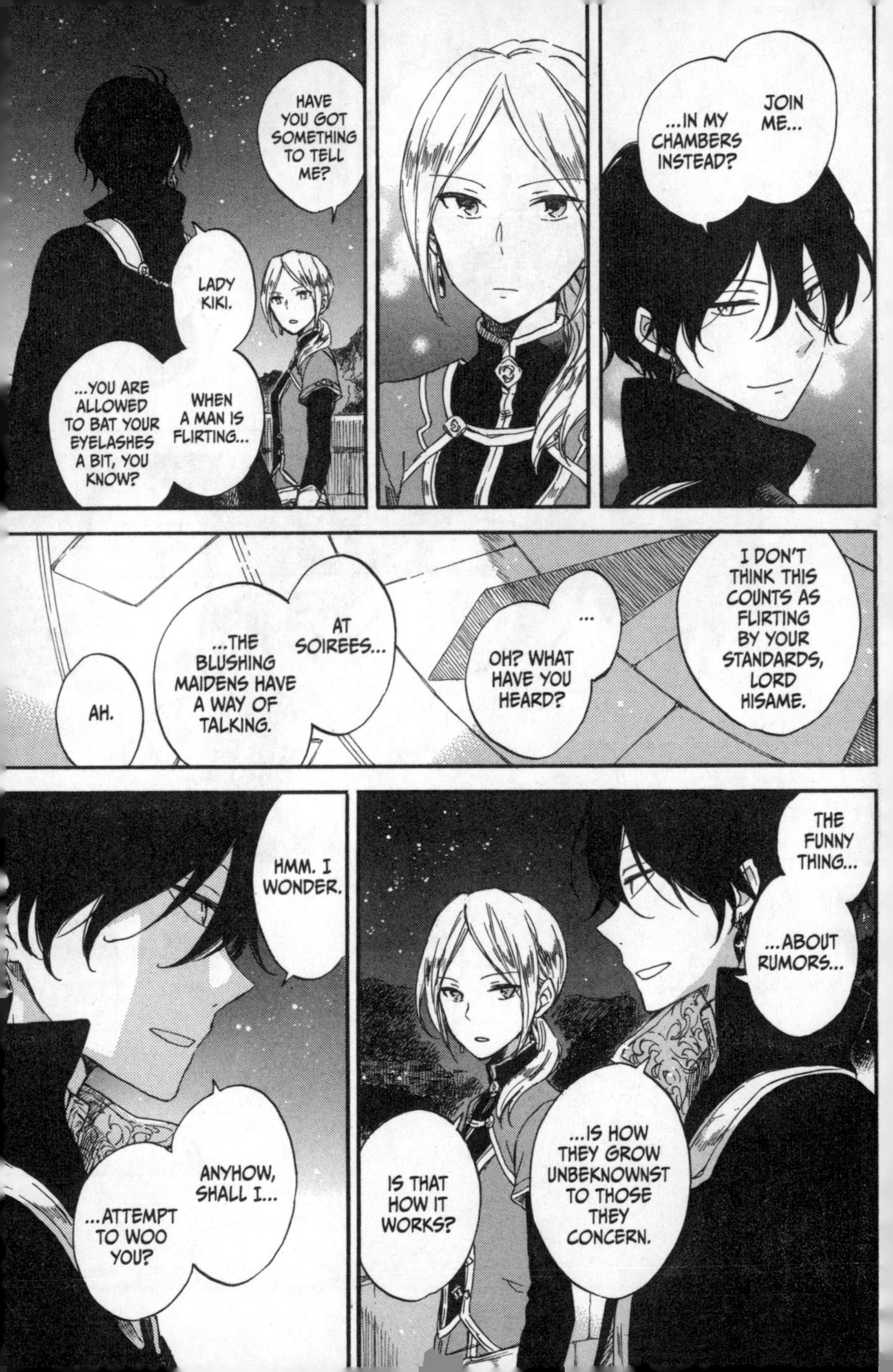
JOIN ME...
...IN MY CHAMBERS INSTEAD?
HAVE YOU GOT SOMETHING TO TELL ME?
LADY KIKI.
WHEN A MAN IS FLIRTING...
...YOU ARE ALLOWED TO BAT YOUR EYELASHES A BIT, YOU KNOW?
I DON'T THINK THIS COUNTS AS FLIRTING BY YOUR STANDARDS, LORD HISAME.
...
OH? WHAT HAVE YOU HEARD?
AT SOIREES...
...THE BLUSHING MAIDENS HAVE A WAY OF TALKING.
AH.
THE FUNNY THING...
...ABOUT RUMORS...
...IS HOW THEY GROW UNBEKNOWNST TO THOSE THEY CONCERN.
IS THAT HOW IT WORKS?
HMM. I WONDER.
ANYHOW, SHALL I...
...ATTEMPT TO WOO YOU?

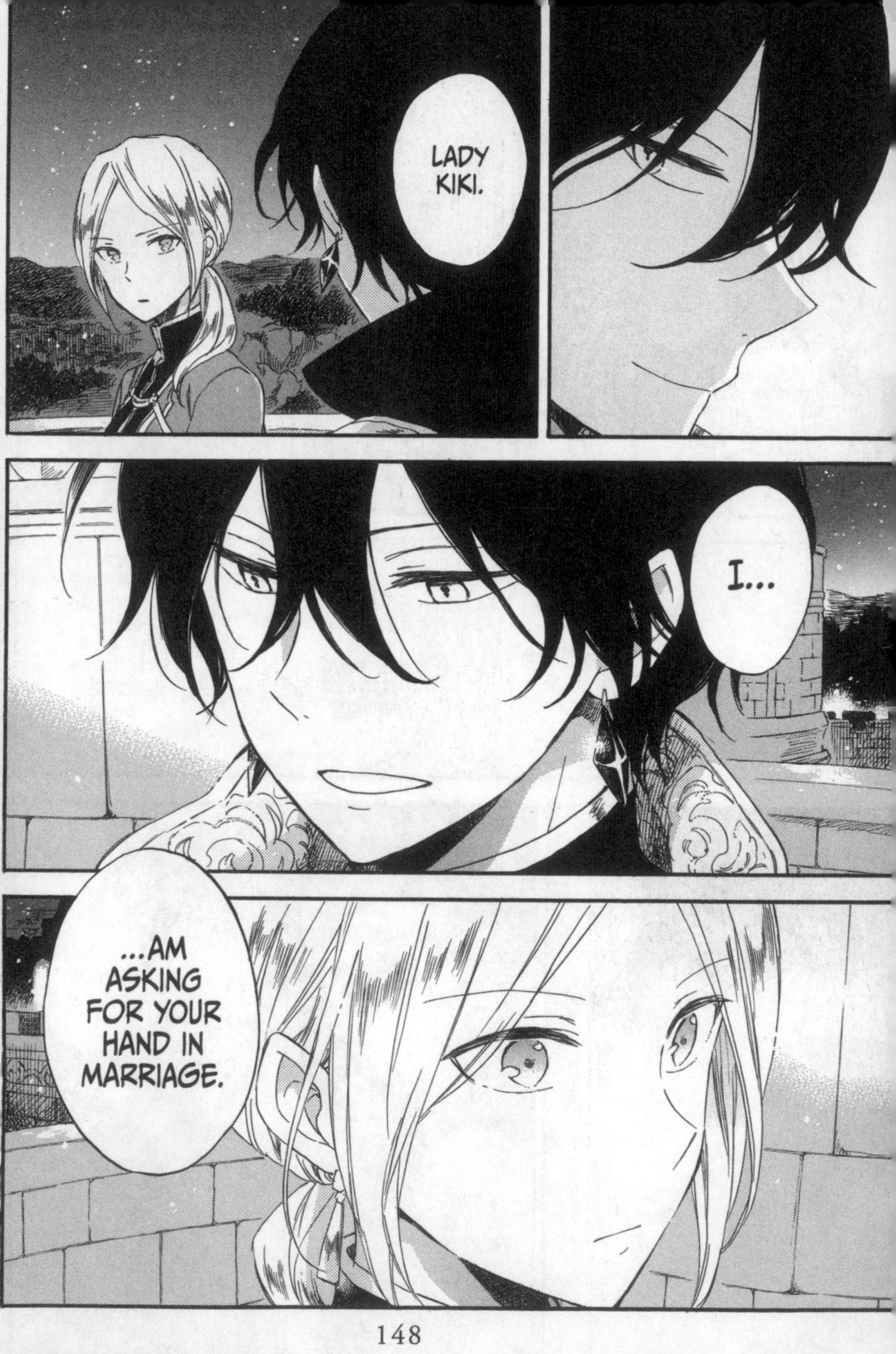
LADY KIKI.
I...
...AM ASKING FOR YOUR HAND IN MARRIAGE.

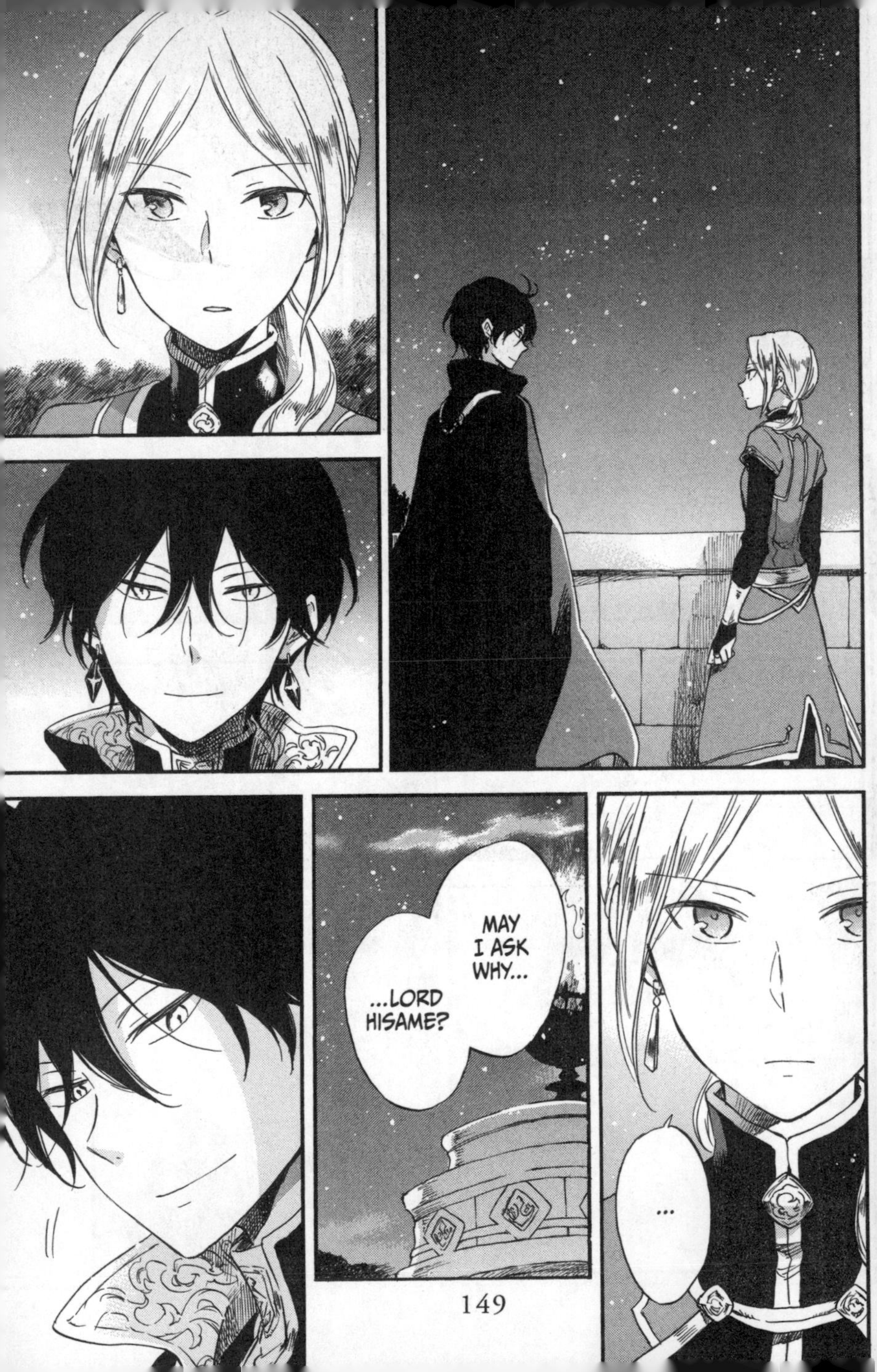
...
MAY I ASK WHY...
...LORD HISAME?

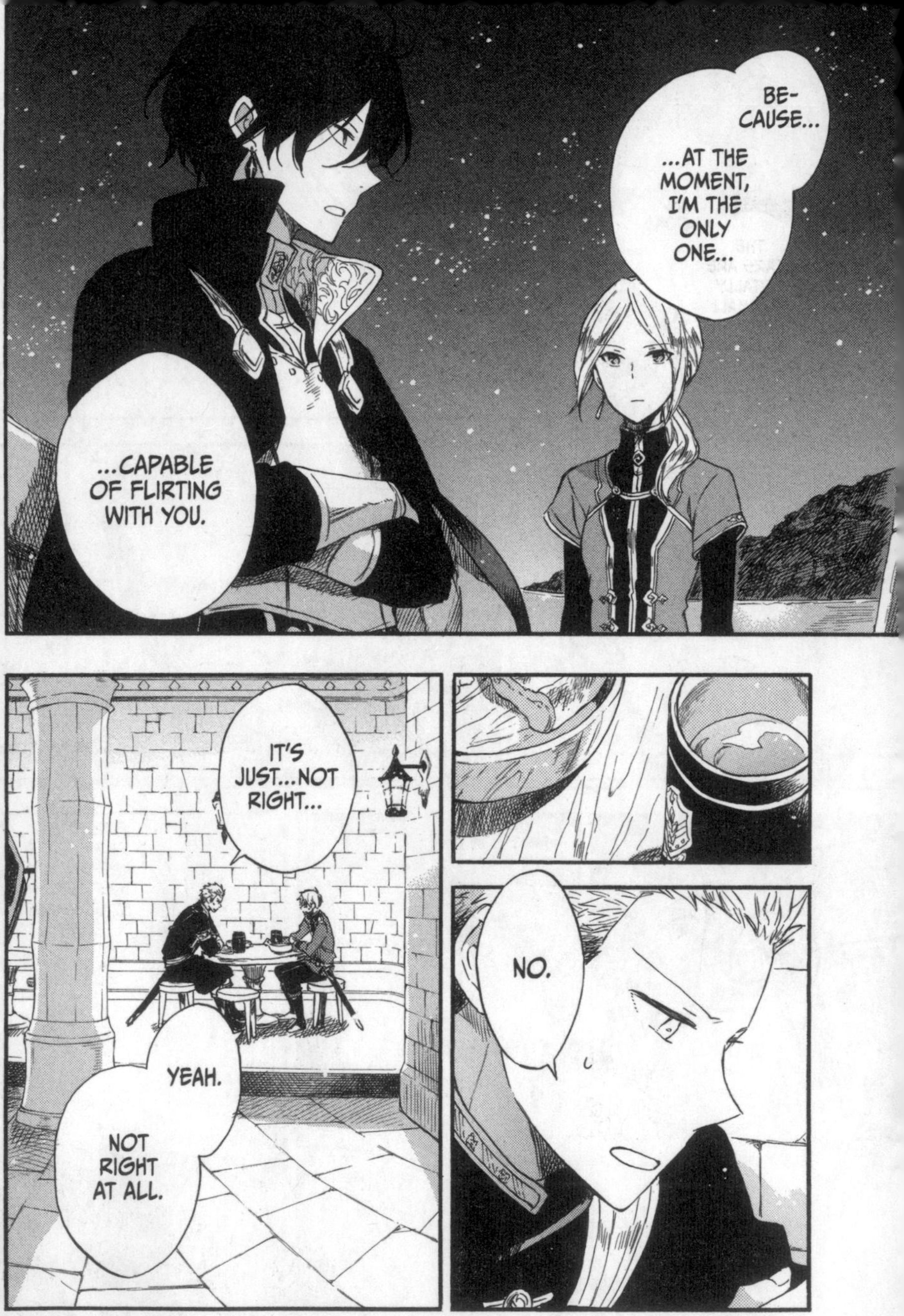
BE-
CAUSE...
...AT THE MOMENT, I'M THE ONLY ONE...
...CAPABLE OF FLIRTING WITH YOU.
NO.
IT'S JUST...NOT RIGHT...
YEAH.
NOT RIGHT AT ALL.

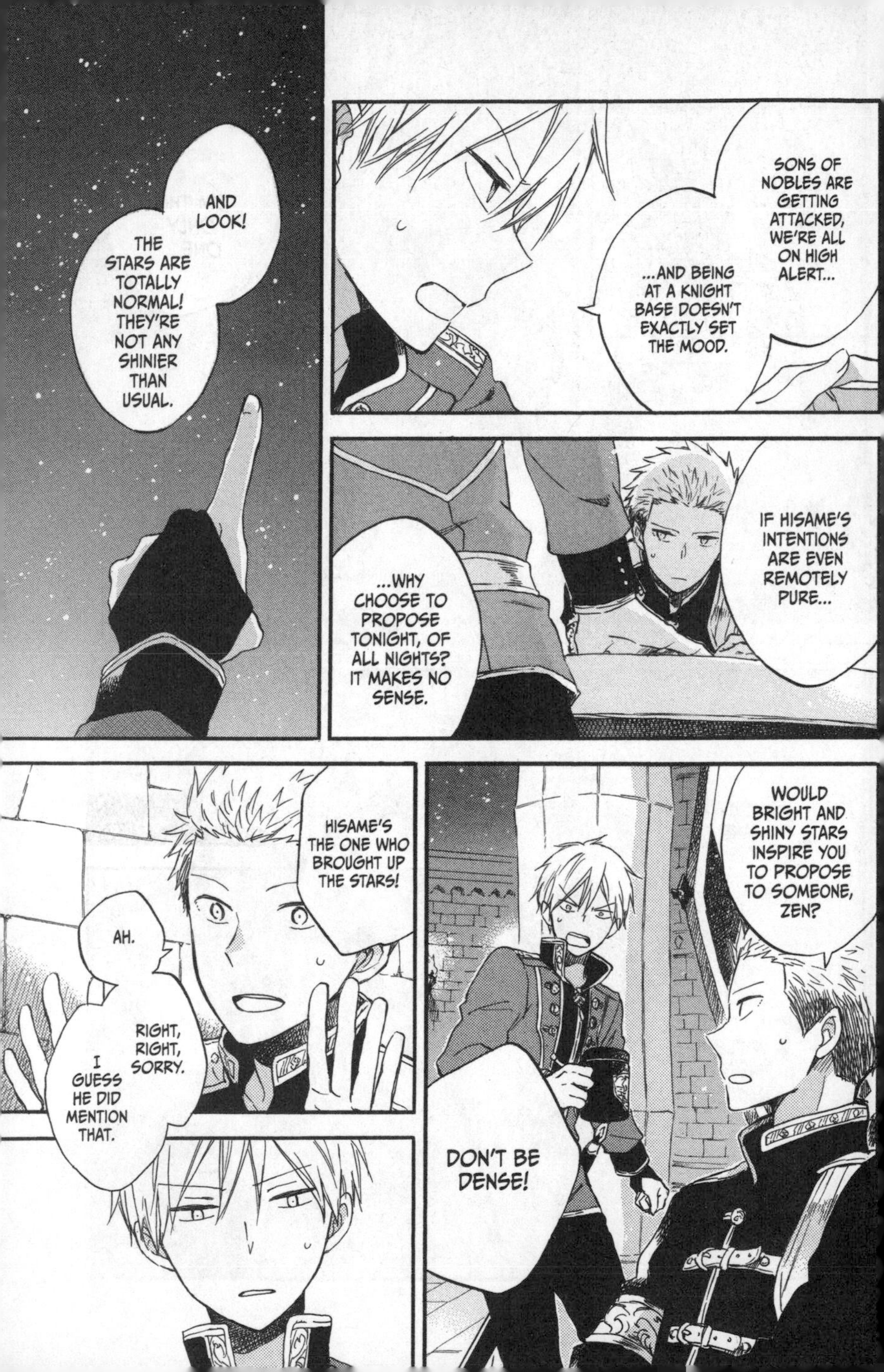
SONS OF NOBLES ARE GETTING ATTACKED, WE'RE ALL ON HIGH ALERT...
...AND BEING AT A KNIGHT BASE DOESN'T EXACTLY SET THE MOOD.
IF HISAME'S INTENTIONS ARE EVEN REMOTELY PURE...
...WHY CHOOSE TO PROPOSE TONIGHT, OF ALL NIGHTS? IT MAKES NO SENSE.
AND LOOK!
THE STARS ARE TOTALLY NORMAL! THEY'RE NOT ANY SHINIER THAN USUAL.
WOULD BRIGHT AND SHINY STARS INSPIRE YOU TO PROPOSE TO SOMEONE, ZEN?
DON'T BE DENSE!
HISAME'S THE ONE WHO BROUGHT UP THE STARS!
AH.
RIGHT, RIGHT, SORRY.
I GUESS HE DID MENTION THAT.

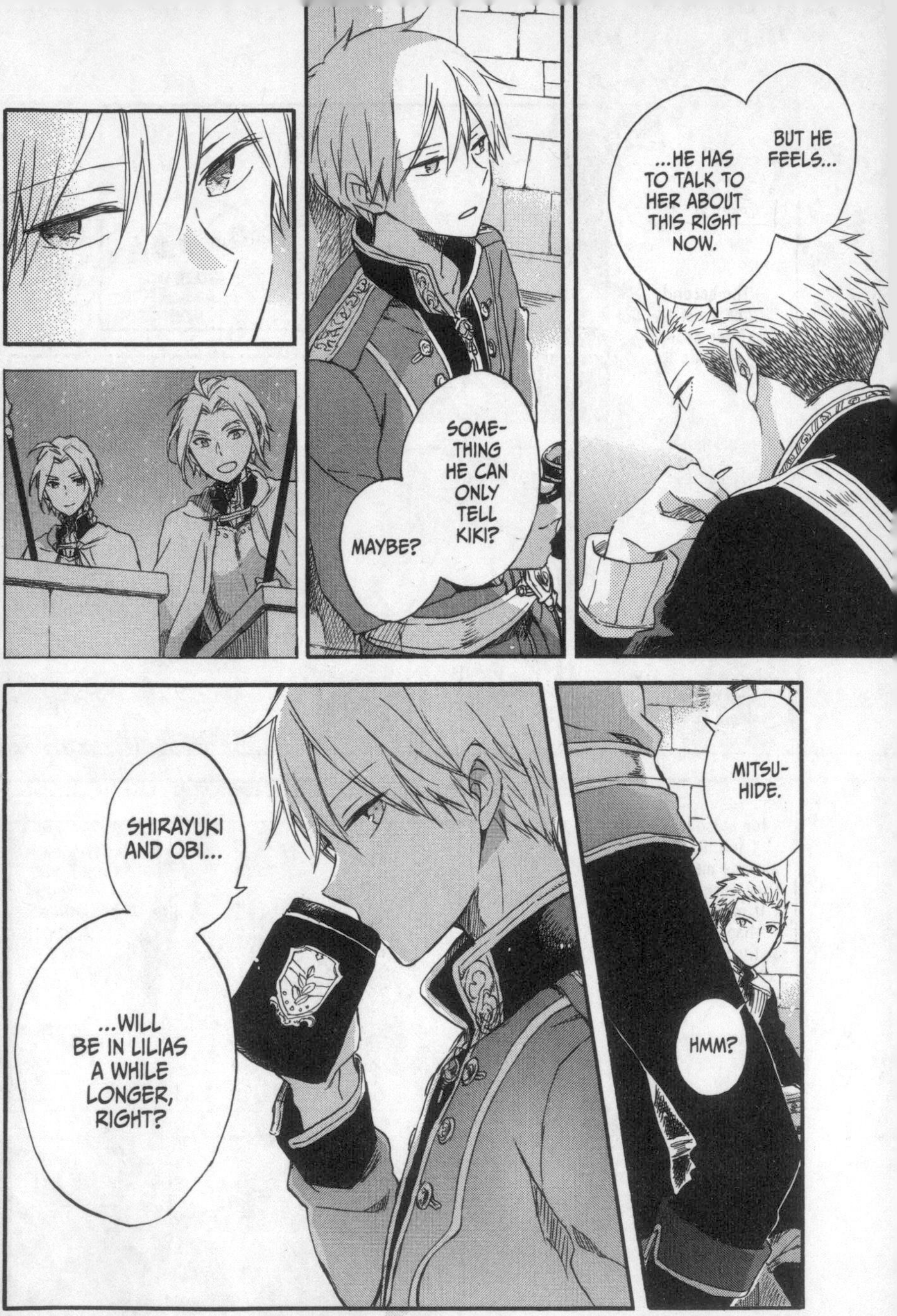
BUT HE FEELS...
...HE HAS TO TALK TO HER ABOUT THIS RIGHT NOW.
SOME-THING HE CAN ONLY TELL KIKI?
MAYBE?
MITSU-HIDE.
HMM?
SHIRAYUKI AND OBI...
...WILL BE IN LILIAS A WHILE LONGER, RIGHT?

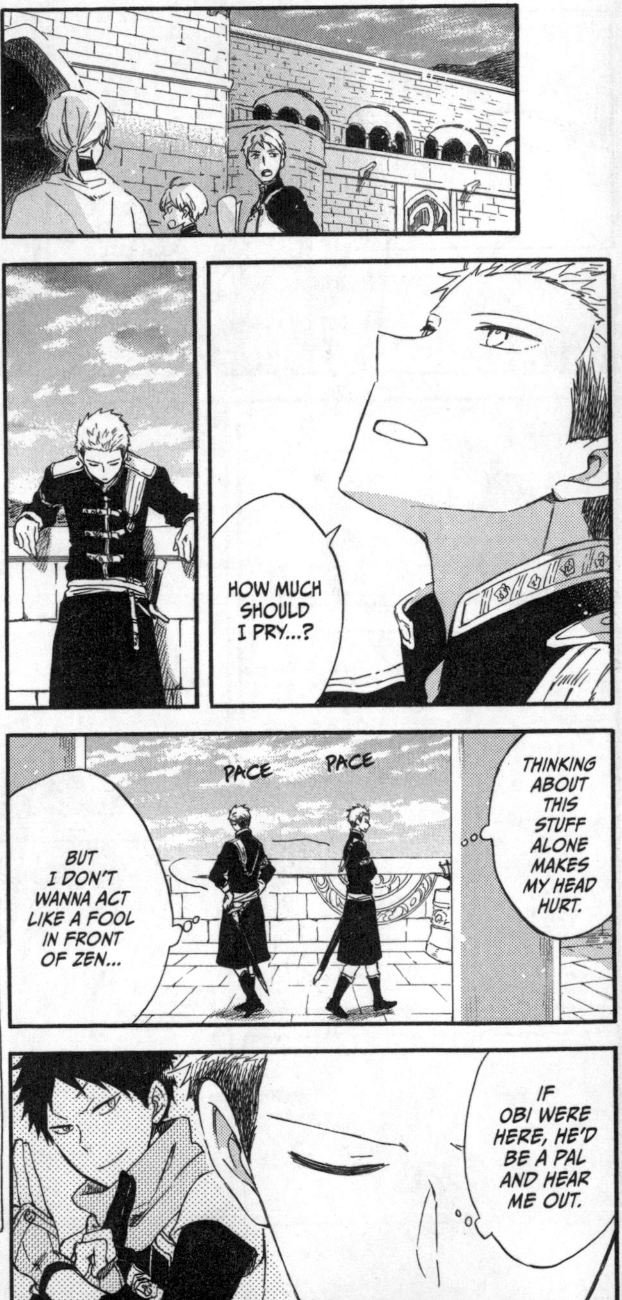
HOW MUCH SHOULD I PRY...?
THINKING ABOUT THIS STUFF ALONE MAKES MY HEAD HURT.
PACE
PACE
BUT I DON'T WANNA ACT LIKE A FOOL IN FRONT OF ZEN...
IF OBI WERE HERE, HE'D BE A PAL AND HEAR ME OUT.

5

RECORDING STUDIO (PART 3)

The final one!

The second time I visited was for season 2, episode 16.

This sidebar is about that time!

It was right after I'd finished watching all of season 1, so the feeling was less, "Wow, that's how Shirayuki and friends sound!" and more like, "Here's Shirayuki and friends, talking right in front of me."

So when they started recording for episode 16, I felt like I'd already met them. They were familiar. It made me so happy to be there for the recording of the last episode.

I got to talk with everyone one-on-one for just a little bit, and by the time it was over, I already missed them so much.

It was a ton of fun though!

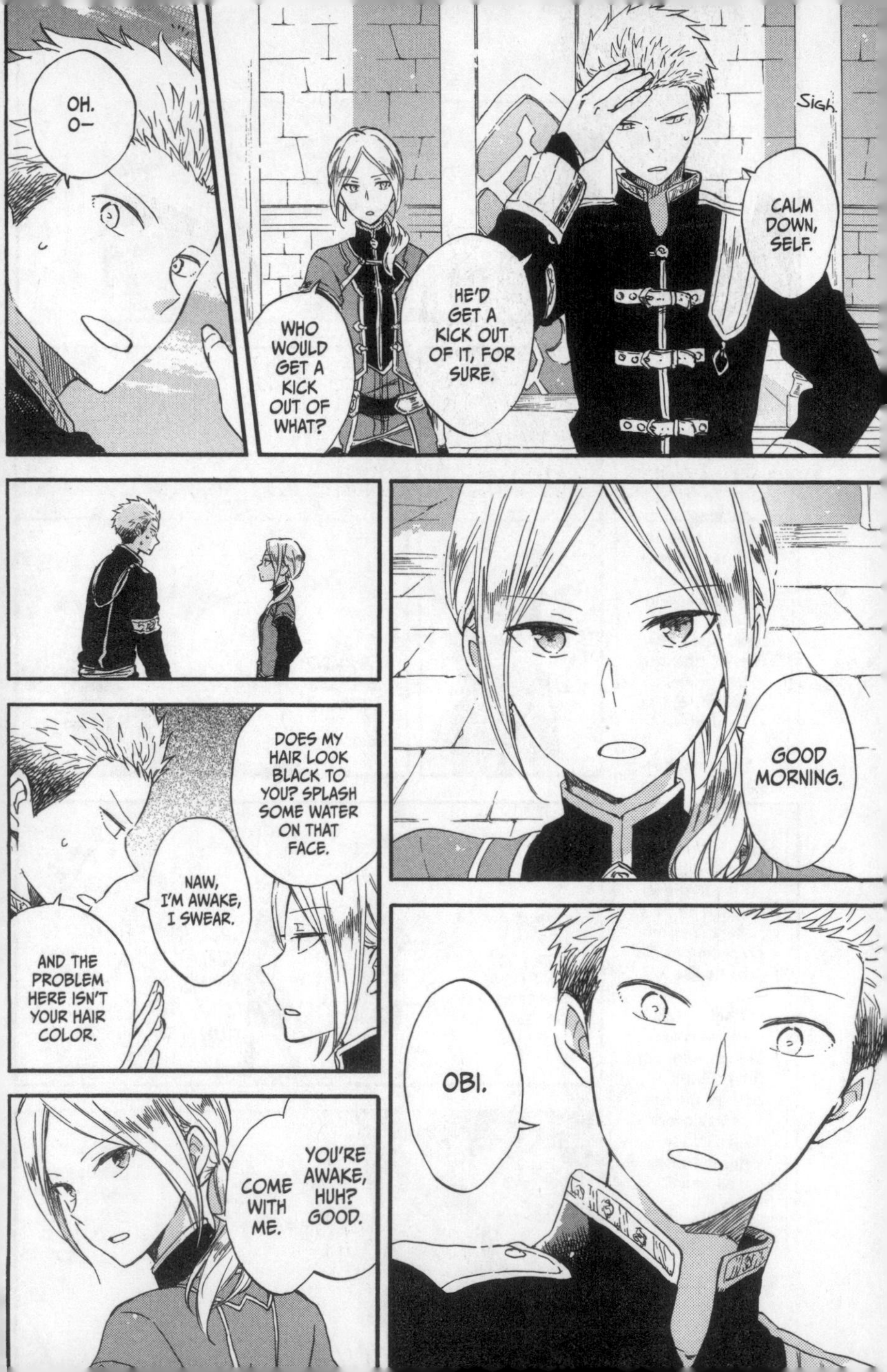
Sigh.
CALM DOWN, SELF.
HE'D GET A KICK OUT OF IT, FOR SURE.
WHO WOULD GET A KICK OUT OF WHAT?
OH. O—
GOOD MORNING.
OBI.
DOES MY HAIR LOOK BLACK TO YOU? SPLASH SOME WATER ON THAT FACE.
NAW, I'M AWAKE, I SWEAR.
AND THE PROBLEM HERE ISN'T YOUR HAIR COLOR.
YOU'RE AWAKE, HUH? GOOD.
COME WITH ME.

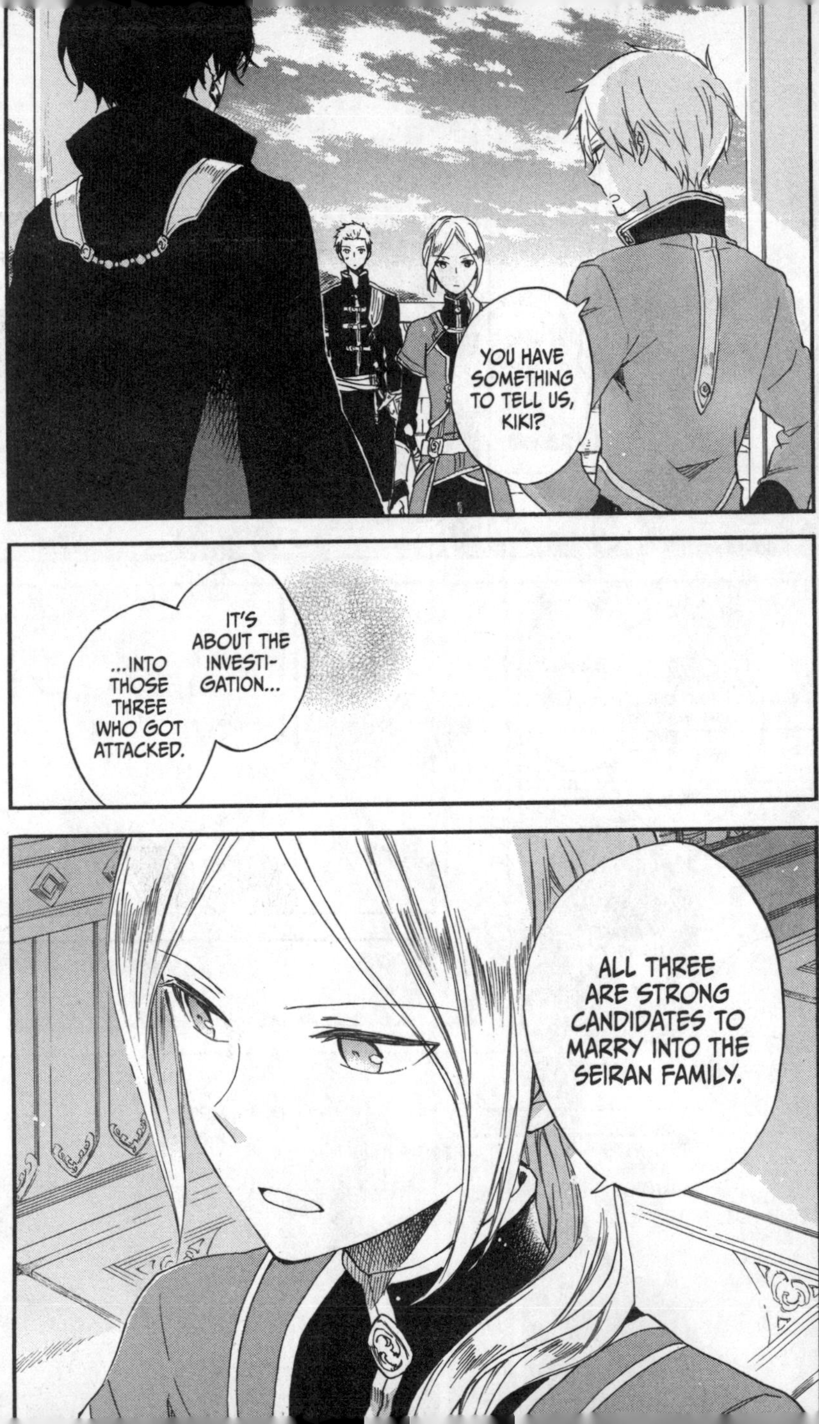
YOU HAVE SOMETHING TO TELL US, KIKI?
IT'S ABOUT THE INVESTI-GATION...
...INTO THOSE THREE WHO GOT ATTACKED.
ALL THREE ARE STRONG CANDIDATES TO MARRY INTO THE SEIRAN FAMILY.

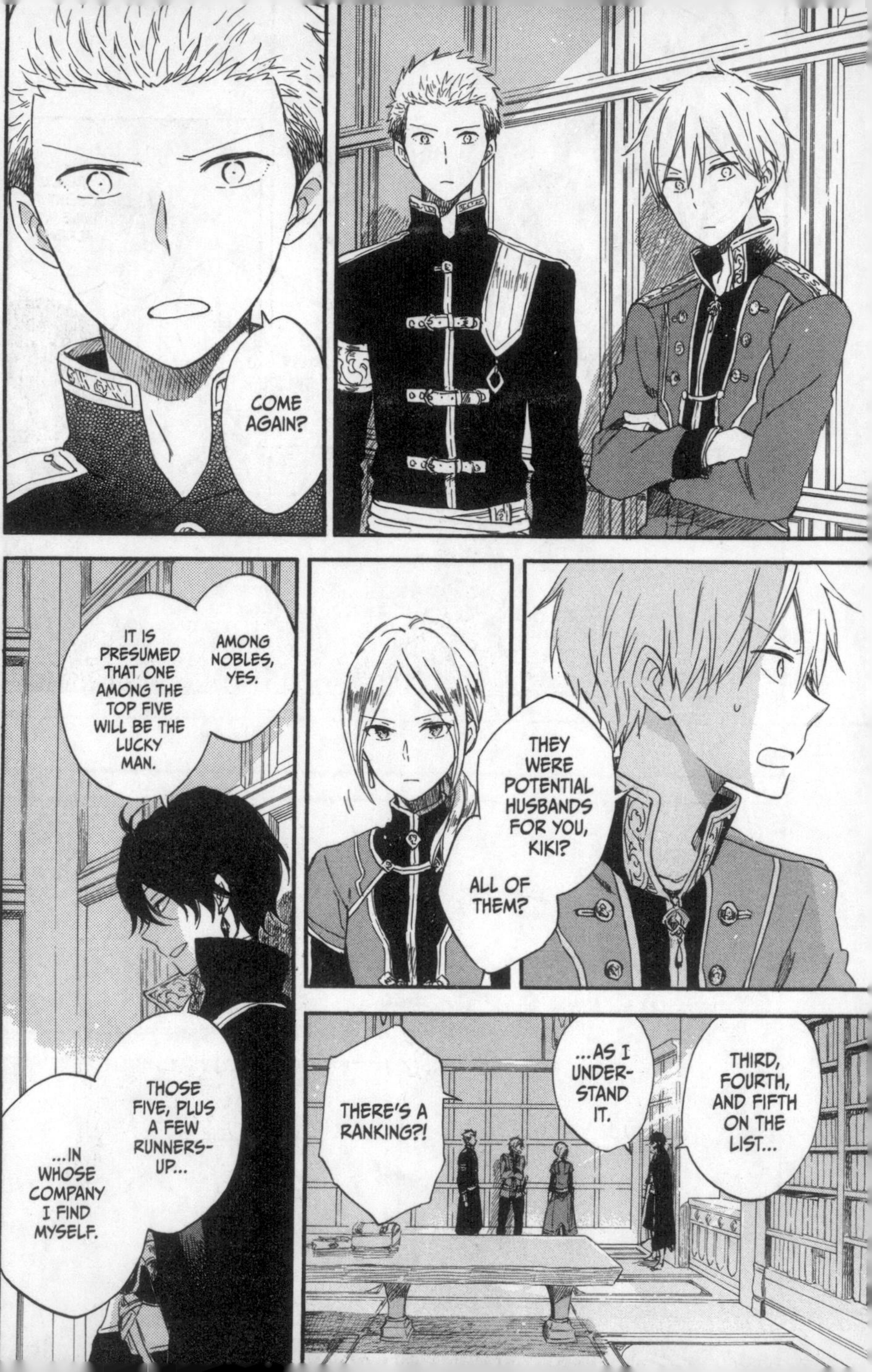
COME AGAIN?
THEY WERE POTENTIAL HUSBANDS FOR YOU, KIKI?
ALL OF THEM?
THIRD, FOURTH, AND FIFTH ON THE LIST...
...AS I UNDER-STAND IT.
THERE'S A RANKING?!
AMONG NOBLES, YES.
IT IS PRESUMED THAT ONE AMONG THE TOP FIVE WILL BE THE LUCKY MAN.
THOSE FIVE, PLUS A FEW RUNNERS-UP...
...IN WHOSE COMPANY I FIND MYSELF.

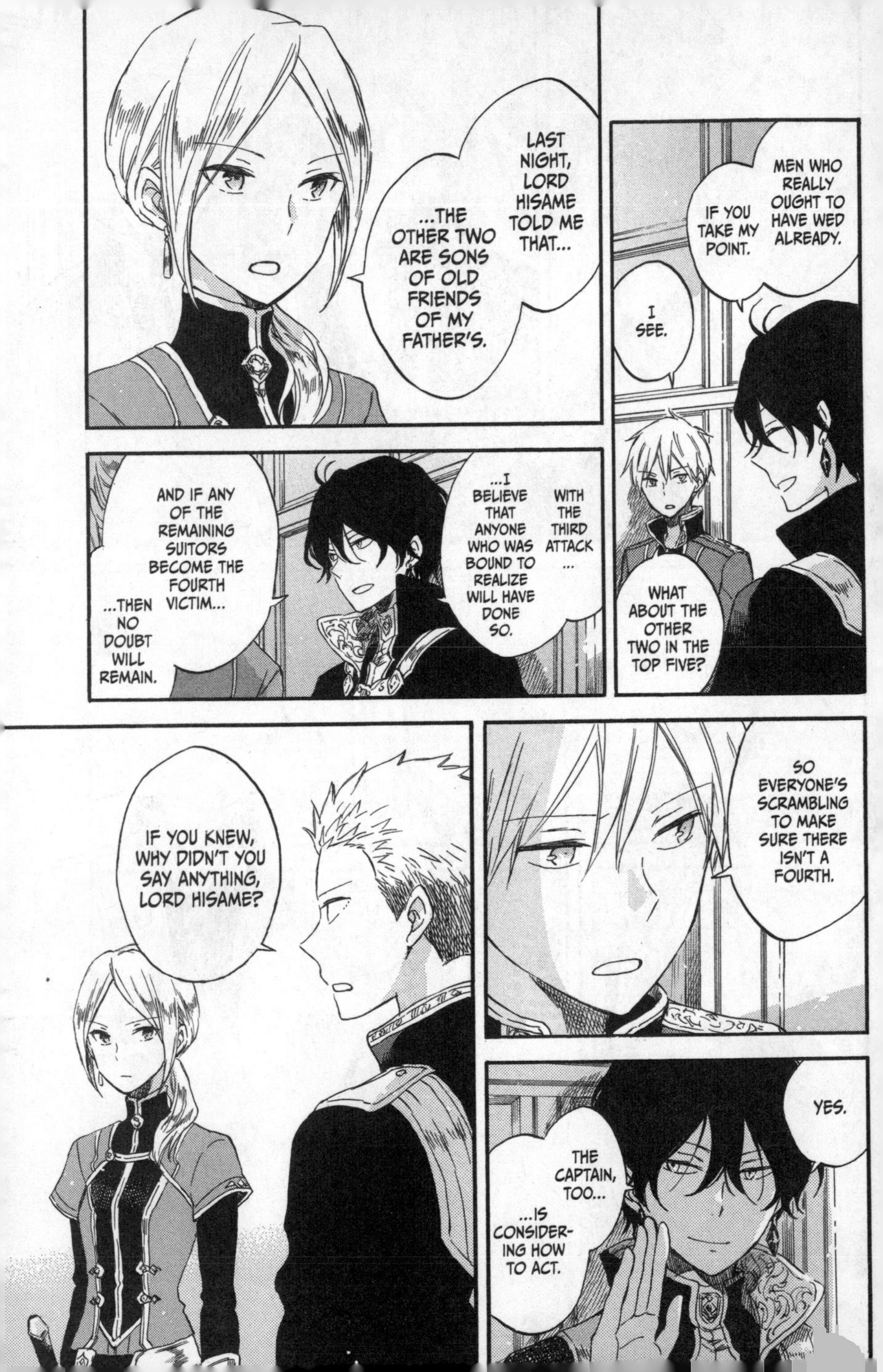
MEN WHO REALLY OUGHT TO HAVE WED ALREADY.
IF YOU TAKE MY POINT.
I SEE.
WHAT ABOUT THE OTHER TWO IN THE TOP FIVE?
LAST NIGHT, LORD HISAME TOLD ME THAT...
...THE OTHER TWO ARE SONS OF OLD FRIENDS OF MY FATHER'S.
WITH THE THIRD ATTACK...
...I BELIEVE THAT ANYONE WHO WAS BOUND TO REALIZE WILL HAVE DONE SO.
AND IF ANY OF THE REMAINING SUITORS BECOME THE FOURTH VICTIM...
...THEN NO DOUBT WILL REMAIN.
SO EVERYONE'S SCRAMBLING TO MAKE SURE THERE ISN'T A FOURTH.
YES.
THE CAPTAIN, TOO...
...IS CONSIDERING HOW TO ACT.
IF YOU KNEW, WHY DIDN'T YOU SAY ANYTHING, LORD HISAME?

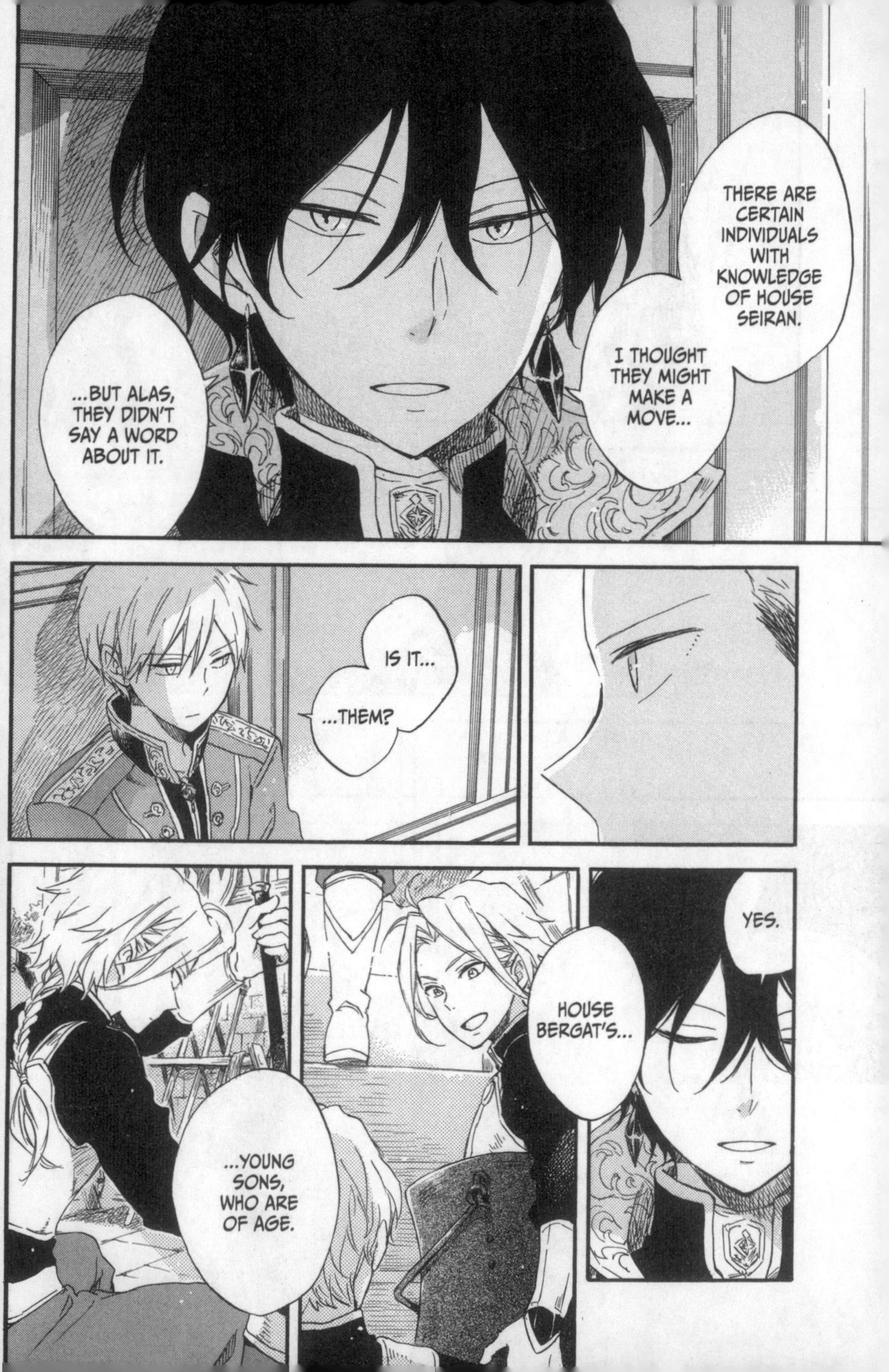
THERE ARE CERTAIN INDIVIDUALS WITH KNOWLEDGE OF HOUSE SEIRAN.
I THOUGHT THEY MIGHT MAKE A MOVE...
...BUT ALAS, THEY DIDN'T SAY A WORD ABOUT IT.
IS IT...
...THEM?
YES.
HOUSE BERGAT'S...
...YOUNG SONS, WHO ARE OF AGE.

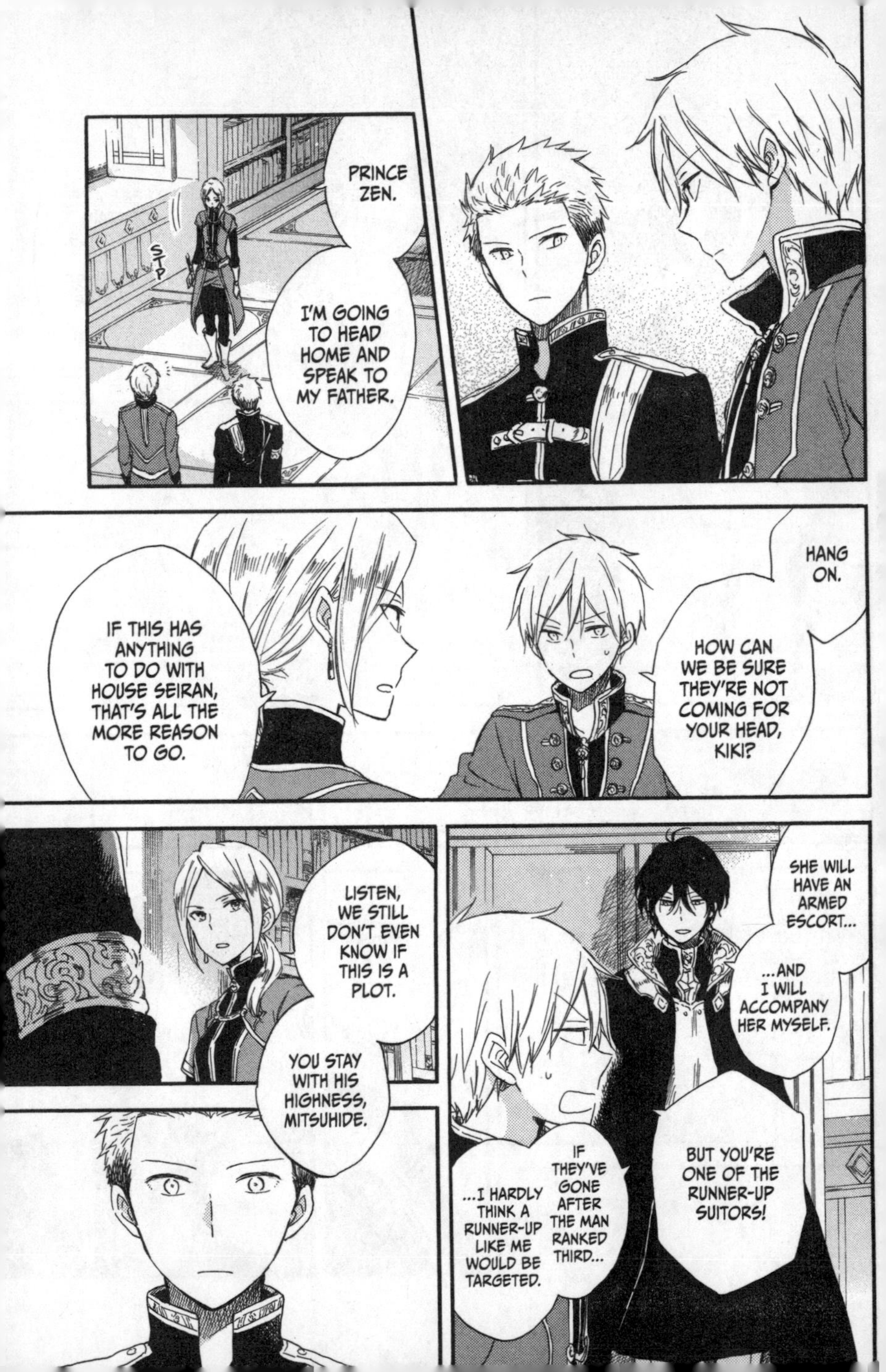
STP
PRINCE ZEN.
I'M GOING TO HEAD HOME AND SPEAK TO MY FATHER.
HANG ON.
HOW CAN WE BE SURE THEY'RE NOT COMING FOR YOUR HEAD, KIKI?
IF THIS HAS ANYTHING TO DO WITH HOUSE SEIRAN, THAT'S ALL THE MORE REASON TO GO.
SHE WILL HAVE AN ARMED ESCORT...
...AND I WILL ACCOMPANY HER MYSELF.
BUT YOU'RE ONE OF THE RUNNER-UP SUITORS!
IF THEY'VE GONE AFTER THE MAN RANKED THIRD...
...I HARDLY THINK A RUNNER-UP LIKE ME WOULD BE TARGETED.
LISTEN, WE STILL DON'T EVEN KNOW IF THIS IS A PLOT.
YOU STAY WITH HIS HIGHNESS, MITSUHIDE.

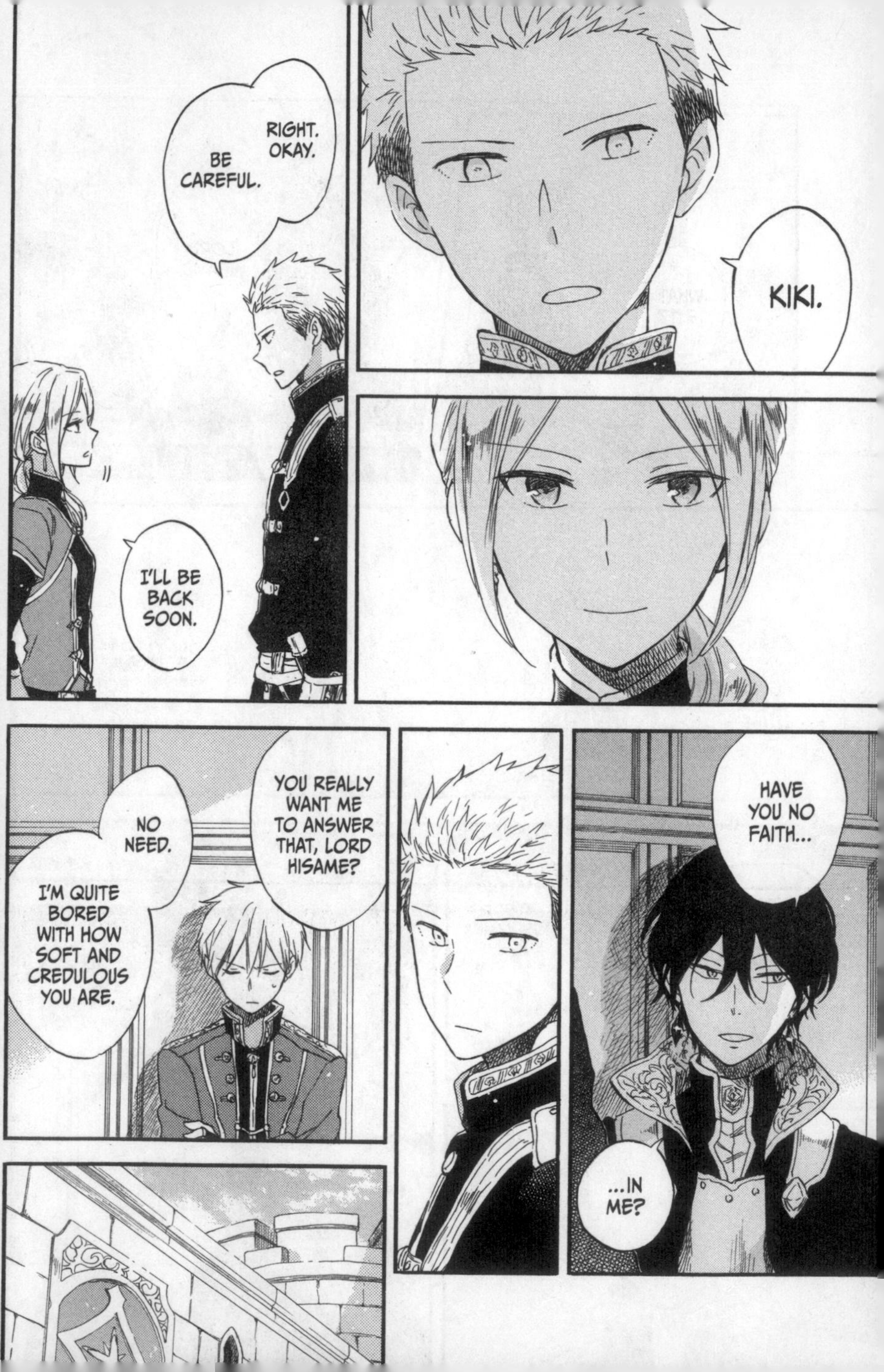
KIKI.
RIGHT. OKAY. BE CAREFUL.
I'LL BE BACK SOON.
HAVE YOU NO FAITH...
...IN ME?
YOU REALLY WANT ME TO ANSWER THAT, LORD HISAME?
NO NEED.
I'M QUITE BORED WITH HOW SOFT AND CREDULOUS YOU ARE.

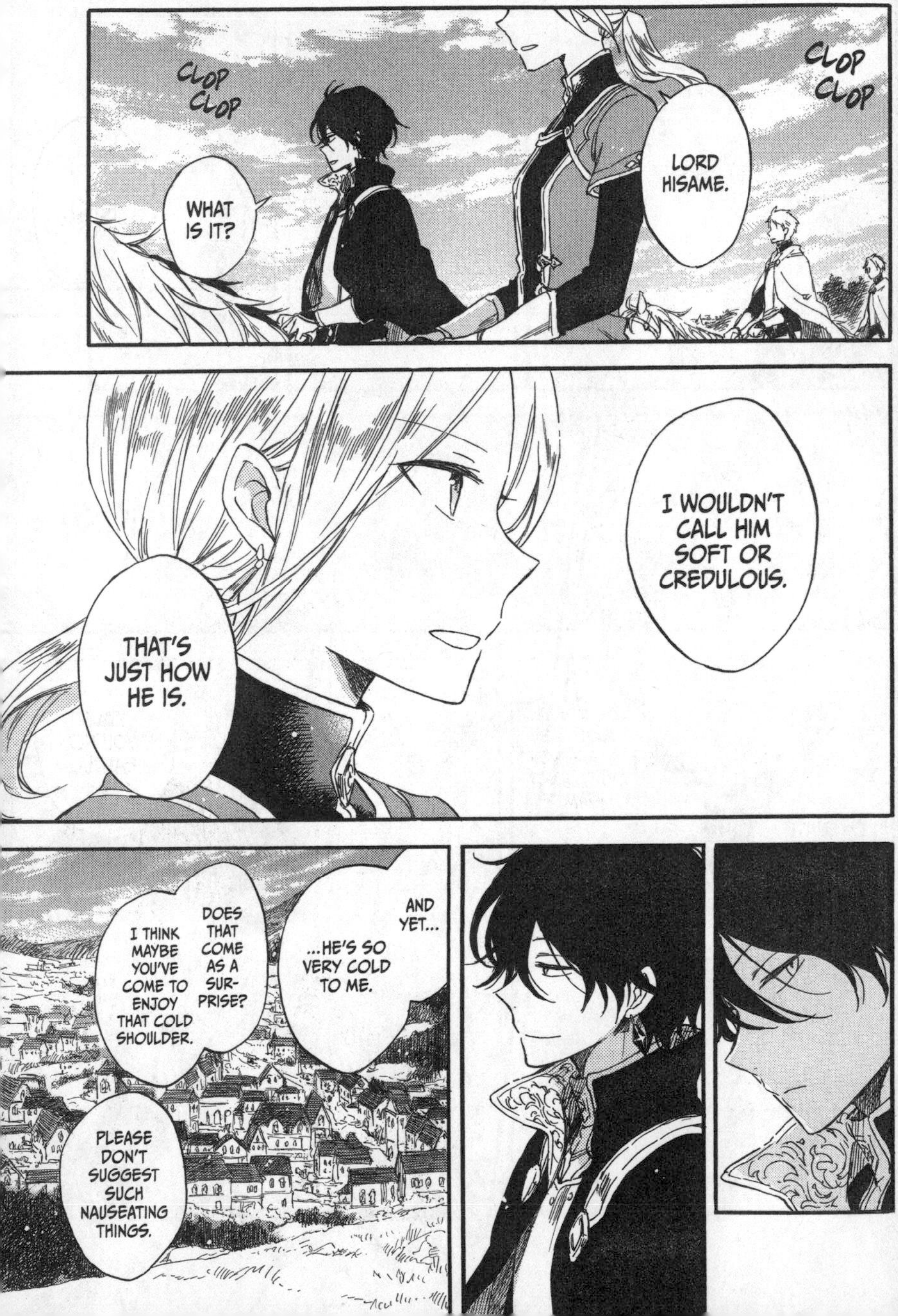
CLOP CLOP
LORD HISAME.
WHAT IS IT?
CLOP CLOP
I WOULDN'T CALL HIM SOFT OR CREDULOUS.
THAT'S JUST HOW HE IS.
AND YET...
...HE'S SO VERY COLD TO ME.
DOES THAT COME AS A SUR-PRISE?
I THINK MAYBE YOU'VE COME TO ENJOY THAT COLD SHOULDER.
PLEASE DON'T SUGGEST SUCH NAUSEATING THINGS.

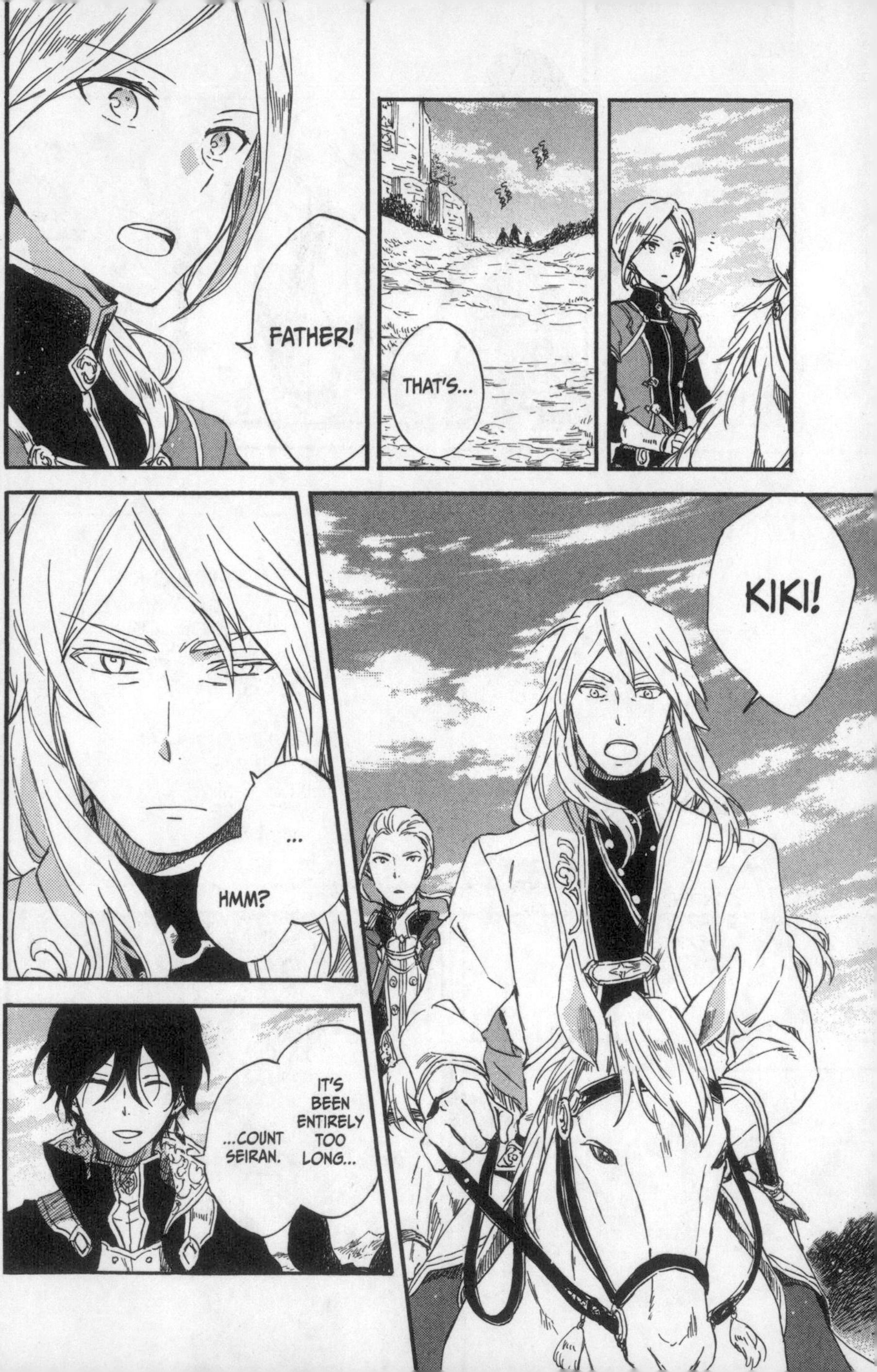
THAT'S...
FATHER!
KIKI!
...
HMM?
IT'S BEEN ENTIRELY TOO LONG...
...COUNT SEIRAN.

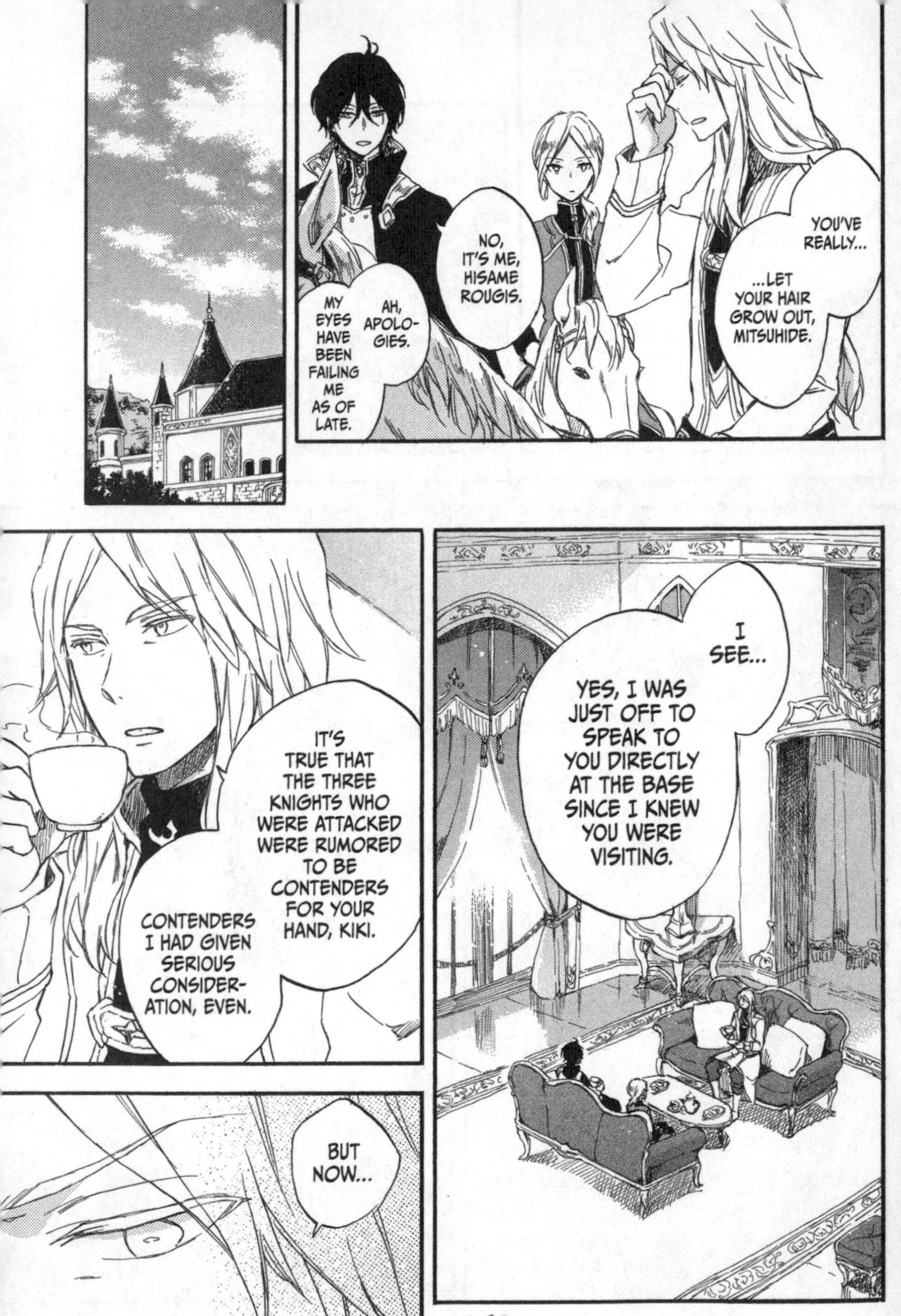
YOU'VE REALLY...
...LET YOUR HAIR GROW OUT, MITSUHIDE.
NO, IT'S ME, HISAME ROUGIS.
AH, APOLOGIES.
MY EYES HAVE BEEN FAILING ME AS OF LATE.
I SEE...
YES, I WAS JUST OFF TO SPEAK TO YOU DIRECTLY AT THE BASE SINCE I KNEW YOU WERE VISITING.
IT'S TRUE THAT THE THREE KNIGHTS WHO WERE ATTACKED WERE RUMORED TO BE CONTENDERS FOR YOUR HAND, KIKI.
CONTENDERS I HAD GIVEN SERIOUS CONSIDER-ATION, EVEN.
BUT NOW...

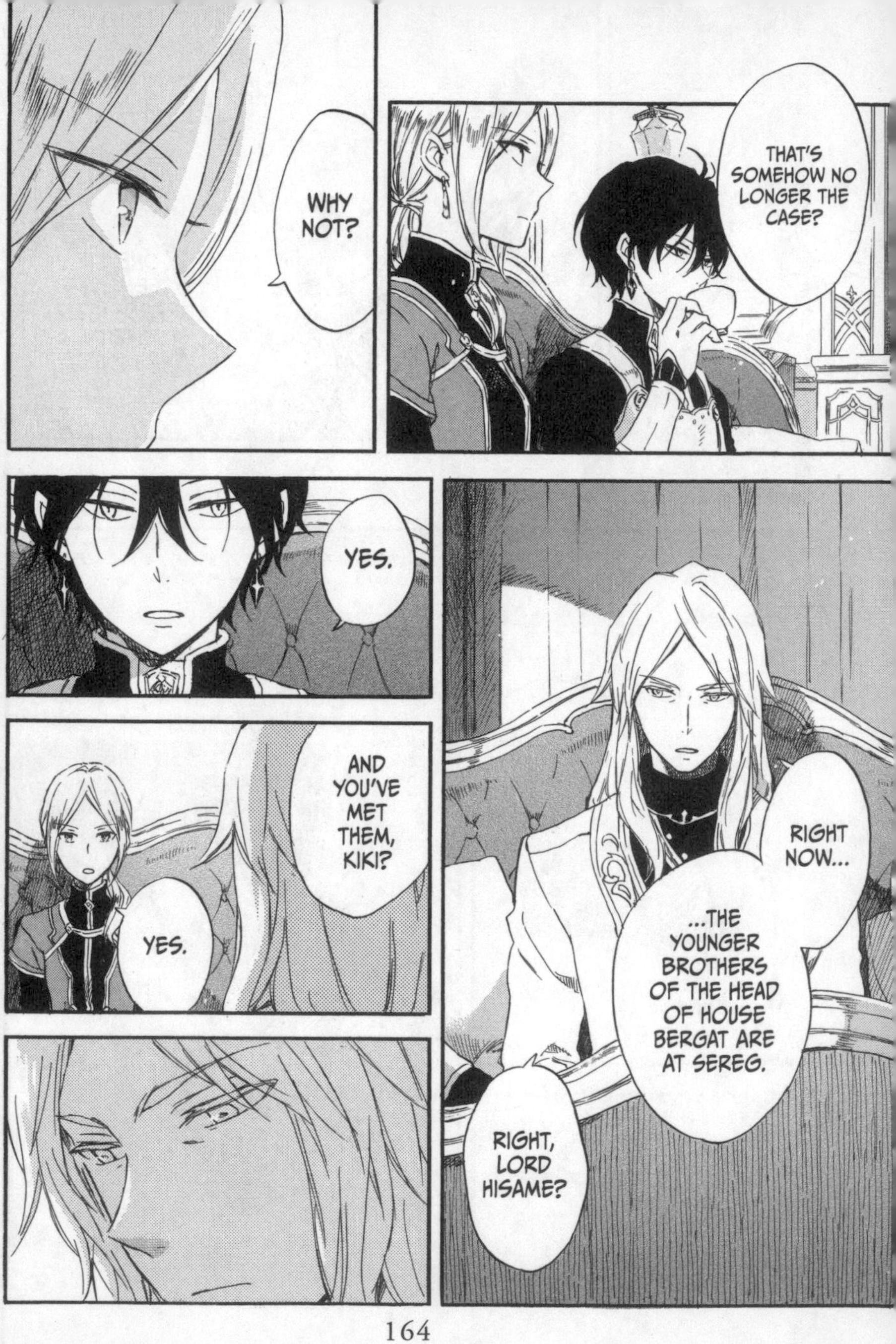
THAT'S SOMEHOW NO LONGER THE CASE?
WHY NOT?
RIGHT NOW...
...THE YOUNGER BROTHERS OF THE HEAD OF HOUSE BERGAT ARE AT SEREG.
RIGHT, LORD HISAME?
YES.
AND YOU'VE MET THEM, KIKI?
YES.

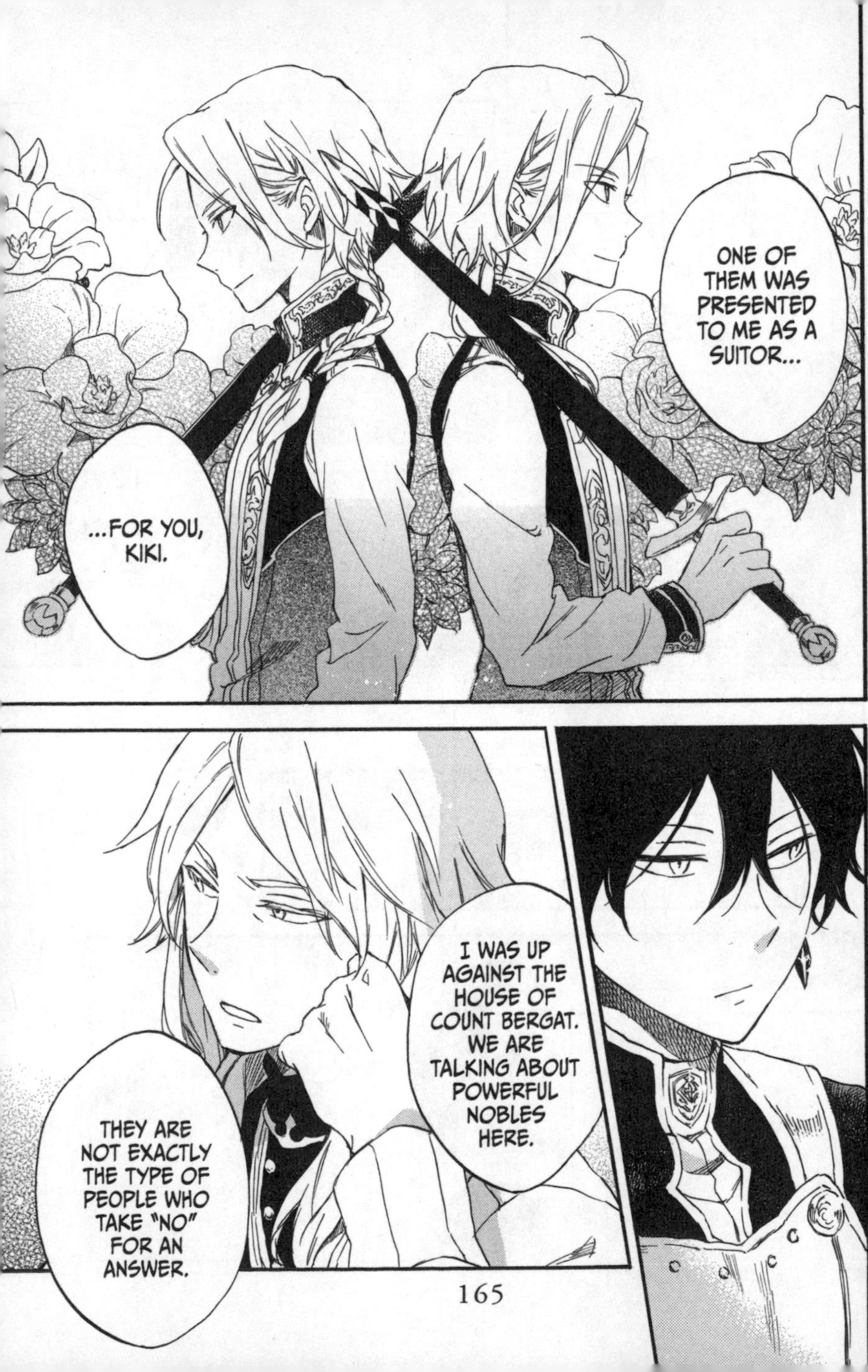
ONE OF THEM WAS PRESENTED TO ME AS A SUITOR...
...FOR YOU, KIKI.
I WAS UP AGAINST THE HOUSE OF COUNT BERGAT. WE ARE TALKING ABOUT POWERFUL NOBLES HERE.
THEY ARE NOT EXACTLY THE TYPE OF PEOPLE WHO TAKE "NO" FOR AN ANSWER.

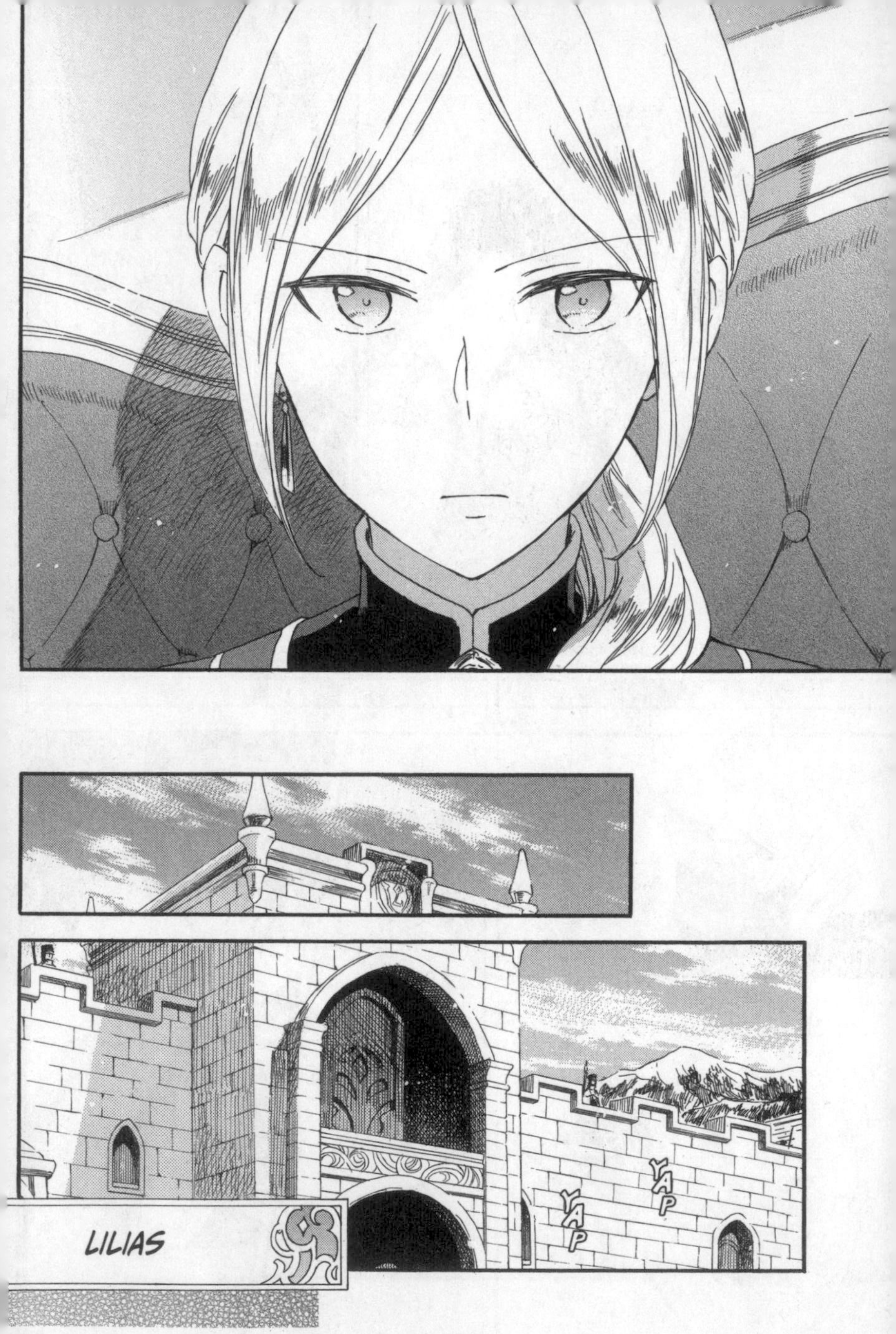
YAP
YAP
LILIAS

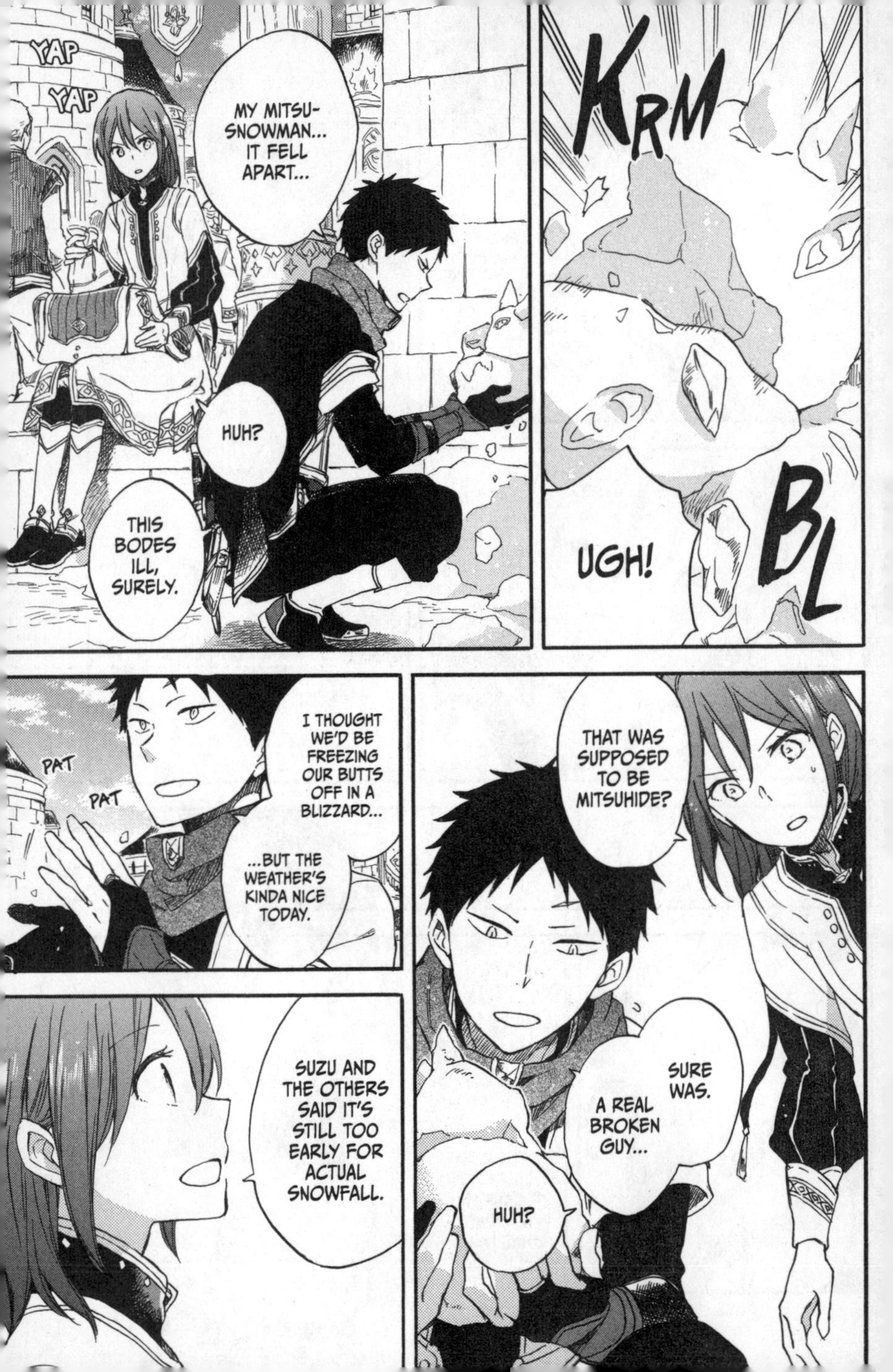
KRM
UGH!
BL
MY MITSU-SNOWMAN... IT FELL APART...
YAP
YAP
HUH?
THIS BODES ILL, SURELY.
THAT WAS SUPPOSED TO BE MITSUHIDE?
SURE WAS. A REAL BROKEN GUY...
HUH?
I THOUGHT WE'D BE FREEZING OUR BUTTS OFF IN A BLIZZARD...
...BUT THE WEATHER'S KINDA NICE TODAY.
PAT
PAT
SUZU AND THE OTHERS SAID IT'S STILL TOO EARLY FOR ACTUAL SNOWFALL.

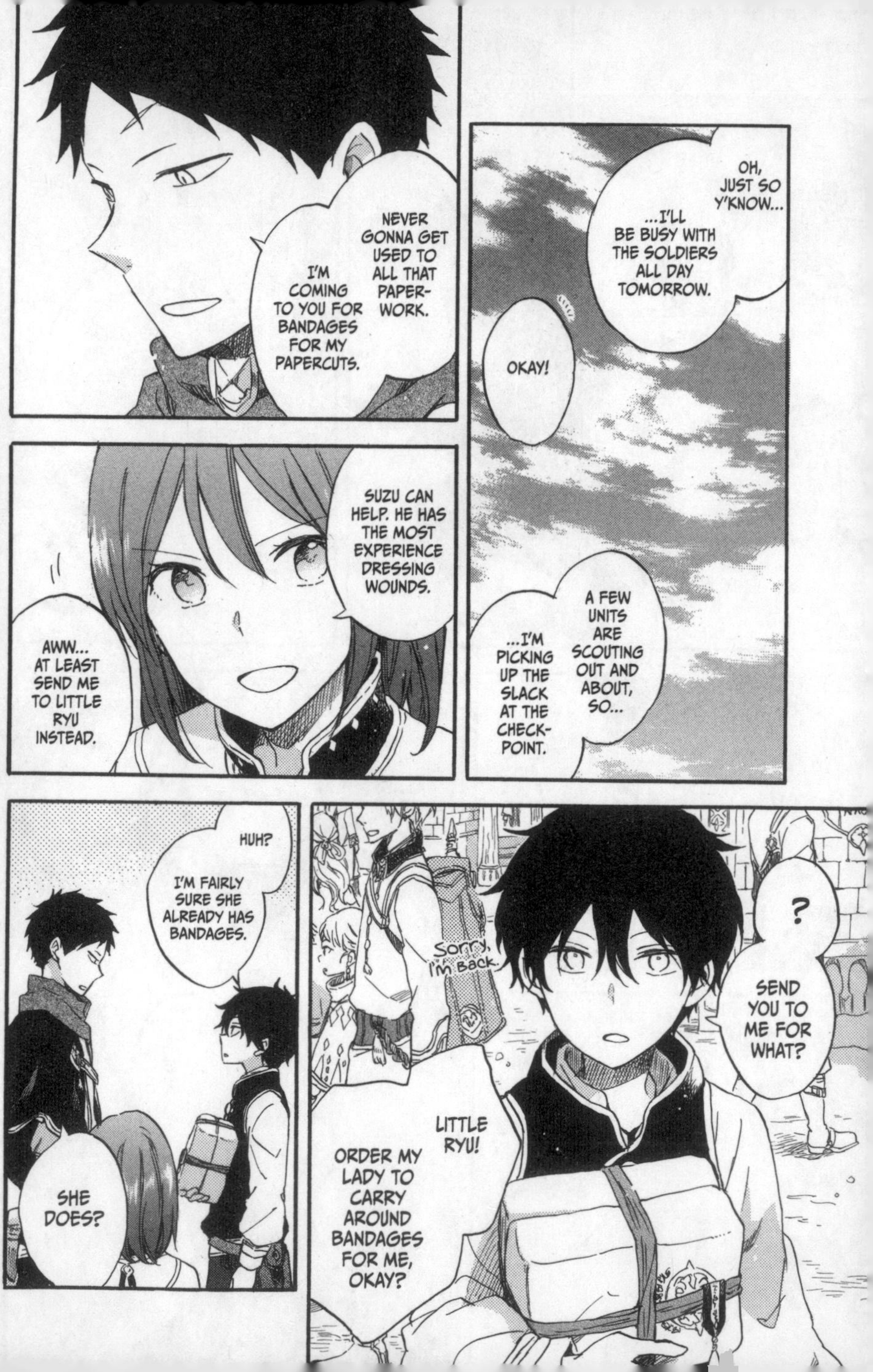
OH, JUST SO Y'KNOW...
...I'LL BE BUSY WITH THE SOLDIERS ALL DAY TOMORROW.
OKAY!
A FEW UNITS ARE SCOUTING OUT AND ABOUT, SO...
...I'M PICKING UP THE SLACK AT THE CHECK-POINT.
NEVER GONNA GET USED TO ALL THAT PAPER-WORK.
I'M COMING TO YOU FOR BANDAGES FOR MY PAPERCUTS.
SUZU CAN HELP. HE HAS THE MOST EXPERIENCE DRESSING WOUNDS.
AWW... AT LEAST SEND ME TO LITTLE RYU INSTEAD.
?
SEND YOU TO ME FOR WHAT?
Sorry, I'm back.
LITTLE RYU!
ORDER MY LADY TO CARRY AROUND BANDAGES FOR ME, OKAY?
HUH?
I'M FAIRLY SURE SHE ALREADY HAS BANDAGES.
SHE DOES?

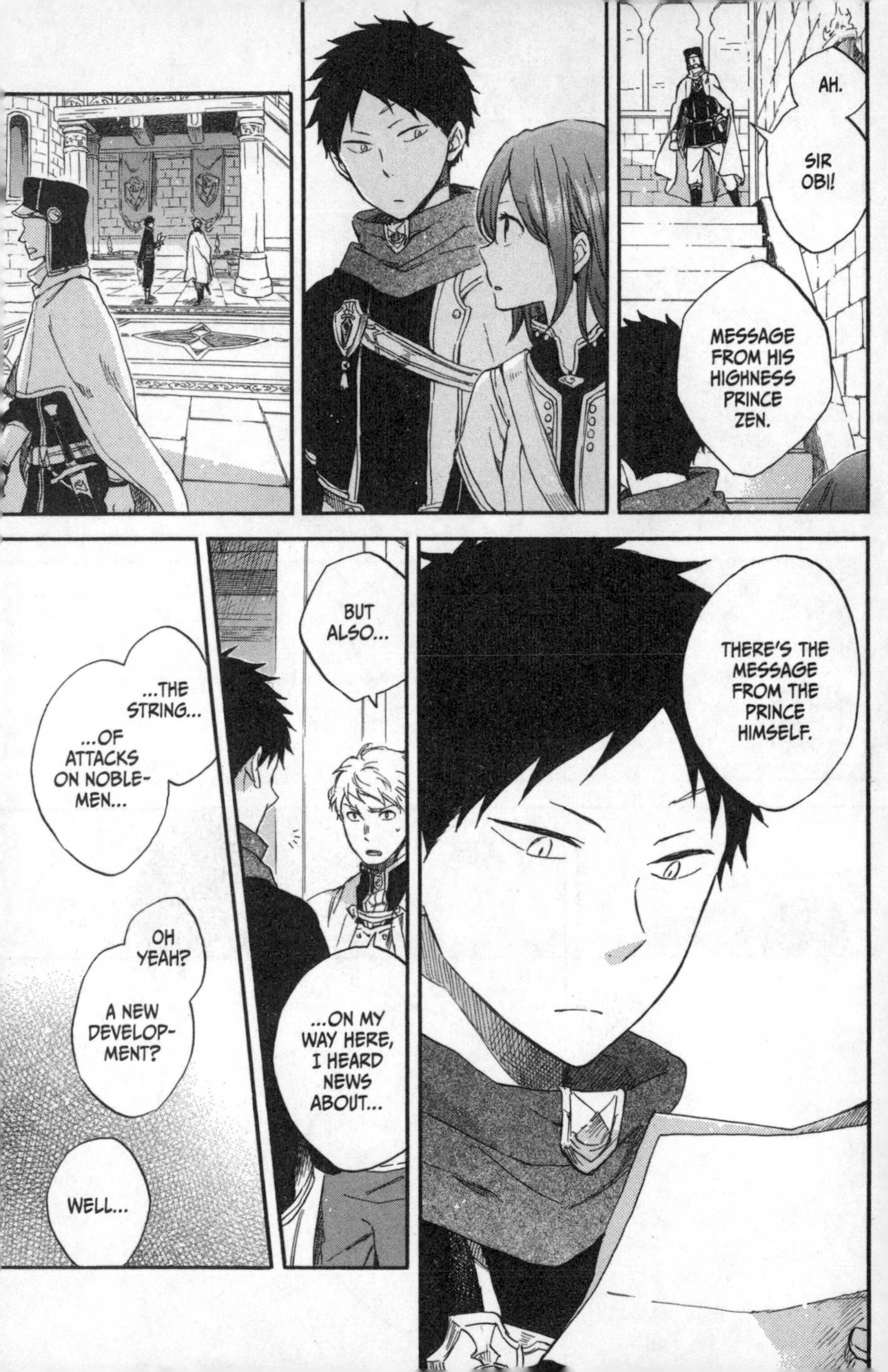
AH.
SIR OBI!
MESSAGE FROM HIS HIGHNESS PRINCE ZEN.
THERE'S THE MESSAGE FROM THE PRINCE HIMSELF.
BUT ALSO...
...ON MY WAY HERE, I HEARD NEWS ABOUT...
...THE STRING...
...OF ATTACKS ON NOBLE-MEN...
OH YEAH?
A NEW DEVELOP-MENT?
WELL...

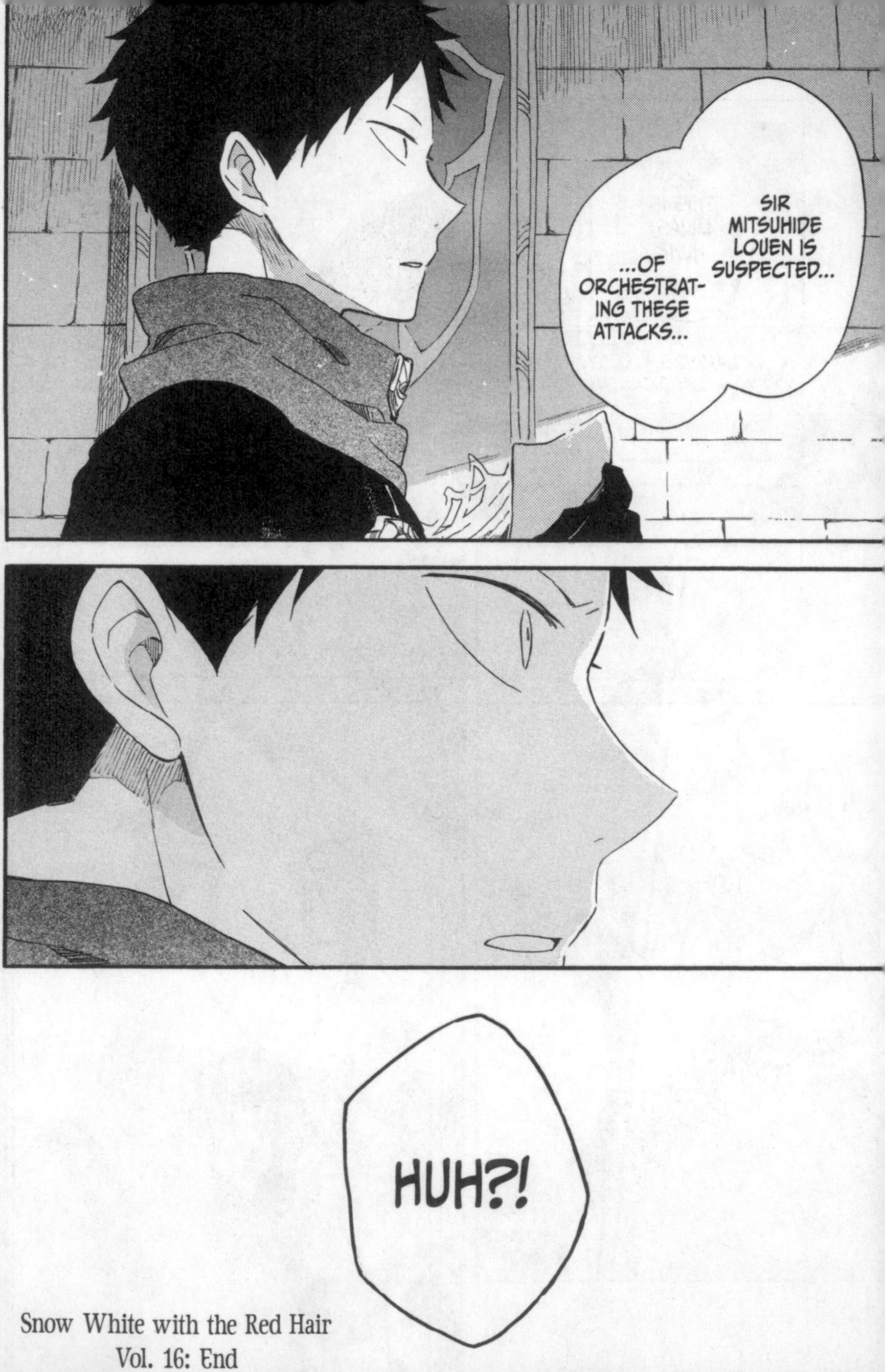
SIR MITSUHIDE LOUEN IS SUSPECTED... ...OF ORCHESTRATING THESE ATTACKS...
HUH?!

Snow White with the Red Hair
Vol. 16: End

Bonus Chapter

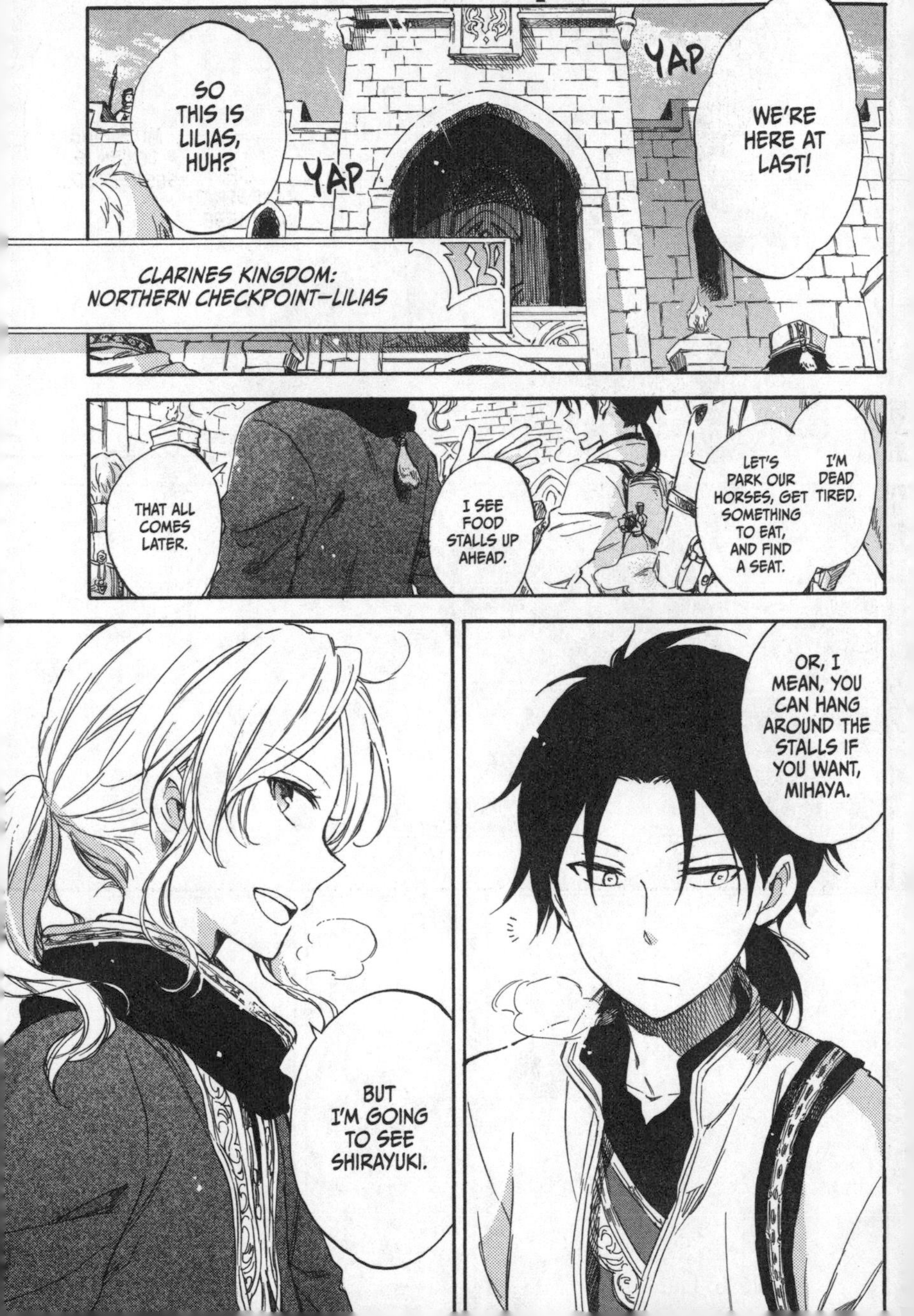
WE'RE HERE AT LAST!
YAP
SO THIS IS LILIAS, HUH?
YAP
CLARINES KINGDOM: NORTHERN CHECKPOINT—LILIAS
I'M DEAD TIRED.
LET'S PARK OUR HORSES, GET SOMETHING TO EAT, AND FIND A SEAT.
I SEE FOOD STALLS UP AHEAD.
THAT ALL COMES LATER.
OR, I MEAN, YOU CAN HANG AROUND THE STALLS IF YOU WANT, MIHAYA.
BUT I'M GOING TO SEE SHIRAYUKI.

Snow White with the Red Hair

Bonus Chapter

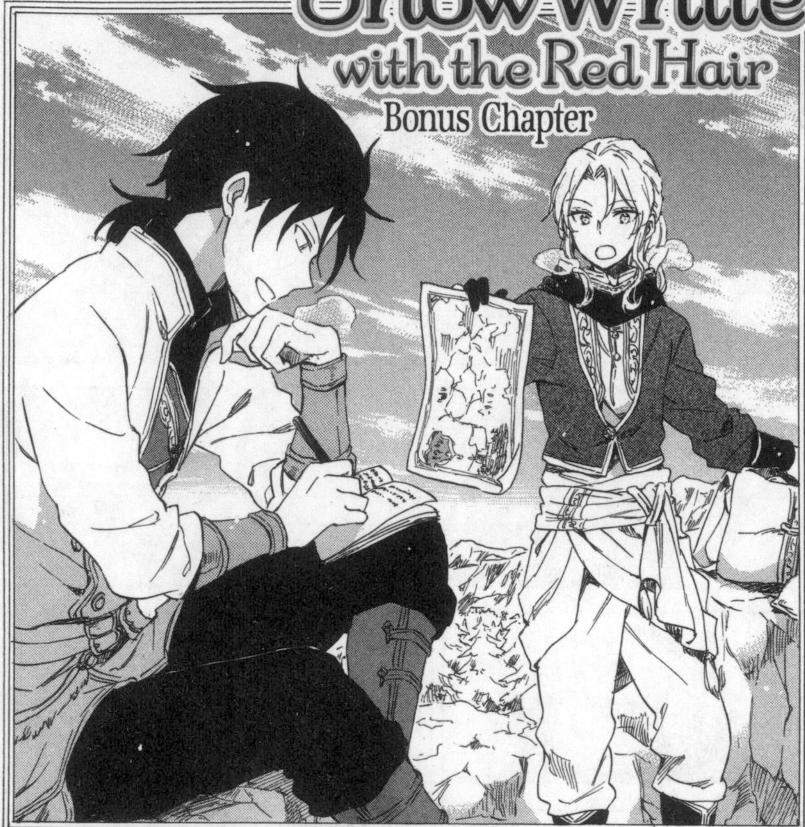

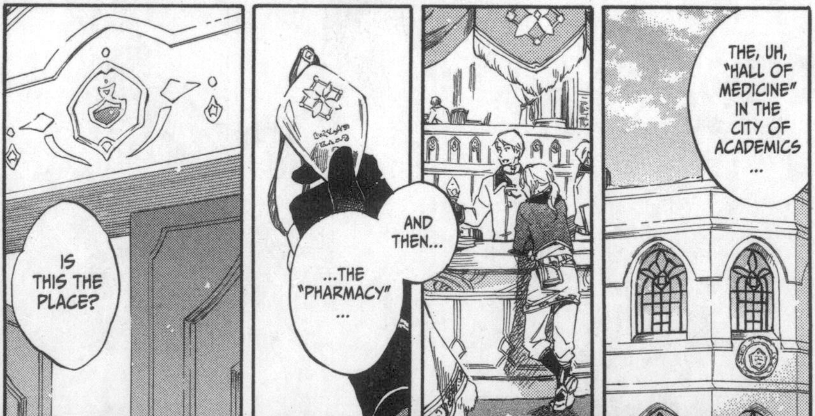
THE, UH, "HALL OF MEDICINE" IN THE CITY OF ACADEMICS ...
AND THEN...
...THE "PHARMACY" ...
IS THIS THE PLACE?

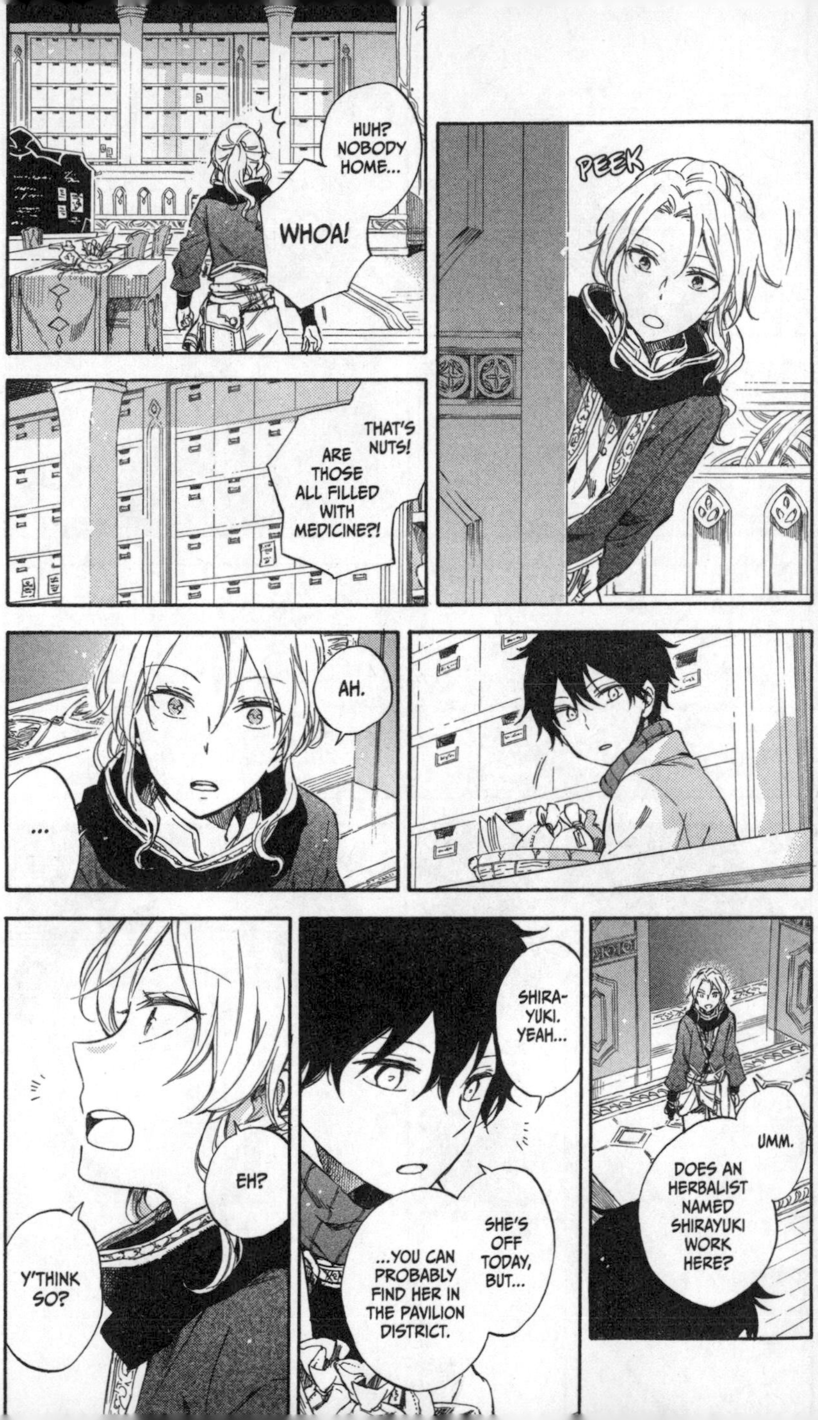
PEEK
HUH? NOBODY HOME...
WHOA!
THAT'S NUTS! ARE THOSE ALL FILLED WITH MEDICINE?!
AH.
...
UMM.
DOES AN HERBALIST NAMED SHIRAYUKI WORK HERE?
SHIRA-YUKI. YEAH...
SHE'S OFF TODAY, BUT...
...YOU CAN PROBABLY FIND HER IN THE PAVILION DISTRICT.
EH?
Y'THINK SO?

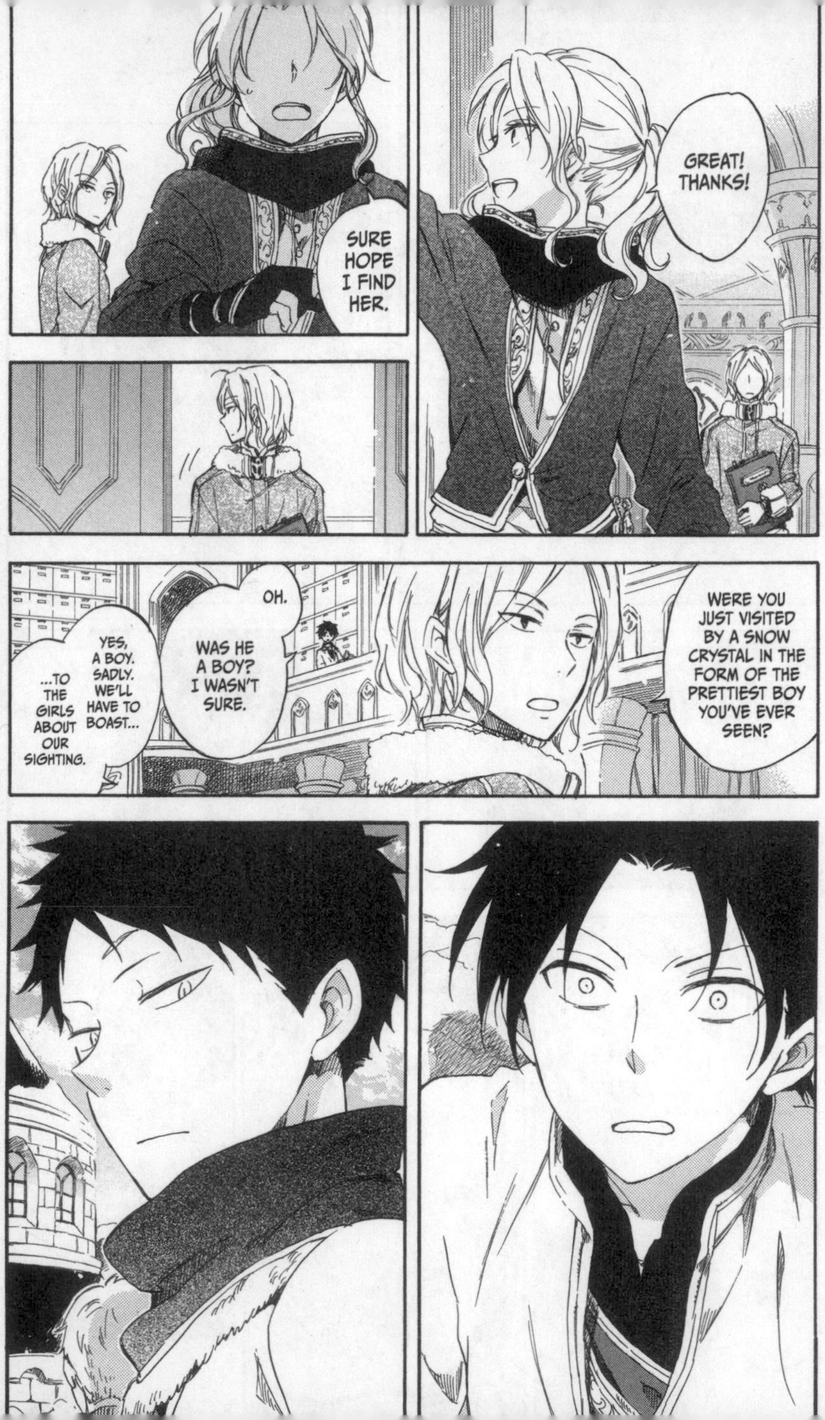
GREAT! THANKS!
SURE HOPE I FIND HER.
WERE YOU JUST VISITED BY A SNOW CRYSTAL IN THE FORM OF THE PRETTIEST BOY YOU'VE EVER SEEN?
OH.
WAS HE A BOY? I WASN'T SURE.
YES, A BOY. SADLY. WE'LL HAVE TO BOAST...
...TO THE GIRLS ABOUT OUR SIGHTING.

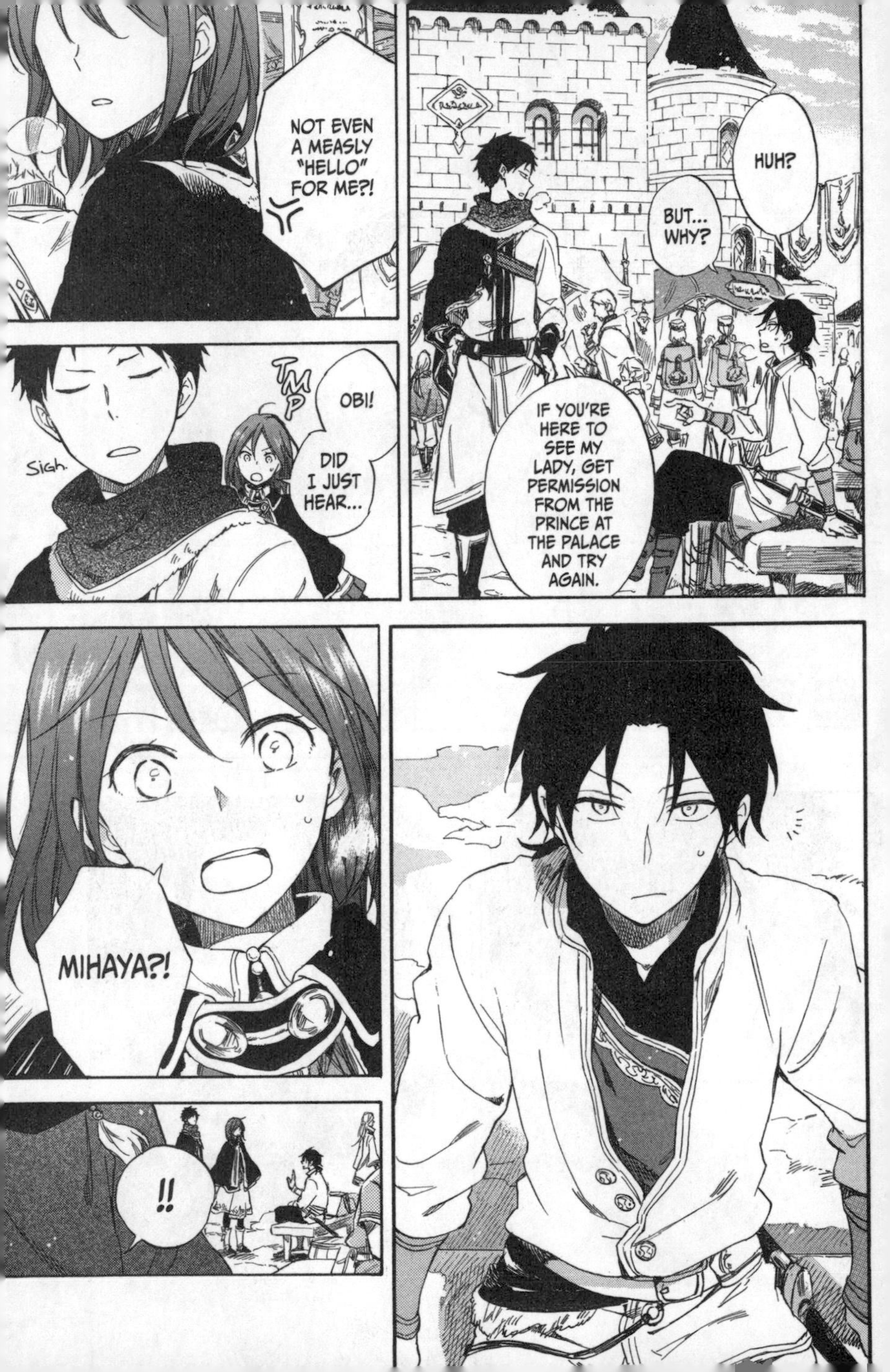
HUH?
BUT... WHY?
IF YOU'RE HERE TO SEE MY LADY, GET PERMISSION FROM THE PRINCE AT THE PALACE AND TRY AGAIN.
NOT EVEN A MEASLY "HELLO" FOR ME?!
TMP
OBI!
DID I JUST HEAR...
Sigh.
MIHAYA?!
!!

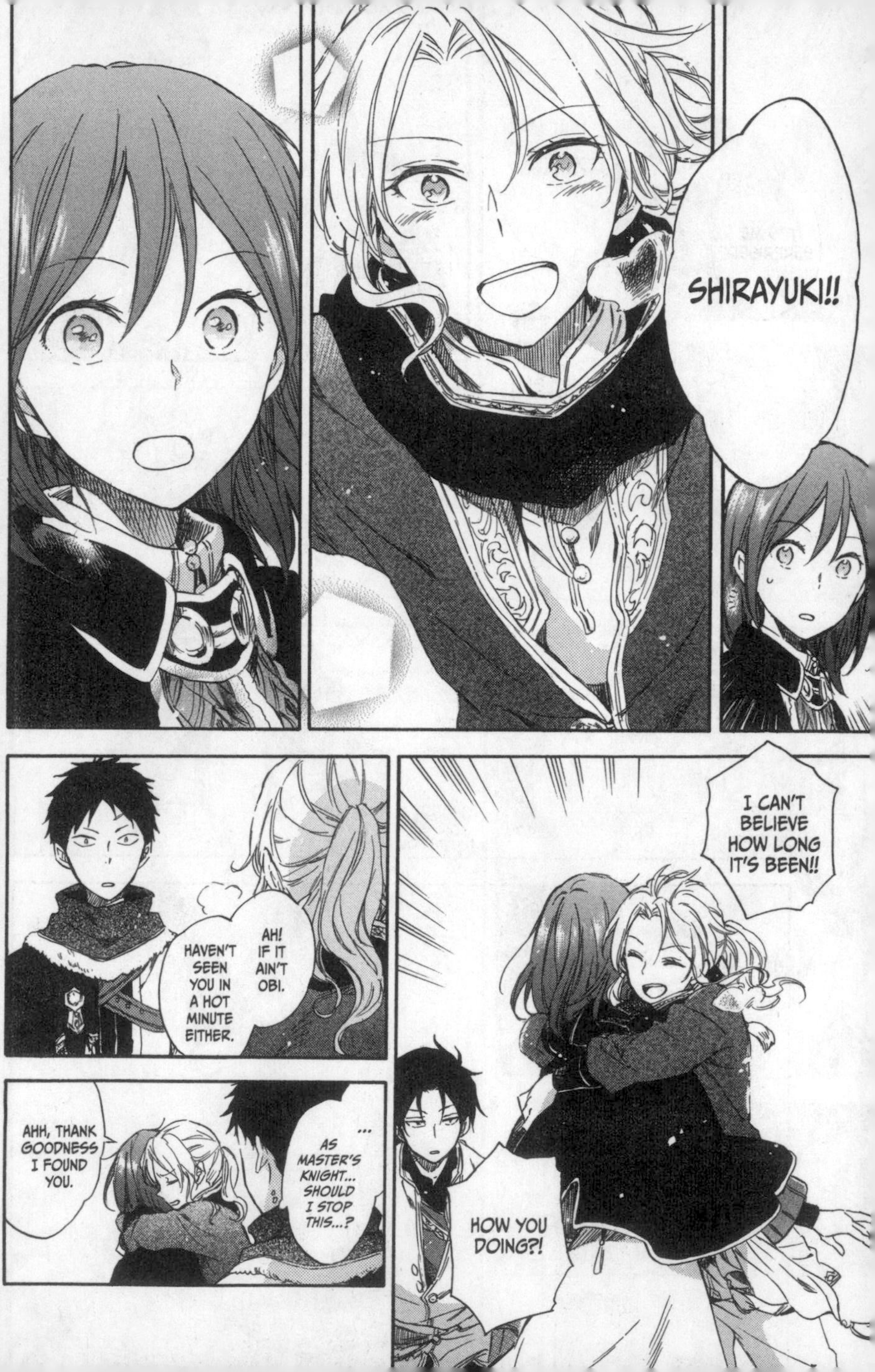
SHIRAYUKI!!
I CAN'T BELIEVE HOW LONG IT'S BEEN!!
HOW YOU DOING?!
AH! IF IT AIN'T OBI.
HAVEN'T SEEN YOU IN A HOT MINUTE EITHER.
... AS MASTER'S KNIGHT... SHOULD I STOP THIS...?
AHH, THANK GOODNESS I FOUND YOU.

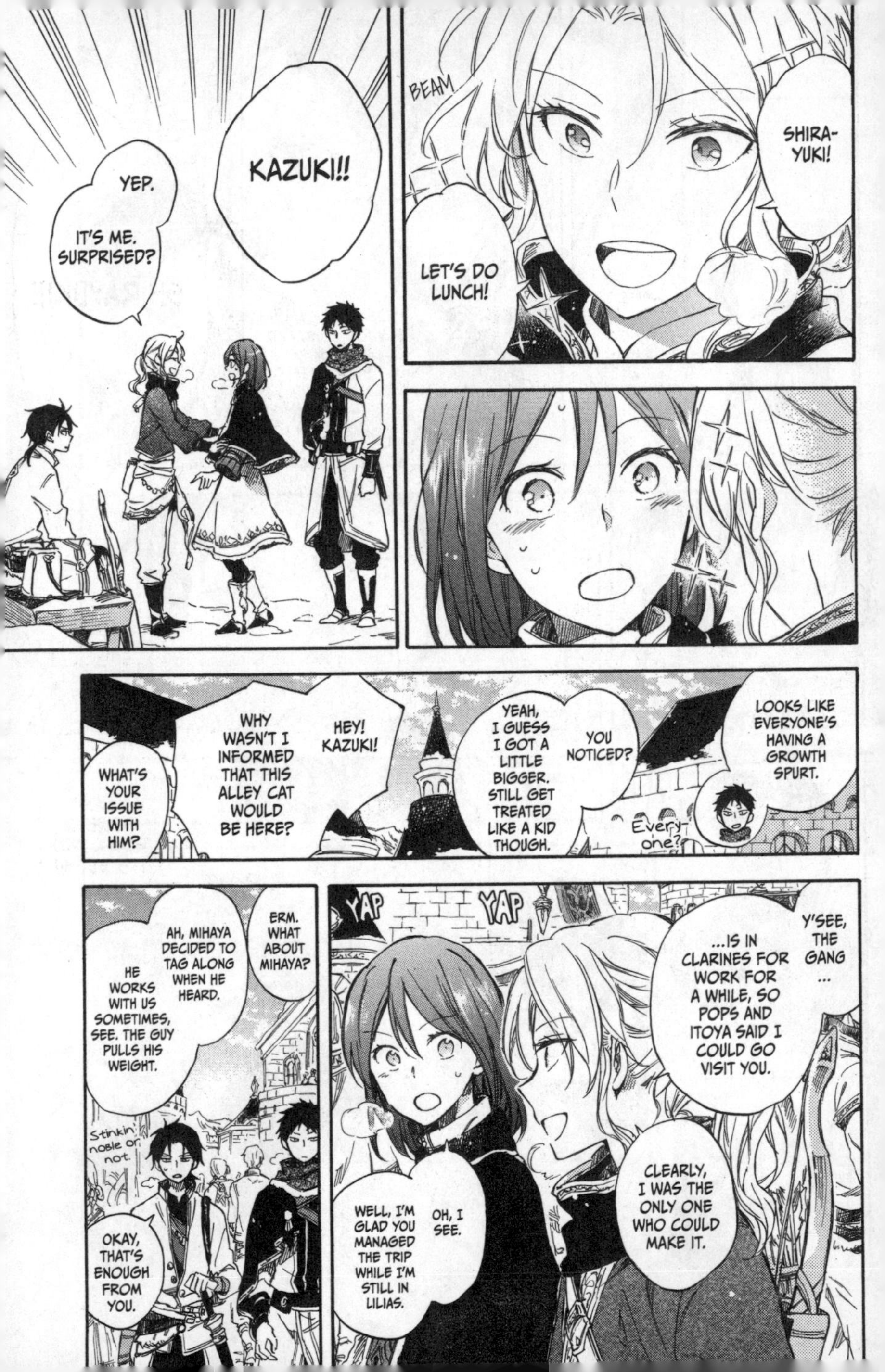
BEAM
SHIRA-YUKI!
LET'S DO LUNCH!
KAZUKI!!
YEP.
IT'S ME. SURPRISED?
LOOKS LIKE EVERYONE'S HAVING A GROWTH SPURT.
Every-one?
YOU NOTICED?
YEAH, I GUESS I GOT A LITTLE BIGGER. STILL GET TREATED LIKE A KID THOUGH.
HEY! KAZUKI!
WHY WASN'T I INFORMED THAT THIS ALLEY CAT WOULD BE HERE?
WHAT'S YOUR ISSUE WITH HIM?
YAP
YAP
Y'SEE, THE GANG ...
...IS IN CLARINES FOR WORK FOR A WHILE, SO POPS AND ITOYA SAID I COULD GO VISIT YOU.
CLEARLY, I WAS THE ONLY ONE WHO COULD MAKE IT.
OH, I SEE.
WELL, I'M GLAD YOU MANAGED THE TRIP WHILE I'M STILL IN LILIAS.
ERM. WHAT ABOUT MIHAYA?
AH, MIHAYA DECIDED TO TAG ALONG WHEN HE HEARD.
HE WORKS WITH US SOMETIMES, SEE. THE GUY PULLS HIS WEIGHT.
Stinkin' noble or not.
OKAY, THAT'S ENOUGH FROM YOU.

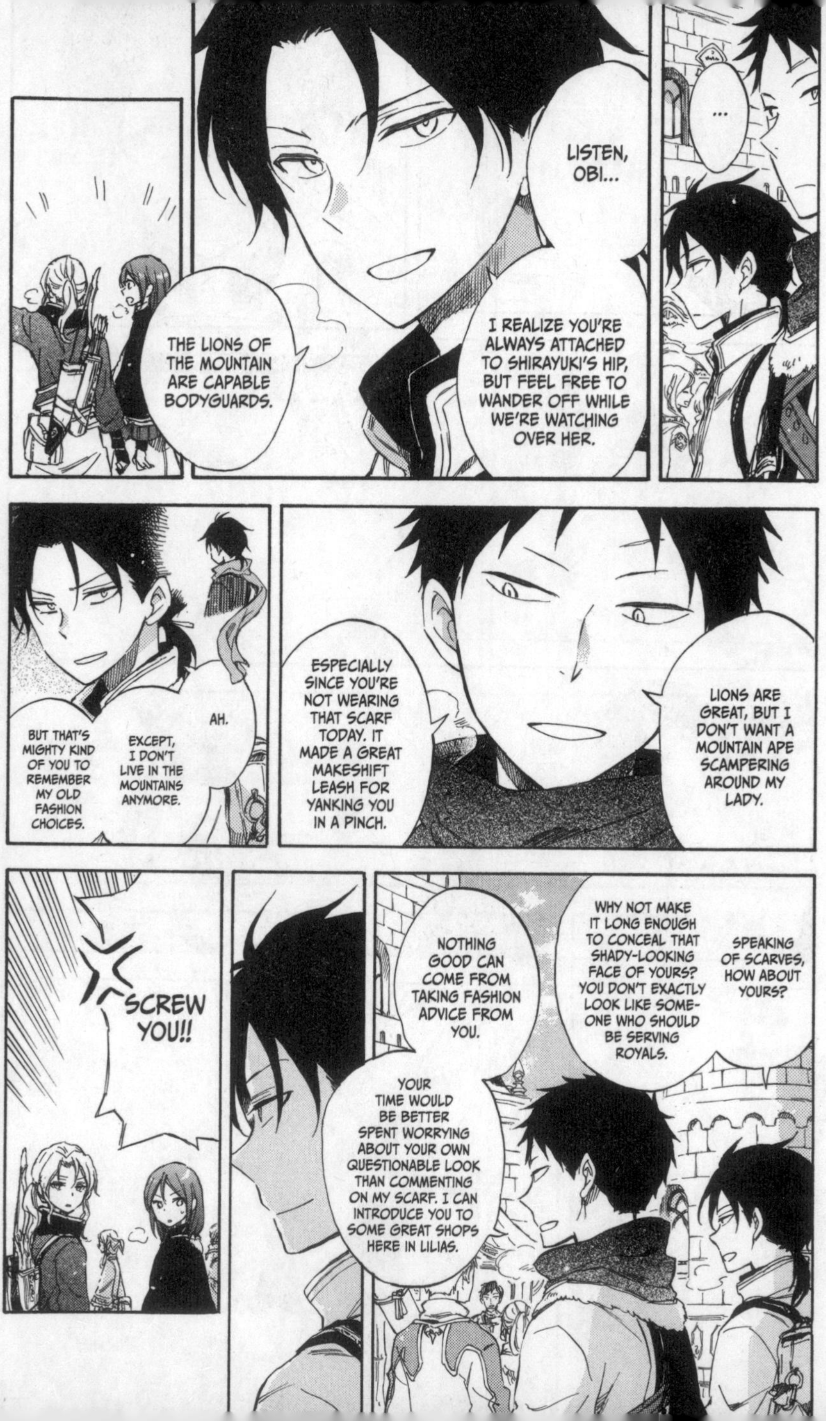
...
LISTEN, OBI...
I REALIZE YOU'RE ALWAYS ATTACHED TO SHIRAYUKI'S HIP, BUT FEEL FREE TO WANDER OFF WHILE WE'RE WATCHING OVER HER.
THE LIONS OF THE MOUNTAIN ARE CAPABLE BODYGUARDS.
LIONS ARE GREAT, BUT I DON'T WANT A MOUNTAIN APE SCAMPERING AROUND MY LADY.
ESPECIALLY SINCE YOU'RE NOT WEARING THAT SCARF TODAY. IT MADE A GREAT MAKESHIFT LEASH FOR YANKING YOU IN A PINCH.
AH.
EXCEPT, I DON'T LIVE IN THE MOUNTAINS ANYMORE.
BUT THAT'S MIGHTY KIND OF YOU TO REMEMBER MY OLD FASHION CHOICES.
SPEAKING OF SCARVES, HOW ABOUT YOURS?
WHY NOT MAKE IT LONG ENOUGH TO CONCEAL THAT SHADY-LOOKING FACE OF YOURS? YOU DON'T EXACTLY LOOK LIKE SOME-ONE WHO SHOULD BE SERVING ROYALS.
NOTHING GOOD CAN COME FROM TAKING FASHION ADVICE FROM YOU.
YOUR TIME WOULD BE BETTER SPENT WORRYING ABOUT YOUR OWN QUESTIONABLE LOOK THAN COMMENTING ON MY SCARF. I CAN INTRODUCE YOU TO SOME GREAT SHOPS HERE IN LILIAS.
SCREW YOU!!

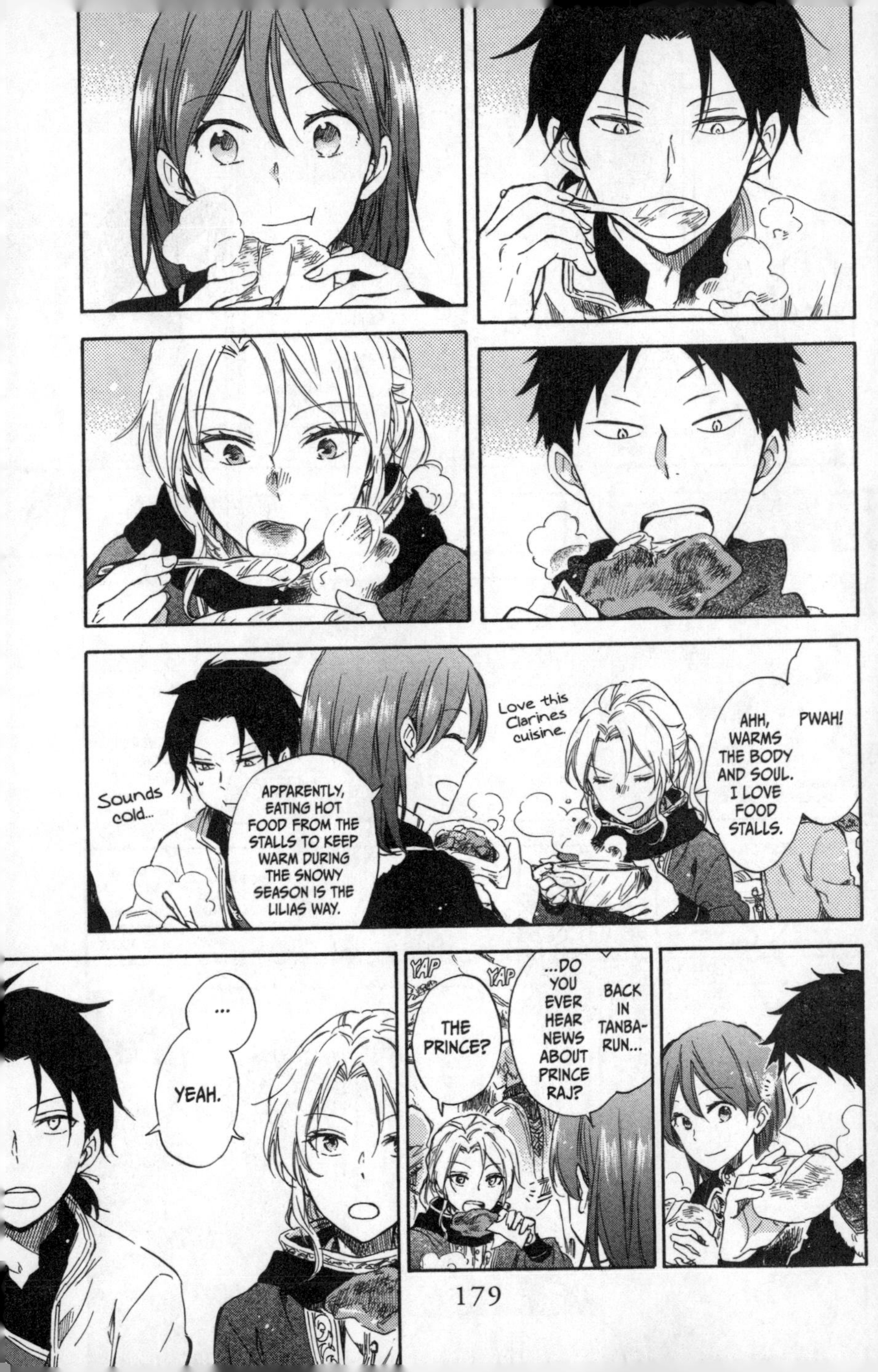
PWAH!
AHH, WARMS THE BODY AND SOUL. I LOVE FOOD STALLS.
Love this Clarines cuisine.
APPARENTLY, EATING HOT FOOD FROM THE STALLS TO KEEP WARM DURING THE SNOWY SEASON IS THE LILIAS WAY.
Sounds cold...
BACK IN TANBA-RUN...
...DO YOU EVER HEAR NEWS ABOUT PRINCE RAJ?
YAP
YAP
THE PRINCE?
...
YEAH.

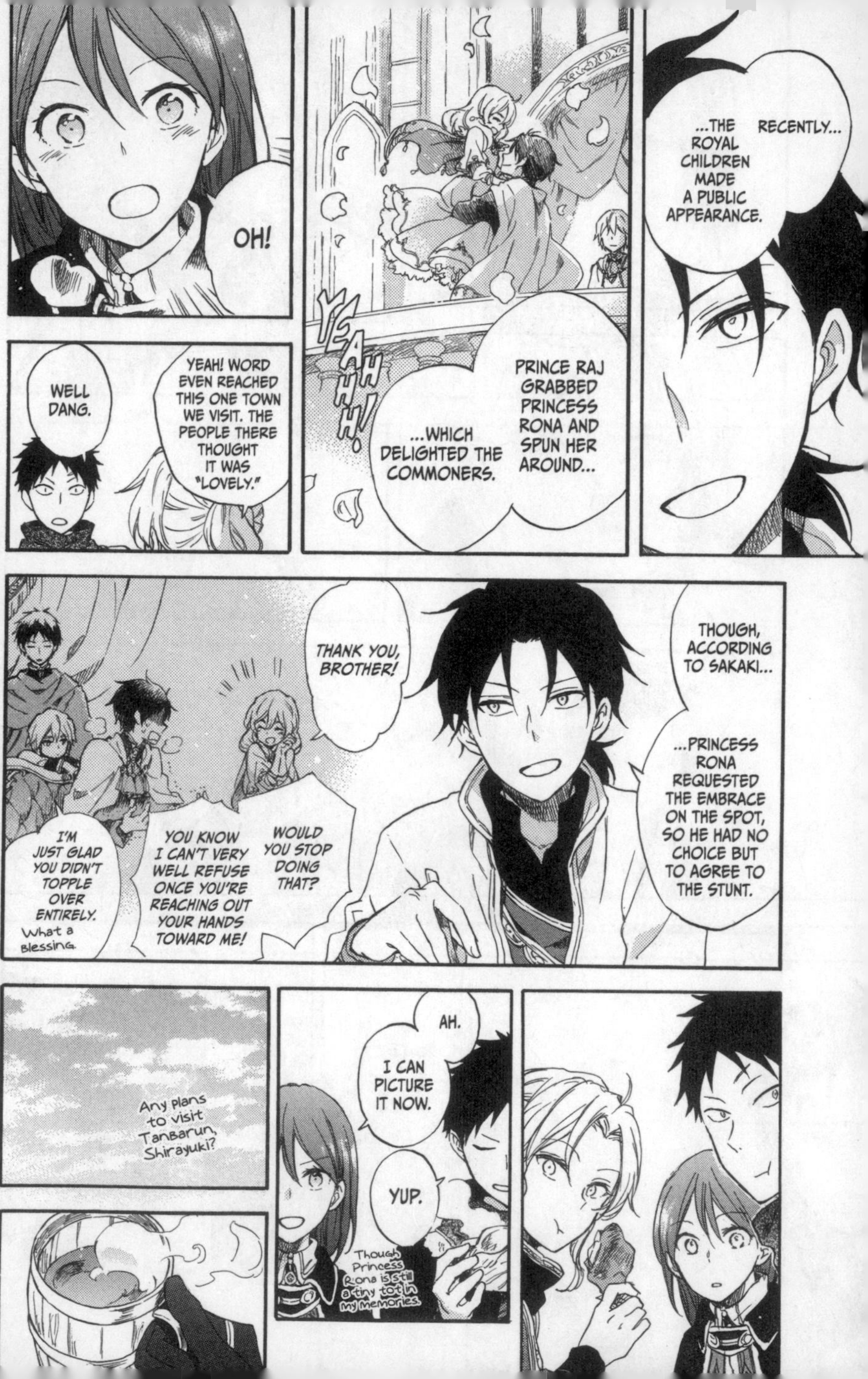
RECENTLY...
...THE ROYAL CHILDREN MADE A PUBLIC APPEARANCE.
PRINCE RAJ GRABBED PRINCESS RONA AND SPUN HER AROUND...
...WHICH DELIGHTED THE COMMONERS.
YEAHHH!
OH!
YEAH! WORD EVEN REACHED THIS ONE TOWN WE VISIT. THE PEOPLE THERE THOUGHT IT WAS "LOVELY."
WELL DANG.
THOUGH, ACCORDING TO SAKAKI...
...PRINCESS RONA REQUESTED THE EMBRACE ON THE SPOT, SO HE HAD NO CHOICE BUT TO AGREE TO THE STUNT.
THANK YOU, BROTHER!
WOULD YOU STOP DOING THAT?
YOU KNOW I CAN'T VERY WELL REFUSE ONCE YOU'RE REACHING OUT YOUR HANDS TOWARD ME!
I'M JUST GLAD YOU DIDN'T TOPPLE OVER ENTIRELY.
What a blessing.
AH.
I CAN PICTURE IT NOW.
YUP.
Though Princess Rona is still a tiny tot in my memories.
Any plans to visit Tanbarun, Shirayuki?

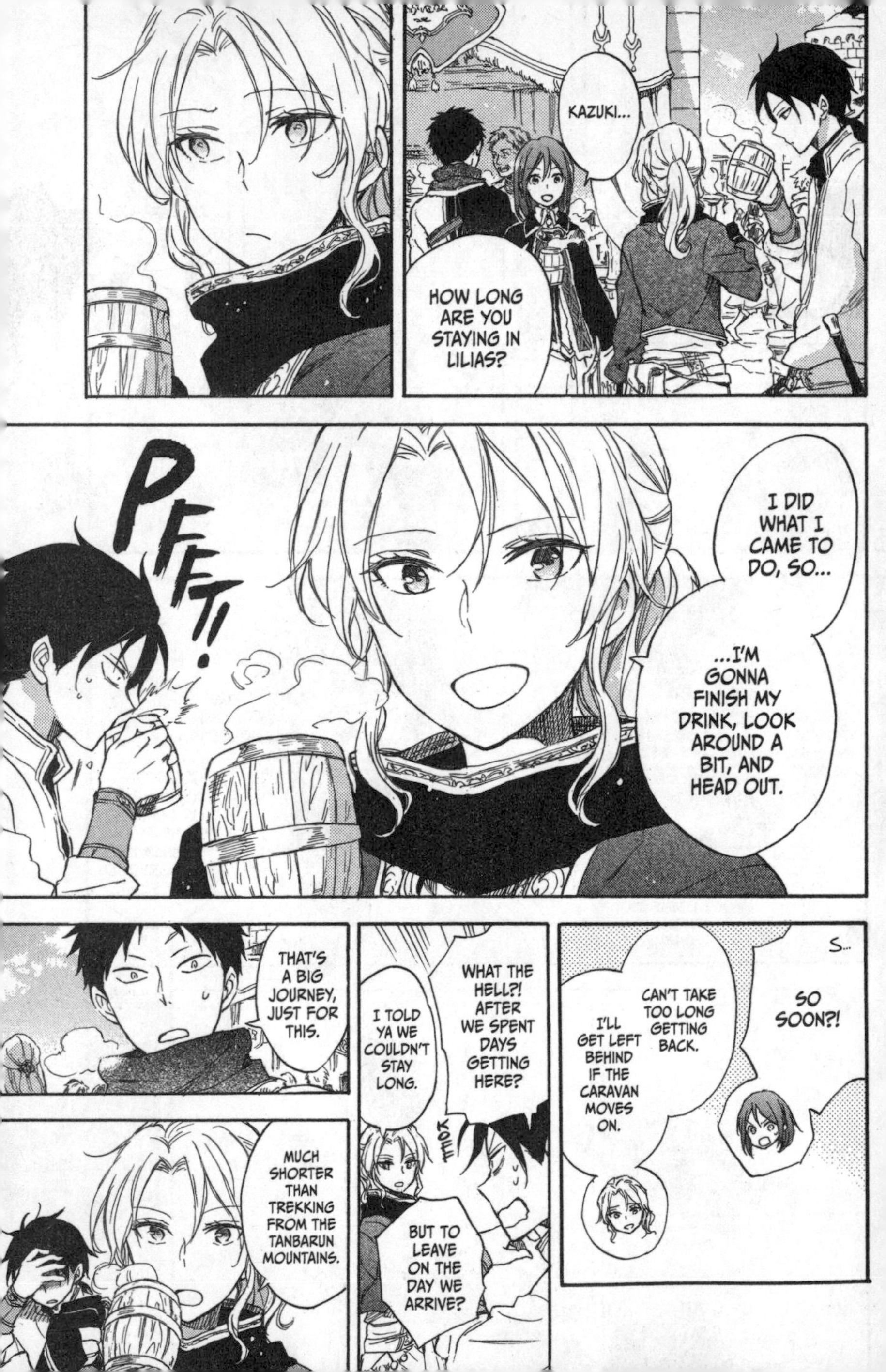
KAZUKI...
HOW LONG ARE YOU STAYING IN LILIAS?
I DID WHAT I CAME TO DO, SO...
...I'M GONNA FINISH MY DRINK, LOOK AROUND A BIT, AND HEAD OUT.
PFFT!!
S...
SO SOON?!
CAN'T TAKE TOO LONG GETTING BACK.
I'LL GET LEFT BEHIND IF THE CARAVAN MOVES ON.
WHAT THE HELL?! AFTER WE SPENT DAYS GETTING HERE?
I TOLD YA WE COULDN'T STAY LONG.
THAT'S A BIG JOURNEY, JUST FOR THIS.
KOFF
BUT TO LEAVE ON THE DAY WE ARRIVE?
MUCH SHORTER THAN TREKKING FROM THE TANBARUN MOUNTAINS.

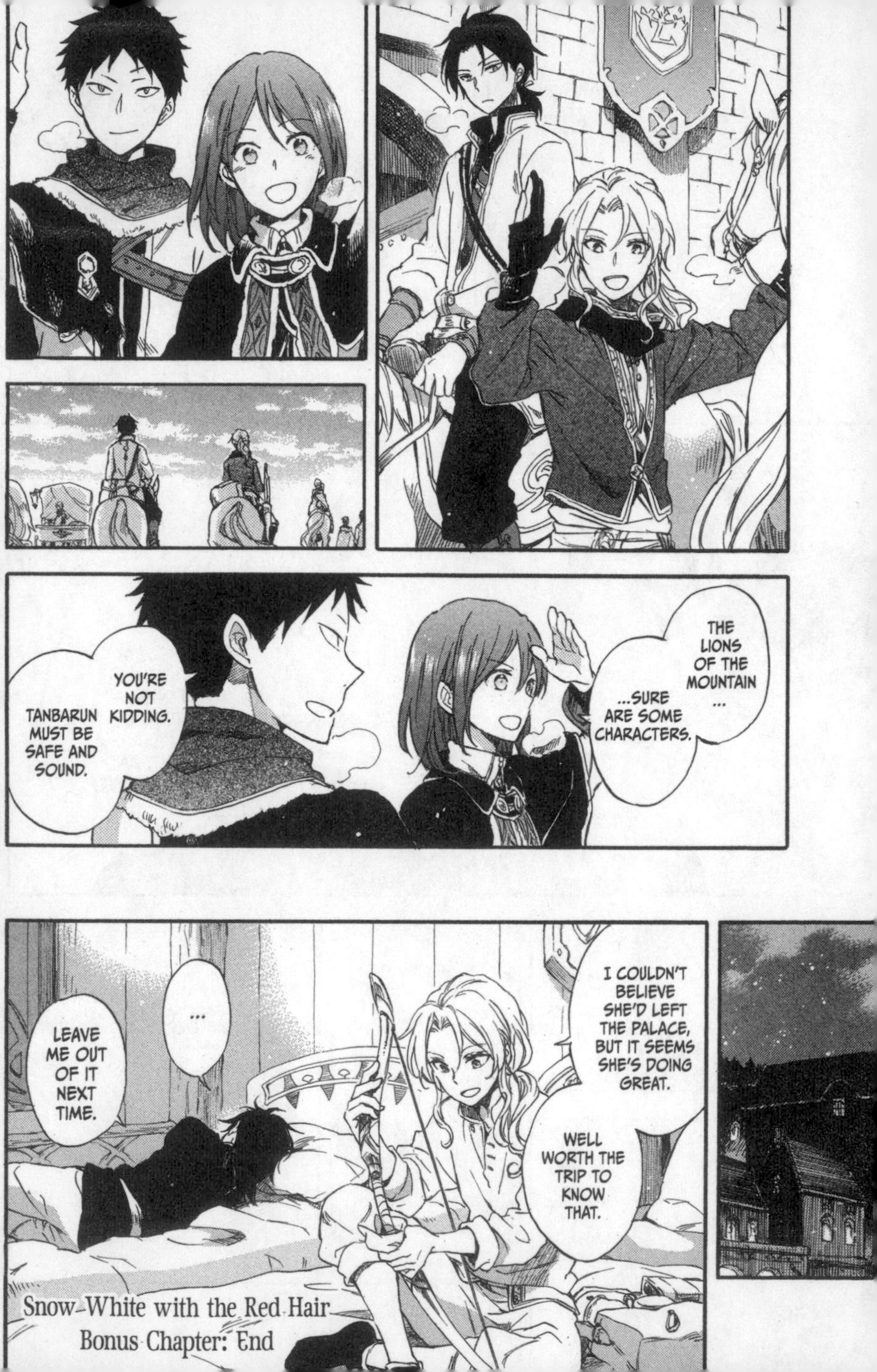
THE LIONS OF THE MOUNTAIN ...
...SURE ARE SOME CHARACTERS.
YOU'RE NOT KIDDING.
TANBARUN MUST BE SAFE AND SOUND.
I COULDN'T BELIEVE SHE'D LEFT THE PALACE, BUT IT SEEMS SHE'S DOING GREAT.
WELL WORTH THE TRIP TO KNOW THAT.
...
LEAVE ME OUT OF IT NEXT TIME.
Snow White with the Red Hair
Bonus Chapter: End

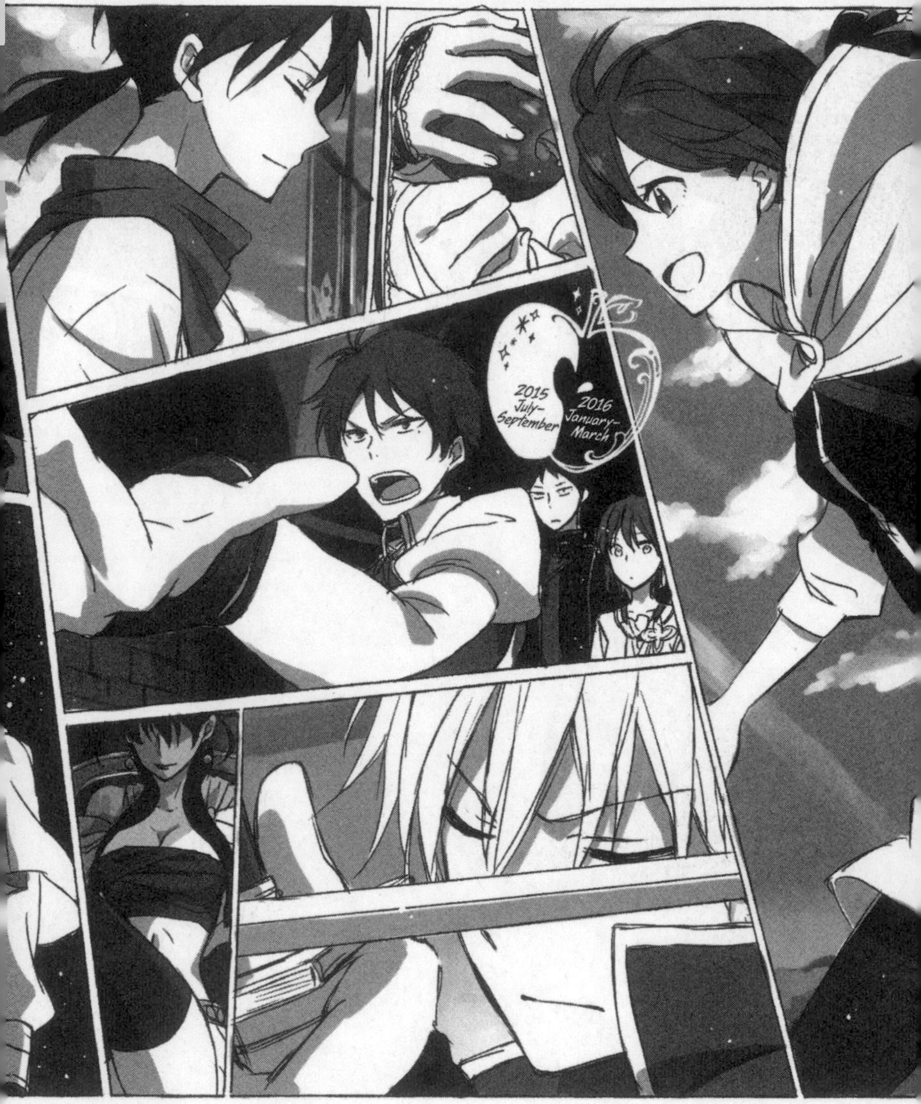
2016
January-
March
2015
July-
September

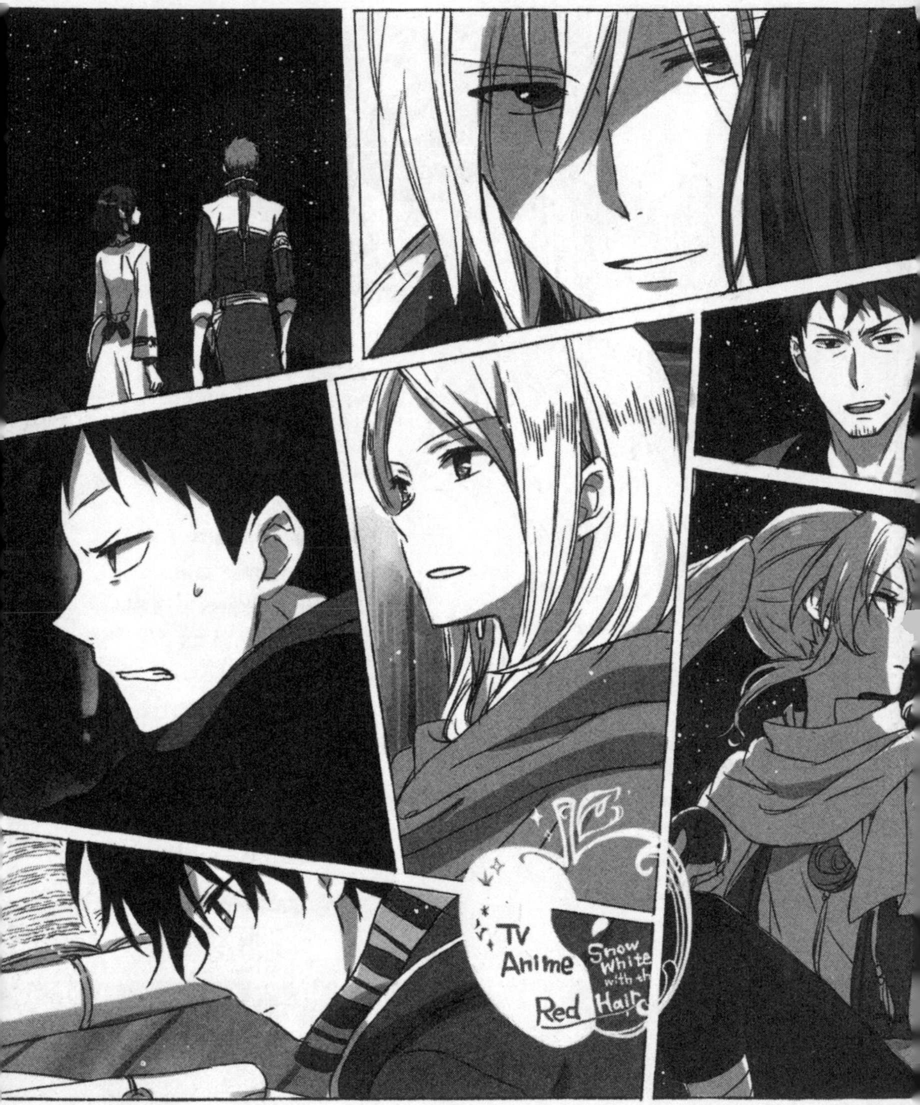
TV Anime
Snow White with the Red Hair

Special thanks

Masahiro Ando-sama

-The anime staff
-The anime cast
-eyelis-sama
-Ide-sama, Iwakiri-sama
-My editor
-The editorial staff at LaLa
-Everyone in Publishing/Sales
-Yamashita-sama
-Noro-sama, Kawatani-sama
-My big sister, mother, and father

Drama CD Contributors:

-Saori Hayami-sama
-Ryota Ohsaka-sama
-Yuichiro Umehara-sama
-Kaori Nazuka-sama
-Nobuhiko Okamoto-sama
-Akira Ishida-sama

-Kazuhiro Wakabayashi-sama
-Akao Deko-sama
-The staff

-And you—the readers!

Sorata Akiduki
July 2016

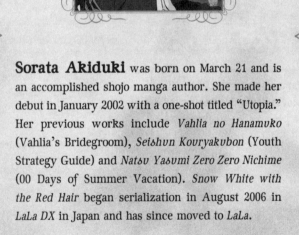

Sorata Akiduki was born on March 21 and is an accomplished shojo manga author. She made her debut in January 2002 with a one-shot titled "Utopia." Her previous works include *Vahlia no Hanamuko* (Vahlia's Bridegroom), *Seishun Kouryakubon* (Youth Strategy Guide) and *Natsu Yasumi Zero Zero Nichime* (00 Days of Summer Vacation). *Snow White with the Red Hair* began serialization in August 2006 in *LaLa DX* in Japan and has since moved to *LaLa*.

Snow White
with the Red Hair

SHOJO BEAT EDITION

STORY AND ART BY
Sorata Akiduki

TRANSLATION **Caleb Cook**
TOUCH-UP ART & LETTERING **Brandon Bovia**
DESIGN **Alice Lewis**
EDITOR **Karla Clark**

Akagami no Shirayukihime by Sorata Akiduki
© Sorata Akiduki 2016
All rights reserved.
First published in Japan in 2016 by HAKUSENSHA, Inc., Tokyo.
English language translation rights arranged with HAKUSENSHA, Inc., Tokyo.

The stories, characters and incidents mentioned
in this publication are entirely fictional.

Printed in Canada

Published by VIZ Media, LLC
P.O. Box 77010
San Francisco, CA 94107

10 9 8 7 6 5 4 3 2 1
First printing, November 2021

viz.com   shojobeat.com

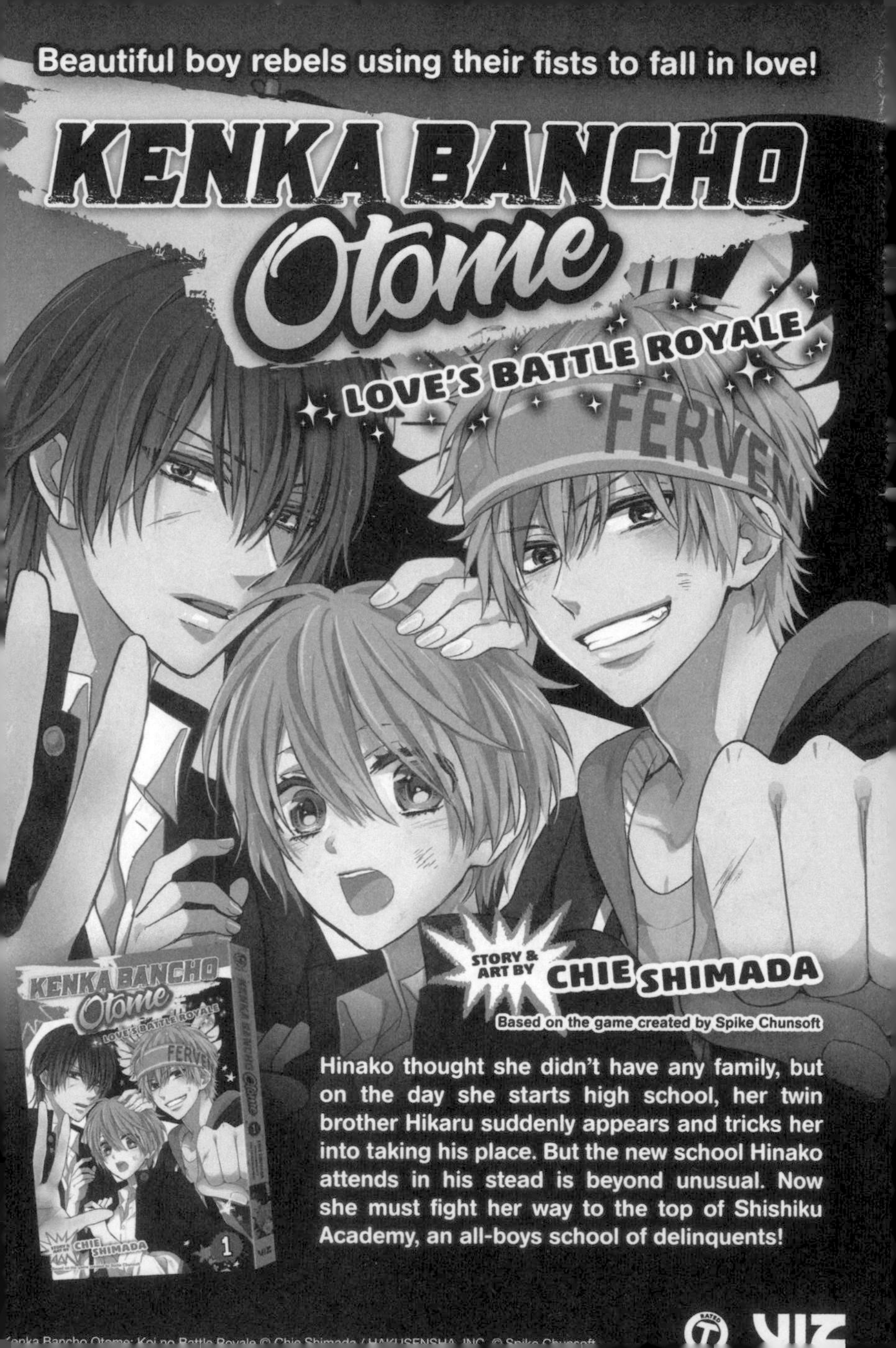
Beautiful boy rebels using their fists to fall in love!
KENKA BANCHO Otome
LOVE'S BATTLE ROYALE
FERVENT
STORY & ART BY CHIE SHIMADA
Based on the game created by Spike Chunsoft
Hinako thought she didn't have any family, but on the day she starts high school, her twin brother Hikaru suddenly appears and tricks her into taking his place. But the new school Hinako attends in his stead is beyond unusual. Now she must fight her way to the top of Shishiku Academy, an all-boys school of delinquents!
KENKA BANCHO Otome
LOVE'S BATTLE ROYALE
CHIE SHIMADA
1
RATED T
VIZ
Kenka Bancho Otome: Koi no Battle Royale © Chie Shimada / HAKUSENSHA, INC. © Spike Chunsoft

YOU'RE READING THE WRONG WAY!

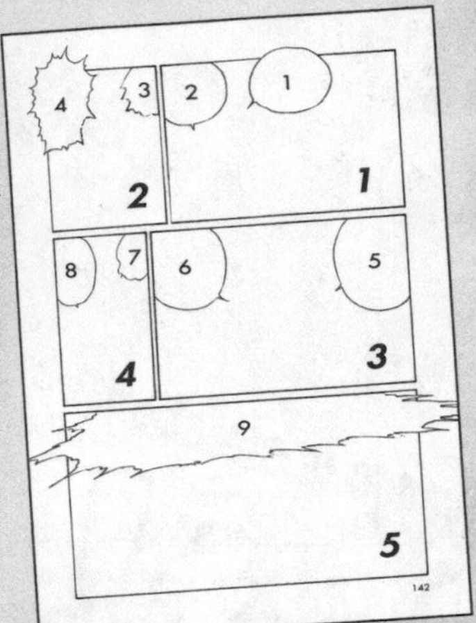
1
2
3
4
1
2
5
6
7
8
3
4
9
5
142

Snow White with the Red Hair reads from right to left, starting in the upper-right corner. Japanese is read from right to left, meaning that action, sound effects and word-balloon order are completely reversed from English order.

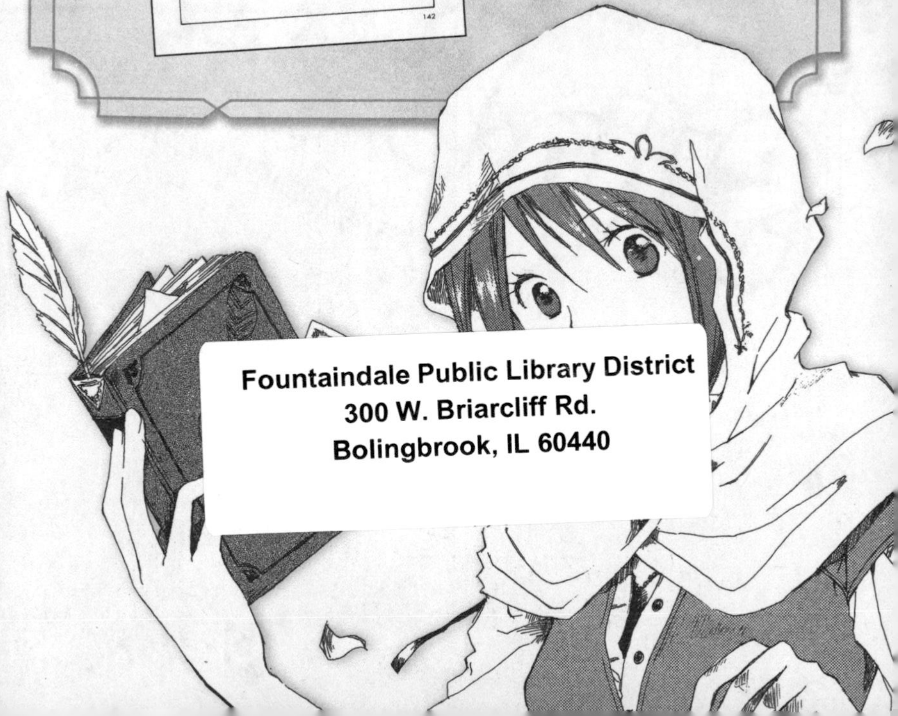

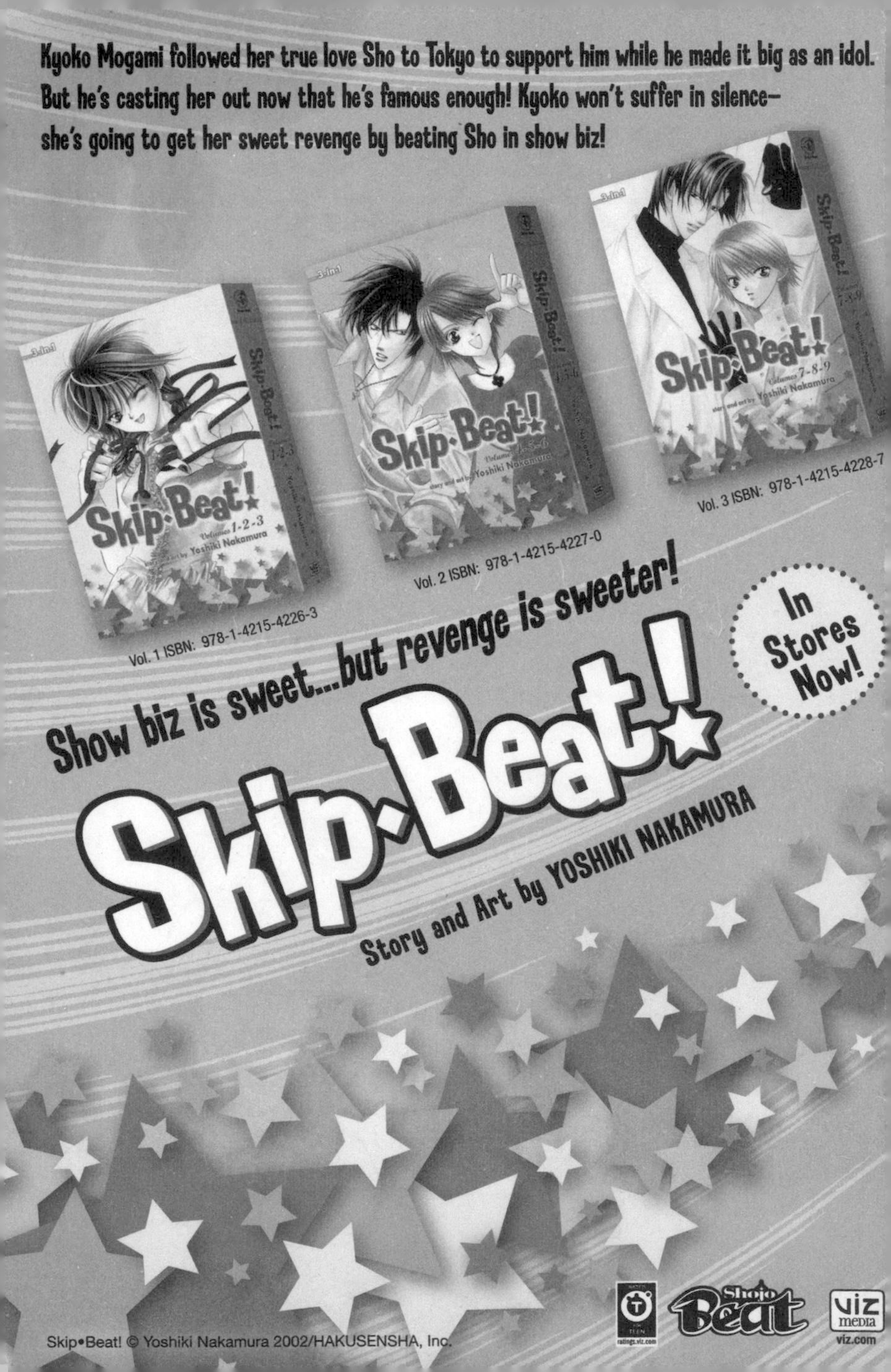
Kyoko Mogami followed her true love Sho to Tokyo to support him while he made it big as an idol. But he's casting her out now that he's famous enough! Kyoko won't suffer in silence—she's going to get her sweet revenge by beating Sho in show biz!
Skip·Beat! Volumes 1-2-3 story and art by Yoshiki Nakamura
Vol. 1 ISBN: 978-1-4215-4226-3
Skip·Beat! Volumes 4-5-6 story and art by Yoshiki Nakamura
Vol. 2 ISBN: 978-1-4215-4227-0
Skip·Beat! Volumes 7-8-9 story and art by Yoshiki Nakamura
Vol. 3 ISBN: 978-1-4215-4228-7
In Stores Now!
Show biz is sweet...but revenge is sweeter!
Skip·Beat!
Story and Art by YOSHIKI NAKAMURA
Skip•Beat! © Yoshiki Nakamura 2002/HAKUSENSHA, Inc.
Shojo Beat
viz media
viz.com